The Civil War

State by State

J. O. Davidson's painting of the capture of Fort Fisher was published in
Prang's War Pictures (1886).

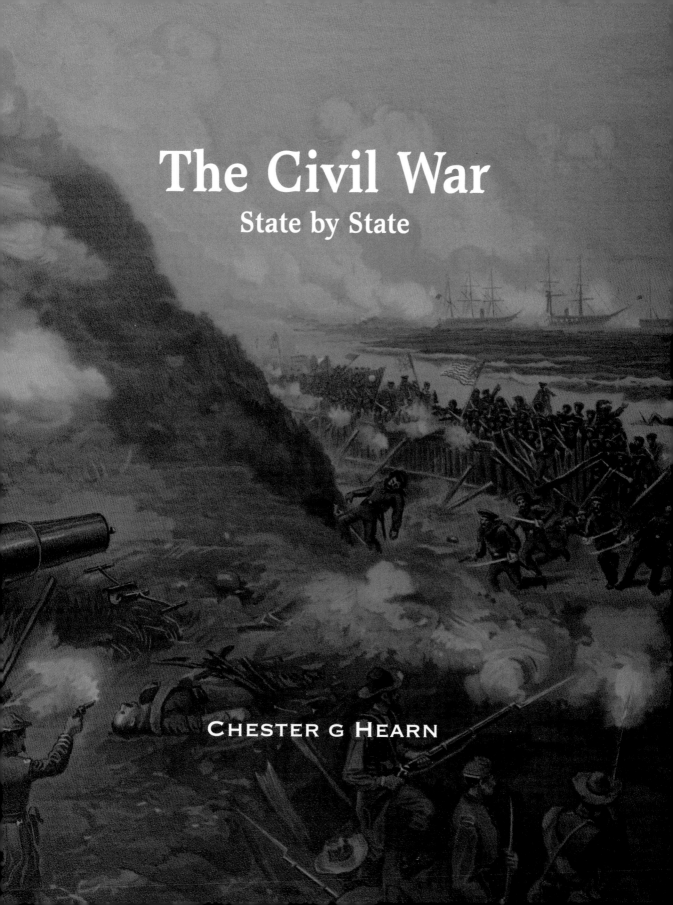

The Civil War
State by State

CHESTER G HEARN

Published by BlueRed Press, 6 South Street, Totnes, Devon, TQ9 5DZ.
This edition printed for Books Are Fun 2013.

Copyright © 2011 BlueRed Press
Editor Martin Howard
Design by Diverse Design & Communications

Acknowledgments
All images used in this book come from:
• Library of Congress, Prints & Photographs Online Catalog
• National Archives
• The Photographic History of the Civil War by
  Francis Trevelyan Miller, New York.
• Frank Leslie's illustrated history of the Civil War,
  published in New York by Mrs. F. Leslie, 1895.
They were researched by Mike Marino who also drew all the maps.
Thanks to those who contributed text and caption material: Marcus
Cowper, Simon Forty, Martin Howard, Angus Konstam, Rick Sapp,
Michael Sharpe, Donald Sommerville, and Ian Westwell.

ISBN 978-1-908247-04-9

Manufactured and printed in Shenzhen, China.
First printed, August 2011
10 9 8 7 6 5 4 3 2

Sherman at the siege of Atlanta. A painting by Thure de Thulstrup published in *Prang's War Pictures*.

CONTENTS

Introduction

In 1850 the United States was still less than a century old. Having thrown off British rule, the new nation was, nevertheless, already an economic and political power in its own right, and was beginning to challenge European global dominance.

Immigration from Europe drove westward expansion. This painting by Felix Darley shows "Emigrants Crossing the Plains."

Attracted by the prospect of a new beginning, in the 1840s and 1850s some 4.2 million immigrants arrived from Europe, raising the overall population of the U.S. to twenty-five million people. As well as increasing the urban population of New York, Chicago, and other major cities, this influx of people drove the westward expansion and settlement of the frontier states.

Despite occasional entanglements with European powers, such as the War of 1812, U.S. foreign policy was marked by steady expansion of its foreign trade during the 19th century, and maintained a policy of avoiding wars with and between European powers. Politically, the nation had begun to build its sphere of influence into the Caribbean: at home it underwent industrialization and the transportation revolution changed the economics of the North and West. The economy, once dependent on exports of cash crops to England, was now expanding into new territory. During a comparatively short lifespan, the new nation had, in fact, experienced a period of spectacular growth, not only in terms of its geographical limits but also its economic might and global standing.

The northern states and those on the eastern seaboard had experienced the most rapid expansion, in both economic and population terms. In fact, most of the industrial strength of the nation was focused in the North, drawing on the plentiful resources needed for factories. Although agriculture was still by far the largest industry, by the 1840s the Industrial Revolution was changing the face of the Northeast, through an expanding network of railroads, canals, mills, small industrial cities, and growing commercial centers, with hubs in Boston, New York City, and Philadelphia.

The Midwest region, based on farming (and increasingly on animal production), was also growing rapidly, using the railroads and river systems to ship food to slave plantations in the South and industrial cities in the East, as well as Britain and Europe. While the Northeast was urbanizing, centers such as Cleveland, Cincinnati, and Chicago were also growing rapidly in the Midwest. By 1860, sixteen percent of Americans lived in cities with 2,500 or more people while a third of the nation's income came from manufacturing.

In the South, agriculture was, again, predominant, but focused on the production of cotton, which had a very high price on the world market. Cotton growers in the South, whose own land had been exhausted, looked west to expand. The great wealth generated by slave labor was used to buy new lands, and – inevitably – more slaves. However, even in the South slave ownership was limited to an economic elite. According to the 1860 U.S. census, fewer than 385,000 individuals (i.e. 1.4 percent of whites in the country, or 4.8 percent of Southern whites) owned one or more slaves. Ninety-five percent of blacks lived in the South, comprising one-third of the population there, as opposed to one percent of the population of the North.

SOURCES OF CONFLICT

As the nation grew, clear divisions began to emerge between the North and South. The causes of the war cannot be attributed to one single factor alone, but, rather, an accumulation of separate issues including disagreements over slavery, the expansion and settlement of new territories, sectionalism, nationalism, and the extent of the authority of the Federal government over individual states and the taxation that was levied on imported goods. Although by the late 1840s, relations between North and South had begun to be tested over these issues, from 1850 onward rifts began to deepen. A sequence of events beginning with the Wilmot Proviso (which attempted, and failed, to prevent the adoption of slavery in any territories won during the Mexican-American War) precipitated the secession crisis of 1860, which led quickly to war.

SLAVERY

Although slavery had been a part of life in America since the early colonial period, many Northerners were morally opposed to the practice and called for it to be abolished. Slavery was, however, protected not only under state laws, but Federal law as well. The Constitution guaranteed the right to own property

A slave coffle passing the Capitol.

and protected everyone against the seizure of that property. In the South, where large plantations depended on slaves to gather and process cotton, a slave was viewed as property. Southern states therefore viewed any attack on slavery as an attack on their rights and livelihood.

POPULAR SOVEREIGNTY

With the failure of the Wilmot Proviso to pass through the Southern-dominated Senate in 1846 and, again, in 1847, Senator Lewis Cass introduced the idea of popular sovereignty in Congress. Cass proposed that Congress did not have the power to determine whether territories could allow slavery since this was not an enumerated power listed in the Constitution. Instead, he said that the people living in the territories should decide the slavery issue. The issue split the Democrats. Northern Democrats called for "squatter sovereignty" under which the people living in the territory could decide the issue when a territorial legislature was convened. Southern Democrats disputed the idea, arguing that the issue of slavery must be decided at the time of adoption of a state constitution when the request was made to Congress for admission as a state. Cass and other Democratic leaders failed to clarify the issue so that neither section of the country felt slighted as the election approached.

THE COMPROMISE OF 1850

The influx of new settlers into California during the Gold Rush prompted the territory's application for statehood in 1850. This created a renewal of sectional tension because California's admission – as well as the imminent admission of Oregon, New Mexico, and Utah – threatened to upset the balance of power in Congress. Many Southerners also realized that the climate of those territories did not lend themselves to the extension of slavery. Debate raged in Congress until a compromise solution was negotiated. Under this, California was admitted as a free state, Texas was financially compensated for the loss of its western territories, the slave trade (not slavery) was abolished in the District of

Columbia, and the Fugitive Slave Law was passed as a concession to the South. Most importantly, it was decided that the New Mexico Territory (including modern day Arizona and the Utah Territory) would determine its status (either free or slave) by popular vote. The Compromise of 1850 temporarily defused the divisive issue, but the peace was not to last long.

SECTIONALISM

In the antebellum, the balance of political power in the Federal government was shifting to the Northern and Midwestern states, largely due to their rapid population increases, something the Southern states did not experience. People began to talk of the nation as sections. This was called "sectionalism." Just as the original colonies fought for their independence almost a century earlier, the Southern states felt a growing need for freedom from Washington. Southerners believed that state laws carried more weight than Federal laws, and that they should abide by the state regulations first. "State's Rights" became a very warm topic in Congress.

TARIFFS

Another of the quarrels between North and South concerned taxes, known as tariffs, paid on goods brought in from abroad. Southerners felt tariffs were unfair because the South imported more goods than the North. There were also taxes on many Southern goods shipped abroad, and these were not always applied to Northern goods. The awkward economic structure also affected Southern banks, which paid higher interest rates on loans made with banks in the North. The situation grew worse after several "panics," including one in 1857 that affected more Northern banks than Southern. Southern financiers found themselves burdened with high payments just to save Northern banks that had suffered financial losses through poor investment.

KANSAS-NEBRASKA ACT AND BLEEDING KANSAS

Senator Stephen A. Douglas introduced the Kansas-Nebraska Act of 1854, proposing "organizing" (opening for white settlement) the territories of Kansas and Nebraska. A provision that stated that the status of the new territories would be subject to popular sovereignty. In theory, the new states could become slave states under this condition.

With the opening of Kansas, both pro- and anti-slavery supporters rushed to settle in the new territory. Violent clashes soon erupted. In 1855, elections were held for the territorial legislature and a pro-slavery majority was voted into power, further fueling the conflict, which caused the state to become known as "Bleeding Kansas."

THE ELECTION OF 1856

In the election of 1856, Democrats campaigned heavily in the South, warning voters that the Republicans were extremists and were promoting civil war. The Republicans, meanwhile, nominated John Frémont under the slogan: "Free soil, free labor, free speech, free men, Frémont."

The Republicans won most of the North and very nearly won the election: only a slight shift of in Pennsylvania and Illinois would have resulted in victory for Frémont. As a result, the Republicans abandoned the South and became a predominantly Northern party. The Democrats, who had won the election, responded by turning to the South for support. The United States was becoming ever more polarized along North-South lines.

THE DRED SCOTT DECISION

On March 6, 1857, the Supreme Court became involved in the gathering crisis when Dred Scott, a black slave, attempted to sue his former master's wife for his freedom on the grounds that he was living in a non-slave territory. Supreme Court Chief Justice Taney declared that Dred Scott was a slave, not a citizen, and thus had no rights under the Constitution. In effect, the Supreme Court decided that slaves were not citizens of the United States. This emboldened Southerners and convinced Northerners that there was a vast "slave power conspiracy" to control the Federal government.

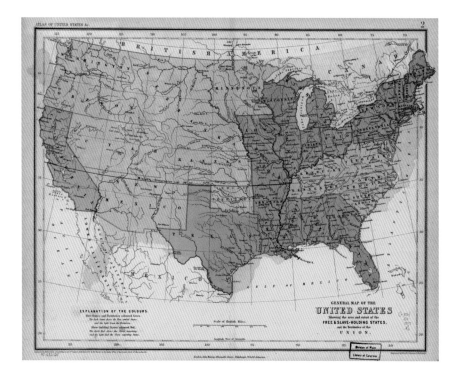

Map showing the free (green) and slave-holding (red) states, the territories (light green), and the boundary of the seceding states. The map differentiates between the dark red (slave importing) and light red (slave exporting) states. Sections of this map are used throughout the book on the opening page of each state's entry.

ABOLITIONISM

Throughout this period clashes over slavery became louder and more persistent. While abolitionist groups called for a total halt to the practice, most debates concerned the constitutionality of the extension of slavery and took the form of arguments over the powers of Congress rather than the morality of slavery. But the Free Soil Movement opposed the "peculiar institution" because it ensured that the economic elite controlled most of the land, property, and capital in the South – which was against the democratic principles upon which the United States was founded. Supporters of slavery justified the practice in many ways. John Calhoun's treatise, "the Pro-Slavery Argument", stated that slavery was a civilizing force for so-called "African savages", because it gave them the lifelong security they were unable to provide for themselves as a "biologically inferior" race.

JOHN BROWN'S RAID

In 1859, a radical abolitionist from Kansas – John Brown – raided the Federal armory at Harpers Ferry, Virginia, in the hopes of supplying weapons to slaves to foment revolt. Brown was cornered with several of his, first by Virginia militia and then by Federal troops sent to arrest him. The troops, commanded by Colonel Robert E. Lee, stormed the building and captured Brown who was tried, found guilty, and hung in Charles Town, WV. The raid fueled the passions of Northern abolitionists who made him a martyr.

THE UNITED STATES GOES TO WAR

The event that lit the touchpaper for the war was the election of Abraham Lincoln. He was elected president (the sixteenth) on November 6, 1860. He won by taking the northern states: he received no ballots in ten of the eleven slave states – and around one percent of the popular vote in the eleventh. The election showed the polarization of the nation. And before Lincoln could even be inaugurated – March 4, 1861 on the steps of the Capitol with an armed guard – the southern states had seceded, South Carolina leading off on December 20, 1860. By February 9, 1861, the South had selected its own president – Jefferson Davis – an act of rebellion that became armed conflict on April 12, 1861, at Fort Sumter.

Alabama

> " The day is now come, and Alabama must make her selection, either to secede from the Union, and assume the position of a sovereign, independent State, or she must submit to a system of policy on the part of the Federal Government that, in a short time, will compel her to abolish African Slavery. "

E. S. Dargen, Delegate to the Secession Convention

First organized as part of the Mississippi Territory in 1798, Alabama became its own territory in 1817 and on December 14, 1819, the twenty-second state.

On January 11, 1861, being part of the agricultural Deep South and dependent on slavery, Alabama became the fourth state to secede from the Union. The action almost created an internal civil war within the state. In northern Alabama, where anti-slavery feeling existed, an effort ensued to create a pro-Union state. The movement failed and a week before formally seceding Governor Andrew B. Moore followed the practice of other secession states, declaring Alabama an independent republic and ordering state troops to seize all Federal property, including Fort Morgan and Fort Gaines at the entrance to Mobile Bay as well as the arsenal at Mount Vernon. Moore then lent five hundred troops to Florida's Governor Madison S. Perry to capture the Union forts and navy yard at Pensacola. At Moore's request, the legislature appropriated $500,000 for defense and another $3,000,000 of indebtedness to prepare the state for war. By February 4th, seven Southern states had seceded and six of them sent delegates to Montgomery, Alabama, to adopt a provisional government and, later, a permanent one fashioned after the United States Constitution. The delegates formed the Confederate States of America and, on February 9th, elected Jefferson Davis of Mississippi president for a six-year term, and, soon after, Alexander H. Stephens of Georgia, vice-president. Governor Moore supported Davis and, because the newly adopted Confederate government had no money, donated the $500,000 recently authorized by Alabama's legislature. Montgomery remained the Confederate capital until May 21st, when President Davis moved the government to Richmond, Virginia.

Governor Andrew Barry Moore.   General Leroy Pope Walker.

GOVERNOR ANDREW BARRY MOORE (1807–1873)

Elected governor in 1857, former judge Andrew B. Moore served the maximum of two two-year terms before yielding the governorship to John G. Shorter late in 1861. Although a moderate Southern rights Democrat, Moore called for a secession convention and facilitated the military build-up in Alabama. Throughout the war he supported Jefferson Davis and continued to work closely with Governor Shorter, encouraging military mobilization and enlistments. Arrested by Federal authorities in 1865, Moore gained his release because of poor health. He practiced law until he passed away on April 5, 1873.

BRIGADIER GENERAL LEROY POPE WALKER (1817–1884)

To fill his cabinet, President Davis attempted to select a man from each state. Alabamans recommended Leroy Pope Walker, a lawyer who would have been a logical choice for attorney general, if the post had not already been filled. Instead, Walker became the first secretary of war. Although he played an important part in mobilizing 200,000 men during the first six months of the war, he was an ineffective administrator, quarrelsome, and soon fell out of favor with the president. Walker resigned on September 16, 1861, and the following day became a brigadier general. Walker never served in the field, however. He resigned in March 1862 and held the post of judge in a military court until the end of the war. Always a power player in Alabama, Walker resumed his law practice after the war and, on August 23, 1884, passed away in Huntsville.

WILLIAM LOWNDES YANCEY (1814–1863)

Yancey excelled as a public speaker and was a fiery advocate for Southern rights. He demanded protection for slave property in the territories opening in the West, but lost some of his following when he engaged in a duel with future Confederate General Thomas L. Clingman. He wrote the "Alabama Platform", which defined property rights to include chattel slavery and organized states-rights organizations throughout the South to run for political office. In 1860, he was also instrumental in a bid to place John C. Breckinridge on the Democratic ballot for president, believing it would ensure a Republican victory and push the South into withdrawal from the Union. Yancey's fierce energy took its toll, however, and he died at the age of forty-eight.

CONFEDERATE RECOGNITION ABROAD

Months before the formation of the Confederate States of America, fiery Southern rights advocate William Lowndes Yancey wrote Alabama's ordinance of secession though, because of his irrepressible radicalism, he did not become a delegate when the first Provisional Confederate Congress met. Yancey expected to be considered for president, but conservatives shut him out. President Davis hesitated to make a place for him in government and, instead, appointed him commissioner to Europe with instructions to obtain recognition for the Confederate government, in particular from the major importers of Southern cotton: England and France. Davis also authorized Yancey to threaten to withhold cotton from the world market. When the strategy failed, Alabama and other cotton-producing states withheld the product in an attempt to force Europe to recognize the Confederacy and perhaps come to the military aid of the South. Yancey's efforts led to the South's cotton embargo, but it also led to the Union blockade of Southern ports, which affected Mobile and Mobile Bay.

After becoming a central figure in early diplomatic relations with Europe, Yancey resigned after a year abroad and took his seat in the Confederate Senate. He soon became a member of the opposition and attempted to limit Davis's policies whenever they encroached on state sovereignty. Yancey died in July 1863, never knowing that his great dream of Southern nationhood would also die two years later.

ALABAMA'S MILITARY

Alabama participated in no major military or naval operation until 1864, yet some 120,000 men – practically the whole of the white population capable of bearing arms – fought for the Confederacy. Recruited locally, they served with men who were friends and neighbors. There is no accurate record of the number of men who died, nor are there accurate records of other Alabama losses in the

Civil War. Although women volunteered to nurse the sick and wounded, the state had few properly equipped hospitals. Estimates range up to 18,000 for those dying from disease because of poor medical conditions. Estimates of battlefield deaths or deaths from wounds top 12,000. Many of the uncounted missing were, however, shoeless stragglers who had no blankets or adequate clothing. These men simply disappeared and never returned to their companies.

Slaves were not entered into the counts, though thousands became involved in the war effort as cooks, launderers, horse tenders, supply wagon drivers, wood cutters, and hospital attendants. They built defensive works, emplaced artillery, hauled ammunition, repaired railroads, worked in iron mines, and labored in foundries. Impressed into work, none was ever paid, and thousands escaped to join the Union army.

Thirty-nine Alabamians attained the rank of general, and Raphael Semmes had the unique distinction of also becoming an admiral. Transplanted from his home in Pennsylvania, Josiah Gorgas was one of the few Northern-born Confederate generals. He married an Alabama woman, became a staunch Southerner and, as the Confederate chief of the Ordnance Bureau, turned Alabama into the munitions manufacturer of the South. He located new munitions plants in Selma that employed 10,000 workers until Major General James Wilson's Union cavalry rampaged through the state in 1865 and burned down the factories. Alabama soldiers fought in hundreds of battles. The state's losses at Gettysburg alone listed 1,750 dead with the famed "Alabama Brigade" taking 781 casualties.

THE ALABAMA BRIGADE

Without ever fighting in Alabama, the famous Alabama Brigade joined Robert E. Lee's Army of Northern Virginia and fought in sixty-nine engagements from First Bull Run (First Battle of Manassas) on July 21, 1861, to the final surrender of General Robert E. Lee's army at Appomattox, Virginia, on April 9, 1865. From June 1862, it was led by Brigadier General Evander McIvor Law, an

BRIGADIER GENERAL JOSIAH GORGAS (1818–1883)

Born in Pennsylvania, Josiah Gorgas married an Alabama girl and eventually settled in Tuscaloosa. Although a graduate of West Point, he joined the Confederate army and became chief of the Ordnance Bureau – a thankless job in a Confederacy without resources – and created what became a huge war industry until the Union army began shrinking the South from all sides. After the war, Gorgas became president of the University of Alabama and never stopped contributing his many skills to the state until his death in 1883.

Right: Fort Gaines, Alabama
Originally named Massacre Island because of bones found there (and, from 1707, called Dauphin Island), this was the headquarters for French colonization along the Gulf coast, which eventually became known as the Louisiana Territory. In 1813, the United States seized the territory around Mobile Bay and began to construct a fort there as part of the comprehensive system of national defense. The designs of Joseph G. Totten were adopted and, in 1853, Congress named the fortification for General Edmund Pendleton Gaines who won lasting fame for his tenacious defense of Fort Erie. Most of the work on the fort had been completed by the outbreak of the Civil War when the building was finished by Confederate forces. Fort Gaines was in active use during the Battle of Mobile (see pages 22–25) and later served in World Wars I and II. One of the best-preserved Civil War-era masonry forts, Fort Gaines has been nominated for listing as a National Historic Landmark.

Alabaman from Tuskegee who rose from captain of the 4th Alabama Regiment to command the brigade that eventually included his own unit as well as the 15th, 44th, 47th, and 48th Alabama regiments. He took command during the Seven Days' Campaign on Virginia's Peninsula.

Perhaps the brigade's finest hour came on June 27, 1862, at Gaines' Mill when the Alabamans and John Bell Hood's Texans broke the Federal center. After the Seven Days Battles brought an end to the Union's Peninsula Campaign, the Alabama Brigade again distinguished itself during major battles fought at Second Bull Run (Second Manassas), Antietam (Battle of Sharpsburg), Fredericksburg, Chancellorsville, Gettysburg, Chickamauga, the Wilderness, Spotsylvania, and Cold Harbor.

General Law did not always agree with his direct superior, Lieutenant General James Longstreet, and after the Battle of Chickamauga demanded a transfer with his brigade to defend Alabama. Longstreet arrested Law, then released him and sent him with the brigade into eastern Tennessee. General Lee interceded and ordered the Alabamans back to the Army of Northern Virginia. Law resigned and William Flank Perry took over the command. After spending the winter of 1864–65 in the Petersburg trenches, Perry led the brigade during General Lee's failed attempt to escape across Virginia. On April 9, 1865, following the surrender at Appomattox, the Alabama Brigade counted only 973 men, the remnant of a famous brigade that once numbered 6,260 Alabamans.

UNIONISTS IN NORTHERN ALABAMA

Alabama experienced little fighting during the first two years of war but by 1863 Federal forces had secured a foothold in northern Alabama. When Union troops moved in, Southern Unionists began emerging from hiding and some 2,500 whites and 10,000 blacks joined the Federal Army. Many of them were fed up with Confederate partisans who stole their food and stock. They sought, and happily received, Union protection. Federal foragers in northern Alabama were equally troublesome, however, and were often assisted by loyal Unionists during raids on pro-Southern farms and homes.

Before Federal troops arrived, Unionist resistance groups operated from underground cells. They received financing from the Union Army, provided local intelligence, and were instrumental in rescuing Federal soldiers held in Confederate camps. Alabama Unionists also formed the 1st Alabama Cavalry Regiment, which became quite prominent during the latter months of the war – gathering intelligence, acting as guides, scouting, and wreaking havoc on Confederate outposts. Their efforts were supplemented by compact Unionist guerrilla bands numbering up to a hundred men who recruited behind enemy lines and fought local pro-Southern bands and roving Confederate cavalry patrols. Even the women became involved. Although many had lost husbands and were struggling to survive, they became part of the Federal communication network, moving freely from town to town delivering messages and collecting intelligence.

THE IRON WORKS OF THE CONFEDERACY

While Virginia had it famous Tredegar Iron Works in Richmond, Alabama supplied most of the iron used by the Confederacy, producing 40,000 tons a year. Sixteen ironworks produced the majority of the South's shot and shell as well as many other products, including iron for the Confederacy's largest and most dangerous ironclad, the C.S.S. ram *Tennessee*. At 209 feet long, forty-eight feet in beam, and with a

Evander McIvor Law was a general who got into the middle of the fighting to lead his men and, for his courage, suffered two dangerous wounds, one at First Bull Run (First Battle of Manassas) and the other at Cold Harbor.

BRIGADIER GENERAL EVANDER MCIVOR LAW (1836–1920)

After graduating from the South Carolina Military Academy (The Citadel) in 1856, Law married and moved to Tuskegee, Alabama, where he helped to establish the Military High School. It was there, when the Civil War began, that he joined the 4th Alabama as captain. Law distinguished himself as a fighter at First Bull Run (First Battle of Manassas), and after recovering from a serious wound returned to the regiment in the fall as its colonel. On October 2, 1862, he became a brigadier general and took command of the famous Alabama Brigade, some of the toughest fighters in General Lee's Army of the Potomac. Law distinguished himself as a no-nonsense general, which led to conflicts with his superior, General Longstreet, who attempted to have Law court-martialed. Lee could not spare Law, however, and while the Alabama Brigade remained with the Army of Northern Virginia, Law eventually transferred to General Joseph E. Johnston's army, which surrendered on April 18, 1865, in the Carolinas.

After the war, Law moved to Florida and spent much of the rest of his life building the state's educational system. He died in Bartow on October 31, 1920.

fourteen-foot draft, much of the ship was built on the banks of the Alabama River near Selma's Confederate Navy Yard. Although delays in getting the ship into Mobile Bay seemed at times interminable, it served as an example of what Alabama's ironworks could produce from foundries unfamiliar with the technology.

The Selma Arsenal produced most of the Confederacy's ammunition, and the Selma Naval Ordnance Works produced artillery – one cannon every five days. Selma's Confederate Nitre Works used slaves to mine niter for gunpowder from limestone caves. When supplies were low, and because urine was rich in organic nitrogen, General Josiah Gorgas encouraged housewives to save the contents of their chamber pots.

THE LAST CAMPAIGN

Major General Dabney H. Maury came to Mobile in July 1863 to command the District of the Gulf and helped to man the forts on Mobile Bay, though playing no direct role in the action. When, on March 17, 1865, Major General Edward R. S. Canby brought 45,000 Federal troops to the area to capture Mobile, Maury had only 10,000 men defending Blakely and Spanish Fort, the city's major fortifications. With support of the navy, Canby's forces drove the Confederates out of both forts and entered Mobile on April 12th. Maury retreated with 4,500 troops toward Montgomery and joined forces with General Richard Taylor, who surrendered the last of the Alabamans on May 4, 1865. All the men received paroles and returned to their homes.

On July 13, 1868, after a lapse of seven and a half years, the United States Congress readmitted Alabama to the Union.

Left: Private Enoch Hooper Cook, Jr. from Company H of the 38th Alabama Infantry Regiment. Organized at Mobile in May 1862, in 1863, the 38th joined the 18th, 36th, and 58th Alabama regiments in General Henry D. Clayton's Brigade. The regiment lost heavily at Chickamauga (nearly forty percent casualties out of 490 engaged). It also fought in the Atlanta Campaign and at Nashville in December 1864. Involved in the defense of Mobile, the regiment battled at Spanish Fort and numbered just eighty men when it surrendered at Meridian, Mississippi.

Robert Knox Sneden's hand-drawn map, the "Rebel defences of Mobile showing Union attack April 3rd-9th 1865 on Spanish Fort."

Semmes of the *Alabama*

Of all the Alabamans who fought in the Civil War, Admiral Raphael Semmes was one of the most daring and resourceful. He virtually destroyed the American carrying trade by driving it off the high seas and, in doing so, arguably won the only Confederate victory achieved during the Civil War. Semmes was also the only officer of the war to become a general as well as an admiral.

Admiral Raphael Semmes.

RAPHAEL SEMMES (1809–1877)

Born in Charles City, Maryland, Raphael Semmes joined the U.S. Navy at the age of sixteen and by 1855 had risen to commander. He became a lawyer while still in the navy and settled in Mobile. When Alabama seceded, Semmes resigned his commission and became a commander in the Confederate navy. Soon after the war began, he went New Orleans, converted and armed a small steamer, named her the C.S.S. *Sumter*, and took her to sea. He captured seventeen American merchant ships before decommissioning the unseaworthy cruiser at Gibraltar.

Raised to the rank of captain and summoned to England, Semmes learned he had been given command of the C.S.S. *Alabama*, a commerce raider secretly built by Confederate agent James Dunwoody Bulloch in a shipyard near Liverpool. Semmes took physical command of the ship in the Azores and spent the next twenty-two months (August 1862 – June 1864) capturing fifty-five American prizes. The fcat made him a hero in the South and a pirate in the North. Being almost constantly at sea took a toll on the *Alabama*, however, and in June 1864 Semmes brought the ship into Cherbourg, France, for major repairs. Challenged by U.S.S. *Kearsarge*, Semmes took the *Alabama*, now badly deteriorated and with defective ammunition, into the English Channel on June 19, 1864, for a famous duel that was watched by thousands. The *Kearsarge* sank the *Florida* in a one-sided fight, though Semmes escaped with many of his officers and took refuge in England.

After finding his way back to the Confederacy through Texas, Semmes arrived in Richmond and met with Secretary of the Navy Stephen R. Mallory. The secretary put Admiral Semmes in charge of the James River Squadron, which in February 1865 consisted of three ironclads and three wooden warships. When the Confederate Government abandoned Richmond on April 2nd, Semmes set the squadron on fire and caught a train to Danville, Virginia. There he found President Davis, who made Semmes a brigadier general and put him in charge of infantry which had been posted in Richmond. A few weeks later Semmes, his officers, and his mini-brigade joined General Joseph E. Johnston's army at Durham, North Carolina, a few days before the final surrender.

The government arrested Semmes, intending to try him for treason and piracy, but the admiral turned general understood the law better than most lawyers in Washington, D.C. and won his release. Semmes spent most of the rest of his life living quietly in Mobile as a lawyer. He wrote his *Memoirs* and passed away in 1877.

This bronze statue of Admiral Raphael Semmes was dedicated in Mobile, Alabama, on June 27, 1900. It stands at the foot of Government Street, just above the Bankhead Tunnel in downtown.

THE U.S. SLOOP OF WAR "KEARSARGE" 7 GUNS, SINKING THE PIRATE "ALABAMA" 8 GUNS.

Semmes' ship, *Alabama,* was what later wars would call a commerce raider. Built in England in 1862 by John Laird, she attacked Union merchant and naval ships before being sunk by U.S.S. *Kearsarge* off Cherbourg in 1864. During her two-year life she never laid anchor in a Southern port and captured fifty-five Union vessels. The crews and passengers were then detained until they could be placed aboard a neutral ship or ashore in a friendly or neutral port – something that ensured an excellent reputation for her captain. This image was published by Currier & Ives, c. 1864.

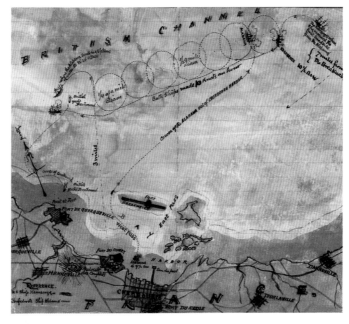

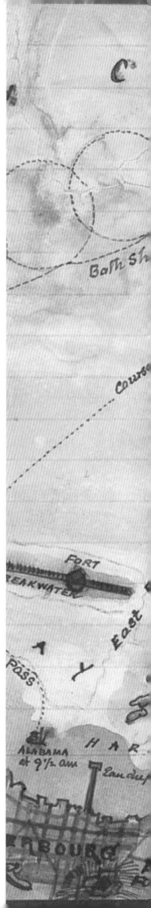

This map shows a plan of the battle between the U.S. Navy's *Kearsarge* under Captain Winslow and the Confederate cruiser *Alabama,* commanded by Captain Raphael Semmes, off Cherbourg, France on Sunday, June 19, 1864. It was drawn by Robert Knox Sneden, a painter who was also a map-maker for the Confederate Army during the Civil War.

"Battle of the U.S.S. *Kearsarge* and the C.S.S. *Alabama*," a color lithograph by
Louis Prang & Company from a sketch or painting by Julian O. Davidson (1853–94).
An exceptional marine artist, Davidson "ran away to sea" and filled many sketch books
with the varied scenes he observed on his world travels.

THE BATTLE OF MOBILE BAY

Since January 1864, Rear Admiral David Glasgow Farragut had been attempting to find enough men and ships to force an entrance into Mobile Bay, the only large port in the Gulf of Mexico still in Confederate hands. By early August, the Union fleet had grown to fourteen wooden ships and four monitors, augmented by General Gordon Granger's XIII Corps. Granger had a special mission. While Farragut steamed into the bay and engaged the Confederate batteries commanded by Brigadier General Richard L. Page at Fort Morgan, infantry from the XIII Corps would land on the opposite side of the channel and invest Fort Gaines. Farragut's task on the morning of August 5, 1864, consisted of silencing Fort Morgan's heavy batteries, skirting three rows of submerged mines, passing through the channel into Mobile Bay, and defeating the Confederate flotilla inside the bay. Although small, the Confederate squadron included the deadly C.S.S. ram *Tennessee*, commanded by Admiral

Franklin Buchanan, and three wooden gunboats: *Morgan*, *Gaines*, and *Powell*.

Farragut's fleet steamed toward the channel at 6:00 a.m. in two columns. His four monitors were on the right flank of the main column with instructions to bombard Fort Morgan. The main column of wooden ships was paired, with the smaller ships protected on the far side of the larger ships. All went well until the leading monitor, *Tecumseh*, wandered into the minefield, struck a so-called "torpedo", and sank. The captain of the leading wooden ship, *Brooklyn*, stopped and caused a jam in the center of the channel directly under Fort Morgan's batteries. Farragut, leaning from the tops of the *Hartford*, shouted his famous order, "Damn the torpedoes, full speed ahead," and led the squadron through the minefield and into Mobile Bay. The *Tennessee* attacked, but fell back as Farragut's squadron steamed into the bay.

The large ironclad off the corner of Fort Morgan is the C.S.S. *Tennessee*. To the right is the approaching U.S. fleet with the sinking monitor U.S.S. *Tecumseh*. Leading the Union ships of war is the U.S.S. *Brooklyn* followed next by the U.S.S. *Hartford*, Admiral Farragut's flagship.

J.O.DAVIDSON

ADMIRAL DAVID GLASGOW FARRAGUT (1801–1870)

Farragut, born in Tennessee, joined the navy as a midshipman at the age of twelve and soon found himself in the middle of the War of 1812. He became the U.S. Navy's first rear admiral by capturing New Orleans in 1862 and its first full admiral after capturing Mobile Bay. A determined and magnificent fighter, Farragut set the standard for every officer in the U.S. Navy for years to come.

Lashed to the shrouds – Farragut passing the forts at Mobile, in his flagship *Hartford*.

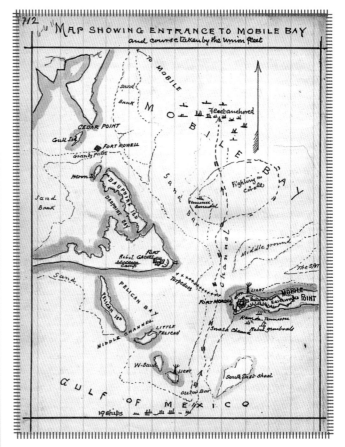

Another of Robert Knox Sneden's beautiful maps, this one showing the entrance to Mobile Bay and the course taken by Farragut and the Union fleet.

The battle resumed at 9:25 a.m. when Buchanan, seeing his other three ships in flames, ordered the *Tennessee*, now at a seventeen to one disadvantage, to attack the entire Union fleet. For thirty-five minutes the largest ships in Farragut's fleet tried ramming the impervious *Tennessee* to no effect. At 10:00 a.m. the exposed steering chains of the *Tennessee* became disabled, and a jarring shot from a Union ram tumbled Buchanan to the deck, breaking his leg. Captain J. D. Johnston surrendered the crippled *Tennessee*, thus ending the Battle of Mobile Bay. Granger's infantry invested Fort Gaines, which surrendered, but General Page at Fort Morgan held out until August 23rd. The Federals suffered 319 casualties, and the Confederates reported 312 killed or wounded and 280 captured, most of whom were Alabamans.

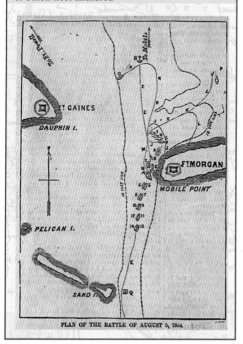

PLAN OF THE BATTLE OF AUGUST 5, 1864.

BRIGADIER GENERAL RICHARD LUCIEN PAGE (1807–1901)

General Page, born in Virginia with the nickname "Ramrod", resembled somewhat his first cousin, General Robert E. Lee. He was an expert in fortifications, sent by the Confederate War Department to Mobile Bay in March 1864 to secure forts Morgan and Gaines from a land-sea attack. Page did his best and waged a gallant defense of Fort Morgan, which Farragut ripped apart with naval guns for two weeks while Granger knocked it to pieces with land-based artillery.

ADMIRAL FRANKLIN BUCHANAN (1800–74)

Born and living Baltimore, Buchanan cast his lot with the Confederacy after an impressive career with the U.S. Navy. He originally commanded the C.S.S. *Virginia* (*Merrimack*) during the first battle of the ironclads on March 8, 1862. Sent to Mobile Bay to command the powerful *Tennessee*, Buchanan attacked the entire Union fleet with unquestionably the finest warship built within the Confederacy. Injured during the battle, Buchanan finished the war by surrendering the city of Mobile in the last battle of the Civil War on April 12, 1865. See also page 187.

The Alabama Confederate Monument is also known as the "Monument to Confederate Soldiers and Sailors," and sits on the Alabama Capitol grounds in Montgomery. The former C.S.A. President Jefferson Davis laid the cornerstone in 1886, but the monument was not completed until 1898. Designed by Alexander Doyle, it commemorates the 122,000 Alabamians who fought for the Confederacy during the Civil War.

Alabama Units Furnished	
Confederate	
Infantry regiments	57
Reserve regiments	3
Infantry battalions	7
Sharpshooter units	2
Misc. infantry units	11
Cavalry regiments	15
Cavalry battalions	8
Reserve cavalry units	2
Independent cavalry units	11
Light artillery battalions	4
Light artillery batteries	20
Union	
Cavalry regiments	1
Independent cavalry unit	1
Light artillery battery	1

ALABAMA UNION ARMY DEATHS

Troops Furnished	Killed/Mortally Wounded	Died of Disease	Died of Other Causes	Total
2,578	50	228	67	345

The Battle of Blakeley was fought at Fort Blakeley on April 9, 1865, at 5:30 p.m. During the battle, 16,000 men led by Brigadier General John P. Hawkins attacked the fort leading to its surrender, one of the last engagements in Alabama. African-American forces played a major role in the successful Union assault. Historic Blakeley State Park was created in 1981 to preserve the National Register Site and its miles of pristine breastworks.

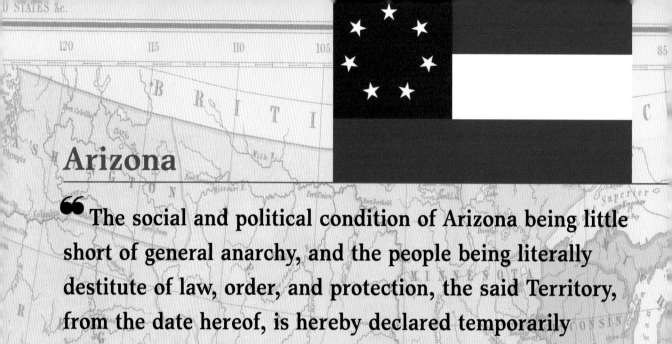

Arizona

“The social and political condition of Arizona being little short of general anarchy, and the people being literally destitute of law, order, and protection, the said Territory, from the date hereof, is hereby declared temporarily organized as a (Confederate) military government until such time as Congress may otherwise provide.”

LIEUTENANT COLONEL JOHN R. BAYLOR

Arizona was formed from New Mexico and seceded from the Union in 1861.

Governor Lewis Sumpter Owings.

Colonel John Robert Baylor.

Granville Henderson Oury.

Under the terms of the Treaty of Guadalupe Hidalgo, signed February 2, 1848, and ending the Mexican-American War, the Federal government purchased, among other lands, the New Mexico Territory, which included a large tract later known as Arizona.

Because of border skirmishes, Indian outrages, and railroad interests, in 1853 the Federal government expanded the New Mexico Territory through the Gadsden Purchase, which enlarged the southern border of New Mexico and Arizona to that of today. Congress also began considering splitting the territory in two, which led to heated debates over the relocation of Indians and the extension of slavery into the Southwest. The debate dragged on until March 16, 1861, when Southern sympathizers held a convention in Mesilla and adopted an ordinance of secession separating Arizona from both New Mexico and the United States. A second convention, held at Tucson on March 28th, ratified the Mesilla ordinance, thus creating the Provisional Territory of Arizona with Dr. Lewis Owings as its governor and Granville H. Oury as its first delegate to the Confederate Congress. When Arizonans petitioned for admission, Jefferson Davis recognized the potential of controlling

GOVERNOR LEWIS SUMPTER OWINGS (1820–75)

A medical doctor by trade, in 1860, Lewis Sumpter Owings became the provisional governor of Arizona, which was then part of the New Mexico Territory. Owings petitioned Congress to pass a law separating Arizona from the New Mexico Territory and, while waiting, continued as Arizona's *de facto* governor. On August 1, 1861, Lieutenant Colonel John R. Baylor entered Arizona, claimed the state for the Confederacy, ousted Owings, and assumed the governorship. In 1862, after the Confederates were driven from Arizona, Owings resumed the governorship, although he was then living in exile in San Antonio, Texas, and never returned.

COLONEL JOHN ROBERT BAYLOR (1822–94)

Born in Kentucky but raised from childhood in the army, John Robert Baylor grew up as a tough individual, and an impetuous and adventurous Texan. He did not wait for formalities to spring into action and followed his own impulses. Frustrated by the lack of support from the government while in Arizona, he returned to Texas as a rancher and died in 1894. Baylor University, though it bears his name, was founded by Robert Baylor, a relative, not by the old Indian fighter.

GRANVILLE HENDERSON OURY (1825–91)

A lawyer, judge, soldier, and miner, who made his home in Tucson, Granville Oury served as Arizona's provisional representative to the Confederate Congress in 1862 and a delegate to the U. S. House of Representatives from Arizona in 1881–85.

BRIGADIER GENERAL HENRY HOPKINS SIBLEY (1816–86)

Born in Louisiana, Henry Hopkins Sibley voiced great plans for converting the Southwest into a Confederate stronghold. Although he had some success during the battles at Valverde, he never had enough men to hold or control the vast New Mexican Territory or to assist Colonel Baylor as he had planned. Sibley is best remembered not for his campaigns during the Civil War but for the Sibley tent (see photo on page 32), which he patented in April 1856. The large conical canvas tent designed for dragoons accommodated twenty soldiers and their personal gear and provided a stove for their comfort. Sibley ended his career as a general of artillery for the khedive of Egypt and died in poverty at Fredericksburg, Virginia, in 1886.

the Southwest and responded quickly by having Congress grant pro-Southern petitioners status as the Territory of Arizona. The action created immediate turmoil in New Mexico, Texas, California, and other parts of Arizona.

JOHN BAYLOR'S WAR

John R. Baylor, a Kentuckian born into an army family, spent much of his early life at Indian Territory posts where his father was stationed. He grew up hating Indians and, at the age of seventeen, went to Texas to fight them. Dismissed from the service for harsh treatment of Native Americans, Baylor raised his own force in 1859 to drive Texas Indians from the Brazos reservation. A natural leader, he served as a delegate to the Texas secession convention and, when the state seceded, independently raised 1,000 men ostensibly for a "buffalo hunt." Instead of hunting buffalo, however, he organized the 2nd Texas Mounted Rifles, designated himself lieutenant colonel, and launched the first Confederate invasion of the New Mexico Territory. Baylor led his cavalry into New Mexico, captured Mesilla, and, on August 1, 1861, declared himself governor of the New Mexico Territory, which included Arizona, and claimed it for the Confederacy. Baylor knew his governorship of the territory was temporary and set his sights on holding Tucson, which he planned to use as a base for operations into both Mexico and west into southern California.

On reaching Arizona, Baylor began dismantling existing Union forts in the territory and left white settlers at the mercy of the Apaches, who rapidly gained control of the area. Forced to seek refuge in Tucson, many settlers did not blame Baylor but continued to support him. Another convention was held in Tucson on August 28, 1861. With Baylor's guidance, Granville H. Oury was re-elected as congressman and on October 1, 1861, Oury was sent to Richmond. He experienced difficulty getting seated in Congress but used his influence with Jefferson Davis to formally proclaim the Confederate Territory of Arizona on February 14, 1862. In 1912, on the same date fifty years later, Arizona officially became the forty-eighth state of the United States.

The Union did not sit by without reacting. On February 24, 1862, President Abraham Lincoln signed into law the official organization of the Arizona Territory as a U.S. territory. For a while the territory had two capitals, Tucson being the Confederate capital and Fort Whipple, later Prescott, being the Union capital in the northern-controlled area.

THE ARIZONA RANGERS

In 1860, three companies of the Arizona Territorial Rangers were formed, primarily to protect settlers against Indian raids. The group disbanded, but Baylor – acting as territorial governor – formed Company A, Arizona Rangers, as the first of three companies to defend the Confederacy's claim to the Arizona Territory. Captain Sherrod Hunter commanded the unit in the Tucson area. Although defeated when the California Column drove the Confederates out of Arizona, the name stuck and in 1901 became the name of Arizona's law enforcement agency, modeled after the Texas Rangers.

GENERAL SIBLEY'S OPERATIONS IN ARIZONA

Unlike Baylor, Brigadier General Henry Hopkins Sibley held a legitimate Confederate commission, conferred on him by Jefferson Davis on June 16, 1861. Davis directed him to recruit a Texas brigade for operations in the New Mexico Territory and California. Arriving at Mesilla in December 1861, Sibley's Texans routed Union forces at Valverde. Sibley took advantage of the victory to declare New Mexico a Confederate territory. Baylor in Arizona and Sibley in New Mexico now relied to some

Richard Cunningham McCormick served as a correspondent for the *New York Evening Post* and *New York Commercial Advertiser* with the Army of the Potomac in 1861–62. Appointed Secretary of Arizona Territory by President Lincoln on March 7, 1863, he traveled with Governor Goodwin's party to the territory. McCormick took his oath of office on December 29, 1863, as part of the Navajo Springs ceremony that officially established Arizona Territory.

The ruins of Fort Bowie, Cochise, Arizona. Established on July 28, 1862, by a hundred men of Company G, 5th California Volunteer Infantry under the command of Major T. A. Coult, Fort Bowie was the center of operations against the Chiricahua Apaches until the final surrender of Geronimo in 1886. The first fort, named in honor of Colonel George Washington Bowie, commander of the 5th California Infantry, consisted of stone breastwork and a few crude adobe buildings. Construction of the second fort, a few hundred yards to the east, began in the mid 1860s and continued sporadically until the fort's abandonment in 1894. Most of the buildings were of adobe; the magazine was of stone. Garrisoned during the Civil War by companies of the 5th California Infantry, the ruins of Fort Bowie are now preserved as part of Fort Bowie National Historic Site.

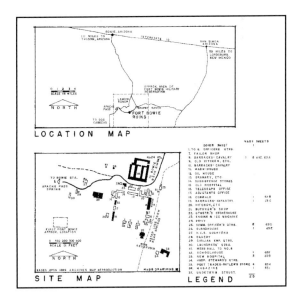

Group of soldiers of Company G, 71st New York Volunteers in front of a Sibley tent. Invented by Henry Hopkins Sibley, the tents were about twelve feet high and eighteen feet in diameter and could accommodate about twenty men.

degree on help from each other. Instead of moving his Army of New Mexico into Arizona, however, Sibley sent only fifty-four men to occupy Tucson while, on March 28th, he engaged Union forces at La Glorietta Pass. Sibley's Texans pushed Union forces through the pass but had to retreat after losing their supplies, ammunition, and wagon train. Sibley retired, but left the battalion of 1st Arizona Mounted Rifles behind. The unit, heavily outnumbered by forces arriving from California and Kansas, retreated into Texas. Sibley's army of New Mexico never reached Tucson, leaving Baylor without support and scotching plans by both men to use Arizona as a launching pad into southern California. When Brigadier General James Henry Carleton threatened Texas, Sibley retreated to San Antonio. For the remainder of the war, he served in obscure commands in Louisiana and never achieved much success.

THE CALIFORNIA COLUMN IN ARIZONA

At Fort Yuma along the Colorado River, Brigadier General Carleton formed ten companies of 1,500 California volunteers for the purpose of driving Baylor and Sibley's Confederates out of present-day Arizona and New Mexico. His force would later be augmented by the 5th California Infantry, commanded by Lieutenant Colonel George W. Bowie, bringing the total strength of the California Column to 2,350 men. Much like Sibley's Army of New Mexico, Carleton's column traveled in small groups at intervals of a few days so as not to exhaust the springs and wells along the way. Earlier, the Butterfield Overland Mail had established a route to California through the territory and, though it had been abandoned when Baylor entered the territory, Unionists had stocked the mail depots with food and grain before Carleton marched out of Fort Yuma. Baylor's Arizona Rangers had destroyed some of the supplies, which slowed Carleton's progress, and the general received little help from General Edward Canby, whose forces were being harassed by Sibley's army.

Carleton's first contact with Confederates occurred on March 30, 1862, when Captain William P. Calloway and a vanguard of 272 troops from the California Column discovered a small detachment of Confederates burning hay intended for the Federals' animals at Stanwix Station. After a brief exchange of gun fire, Baylor's Confederates retreated to Tucson.

On April 15, 1862, Carleton encountered another Confederate party at Pichaco Pass, about fifty miles northwest of Tucson. The skirmish marked the westernmost battle of the Civil War. Only thirteen Union cavalry and ten Confederate cavalry participated in the skirmish, and both commands fell back slightly bruised. The Confederates reported the fight to the Tucson garrison, which hurriedly abandoned the town. This small skirmish represented the high-water mark of the Confederate invasion of present-day Arizona, and Carleton's California Column continued the eastward march into present-day New Mexico and eventually Texas. This did not end the fighting in Arizona, though a different enemy now had to be engaged. A detachment from the California Column remained behind and on July 15, 1862, was attacked by 500 warriors at Apache Pass in Cochise County.

In 1864, the Union reorganized the territory of Arizona, dividing New Mexico along the state's current north-south border, and extending control southward from the new provisional capital of Prescott. For Arizona, the war with the Confederacy had ended, but the war with the Indians continued for years to come.

BREVET MAJOR GENERAL JAMES HENRY CARLETON (1814–73)

Although born in Lubec, Maine, James Henry Carleton became a colorful character of the Old West. He always wanted to be an author and, after becoming a dragoon, frontiersman, Indian fighter, and military governor of the Arizona Territory, he began writing military books. *The Battle of Buena Vista,* written in 1848, received the widest attention. Carleton remained in the army after the war ended and served in the 4th U.S. Cavalry. He retired to San Antonio, Texas, where he passed way. His son, Henry Guy Carleton, became a successful journalist, playwright, and inventor, and is buried beside him.

Arizona Confederate Units Furnished	
Arizona Brigade	1
Infantry battalions	1
Herbert's cavalry battalion	1

Arizona Union Units Furnished	
Infantry battalions	1

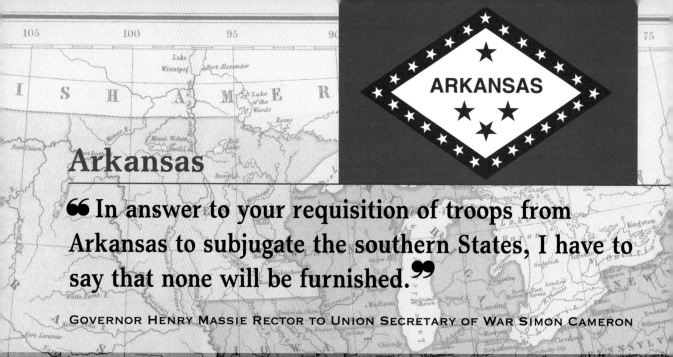

Arkansas

❝ In answer to your requisition of troops from Arkansas to subjugate the southern States, I have to say that none will be furnished. ❞

GOVERNOR HENRY MASSIE RECTOR TO UNION SECRETARY OF WAR SIMON CAMERON

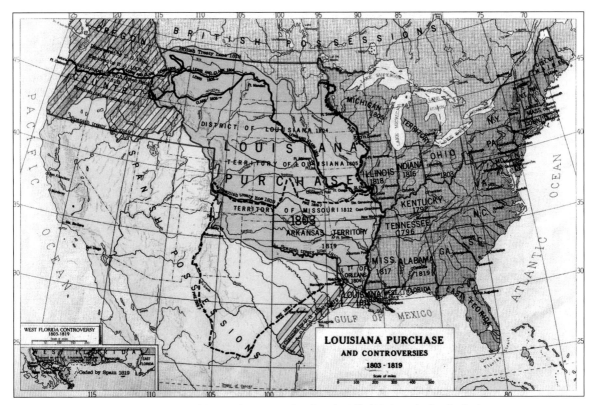

The Louisiana Purchase almost doubled the size of the United States, stretching from the Gulf of Mexico to the Canadian border.

By a treaty signed on April 30, 1803, the United States purchased from France the Louisiana Territory – 800,000 square miles of land extending west from the Mississippi River to the Rocky Mountains.

At a price of $15,000,000, President Thomas Jefferson doubled the size of the United States, opening it for settlement and guaranteeing free navigation of the Mississippi. The deal was consummated, ratified by the Senate, and, on December 20th, France turned the Louisiana Purchase over to the United States. From the acquired lands came the Arkansas Territory, the western border of which included present-day Oklahoma. On June 15, 1836, slave-holding Arkansas became the 25th state of the Union, a trade-off for free state Michigan's entry as the 26th state.

Tension over slavery and states' rights continued to grow, tying Arkansas's interests with those of her Southern neighbors. On February 18, 1861, though Arkansas had not seceded, Governor Henry Massie Rector dispatched state troops to take possession of the Federal arsenal at Little Rock, thus creating the first flashpoint. However, most officials – as well as the populace – hoped differences between the North and South could be settled without bloodshed and when delegates convened in March 1861 to discuss the issues, they voted against secession. A month later, on April 12th, South Carolina's Confederate batteries opened and two days later forced the surrender of Fort Sumter. When Abraham Lincoln called for 75,000 troops to stop the rebellion, Governor Rector called a second convention. On April 25th, before the delegates met, state troops attacked Fort Smith, driving Captain Samuel D. Sturgis and two troops of cavalry into the Indian Territory (present-day Oklahoma). On May 6th, the delegates passed, but for one contrary vote, a secession ordinance, and Arkansas became the ninth state to join the Confederacy.

Major General Patrick Ronayne
Cleburne.

Governor Henry Massie Rector.

MAJOR GENERAL PATRICK RONAYNE CLEBURNE (1828–64)

Born in Cork County, Ireland, Cleburne joined His Majesty's 41st Regiment around 1845 and served for three years before emigrating to the United States in 1849. He eventually moved to Helena, Arkansas, where he became a partner in a drugstore. At the outbreak of war, Cleburne joined the 15th Arkansas Infantry, where his friends elected him captain. He soon became the regiment's colonel, after which he joined Major General William J. Hardee's division in Kentucky. The only time Cleburne performed a warlike act in Arkansas was when he organized the Yell Rifles and seized the Little Rock Arsenal.

Cleburne soon distinguished himself on the battlefield, received promotion to brigadier general, and became one of the South's foremost infantry commanders. In April 1862, he fought at Shiloh and in August at Richmond, Kentucky, where a bullet entered his left cheek and tore away several teeth as it exited, leaving him unable to speak. Two months later, and still on the mend, he fought with distinction at Perryville, Kentucky, and received

promotion to major general. He led a division at Stones River, Tennessee, in December 1862, and at Chickamauga, Georgia, in August and September. He served under General Joseph E. Johnston during the 1864 Atlanta Campaign and under General John B. Hood during the Battle of Franklin. Cleburne was too much of a fighter to not be in the midst of the fighting and, on November 30, 1864, after having two horses shot beneath him, died while raising his sword as he led his men on foot to within fifty yards of the Union line.

Cleburne never owned a slave and never wanted one. He believed slaves deserved freedom and angered Confederate officials by suggesting that blacks be recruited to serve in the army. When Cleburne died in battle, those who knew him grieved over the loss. In a final tribute, Jefferson Davis called him the "Stonewall Jackson of the West."

GOVERNOR HENRY MASSIE RECTOR (1816–99)

Born in Louisville, Kentucky, Henry M. Massey grew up in St. Louis, where he drove a freight wagon for his stepfather while receiving a brief education at home from his mother. He moved to Arkansas in 1835 to manage land inherited from his father and eventually settled into farming and politics. More interested in the latter, Rector studied law, became a state senator in 1848, a Supreme Court judge in 1859, and governor in 1860. In April 1861, after Lincoln called for 75,000 troops, Rector received a letter from Secretary of War Simon Cameron specifying the number of regiments Arkansas was to supply for the defense of the Union. Rector replied, "In answer to your requisition of troops from Arkansas to subjugate the southern States, I have to say that none will be furnished. The people of this commonwealth are freemen, not slaves, and will defend to the last extremity their honor, lives, and property against Northern mendacity and usurpation." On May 6th, with Rector's blessing, Arkansas passed an ordinance of secession and did defend their state with the tenacity promised by the governor.

The battle of Wilson's Creek saw Arkansas units blooded in the first major battle west of the Mississippi.

Battle of Wilson's Creek

AUGUST 10, 1861

One of the first major battles involving troops from Arkansas occurred at Wilson's Creek, Missouri, on August 10, 1861. At the time, Brigadier General Ben McCulloch commanded all military units in northern Arkansas and southern Missouri. A former Texas Ranger and frontier fighter, McCulloch had a quarrelsome streak and little regard for military protocol. At Wilson's Creek he served with Brigadier General Sterling Price, a portly, handsome aristocrat and politician with moderate military experience. Arkansans soon observed tension brewing between them.

During the battle, Colonel James M. McIntosh, commanding the 2nd Arkansas Mounted Rifles and with help from the Pulaski Arkansas Battery, assaulted the Union left flank, driving back the Federals. When Price failed to throw in reinforcements, a Union counterattack collapsed the gains made by the 2nd Arkansas. Although McCulloch had routed part of the Union force, Price failed to take advantage and while they argued about tactics, the Confederate force became badly disorganized. Although Price claimed victory at Wilson's Creek, men from Arkansas knew that much more could have been accomplished had the two generals worked together instead of impeding each other.

BRIGADIER GENERAL ALBERT PIKE (1809–91)

Born in Boston, Massachusetts, Albert Pike was originally a teacher but, finding the job dull, he traveled to Independence, Missouri, to become a hunter and a trader instead. By 1833, he tired of life on the trail, settled in Arkansas, and became a lawyer, planter, newspaper publisher, and poet. He also became a 300-pound Confederate brigadier general who should have remained a civilian.

Although Pike at first opposed secession, he believed he could help the Confederate cause by recruiting Creek Indian tribal leaders, whose interests he successfully represented as a lawyer. As a reward for raising Indian regiments, Pike became a brigadier general and, without any military experience himself, commenced training about 2,000 warriors.

On April 7, 1862, Pike led them into battle at Pea Ridge. The warriors furiously attacked and routed Colonel Peter Osterhaus's gunners, who fled in fear of being scalped. Instead of following up their victory, the warriors paused to celebrate and were driven off by a Federal counterattack. Pike was unable to regroup his warriors and General Earl Van Dorn blamed him for losing the battle. Federals claimed that some of their men had been scalped and, after other issues surfaced over the mishandling of money, Pike disappeared into the hills to avoid arrest. He escaped court-martial by resigning his commission on November 11, 1862.

MOBILIZATION IN ARKANSAS

At the outset of the war, Arkansas already had twenty-seven state militia units trained and uniformed. Governor Rector demanded more and over the course of the war some 120 military units, including infantry, cavalry, and artillery, fought for the Confederacy. The 1st Arkansas Mounted Rifles and the 1st, 4th, and 6th Arkansas Infantry Regiments joined Major General Braxton Bragg's Army of the Tennessee. Only one regiment, the 3rd Arkansas, served in the Eastern Theater with General Robert E. Lee's Army of Northern Virginia, the men distinguishing themselves during the campaigns on Virginia's Peninsula, Antietam (Battle of Sharpsburg), Fredericksburg, Gettysburg, Chickamauga, the Wilderness, and to the final surrender at Appomattox. Most Arkansas units remained in the Western Theater, where few battles ever reached the size and intensity of those fought by Bragg and Lee.

SUPPORTING THE UNION

Not all Arkansans supported the Confederate cause. After the fall of Little Rock to Union forces in 1863, support for the Union increased. Arkansans formed eleven infantry regiments, four cavalry regiments, and two artillery batteries to serve with the Union in the Western Theater though few of the units became involved in major battles. The men concentrated their efforts on patrolling small towns and the countryside to protect the people from guerrilla raids.

As Arkansas gradually fell under the control of Union troops, Governor Rector moved the state capital to Hot Springs, and when that town was threatened, the capital moved again, this time to Washington, Arkansas, where it remained for the balance of the war. By the time the Civil War ended Arkansans were thoroughly demoralized.

BRIGADIER GENERAL JAMES MCQUEEN MCINTOSH (1828–62)

A graduate of West Point in 1849, James McIntosh had spent his army career on the frontier. Although born in Florida, he called Arkansas his home and lost his life during the fighting at Pea Ridge on April 7, 1862. His brother, John Baillie McIntosh, also became a general, but in the Union Army.

BEN MCCULLOCH (1811–62)

Ben McCulloch had a famous neighbor, Davy Crockett, whom he followed into Texas. There, he became a Texas Ranger and fought in the Mexican war. At the outbreak of the Civil War, he became a brigadier general in the Confederate army. A natural leader and fighter, McCulloch was very popular with his men but quarrelsome with his less-experienced superiors. He led his brigade at Pea Ridge and lost his life on April 7, 1862.

MAJOR GENERAL FRANZ SIGEL (1824–1902)

Sigel was not the most successful general in the Federal Army although he played a significant role in the victory at Pea Ridge. A German revolutionary, Sigel emigrated to the United States in 1852, as did many other German "Forty-Eighters", and his anti-slavery influence in the Missouri immigrant community led to his commission as colonel of the 3rd Missouri Infantry on May 4, 1861, and speedy promotion to brigadier general on August 7, 1861 – a political appointment endorsed by Lincoln.

At Wilson's Creek, his command was routed after making a march around the Confederate camp and attacking from the rear, but at Pea Ridge, he commanded two divisions and personally directed the Union artillery on the second day of the battle. Promoted to major general on March 21, 1862, in February 1863 another political promotion saw him commanding the new Department of West Virginia. He was defeated by Breckenridge at New Market, on May 15, 1864, and that summer was replaced by Major General David Hunter because of his "lack of aggression." He would not receive an active command for the rest of the war.

The Battle of Pea Ridge

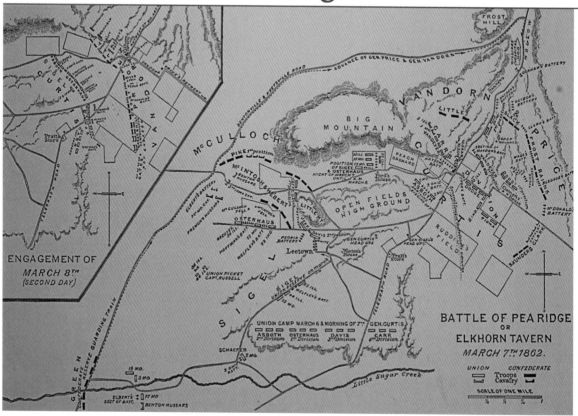

Although nineteen battles were fought in Arkansas, none were as devastating to the welfare of the state as the Battle of Pea Ridge. On February 10, 1862, Union Major General Samuel R. Curtis designed a movement to drive General Price out of Missouri. The campaign succeeded and Price took his 8,000 Missourians into Arkansas to join forces with McCulloch. Since the last dispute between Price and McCulloch, the Confederate War Department had placed Major General Earl Van Dorn as overall commander of the Trans-Mississippi District.

By March 6th, Van Dorn had 17,000 troops available, including Brigadier General Albert Pike's Cherokees from the Indian Territory. While McCulloch's Arkansans and Pike's Cherokees feinted against the Union right, Price marched his Missourians

all night to strike Curtis's left near Elkhorn Tavern. Although late for the attack, Price eventually made progress, but Pike's Cherokees were thrown back and a sharpshooter killed Ben McCulloch, taking the steam out of the attack.

In the morning, Curtis attacked Van Dorn's line, which had reformed around McCulloch's former position. Having depleted most of his ammunition on the previous day, Van Dorn retreated, leaving the field to Curtis. The Confederate defeat at Pea Ridge accomplished two Union strategic goals: Price had been driven completely out of Missouri, and a section of Arkansas now fell under Union control. To make matters worse for Arkansas, Van Dorn received orders to bring his army across the Mississippi and join the Army of Mississippi at Corinth.

THE BATTLE OF PEA RIDGE, ARKANSAS, MARCH 8TH 1862.

Right: Pea Ridge was Major General Sigel's only significant success of the war, but his fame endured. The "Pea Ridge March" was dedicated to him.

Arkansas Confederate Units Furnished	
Infantry regiments	35
Infantry battalions	12
State infantry	3
Militia units	13
Misc. infantry units	16
Cavalry regiments	10
Cavalry Battalions	3
Mounted rifles	2
Misc. mounted units	4
Misc. cavalry units	11
State cavalry	1
Light artillery batteries	5
Misc. artillery batteries	9

The Battle of Prairie Grove

On a bitter cold December day in northwest Arkansas, 11,000 grayclads commanded by Major General Thomas C. Hindman prepared to move against 7,000 bluecoats commanded by Brigadier General James G. Blunt. Knowing he was outmatched, Blunt appealed to Major General Samuel R. Curtis, commanding the Department of the Missouri, for help. Curtis responded by sending Brigadier General Francis J. Herron's brigade, which was 110 miles away. On December 6th, Herron's troops arrived at Fayetteville completely exhausted. Hindman saw an opportunity to move into an eight mile gap between the two Union commands and destroy Herron before the latter united with Blunt in the morning and then crush Blunt.

Before dawn on December 7th, Hindman sent his cavalry to demonstrate against Blunt while his main force struck Herron at Prairie Grove Church, southwest of Fayetteville. The surprise attack, led by Brigadier General John S. Marmaduke's cavalry, drove back Herron's leading elements. With victory in his grasp, Hindman inexplicably took a defensive position. Herron formed a battle line and counterattacked. Blunt heard heavy fighting in the distance and marched quickly toward Prairie Grove. Arriving during the afternoon, Blunt struck Hindman's flank with enfilading fire and collapsed the Confederate line. Hindman called up a newly recruited Arkansas regiment but found it had deserted. The fighting continued until dark, with 1,300 casualties on both sides.

Hindman's demoralized grayclads slipped away during the night, leaving behind many uninjured men who had frozen to death on the battlefield. Hindman also learned that some of his malcontents had removed the bullets from their cartridges and fired blanks. The day following the Battle of Prairie Grove, General Blunt pursued Hindman, captured the town of Van Buren, and gained full possession of northwest Arkansas and western Missouri.

Brigadier General Thomas Carmichael Hindman.

John Sappington Marmaduke.

JOHN SAPPINGTON MARMADUKE (1833–87)

An 1857 graduate of West Point, Marmaduke was serving on the frontier when war began. He resigned his commission in the Union Army and served as colonel of the 3rd Missouri in the Confederate Army. Promoted to major general in 1863, Marmaduke commanded a cavalry division that participated in much of the fighting in Arkansas.

BRIGADIER GENERAL THOMAS CARMICHAEL HINDMAN (1828–68)

During the first twenty-eight years of Thomas Hindman's life, he lived in Kentucky, Alabama, Mississippi, New Jersey, and, in 1856, finally settled as a lawyer in Helena, Arkansas. Elected to Congress in 1858 and 1860, he spent most of his time agitating for secession. Having succeeded in his efforts, he resigned from Congress, raised a regiment, and became the colonel of the 2nd Arkansas Infantry. Promoted to brigadier general in September 28, 1861, he suffered a disabling wound while leading a division on April 6–7, 1862, at Shiloh.

Hindman recovered and, in late May, returned to Arkansas as a major general in charge of the Trans-Mississippi Department. Standing five feet one-inch tall, and with behavior resembling that of a martinet, he quickly became unpopular because of his vigorous enforcement of conscription and martial law. Replaced by Lieutenant General Theophilus H. Holmes to appease the public, Hindman took command of Confederate forces in northwest Arkansas and lost the Battle of Prairie Grove on December 7, 1862. The War Department removed Hindman from Arkansas at his own request and reassigned him to General Braxton Bragg's Army of Tennessee. Hindman led a division at Chickamauga, where he received a wound, and during the Atlanta Campaign, where he received another wound, which incapacitated him for further duty.

When the Confederacy collapsed, Hindman escaped to Mexico to become a coffee planter but ran out of money. Although disliked by many Arkansans, he returned to Helena in 1867 and became involved in Reconstruction issues. On September 28, 1868, an assassin entered his home and killed him.

THE CAPTURE OF LITTLE ROCK SEPTEMBER 10, 1863

After the Battle of Helena on July 4, 1863, which came at great cost to the Confederates in men and morale, the fight for control of Southern capitals swung into full gear. Union Major General Frederick Steele set his sights on capturing the state capital of Little Rock in Pulaski County and began maneuvering Major General Sterling Price's Confederates out of Arkansas. Helena gave Steele a supply base on the Mississippi River and the recent Union victory at Vicksburg gave the Union army unlimited reinforcements. General Price had assumed command of the Confederate District of Arkansas on July 23rd, and deployed his troops in defensive positions near present-day Jacksonville in Pulaski County. He ordered his cavalry to delay the approach of Union troops as long as possible and used the remainder of his command to build fortifications on high ground opposite Little Rock.

On August 10th–11th, Steele sent some 7,000 Union infantry, cavalry, and artillery troops across the swamps of east Arkansas to join Brigadier John Davidson's command at Clarendon. (Unknown at the time, the majority of the fighting for Little Rock would be between Union cavalry and Brigadier General John S. Marmaduke's Confederate cavalry.) Marmaduke slowed the Union advance along the military road leading to Little Rock about the same time Davidson's cavalry struck Price's fortifications opposite the capital. Union troops fell back, and Price withdrew to Little Rock. Steele waited for reinforcements to arrive from Helena, bringing the Union strength to 15,000 by September 2nd. Meanwhile, Price ordered Marmaduke to join forces with Brigadier General Lucius M. Walker. The two generals thoroughly disliked each other. A duel ensued on the morning of September 6th, during which Marmaduke killed Walker, his superior. Price arrested Marmaduke but released him as the final battle for Little Rock began. The incident seemed to demoralize the Confederates and they retreated hastily when they saw the Union infantry approaching. At 7:00 p.m. on September 10th, civilian authorities formally surrendered the capital.

Successful attack on Fort Hindman on January 9–11, 1863, by Union troops under Major General John McClernand.

EPILOG

The loss of Little Rock should have ended the war in Arkansas, but the southern part of the state continued to be occupied by Confederates while the northern section suffered harassment from guerrilla raids. Those Confederates that continued the fight became part of the Trans-Mississippi Department under General E. Kirby Smith, whose command encompassed Confederate activities in Missouri, Arkansas, western Louisiana, Texas, and the Indian Territory. Smith held out until May 26, 1865, but ordered one of his subordinates the chore of surrendering. However, with Arkansas's capital under Union control – along with Nashville, Tennessee, Baton Rouge, Louisiana, and Jackson, Mississippi – President Lincoln issued a "Proclamation of Amnesty and Reconstruction" on December 8, 1863.

The fall of Little Rock had a direct effect on President Abraham Lincoln's decision.

ARKANSAS UNION ARMY DEATHS

Troops Furnished	Killed/Mortally Wounded	Died of Disease	Died of Other Causes	Total
8,289	305	1,254	154	1,713

The proclamation provided that when ten percent of the 1860 voters in a secession state had taken an oath of loyalty to the United States, the state could then establish a Unionist government. That happened in Arkansas on January 4, 1864, with the swearing in of Isaac Murphy as governor. Despite opposition in Congress, this was Lincoln's gentle way of welcoming back the nation's wayward sisters.

A Currier & Ives print showing the bombardment by Union ironclads of Fort Hindman, Arkansas Post, during the 1863 attack led by Union Major General John McClernand, which General Grant later described as a "wild goose chase."

BATTLES IN ARKANSAS

Battle of Arkansas Post	January 9-11, 1863
Battle of Bayou Fourche	September 10, 1863
Battle of Cane Hill	November 28, 1862
Battle of Chalk Bluff	May 1-2, 1863
Battle of Devil's Backbone	August 31, 1863
Battle of Elkin's Ferry	April 3-4, 1864
Battle of Helena	July 4, 1864
Battle of Hill's Plantation	July 7, 1862
Battle of Jenkin's Ferry	April 30, 1864
Battle of Marks' Mills	April 25, 1864
Battle of Old River Lake	June 5-6, 1864
Battle of Pea Ridge	March 6-8, 1862
Battle of Pine Bluff	October 25, 1863
Battle of Poison Spring	April 18, 1864
Battle of Prairie D'Ane	April 9-13, 1864
Battle of Prairie Grove	December 7, 1862
Battle of Reed's Bridge	August 27, 1863
Battle of Saint Charles	June 17, 1862
Battle of Whitney's Lane	May 19, 1862

The *Sultana* at Helena, Arkansas, on April 27, 1865. This photograph shows the steamboat on the Mississippi River the day before she sank. On the 28th her boilers exploded and over 1,100 of her ca. 1,880 passengers – including many Union soldiers heading home at the end of the Civil War – died.

ARKANSAS CONFEDERATE ARMY DEATHS

	Killed	Died of Wounds	Died of Disease	Total
Officers	104	27	74	205
Enlisted	2,016	888	3,708	6,612
Total	2,120	915	3,782	6,817

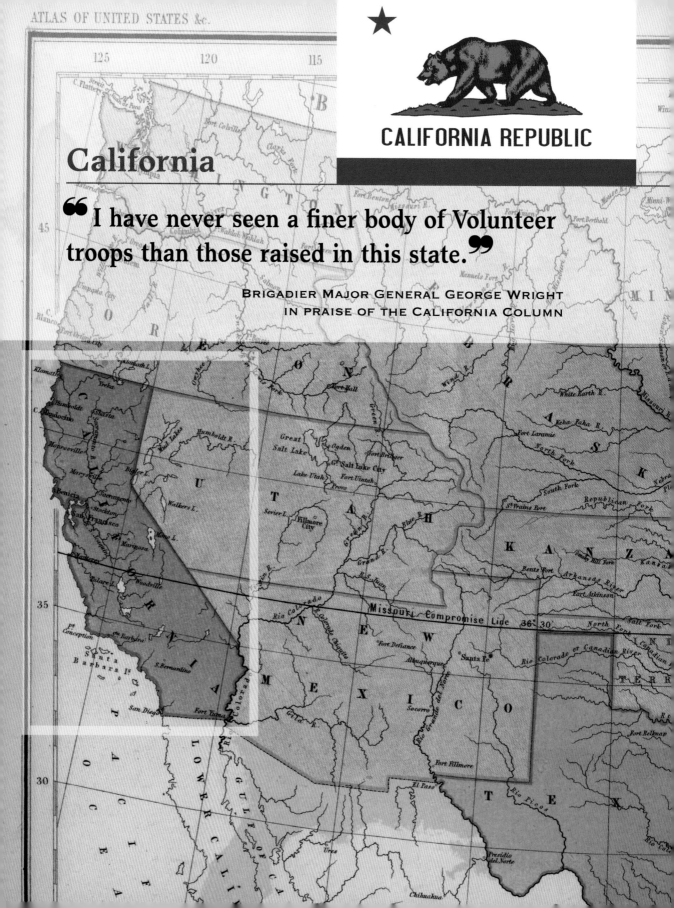

CALIFORNIA REPUBLIC

California

> 66 I have never seen a finer body of Volunteer troops than those raised in this state. 99

BRIGADIER MAJOR GENERAL GEORGE WRIGHT
IN PRAISE OF THE CALIFORNIA COLUMN

The United States acquired California from Mexico on February 2, 1848, under the Treaty of Guadalupe Hidalgo, which ended two years of war with Mexico.

The Gold Rush of 1849 brought more than 15,000 miners and settlers to the state and, over time, those of Mexican ancestry lost touch with their government officials in Mexico City. In 1848, the only other souls populating California were 24,000 Native-Americans scattered about the territory. Because of the unfriendly Indian and Mexican population, and to protect the transportation of gold from California and silver from Nevada, the Federal government established military control of the territory with headquarters in San Francisco. With the signing of the Compromise of 1850, California rejected slavery and on September 9th of that year joined the Union as the nation's 31st state with Sacramento as its capital. The third largest state by area, California's population expanded rapidly to 380,000 by 1860. Military control ceased on January 1, 1861, but after the firing on Fort Sumter in April 1861, California became part of the military Department of the Pacific.

In all, California provided 15,725 volunteers for her own units, plus five companies for the Massachusetts Cavalry and eight for the Washington Territory Infantry. Other units sprang up when New Mexico and Arizona added another 3,500 men to the California roles. Over the course of the war, little would have been accomplished by the Union in the territories of Arizona and New Mexico had it not been for the seminal success of General Carleton's California Column.

JOHN CHARLES FRÉMONT AND THE BEAR FLAGGERS

Of four generals named by President Abraham Lincoln at the outbreak of the Civil War, Major John Charles Frémont earned top billing as the most celebrated. He had become a national hero in 1840 after entering present-day California. Ostensibly

JOHN C. FRÉMONT (1813–90)

John C. Frémont earned a distinguished reputation as the California "Pathfinder", but as a major general during the Civil War he never reached expectations.

For operations in California, Frémont adopted his own flag, which he continued to use for years to come.

there as an explorer in search of a route to the Pacific, Frémont had taken a leading part in a military campaign to win California from Mexico. Although he had attempted to remain in the background, his small band of settlers instigated what became known as the "Bear Flag Revolt". At that time, Frémont intended to turn California into a republic, much as Sam Huston and others had done in Texas. Shortly after the Bear Flaggers succeeded in their revolt, however, Frémont interceded with sixty soldiers, raised his own flag, and took command in the name of the United States. Frémont's popularity soared, and the so-called "Pathfinder" returned home to be nominated as the first Republican president in 1856. He lost the election to James Buchanan, and during the Civil War fumbled every post he held.

UNION DEPARTMENT OF THE PACIFIC

On January 1, 1861, the military departments of California, Oregon, and the Washington Territory were merged into the Union Department of the Pacific at Los Angeles with Brigadier General Albert Sidney Johnston in command. When Johnston resigned to join the Confederacy, Colonel Edwin V. Sumner took his place and held the post until Colonel George Wright arrived from the East and relocated headquarters to San Francisco. Wright raised regiments and sent several of them to Washington, D.C. to serve in the Eastern Theatre. He also built forts up and down the Pacific coast and promulgated treaties with the Indians to encourage peace. In addition to protecting settlers, he maintained the telegraph, kept the overland mail operating, and organized several expeditions, including Colonel James H. Carleton's mid-1862 invasion of Arizona and New Mexico. Relieved by Major General Irvin McDowell on July 1, 1864, Wright lost his life *en route* to taking command of the Department of the Columbia when the steamer transporting him struck a rock off Crescent City, California, and sank.

THE CALIFORNIA COLUMN

After President Lincoln's call for 75,000 troops, Governor Downey authorized the 1st California Regiment and five cavalry companies and placed them under the command of Colonel James H. Carleton, a twenty-year career officer in the Regular Army. Carleton's initial orders were to keep the overland mail route through Nevada and Utah open. A month later, Brigadier General Edwin V. Sumner, commanding the Department of the Pacific, learned of Lieutenant Colonel John R. Baylor's Confederate invasion of the New Mexico Territory and redirected part of Carleton's force to Fort Yuma, a weakly garrisoned fort in western Arizona. Carleton remained at San Francisco, recruiting more volunteers and collecting enough men and supplies to launch a three-stage expedition to drive the Confederates out of the New Mexico Territory.

In February, 1862, Carleton learned that Colonel Edward R. S. Canby's Union column had been defeated at Valverde by Brigadier General Henry H. Sibley's Confederates in New Mexico and that Colonel Baylor had posted 100 Confederate cavalrymen at Tucson. With the southern tier of the New Mexico Territory now in Confederate hands, Carleton recognized the threat to California and asked for reinforcements. Sumner detached the 5th California Infantry, a company from the 2nd California Cavalry, and Company A from the 3rd U.S. Light Artillery. Setting off in early April with 2,000 men and 200

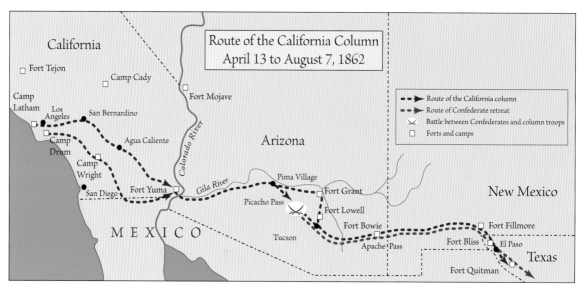

Governor John Gately Downey.

James Henry Carleton seen as a brigadier general.

Brigadier General George Wright.

Major General Edwin V. Sumner.

supply wagons, Carleton reached Fort Yuma on May 2nd and named the expedition "The Column from California." The column continued marching at a steady pace along the old Gila River Trail, fought the Battle of Picacho Pass, whipped Baylor's Texans thoroughly, and entered Tucson on June 8th. He then established martial law and named himself military governor of the Arizona Territory.

After stabilizing Arizona, the California Column headed east, fighting Indians at Apache Pass before moving into New Mexico. Promoted to brigadier general on August 21st, Carleton moved on to Santa Fe and assumed command of the Department of New Mexico without ever engaging in heavy battle. After driving all the organized Confederates out of the territory, Carleton moved into western Texas and captured forts Bliss, Davis, Quitman, and Thorn. Later, Major General Henry W. Halleck, a Californian serving as Lieutenant General Ulysses S. Grant's chief of staff, praised the California Column: "It is one of the most creditable marches on record. I only wish our Army here (in the East) had the mobility and endurance of the California troops."

California Union Units Furnished	
Infantry regiments	8
Infantry battalions	1
Infantry mounted	1
Cavalry regiments	2
Cavalry battalions	1

GOVERNOR JOHN GATELY DOWNEY (1827–94)

Seventh governor of California 1860–1862, John Gately Downey expressed ambivalence over the slavery issue, but responded favorably to Secretary of War Simon Cameron's call for troops though leaving recruiting mainly in the hands of General Wright.

JAMES HENRY CARLETON (1814–73)

An Indian fighter on the frontier during the 1830s, James Henry Carleton raised the California Column around the 1st California Infantry Regiment and in an epic march led 2,000 volunteers into Arizona, New Mexico, and West Texas. He ended the war as a Brevet Major General. See also page 33.

BRIGADIER GENERAL GEORGE WRIGHT (1803–65)

Despite California's distance from the seat of the Civil War, General Wright raised troops to deter Confederate incursions into the New Mexico Territory and French efforts in Mexico to destabilize California.

MAJOR GENERAL EDWIN V. SUMNER (1797–1863)

Lincoln promoted Sumner to brigadier general and sent him to replace Johnston in command of the Department of the Pacific. He returned east in November 1861 and became the oldest field commander of any army corps on either side as leader of the II Corps of the Army of the Potomac.

The California Battalion

The California Battalion evolved from a group of volunteers known as the California Hundred, every man of which had traveled to Massachusetts from California. J. Sewall Reed, among others, hatched the idea and contacted Massachusetts Governor John A. Andrew, offering to help fill the Bay State's quota by raising a company of cavalry. Andrew agreed. The California Hundred used their enlistment bonuses to buy their transportation and, on arrival, merged into the 2nd Massachusetts Cavalry Regiment as Company A.

Four hundred more volunteers from California signed up under the same terms and in March–April 1863 arrived at Fort Meigs, where they were assigned to the defenses of Washington, D.C. When the 2nd Massachusetts Cavalry was sent to Washington, the recently arrived Californians were assimilated into the regiment as companies E, F, L, and M, and the unit became known as the California Battalion. They defended Washington, D.C. in July 1864 when Lieutenant General Jubal Early's Confederates threatened to attack. In August, the battalion joined Major General Philip Sheridan's Army of the Shenandoah for the fall campaign. The Californians soon engaged in bitter battles in Virginia's Shenandoah Valley, fighting at Winchester, Fisher's Hill, and Cedar Creek, and in 1865 they engaged in the final battles at Five Forks and Saylor's Creek. Unlike other California units, the battalion saw real war in the battlefields of the East. They also witnessed the end of the war when General Robert E. Lee surrendered on April 9, 1865, at Appomattox. Three months later, the battalion mustered out of the army and received their final pay. Most of them returned to California.

CAPTAIN J. SEWALL REED (1832–64)

Sewall Reed brought a hundred Californians to Massachusetts to serve with the 2nd Massachusetts Cavalry. Other Californians followed and formed the California Battalion.

CALIFORNIA UNION ARMY DEATHS

Troops Furnished	Killed/Mortally Wounded	Died of Disease	Died of Other Causes	Total
15,725	108	344	121	573

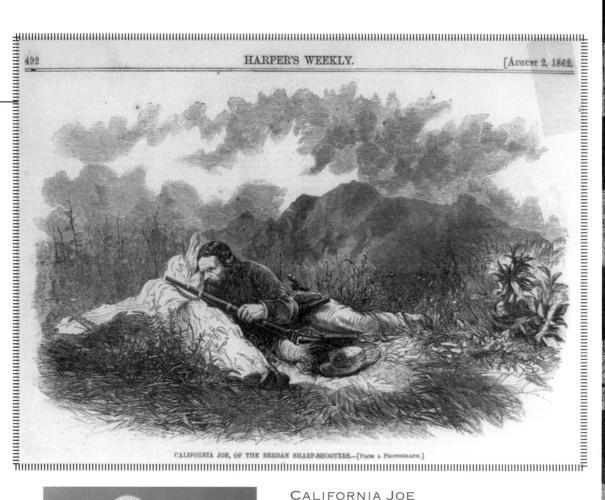

CALIFORNIA JOE, OF THE BERDAN SHARP-SHOOTERS.—[From a Photograph.]

Joseph Rodman West was lieutenant colonel of the 1st California Infantry Regiment, August 1861.

CALIFORNIA JOE

Truman Head served in Company C of the First Regiment of Berdan's Sharpshooters – the famous unit who dressed in distinctive green uniforms and were equipped with the most advanced long-range rifles. Nicknamed "California Joe," he was at least fifty-two years old at the time he enlisted, and was greatly loved by the press because his exploits made for good reading at a time when the Union was sorely lacking heroes and good news from the war. Sadly, Joe didn't spend long with the sharpshooters – his sight was starting to fail him and he was discharged on November 4, 1862. He returned to California and became a customs inspector in San Francisco. He died November 24, 1874. This image above is from *Harper's Weekly* of August 2, 1862, before his discharge.

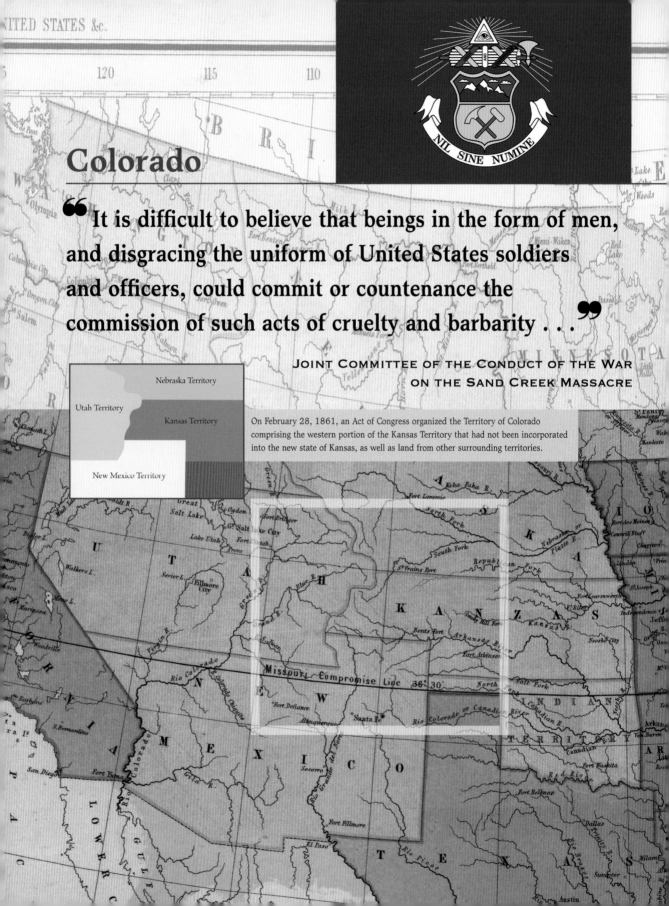

Colorado

"It is difficult to believe that beings in the form of men, and disgracing the uniform of United States soldiers and officers, could commit or countenance the commission of such acts of cruelty and barbarity . . ."

JOINT COMMITTEE OF THE CONDUCT OF THE WAR
ON THE SAND CREEK MASSACRE

NIL SINE NUMINE

Nebraska Territory

Utah Territory

Kansas Territory

New Mexico Territory

On February 28, 1861, an Act of Congress organized the Territory of Colorado comprising the western portion of the Kansas Territory that had not been incorporated into the new state of Kansas, as well as land from other surrounding territories.

Organized as a territory on February 28, 1861, Colorado's population held mixed opinions about the war, with a slightly larger element espousing Unionist rather than Confederate views.

Those sympathizing with the South, however, successfully blocked efforts by Colorado to achieve statehood in 1862, 1863, and 1864. While 4,903 troops served the Union cause, about the same number joined Confederate units though both Colorado governors – William Gilpin in 1861–62 and John Evans in 1862–65 – supported the Union.

There were no major battles in the territory, but both the Union and the Confederacy considered it strategically important because Colorado's gold and silver mines represented mineral wealth to finance the war. Colorado troops served in New Mexico, Kansas, Missouri, and the Indian Territory (present-day Oklahoma) suppressing Indian and guerrilla raids, protecting stage lines, and defending army forts. From February to April 1862, the First Colorado Regiment of Volunteers, raised by Governor Gilpin, saw plenty of action in New Mexico when Brigadier General Henry H. Sibley's Confederates attempted to take control of the territory. Sibley intended to invade the Colorado Territory and to cut the supply lines between California and the rest of the Union, but – largely thanks to Colorado's troops – Confederate forces never reached as far as the future state's territorial border.

GOVERNOR WILLIAM GILPIN (1813–94)

Born in Pennsylvania, William Gilpin graduated from West Point in 1836 and seven years later joined John C. Frémont's 1843 expedition in search of a route over the Continental Divide. Gilpin served as a major in the Mexican-American War and, as a result of his military experience, received command of a volunteer force to suppress Indian uprisings along the Santa Fe Trail. When Colorado became a territory in 1861, President Abraham Lincoln wanted a man with military experience in the West and selected Gilpin as the governor.

Gilpin made excellent progress in getting the Colorado Territory organized. A futurist at heart, he recognized the enormous potential for Colorado, though he is best known for raising troops to defend the region from Confederate invasion. In July 1861, he asked the War Department for permission to raise Union troops to defend the territory. Secretary of War Simon Cameron, unaware of the Confederate buildup in New Mexico and Western Texas, inexplicably turned him down. Gilpin ignored him and, in August, organized the 1st Colorado Regiment of Volunteers. Officers of the regiment included Colonel John Slough, Major John Chivington, Captain Edward Wynkoop, Captain Samuel Cook, Captain Samuel Logan, and several others who earned distinction during and after the war.

Gilpin had no money to arm and equip the regiment, so he issued negotiable drafts directly upon the national treasury. Although illegal, the move worked temporarily. After the Treasury Department discovered $375,000 in unauthorized drafts, President Lincoln removed Gilpin from his gubernatorial post and replaced him with John Evans. Nonetheless, the illegally funded 1st Colorado Regiment – otherwise known as "Gilpin's Pet Lambs" – distinguished itself in the battles of Apache Canyon, La Glorietta Pass, and Peralta.

REVEREND COLONEL JOHN MILTON CHIVINGTON (1821–94)

Chivington emigrated from Ohio, became an elder in the Rocky Mountain Methodist Church, and began following an interest in politics. Believing he could advance by getting attention in the press through military achievement, he joined Governor Gilpin's 1st Colorado Volunteers as a major and made a name for himself at the battle of La Glorietta Pass, New Mexico. Elevated to the rank of colonel after former commander John P. Slough resigned, Chivington envisioned himself as a congressman and hoped to win more attention by exaggerating troubles with the Indians. Governor John Evans, then lobbying for statehood, bought into Chivington's scheme and asked Secretary of War Edwin M. Stanton for more troops to fight Indians. When Stanton denied the request, Chivington appealed to Evans, who agreed to raise the 3rd Colorado – the 2nd Colorado having been sent to Kansas.

Having no Confederates to fight, Chivington attacked peaceful Indians. On November 29, 1864, he struck Black Kettle's Cheyenne village, which was supposedly under the protection of the Federal government. The scandal became known as the Sand Creek Massacre and resulted in a Congressional investigation. After being charged as a pathological racist, Chivington resigned his commission and shed his political ambitions. The former "Fighting Parson" spent the rest of his life traveling through the Western states until his death in Denver on October 4, 1894.

ENGAGEMENT AT VALVERDE

A Confederate cavalry company from Colorado participated in its first action at Valverde on February 21, 1862, when Brigadier General Henry H. Sibley attempted to take control of New Mexico. Around 2:00 p.m. Colonel Thomas Green, leading the 5th Texas Mounted Rifles, sent the Colorado lancers against Union Colonel Edward R. S. Canby's extreme right. Twenty lancers were killed and wounded during the charge along with most of their horses. The lancers then went to the rear, rearmed themselves with pistols and shotguns, and continued fighting. The engagement turned into a defeat for Union forces and the Colorado Lancers, which had been mistaken by Green as an untested New Mexico unit, received praise for preventing Canby from turning the Confederate left flank. The Battle of Valverde, however, represented the high water mark of Sibley's success in New Mexico.

Two Union companies joined Canby's force late and never participated to any degree in the fighting. On March 11, 1862, Colonel Chivington reached Fort Union in northern New Mexico with the 1st Colorado Regiment after a forced march from Denver – too late to be of any service to Canby.

Known as the "Fighting Parson", Chivington wanted a chance of gaining military glory and public advancement but eventually went too far and was disgraced.

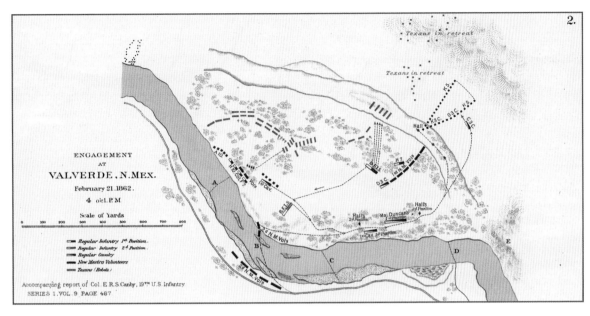

ABOVE: Engagement at Valerde, February 21, 1862, at 4:00 pm. BELOW: at midnight.

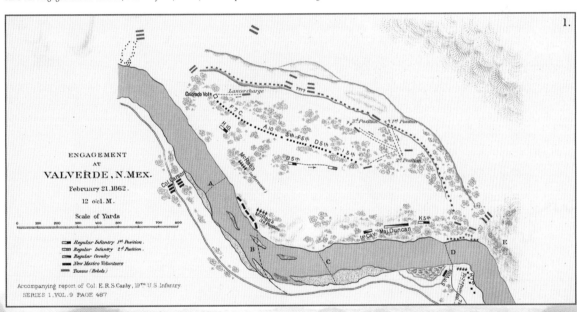

The old battleground of Valverde, on the Rio Grande from *Frank Leslie's Illustrated Newspaper*, July 4, 1885.

The Battle of La Glorieta Pass

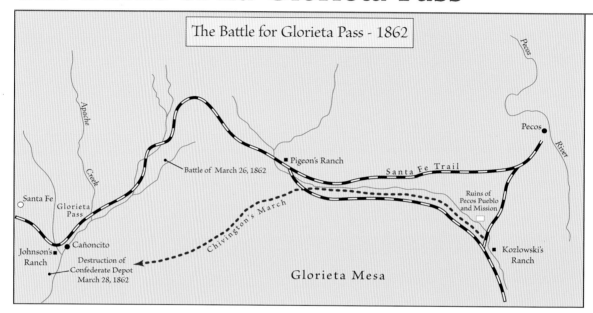

The Battle for Glorieta Pass - 1862

Sometimes called Apache Canyon, La Glorieta Pass ran along the old Santa Fe Trail at the southern tip of the Sangre de Cristo Mountains. On March 25, 1862, Major John Chivington received orders from Colonel Slough to take 418 men and reconnoiter it. From captured Confederate pickets, Chivington learned that a force of roughly 300 Texans under Major Charles L. Pyron had bivouacked at a nearby ranch at the far end of the pass.

During the early morning of March 26th, Chivington fell upon Pyron's camp but was driven off by artillery fire. Chivington redeployed his men among the rocks and created a cross-fire, forcing Pyron to retire to a narrower section of the pass. Chivington sent his men up the slopes, flanked the Texans, and sprayed the defenders with enfilading fire. When the Texans broke, Chivington's men remounted their horses, chased the fleeing Confederates, and captured more than sixty prisoners.

Pyron sent for reinforcements from Sibley while Colonel Slough arrived with the rest of his Union regiment. Lieutenant Colonel William R. Scurry reinforced Pyron with more Texans, bringing the Confederate force to 1,100 men. Slough's force, combined with Chivington's men, numbered about 1,300. Slough moved toward La Glorieta Pass with 900 men while Chivington took his troopers around the pass intending to catch the Confederates between two Federal commands. Scurry realized he was in trouble when Slough opened fire with eight field guns. The fighting, which was fierce at times, ended at 5:00 p.m. when Slough and Scurry both retired. Scurry believed he had bettered Slough until he learned that Chivington had descended on the Confederate rear and captured the supply trains. Scurry returned to Sibley's encampment, reported the loss, and the Confederates retired into Texas. Chivington's blow ended Sibley's designs on the New Mexico Territory – a blow from which the Southerners never recovered. The Battle of La Glorieta Pass ended Confederate efforts to occupy the New Mexico Territory and advance into Colorado. Governor Evans continued to lobby for Colorado statehood, but twenty years passed before Congress finally admitted the territory to the Union in 1876 as the 38th state.

John Potts Slough, who pronounced his name "slow," moved from Ohio to Denver, Colorado, around 1860. Although he became colonel of Colorado's 1st Regiment, he had the annoying habit of acting impulsively and behaving rudely to others.

COLONEL JOHN POTTS SLOUGH (1829–67)

An Ohio state legislator at the age of twenty-one, John Potts Slough moved west after the legislature expelled him for a fistfight with a political rival. In mid 1861, his Democratic antecedents made him a likely Southern sympathizer but he showed his colors by raising a company of Union volunteers. Moving his men into Fort Garland in the Colorado Territory he whipped them into shape and when Governor Gilpin organized the 1st Colorado Regiment of Volunteers, he named Slough colonel.

Colorado Union Units Furnished	
Infantry regiments	3
Cavalry regiments	3
Light artillery battery	1

In March 1862, the 1st Colorado became part of Brigadier General Edward R. S. Canby's army in New Mexico. Canby's assignment was to force Brigadier General Henry H. Sibley's Confederates out of the New Mexico Territory. Placed in command of 1,340 troops detached troops from Canby's army, Slough led an expedition from Fort Union into La Glorietta Pass, where, on March 28th, he collided with Sibley's force. Although under orders not to bring on an engagement, Slough pressed ahead against superior numbers. On the verge of defeat, Chivington's flanking column saved Slough by striking the Confederate rear and capturing Sibley's ammunition and supply wagons. Sibley retreated into Texas, thus ending the Confederate campaign in New Mexico.

Success brought Slough a brigadier generalship and command of a brigade in Virginia. Mustered out in August 1865, he returned to New Mexico as a justice, but his constant feuding with officials led to an altercation with a Santa Fe lawmaker, who shot him. Slough died two days later, unmissed by those who knew him.

COLORADO UNION ARMY DEATHS

Troops Furnished	Killed/Mortally Wounded	Died of Disease	Died of Other Causes	Total
4,903	153	120	50	323

Connecticut

> **At seven o'clock on Tuesday evening, I saw the three Connecticut regiments, with two thousand bayonets, march under the guns of Fort Corcoran in good order, after having saved us not only a large amount of public property, but the mortification of seeing our standing camps fall into the hands of the enemy.**

BRIGADIER GENERAL DANIEL TYLER REPORT AT
FIRST BULL RUN (FIRST MANASSAS)

One of the original thirteen colonies, Connecticut had already begun phasing out slavery before the legislature completely outlawed the practice in 1848.

Along with the rest of New England, the state turned Republican and, in 1856, voted for the party's first presidential candidate, John C. Frémont, giving him all six electoral votes. Republicans opposed extending slavery into the territories, and Connecticut residents agreed, adopting the slogan "Free speech, free press, free soil, free men, Frémont and victory!" Frémont lost the election to James Buchanan of Pennsylvania, but Connecticut remained Republican and in 1860 cast fifty-eight percent of their ballots for Abraham Lincoln, a lawyer from Illinois they knew little about.

According to the 1860 census there were 460,147 people living in Connecticut: 451,504 whites, 8,627 blacks, and sixteen Indians. Twenty percent of the population was foreign-born, with most coming from Ireland. Another twenty percent of the population owned farms, but industrialization had begun drawing people into the cities. Fighting during the Civil War never reached Connecticut, but the state supplied a large number of fighting men and its industry was a major contributor to the war effort.

THE WAR EFFORT

In military and economic support, Connecticut played a larger part in the Civil War, and the ultimate Union victory, than is often acknowledged. Three days after the firing on Fort Sumter, Governor Buckingham formed the 1st Connecticut Infantry under the command of Colonel Daniel Tyler. Two more regiments of ninety-day volunteers quickly followed. During the course of the war, the state furnished thirty full regiments of infantry, including two formed from African-American volunteers. The governor dedicated Fort Trumbull in New London as an organizing center for Connecticut troops and headquarters for the U.S. 14th Infantry Regiment, which handled recruiting and training before sending men off to war.

GOVERNOR WILLIAM ALFRED BUCKINGHAM (1804–75)

Born in Hartford, Connecticut, in 1804, William Alfred Buckingham was a prosperous businessman before he became governor in 1858, a post he would hold for eight years. He met Abraham Lincoln in March 1860 and liked the man's warmth, wit, and integrity. When Lincoln became president and began mobilizing the North, Governor Buckingham proved to be a determined organizer. When, in April 1861, the War Department asked for one regiment to fill the state's quota, Buckingham authorized five. From a population of only 461,000, he eventually raised 54,882 volunteers for military service in the Union army. In 1868, Buckingham ran for the U.S. Senate, won the seat easily, and served until his death in 1875.

Many of the regiments trained at Fort Trumbull distinguished themselves on numerous battlefields. The 14th Connecticut Infantry played a prominent role in the Army of the Potomac's defense of Cemetery Ridge during the Battle of Gettysburg, while the 2nd Connecticut Heavy Artillery fought bravely and suffered heavy casualties during Lieutenant General Ulysses S. Grant's 1864 Overland Campaign, which culminated in the Siege of Petersburg. Not all Connecticut troops fought in the Eastern Theatre, however. The 9th Connecticut Infantry participated in the capture of New Orleans as part of Major General Benjamin F. Butler's "New England Brigade".

Famous Admirals and Generals

Brigadier General Joseph Gilbert Totten.

Major General John Sedgwick.

Major General Alfred Howe Terry.

Rear Admiral Andrew Hull Foote.

BRIGADIER GENERAL JOSEPH GILBERT TOTTEN (1788–1864)

Graduating from West Point as an engineer in 1805, Joseph G. Totten had performed many complicated engineering duties during the War of 1812. He served as General Winfield Scott's chief engineer during the Mexican War and earned a brevet to brigadier general. Prior to the outbreak of the Civil War, Totten toured the country inspecting the nation's harbors and improving coastal defenses, some of which later fell into the hands of the Confederates. Considered as one of the foremost military engineers of his era, Totten continued in command of the Army Corps of Engineers in Washington, where he supervised the construction of the capital's defenses and continued throughout the war to make improvements. The War Department relied on his advice and, on March 3, 1863, boosted his permanent rank to brigadier general in the Regular Army. On April 22, 1864, one day before his death in Washington, D.C., Totten received a brevet to major general. By then, few people remembered that he had come from Connecticut.

REAR ADMIRAL ANDREW HULL FOOTE (1806–63)

Born in New Haven, Connecticut, Andrew Hull Foote attended West Point in 1822 but left to accept an appointment as a midshipman in the navy. He spent the next thirty-nine years sailing the world. In 1861,

Secretary of the Navy Gideon Welles, one of Foote's old friends, put him in charge of the Union fleet in the upper Mississippi. Flag Officer Foote collaborated with Brigadier General Ulysses S. Grant in capturing Fort Henry and Fort Donelson in February 1862, at a time when no other engagements were taking place anywhere in the country. During the action at Fort Donelson, shell fragments struck the flag officer in the foot, but he ignored the wound and kept on fighting.

Foote was still on crutches in March when he attacked Island No. 10. Unable to continue commanding on the Mississippi River, he traveled to Washington, D.C. to serve in an administrative capacity. He disliked the duty, however, and told Welles he wanted to get back into the action. The secretary duly put the rear admiral in charge of the South Atlantic Blockading Squadron but, on the way to his new command, Foote died from his wound on June 26, 1863.

MAJOR GENERAL JOHN SEDGWICK (1813–64)

John Sedgwick entered West Point at the age of twenty and graduated in 1837 as an artillerist. He won distinction fighting under General Winfield Scott in the Mexican War and spent the next several years on the frontier. Appointed brigadier general on August 31, 1861, Sedgwick commanded a division during the 1862 Peninsula Campaign, after which he

Alfred Waud's drawing of the spot where General Sedgwick was killed.

became a major general in the Army of the Potomac. Wounded at Antietam (Battle of Sharpsburg), he recovered and assumed command of the VI Corps.

Sedgwick achieved the reputation of being a dependable leader and distinguished himself at Gettysburg. When Major General George G. Meade failed to follow up the Gettysburg victory, rumors pointed to Sedgwick as the next commander of the Army of the Potomac. The general expressed no interest, however, but retained command of his corps and lost his life when struck in the head by a bullet while supervising the placement of artillery. His remains were returned to Cornwall Hollow, Connecticut, the place of his birth, for burial.

MAJOR GENERAL ALFRED HOWE TERRY (1827–90)

Alfred Terry passed up West Point and went to Yale Law School instead. Nevertheless, he lost interest in his studies and when war broke out raised the 2nd Connecticut, a ninety-day regiment. He led it at First Bull Run (First Battle of Manassas) and, when the unit disbanded, raised the 7th Connecticut for the duration of the war.

After sharing in the capture of Port Royal, South Carolina, in November 1861, and Fort Pulaski, Georgia, in April 1862, Terry became a brigadier general. In the autumn of 1862, he assumed command of the X Corps in General Butler's Army of the James. Unfortunately, Butler mishandled the army, like he had almost everything else. Terry stultified near the Petersburg trenches along with the most of Butler's generals, until assigned to the capture of Fort Fisher, North Carolina, in early January 1865. Cooperating with Rear Admiral David D. Porter in the assault, Terry carried the works and won the thanks of Congress. After the war, he remained in the army and became a major general in the Regular Army.

THE HOME FRONT

What Connecticut could not supply in men the state supplied in manufacturing capacity. Benjamin Tyler Henry of New Haven produced the Henry rifle, one of the most accurate long-range weapons manufactured during the Civil War. Hartford-born Samuel Colt founded Colt's Manufacturing Company and provided the Union with munitions and a variety of handguns. (Naval personnel carried the famous Colt Navy .45 caliber revolver, and so did many Army officers.) Pratt and Whitney, a Hartford company that today produces jet engines, provided arms-making machinery. Connecticut also had a shipyard at Mystic, where warships launched for the navy included the U.S.S. *Monticello* in 1859, the U.S.S. *Varuna* in 1861, and the U.S.S. *Galena* in 1862. In Connecticut, everyone played a role in the war, including the financing that kept the war machine in operation. Compared with other states in the Union, Connecticut did more than its share on the home front.

Above: Colonel Samuel Colt from the *Illustrated London News*, November 29, 1856.
Below: Battery of Parrott guns manned by Company C, 1st Connecticut Heavy Artillery, Fort Brady, Virginia.

CONNECTICUT UNION ARMY DEATHS	
Troops Furnished	51,937
Killed/Mortally Wounded	1,947
Died of Disease	2,542
Died of Other Causes	865
Total	5,354

Connecticut Union Units Furnished	
Infantry regiments	27
Infantry regiments colored	2
Cavalry regiments	1
Heavy artillery regiments	2
Light artillery regiments	3
Garrison guards	1
Unassigned regiment	1
Sailors/marines personnel	2,163
Colored troops	1,784

After serving as colonel of the 1st Connecticut Infantry, Daniel Tyler was appointed brigadier general in the Connecticut militia and commanded a division in Irvin McDowell's Army of Northeastern Virginia.

Gideon Welles was secretary of the navy until 1869. Probably no cabinet member served Lincoln with more loyalty.

SECRETARY OF THE NAVY GIDEON WELLES (1802–78)

Born in Connecticut and educated at present-day Norwich University, Gideon Welles became an Andrew Jackson Democrat. Jackson rewarded Welles by making him Hartford's postmaster and on the outbreak of the war with Mexico, Welles became the head of the Naval Bureau of Provisions and Clothing. Because of his strong antislavery feelings, Welles turned away from Democrats in 1856, became a Republican, and supported Lincoln. When the new president wanted four former Democrats in his cabinet, he chose Welles to represent New England.

Through four years of the Civil War, Welles shouldered the thankless task of mobilizing a navy to blockade Southern ports, fight Confederate ironclads on inland waterways, and clear the high seas of enemy commerce destroyers. Unlike the War Department, he ran a clean operation free of corruption and became one of the most reliable secretaries in Lincoln's cabinet. The president fondly referred to him as "Father Neptune" and sometimes, because of the secretary's silvery wig and beard, called him "Grandfather Welles".

Dakota Territory

> **"I could not afford to hang men for votes."**

ABRAHAM LINCOLN PRIOR TO THE 1864 ELECTION ON THE POPULAR MOVEMENT
IN THE DAKOTAS TO HANG SIOUX RENEGADES

The Dakota Territory did not officially exist until March 2, 1861, though the vast area represented the northernmost lands acquired as part of the Louisiana Purchase in 1803.

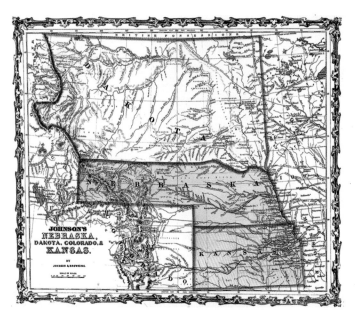

Map of the Dakota Territory, 1861.

The name "Dakota" referred to the various Sioux tribes occupying the area. Sections of the Dakota Territory belonged to the Nebraska and Minnesota territories, though when Minnesota became a state, in 1858, part of its western area remained unorganized until becoming the eastern sector of the Dakota Territory. Two West Pointers, and veterans of the war with Mexico, Daniel M. Frost and John B.S. Todd, resigned their commissions in the late 1850s and formed the Frost-Todd Company to trade with Dakota settlers and establish town sites. After lobbying the government for three years to establish the territory of the Dakotas, Todd used his influence with cousin-in-law President-elect Abraham Lincoln and succeeded in gaining territory status two days before the latter's March 4th inauguration. The territory, by 1860 census, contained a white population of around 900 settlers and included present-day North and South Dakota and most of Montana and Wyoming.

ORGANIZING THE DAKOTA TERRITORY

Abraham Lincoln named William Jayne, a physician from Springfield, Illinois, who had served as the Lincoln family's personal physician, as first governor of the Dakota Territory. Jayne moved to Yankton, the territory's capital and largest town with a population of 300 settlers and found the rugged dirty and dusty town much different from the improved streets and fine homes of Springfield. In the fall of 1861, the War Department authorized the new governor to raise two companies of cavalry, mainly to protect the settlers from Sioux uprisings spreading west from Minnesota. Because the War Department had removed Army regulars from forts Randall and Abercrombie, Jayne also needed men for garrison duty. On December 7, 1861, he established recruiting stations at Yankton, Vermillion, and Bon Homme and placed men in each town to raise volunteers. Recruiting agents in the three towns spent the winter raising troops and, on April 29, 1862, Company A mustered into the service at Yankton for a term of three years with Nelson Miner, captain, J. K. Fowler, 1st lieutenant, and Frederick Ploghoff, 2nd lieutenant. Some of the volunteers had been former members of the Regular Army and knew how to whip the greenhorns into shape.

As Sioux raids intensified, Jayne kept recruiting stations open and called for more men. In addition to Company A, the Dakota Territory recruited the Frontier Rangers, the Yankton Home Guard, and the Vermillion Home Guard. All three units remained at home to protect the settlers but other Dakotans showed more interest in going to war. They joined regiments being formed in Nebraska and Iowa and fought in several major engagements during the Civil War.

"Our Camp at Cha-ink-pah River", watercolor, by Alfred Sully, c. 1856.

THE DAKOTA FORTS

In 1861, the vast Dakota Territory contained only two forts – Abercrombie and Randall. At the outbreak of war, ten officers resigned from the forts and joined the Confederacy. The War Department called most of the remaining troopers to Washington, D.C. to train recruits piling into the capital, leaving Governor Jayne to recruit more Dakotans to garrison the forts. Because of an increase in Sioux uprisings, the governor also recognized the need for increased protection and, over time, new forts such as Rice, Sully, Thompson, and Dakota spread out across the territory. In 1861, the Dakotas became part of the Union District of Kansas, but in 1863 Brigadier General Alfred Sully arrived to take command of the Dakota District and to direct the Indian fighting for the next three years.

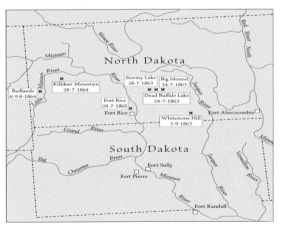

FIRST BATTALION, DAKOTA CAVALRY

After Governor Jayne authorized the formation of Company A at Yankton, Alpheus G. Fuller, an early settler in Dakota's Bon Homme County, recruited a small cavalry command called the Militia Brigade of Dakota. When Fuller failed to get the War Department to accept the company, the volunteers merged with another militia unit at Elk Point. Both units went to Sioux City, Iowa, and became Company B with Captain William Tripp commanding.

The battalion carried the dual assignment of duties in the District of Iowa as well as in the Dakotas and neither command ever exceeded 206 men. Sully split the companies into smaller detachments to operate against marauding Indians throughout the territory and to defend the frontier from Confederate incursions. He called the battalion the 1st Dakota Cavalry, but the two companies fell considerably short of being a regiment.

One of the rare times both companies served together occurred between July 25th and October 8, 1864, when Sully launched a major expedition against hostile Sioux in the Dakota Territory. Two significant engagements occurred, one on July 28th at Tahkaha-kuty and the other on May 9, 1865, at Two Hills in the Badlands on the Little Missouri River. Company A mustered out after the May 9th engagement, but Company B remained active until November 15, 1865.

Brigadier General Daniel Marsh Frost.

Dr. William Jayne.

Brigadier General Alfred Sully.

BRIGADIER GENERAL DANIEL MARSH FROST (1823–1900)

Frost served in the Dakota Territory as an antebellum officer in the U.S. Army and as a brigadier general in the Confederate States Army during the Civil War. He spent many years in Missouri politics and developed a personal friendship with Missouri Governor Claiborne F. Jackson, a secessionist. Through this relationship, Frost joined the Confederacy.

DR. WILLIAM JAYNE (1826–1916)

Jayne mixed his medical practice with politics and, in 1861, became governor of the Dakota Territory. In 1863, he replaced John Todd as delegate to the U. S House of Representatives.

BRIGADIER GENERAL ALFRED SULLY (1821–79)

Born in Pennsylvania, and a graduate of the West Point class of 1841, Sully spent most of his life as an officer in the Plains States, where he earned a reputation as an Indian fighter. Being an oil and watercolorist, Sully liked the Western scenery and painted it wherever he went. On February 3, 1862, he became colonel of the 1st Minnesota Volunteer Infantry and was ordered east. Sully led the regiment in Virginia's Peninsula Campaign and became a brigade commander. The War Department raised him to brigadier general and sent him back to the frontier in command of the Dakota Territory during the Sioux uprising of 1862 in Minnesota. When the trouble spread to the Dakotas, Sully sent cavalry after Sioux parties raiding settler encampments. Some actions became major engagements. During the Battle of White Stone Hill on September 3–5, 1863, for example, Sully's troopers suffered seventy-two casualties while destroying 500 tipis and killing or wounding 750 warriors, women, and children.

While at Fort Randall, South Dakota, Sully met and married a French-Indian girl from the Yankton Sioux tribe who reminded him of his young Mexican wife, who had died from a cholera epidemic in California. The marriage made him the son-in-law of Saswe, a powerful Yankton medicine man and chief of the half breeds. Sully fit right in with the Indians, so long as they behaved, protected the settlers, and brought order to the territories. He also raised a daughter, whom he named Mary. The Yankton Sioux called her Akicita Win, which translated meant "Soldier Woman". She later became the wife of Reverend Philip Joseph Deloria, an Episcopal priest and leader of the Sioux nation's Yankton-Nakota tribe.

DAKOTA TERRITORY UNION ARMY DEATHS

Troops Furnished	Killed/Mortally Wounded	Died of Disease	Died of Other Causes	Total
206	2	4	0	6

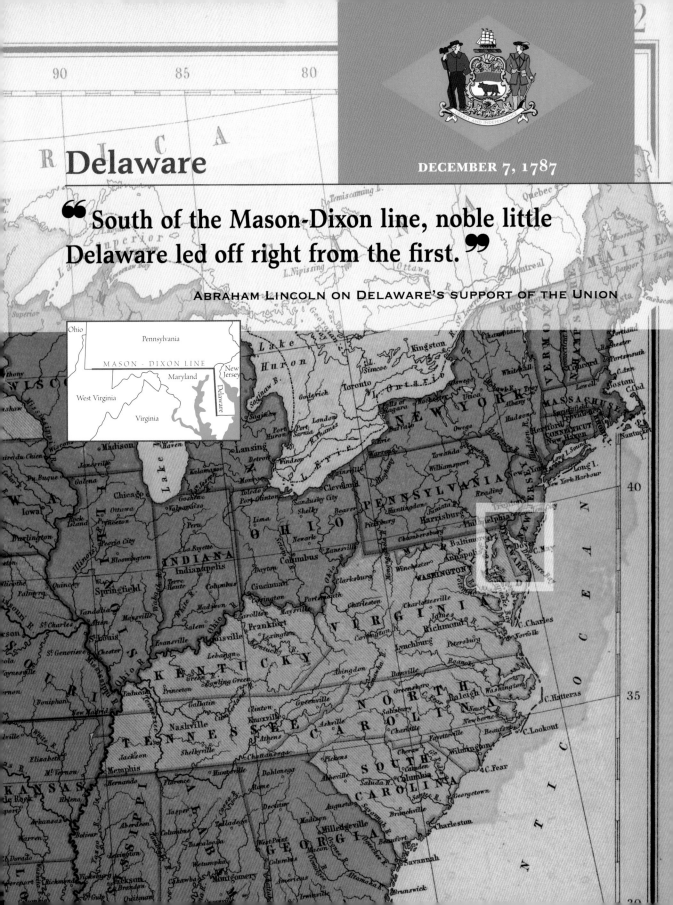

Delaware

> **"South of the Mason-Dixon line, noble little Delaware led off right from the first."**

ABRAHAM LINCOLN ON DELAWARE'S SUPPORT OF THE UNION

One of the original thirteen British colonies and member of the Continental Congress, Delaware became a sovereign state in 1776, signed the Articles of Confederation on February 22, 1779, and, on December 7, 1787, became the first state to ratify the Constitution.

Governor William Burton (1789–1866). Born in Delaware and a practicing physician, Burton turned to politics in 1830 and became sheriff of Kent County.

Considered a border state, it allowed slavery but was less divided in its loyalties than Maryland, the neighboring state, or the mid-western states of Kentucky and Missouri. Delaware had only one major city, industrial Wilmington, and much of the rest of the state relied on agriculture. With only 1,800 slaves, Delaware nonetheless met the official 1860 definition of a slave state, but though the majority of the population disapproved of any military action by the Federal government to force Southern states back into the Union, they also disapproved of secession.

During the 1860 presidential election, John C. Breckinridge, the Democratic candidate and former vice-president under James Buchanan, received the most votes with 7,320. Abraham Lincoln, with 3,810 votes, came in third behind Constitutional Unionist John Bell, who tallied 3,830 votes. After taking office, Lincoln offered to compensate owners for the emancipation of their slaves, but Delaware's state legislature rejected the proposal. Nevertheless, despite some support for the South, Delaware remained loyal and furnished some 11,236 soldiers to the Union. Most of the volunteers served in the Army of the Potomac. A much smaller number of Delaware's men joined Maryland and Virginia regiments and fought for the South.

Even as the Civil War began petering out, there were still those in Delaware who still enjoyed the privileges of slavery. On February 18, 1865, two months before the end of the war, the Delaware legislature seemed intent on supporting slavery and voted to reject the 13th Amendment to the Constitution, which abolished the practice throughout the nation. When other states ratified the amendment, however, Delaware looked a little foolish.

GOVERNOR WILLIAM BURTON TAKES A STAND

When William Burton ran for governor in 1858, he never considered the possibility of becoming a war governor and during the early months of the Civil War tried to straddle the issue by steering a course down the middle – upsetting neither those sympathetic with the South nor Delaware's Unionists. He opposed secession partly because of Delaware's geographic proximity to Pennsylvania and Maryland. In fact, a Confederate delegation came to Delaware to sway the General Assembly toward secession, but Burton stood fast and the legislature rejected the overture. Delaware thus remained firmly in the Union, but not without scattered pro-Southern factions attempting to gather arms and cause trouble. Burton told the groups to disarm but then withdrew the request. Instead, he appointed West Point graduate Henry A. du Pont, president of E. I. du Pont de Nemours and Company, to take charge of the state militia. Du Pont directed his efforts toward strengthening the loyal militia and made sure that all the gunpowder produced by the Du Pont Company mills went to them and not Southern sympathizers. In fact, Du Pont ended up supplying over half the gunpowder used by the Union armies.

When the War Department called for regiments from Delaware, however, Burton refused to relinquish the militia but agreed to encourage enlistment. By then, support for the Union had strengthened to the point that Delaware provided a larger number of soldiers relative to the size of its population than any other state.

FORT DELAWARE

Pea Patch Island in the Delaware River became the site for building a fort shortly after the War of 1812 but, because of marshy ground and foundation issues, the Army Corps of Engineers tore down the original structure in 1833. Fresh work began around 1848, and, by 1859, Fort Delaware was the largest of its kind in the United States. Though the structure was never intended to be used as a prison, it became one in 1862.

During the Civil War, Delaware first used the fort to organize and muster state troops. That lasted only a short time. Some of the units mustered on Pea Patch Island remained there and performed garrison duty when Fort Delaware became a prison for Confederate troops, Southern sympathizers, and Federal soldiers convicted of crimes. The island soon became overcrowded and wooden barracks resembling sheds began collecting outside the fort though the ground was soggy and many of these shelters started to sink. Nevertheless, the number of prisoners on the island increased. Most of the Confederates captured at Gettysburg were sent to Fort Delaware, which, by 1863, held some 11,000 prisoners. By war's end, that number had increased to 33,000. The conditions were barely tolerable, and more than 2,400 prisoners died at the fort. As one prisoner commented, the chances of dying on Pea Patch Island were greater than dying on the battlefield.

All Civil War prisons were horrible but word was soon spread by the few Confederates released through prisoner exchanges that Fort Delaware ranked among the worse. Indeed, the Hungarian refugee, Brigadier General Albin F. Schoepf, who commanded the prison, became known to the inmates as "General Terror". While Colonel William Hoffman, commissary general for Federal prisons, insisted the prisoners were adequately provisioned, the surgeon general said the men were dangerously packed together without proper cooking implements and some were diseased, sick, emaciated, and on the verge of starvation. General Terror met the surgeon general's concerns with indifference.

"Fort Delaware, Delaware", by Seth Eastman (1808–75), painted 1870–75.

Fort Delaware on Pea Patch Island.

Delaware's Distinguished Officers

MAJOR GENERAL GEORGE SYKES (1822–80)

George Sykes grew up in Dover, Delaware's capital, and at the age of sixteen entered West Point, graduating thirty-ninth in a class of fifty-six. Many of the officers with whom he graduated would later become Union or Confederate generals during the Civil War. As major in the 14th U.S. Infantry, he led "Sykes Regulars" on July 21, 1861, at First Bull Run (First Battle of Manassas). Two months later, on September 28th, he rose in rank to brigadier general. Merged into the Army of the Potomac, Sykes led a brigade at the Battle of Yorktown during the Peninsula Campaign and a division during the Seven Days Battles that followed. He gained particular distinction at Gaines' Mill on June 27th, and at Malvern Hill on July 1st. His command became heavily engaged at Second Bull Run (Second Manassas) on August 30th, and lightly engaged at Antietam (Battle of Sharpsburg) on September 17th. On November 29, 1862, two weeks before the Battle of Fredericksburg, Sykes became a major general.

In June 1863, Major General George G. Meade assumed command of the Army of the Potomac. An irascible and quarrelsome commander, Meade complimented Sykes's management of the V Army Corps on July 2, 1863, at Gettysburg but blamed him for acting too slowly during the Battle of Mine Run in late November. Meade had received much of the blame for the Army of the Potomac's ineffectiveness at Mine Run and the general, with some justification, shifted the resonsibility to Sykes. After nicknames such as "Tardy George" and "Slow Trot Sykes" began resonating through the Army of the Potomac, the general knew he was in trouble. When Lieutenant General Ulysses S. Grant took command of the Union armies in March 1864, he decided Meade might be right and sent Sykes west to command the Department of Kansas.

Sykes remained in the postwar army with a permanent rank of colonel and died while serving in the West on February 8, 1880.

Major General George Sykes. A West Point graduate from the class of 1842, George Sykes fought in the Seminole Wars, the Mexican War, and on the frontier. A corps commander in the Army of the Potomac, he distinguished himself at Gettysburg by repulsing two Confederate attacks.

Major General Alfred Thomas Archimedes Torbert. General Torbert grew in military prowess as the war progressed, advancing from a commander of an infantry regiment to command of the Army of the Shenandoah.

MAJOR GENERAL ALFRED THOMAS ARCHIMEDES TORBERT (1833–80)

Born in Georgetown, Delaware, Alfred Torbert graduated from West Point in 1833 at the age of twenty-two and became a second lieutenant in the infantry-cavalry. His choice of service guaranteed that he would serve in the West, which he did until he took leave and returned home on February 25, 1861. Two months later he received the rank of 1st lieutenant in the Confederate Artillery. Torbert rejected the appointment, recruited New Jersey volunteers, and, on September 16th, became colonel of the 1st New Jersey Infantry Regiment. For the next two years he commanded his regiment, and later a brigade, in all the major battles of the Army of the Potomac. After leading a brigade of the VI Corps on August 29, 1862, and after several months of exceptional performance, Torbert earned the rank of brigadier general on November 29th.

When Lieutenant General Ulysses S. Grant reorganized the Union armies during the spring of 1864, Torbert received command of a cavalry division in Major General Philip Sheridan's Cavalry Corps. Torbert fought in every one of Grant's battles during the 1864 Overland Campaign and when Sheridan assumed command of the Army of the Shenandoah in August 1864, Torbert became a major general and commanded Sheridan's cavalry. He struggled at times during the Shenandoah Valley Campaign during the fall of 1864 but redeemed himself at Tom's Brook by completely routing and permanently disabling the Confederate cavalry.

Torbert resigned from the Army in 1866 and spent much of the rest of his life performing diplomatic duties for the government and dabbling in business. He drowned on August 29, 1880, when the steamer *Vera Cruz* was wrecked off the coast of Cape Canaveral, Florida.

General Torbert (seated center holding saber) and staff at headquarters during the 1864 Shenandoah Valley Campaign.

ADMIRAL SAMUEL FRANCIS DU PONT (1803–65)

Although born at Bergen Point, New Jersey, Du Pont always called Wilmington, Delaware, his home though he was often at sea, serving in European waters, the West Indies, along the South American coast, the Far East, and the Mediterranean. In 1860, he commanded the Philadelphia Navy Yard and, in June 1861, became president of the naval board Secretary of the Navy Gideon Welles convened to plan the Navy's Civil War strategy. Promoted to flag officer in September 1861, Du Pont commanded the South Atlantic Blockading Squadron and led the successful amphibious attack on Port Royal, South Carolina, for which he earned the thanks of Congress and promotion to rear admiral.

Du Pont continued to capture forts along the southern Atlantic coast, but on April 7, 1863, ran into stiff opposition from heavy shore batteries in Charleston Harbor. After two hours of battle, he withdrew. Five ships had suffered damage and one sank the following day. Du Pont had argued against entering Charleston's harbor but Secretary Welles insisted the effort be made. Du Pont blamed his failure on the seven monitors in his command, calling them unfit, and wanted to make the facts public so he could place the responsibility on Welles. When the secretary refused, Du Pont asked to be relieved.

On July 6, 1863, Welles granted the admiral's wishes. In failing health, Du Pont retained his commission and returned to his home in Wilmington. He died on June 23, 1865, while visiting Philadelphia.

Admiral Samuel Francis Du Pont. Appointed midshipman on December 19, 1815, at the age of twelve, Samuel Francis Du Pont spent the balance of his life in the U.S. Navy.

DELAWARE UNION ARMY DEATHS

Troops Furnished	Killed/Mortally Wounded	Died of Disease	Died of Other Causes	Total
11,236	383	356	143	882

General Sykes and his staff at Antietam (Battle of Sharpsburg).

THE CRAZY DELAWARES

The 2nd Infantry Regiment, Delaware Volunteers, were formed after President Lincoln's second call for troops and his first call for three-year regiments. The War Department set new quotas and asked Governor Burton for four regiments. The men began mustering in on May 21, 1861, under Colonel W. H. Wharton and Lieutenant Colonel William P. Bailey. Delawareans responded tepidly, however. Five companies came from Maryland, three from Philadelphia, and only two from Delaware.

There is no account that explains why the regiment bore the name "The Crazy Delawares", other than the fact that most men came from another state. Although some of the companies were still short by a few men when organized into a regiment, the unit took the field with thirty-three officers and 805 men

Delaware Union Units Furnished	
Infantry regiments	10
Cavalry battalion	1
Independent cavalry	1
Heavy artillery regiments	1
Light artillery regiments	2
Unassigned regiment	1
Sailors/marines personnel	94
Colored troops	954

and fought in all the major campaigns of the Army of the Potomac. After three years of fighting and unsustainable losses, the regiment began mustering out in July 1864.

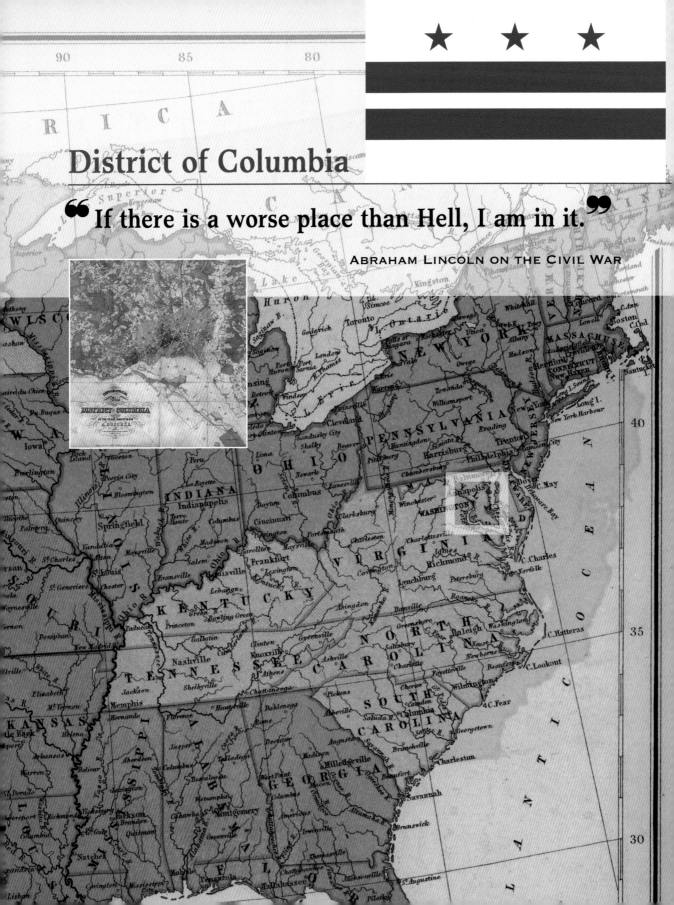

District of Columbia

"If there is a worse place than Hell, I am in it."

ABRAHAM LINCOLN ON THE CIVIL WAR

The United States Constitution, signed by Congress on September 17, 1787, and ratified by the states on June 21, 1788, established a system of government that began to function in 1789.

One provision of the Constitution authorized the creation of a special district, not a part of any state, to serve as the permanent national capital overseen by the Federal government. In compliance, George Washington picked a spot on the north shore of the Potomac River and Maryland and Virginia granted land on opposite sides, including the towns of Alexandria on the Virginia shore and Georgetown on the Maryland shore. During 1791–92, Andrew Ellicott and several assistants surveyed the border of the District – then described as a territory ten miles square – placing boundary stones every mile. Within this area, the government created a new capital city in 1791 and named it in honor of George Washington. Hence, the capital of the United States became Washington, D.C., where on November 17, 1800, Congress met for the first time. The Organic Act of 1801 officially organized the District of Columbia and placed the entire area, including the cities of Washington, Alexandria, and Georgetown under the exclusive control of Congress.

In 1800, the slavery issue had not yet gathered momentum and no politician had the foresight to ask what might happen to the national capital if slavery divided the nation and encased the District of Columbia between two slave-holding states: Maryland and Virginia. The issue came into focus in 1860, however, during the latter months of James Buchanan's presidency. After Abraham Lincoln's election in November, South Carolina seceded from the Union on December 20, 1860. Between December and Lincoln's inauguration on March 4, 1861, six more Southern states seceded, though not Virginia or Maryland.

A Republican but not an abolitionist, Lincoln never appeared on the ballot in the South and by

PRESIDENT JAMES BUCHANAN (1791–1868)

President Buchanan rode with Lincoln to the inauguration ceremonies and then departed from Washington without informing Lincoln of the impending crisis. For most of his administration, he had vacillated on Southern secession and made no effort to curb it or safeguard Federal property being confiscated by the Confederacy. He departed from Washington leaving the government in a state of virtual chaos.

Inauguration Day, tensions were running so high that seventy-five-year-old Lieutenant General Winfield Scott, general in chief of the Army, turned out the Washington regulars to prevent the assassination of Lincoln as he rode in a carriage with President Buchanan to the swearing-in ceremony at the Capitol. Scott knew Southern sympathizers resided in Washington, and many were openly hostile toward the Federal government. Lincoln didn't notice the Union sharpshooters standing on rooftops, or the cavalry posted on side streets. He survived the trip to and from the Capitol and moved into the White House immediately following his inauguration.

LINCOLN'S CABINET

Probably no prior president ever had so much trouble forming a cabinet as Lincoln. On the night of his election he decided the cabinet should represent the true antecedents of the Republican Party and determined to select four former Democrats and three former Whigs with himself as the fourth Whig. Clashes between the men he chose began immediately.

New Yorker William H. Seward, Lincoln's selection as secretary of state, believed the cabinet should be all Whigs. Former governor of Ohio, Salmon P. Chase, the incoming secretary of the treasury, disliked Seward, who he believed would try to run the government. Simon Cameron, a political power-player from Pennsylvania, had never been in Lincoln's original cabinet plan but brokered a deal that put Lincoln on the presidential ballot during the Republican convention in May 1860. As a pay-off, Cameron wanted to head the patronage-rich Treasury Department. That post had gone to Chase, so Cameron had to settle for the War Department. Gideon Welles, a former Democrat from Connecticut, had not bargained for anything and accepted the post of secretary of the navy. Like Chase, Welles disliked Seward and believed the New Yorker, who had lost the presidential nomination to Lincoln, would try to run the government. Caleb Blood Smith of Illinois had also brokered a deal during the Republican convention. He had never been on Lincoln's short-list, but the president relented and made him secretary of the interior. Montgomery Blair

Diagram of the Federal government and American Union by N. Mendal Shafer, dated 1861. It shows the outline of forty-two states and Indian Territory, a Civil War battle scene, and Liberty holding the U.S. flag and sword riding on the back of an eagle, as well as Lincoln and his cabinet (the secretaries linked to images of the Army, Navy, Treasury, Interior, P.O. Deptartment, and State Department) representing the "Executive" branch, the Senate and the House of Representatives representing the "Legislative" branch, and the Supreme Court representing the "Judicial" branch of the Federal government. Also, cameo portraits of "the seven builders and leading spirits of the revolution."

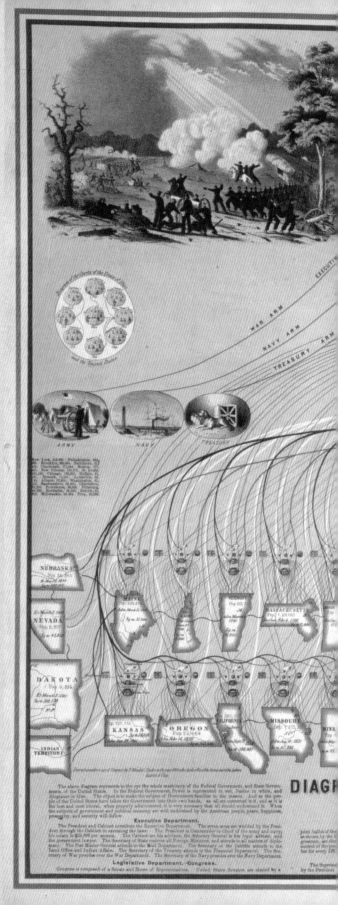

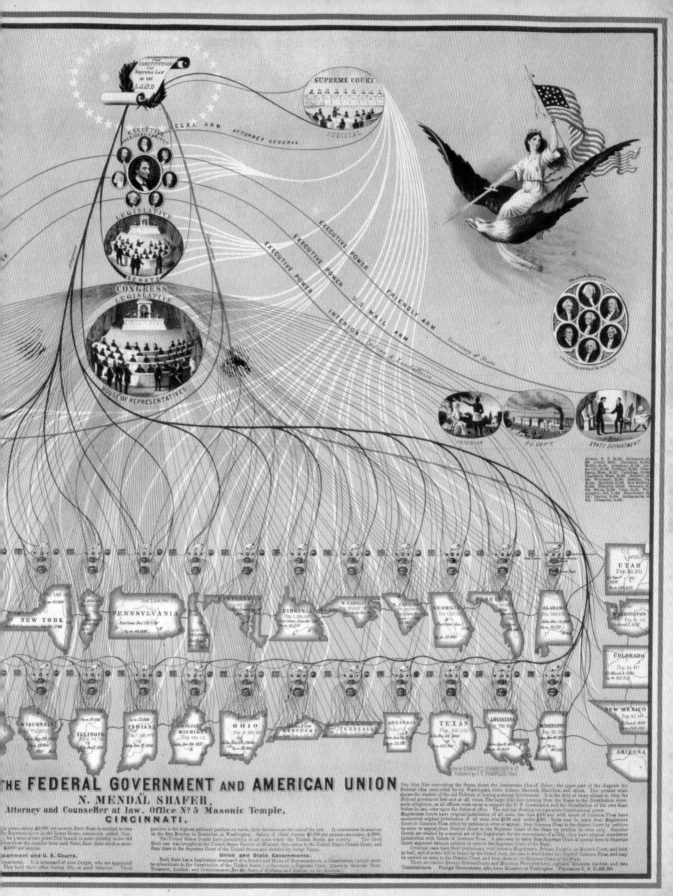

THE FEDERAL GOVERNMENT AND AMERICAN UNION

N. MENDAL SHAFER,
Attorney and Counsellor at Law, Office No 5 Masonic Temple,
CINCINNATI.

The bombardment of Fort Sumter by the batteries of the Confederate states.

of Maryland became postmaster general, and Edward Bates of Missouri became attorney general. A non-cabinet member, Vice-President Hannibal Hamlin of Maine, remained in his home state during most of Lincoln's term and contributed virtually nothing to the administration.

FORT SUMTER

On March 5th, the first day of business in the White House, Lincoln found a note from former Secretary of War Joseph Holt warning that the Fort Sumter garrison in Charleston, South Carolina's Harbor, was running out of provisions. Lincoln called a meeting with the cabinet to ask if the fort should be reinforced or evacuated. Seward took the lead because he believed Fort Sumter should be evacuated to preserve strong Unionist sentiment in the South, which did not actually exist. Most of the cabinet, including General Scott, agreed with him.

After three weeks of presidential arm-twisting and further deliberation, the cabinet finally agreed to re-provision the fort, and, if possible, land reinforcements. Because of Seward's secretive meddling in the relief of Fort Pickens, Florida, however, the secretary inadvertently delayed the Fort Sumter mission by several days. When Union relief ships arrived late off Charleston's harbor on April 13th, Confederate batteries were already pummeling Sumter. Major Robert Anderson surrendered the fort and the following day evacuated the garrison.

Lincoln accepted the loss as a victory, not a defeat. He could now blame South Carolina for starting the war.

Opposite page: The steamship *Star of the West*, with reinforcements for Major Anderson, approaching Fort Sumter while the South Carolinians firing on the fort from batteries on Morris Island and Fort Moultrie. From *Frank Leslie's Illustrated Newspaper*, January 19, 1861.

Joseph Holt (1807–94)

Holt had been secretary of war during the last two months of the Buchanan administration. Lincoln never considered the Kentuckian for a cabinet post, but he continued to serve in that capacity until March 11th, when Simon Cameron arrived in Washington. Over a period of five days, Lincoln recognized too late that Holt was a magnificent organizer who would have cleaned out the dead wood and red tape in the War Department had he remained in charge. In retrospect, Lincoln admitted that Holt would have been a much more effective secretary than Cameron.

Simon Cameron (1799–1889)

As Lincoln's secretary of war, Cameron knew nothing about war, despite calling himself "General", and spent the first months on the job dispensing patronage to his friends. He avoided cabinet meetings on critical issues and seemed content with the department's red-tape system, which was controlled by clerks and officers whose service dated back to the War of 1812. Ten months after his appointment, Cameron resigned under duress, leaving the department in a mess.

LIEUTENANT GENERAL WINFIELD SCOTT (1786–1866)

Born in Virginia, General Scott rose to heroic status during the War of 1812 and became general-in-chief of the Army in 1841. He proved his worth again by defeating the Mexican army in 1847. Although Scott possessed a good military mind, he had not kept current with 1860s technology. Nor was he in good health. Weighing over 300 pounds, stricken with gout and other ailments, he could not take the field or travel far. Even a carriage ride of a few blocks to the White House exhausted him and, after slumping into a chair, he usually fell asleep. Although ridiculed at first for suggesting the Anaconda Plan, it was proved by subsequent events to be sound.

The Call to Arms

On April 15, 1861, President Lincoln used the firing on Fort Sumter as his justification for issuing a proclamation calling for 75,000 three-month volunteers. Confederate President Jefferson Davis had already raised more than 100,000 troops and, on April 17th, upped the ante by granting letters of marque and reprisal to any ship owner willing to arm his vessel to prey on Union commerce. Lincoln called a meeting with his cabinet to discuss possible means of retaliation and announced the blockade of Confederate ports on April 19th. Secretary of the Navy Welles did not have the ships to implement a blockade, however, and began a massive mobilization of the Union Navy. The blockade idea – dubbed the "Anaconda Plan" by the press – had originated in a strategy session with General Winfield Scott, who suggested that the South be squeezed into submission by closing down Confederate ports and obtaining control of the Mississippi River. Although some cabinet members thought it too heavy-handed, Lincoln disagreed and set the strategy in motion.

Lincoln and his cabinet, with Lieutenant General Winfield Scott (center, pointing at map) in the council chamber at the White House.

An 1861 cartoon of General Scott's Anaconda Plan.

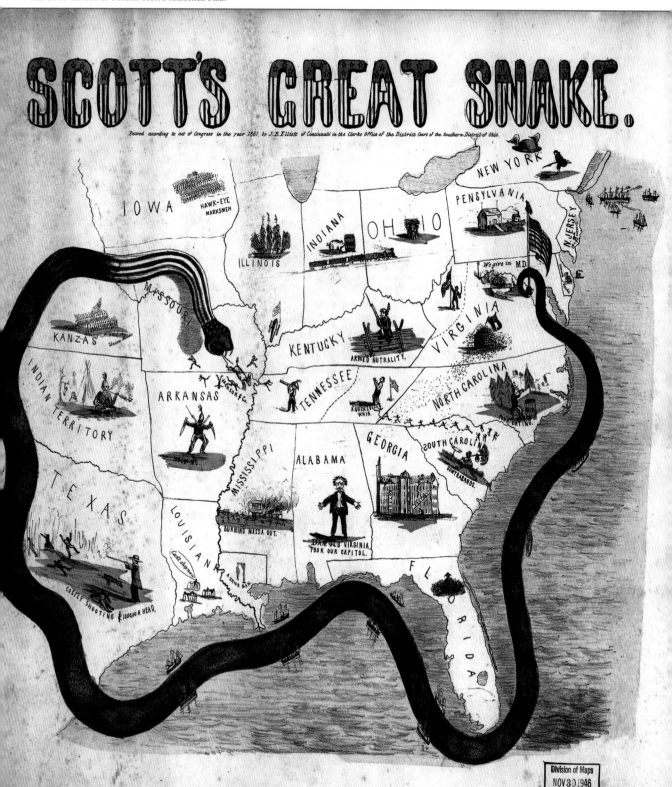

FORTIFYING WASHINGTON

Virginia seceded on April 17th as the direct result of Federal mobilization while secessionists in Maryland became openly hostile to the Union. Baltimore thugs attacked the 6th Massachusetts as the regiment, *en route* to Washington, changed trains. Lincoln succeeded in curbing the secession movement in Maryland, thus preventing the capital from being surrounded by Southern states, but little else had been done to safeguard Washington from attack. It was obvious that because of the capital's precarious geographic location it needed to be fortified.

The task fell to seventy-three-year-old Brigadier General Joseph G. Totten, who held the title of commander, Corps of Engineers, and Brigadier General John G. Barnard, chief engineer. In 1861, Barnard began the construction of Washington's defenses – a frustrating task little appreciated by others but a major engineering feat that made Washington virtually impregnable.

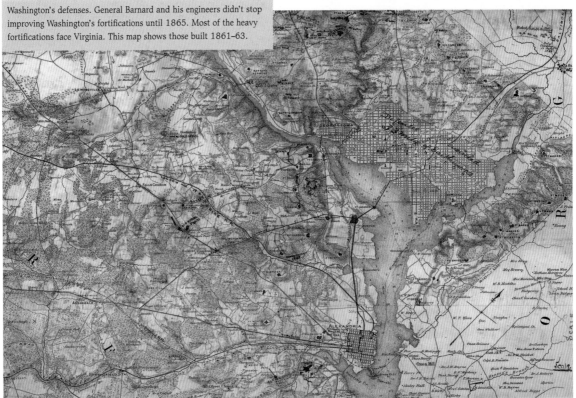

Washington's defenses. General Barnard and his engineers didn't stop improving Washington's fortifications until 1865. Most of the heavy fortifications face Virginia. This map shows those built 1861–63.

Left: Major General John G. Barnard (1815–82). While he was building Washington's fortifications, generals in the field constantly relied on Barnard when confronted with problems. Major General George B. McClellan used him during the 1862 Peninsula Campaign, and Lieutenant General Grant brought him into the field to command engineering operations during the 1864 Petersburg Campaign. Barnard had high regard for Grant and little regard for McClellan as field commanders.

Right: Born in the District of Columbia, Rose O'Neal Greenhow was well-known in Washington society. Every politician and high-ranking officer sought her companionship, making her an effective and useful spy for the Confederacy. Her younger daughter, also named Rose, joined her in prison, later traveled with her, and eventually became an actress in England.

ROSE O'NEAL GREENHOW (1817–64)

When a teenager, Rose O'Neal moved into her aunt's fashionable boarding house and soon became the center of attention in Washington. A beautiful and seductive young lady, she hobnobbed with high society, counting presidents, senators, some of the highest ranking officers in the army, and Southern spies among her admirers. Having cultivated such close relationships with men of influence, she disappointed many when she married Dr. Robert Greenhow. After her husband died, however, Greenhow resumed her social life and used her talents and connections to discover the Union Army's plans, which resulted in the rout of Brigadier General Irvin McDowell's Federals on July 21, 1861, at First Bull Run (First Manassas).

Eventually arrested in February 1862, and brought to trial after spending two months imprisoned, a court deported her to Richmond, where enthusiastic crowds greeted her with cheers. Jefferson Davis believed that Greenhow would make an excellent emissary and sent her to Europe with her daughter, Rose. In France, Greenhow visited with Napoleon III, and in England she met Queen Victoria. During her travels she also wrote *My Imprisonment*, a book that recalled the events leading up to and including her incarceration in Washington's Old Capitol Prison. It became a best-seller.

Summoned back to Richmond by President Davis, Greenhow left her daughter in England and booked passage on the blockade runner *Condor*. Disaster struck when the ship struck a sandbar in the mouth of the Cape Fear River. Greenhow tried to reach shore but was dragged under the waves by $2,000 in gold she was carrying when her lifeboat overturned. She was buried with honors in Wilmington, North Carolina. Her daughter, Rose, remained in England and became an actress.

First Bull Run (First Manassas)

In July 1861, Lincoln faced a political problem. The enlistments of his 75,000 three-month volunteers were about to expire and three-year volunteers were just arriving in the capital for weeks of training before going into the field. Meanwhile, Secretary of the Treasury Chase had been meddling in the affairs of the War Department and convinced Cameron that the man to lead the Union army was Major Irvin McDowell. (Having been governor of Ohio, Chase always recommended Ohioans, and McDowell came from Columbus.) Raised to brigadier general and placed in command of the troops gathered at Washington, McDowell asked for several months to prepare the army for battle. Lincoln refused because, by then, the three-month volunteers would be gone. He consoled McDowell by arguing that the Confederates were equally as green as the Federal troops and, since the Union army of 35,000 men exceeded Brigadier General Pierre G. T. Beauregard's 22,000-man army at Manassas, a quick and successful battle might possibly bring an end to the war. Such assurances by Lincoln, a man without military credentials, at least made numerical sense.

The strategy, rife with complications, depended on Major General Robert Patterson's Pennsylvania militia holding Brigadier General Joseph E. Johnston's 12,000 Confederate troops in the Shenandoah Valley. Patterson did nothing, and when McDowell assaulted Beauregard's army on July 21, 1861, at First Bull Run, Johnston's force arrived by train and joined the battle. With the armies engaged now equal in size, and with the Confederates having the early advantage of fighting defensively, McDowell's army of inexperienced militia turned and fled when the Confederates counterattacked. The rout swept McDowell's troops back to the defenses of Washington, along with hundreds of carriages filled with festive spectators who had followed the army to Bull Run to witness a fight Northern newspapers asserted would win the war.

BRIGADIER GENERAL IRVIN MCDOWELL (1818–85)

A graduate of West Point in 1838, McDowell had spent most of his career with staff work. He never commanded in the field but after being raised to brigadier general on May 14, 1861, and placed in charge of building the Union Army, he put together a credible plan of operations. He also warned that his volunteers were ill-prepared for fighting a major engagement. Lincoln, however, could not be dissuaded from putting the troops into action. The ensuing defeat harmed McDowell's reputation, though he later became a corps commander. General Grant referred to McDowell as the unluckiest general in the army.

The loss stunned Lincoln, and Washingtonians and reporters who witnessed the fight awoke to the reality that the war would not be short, romantic, or bloodless. Meanwhile, thousands of wounded trickled into the city on carts and Washington had neither the hospitals nor the personnel to handle the carnage. This so-called "battle of amateurs" changed the entire country's outlook on war and, while the nation grieved its losses, Lincoln decided that McDowell may not be the right man for the job.

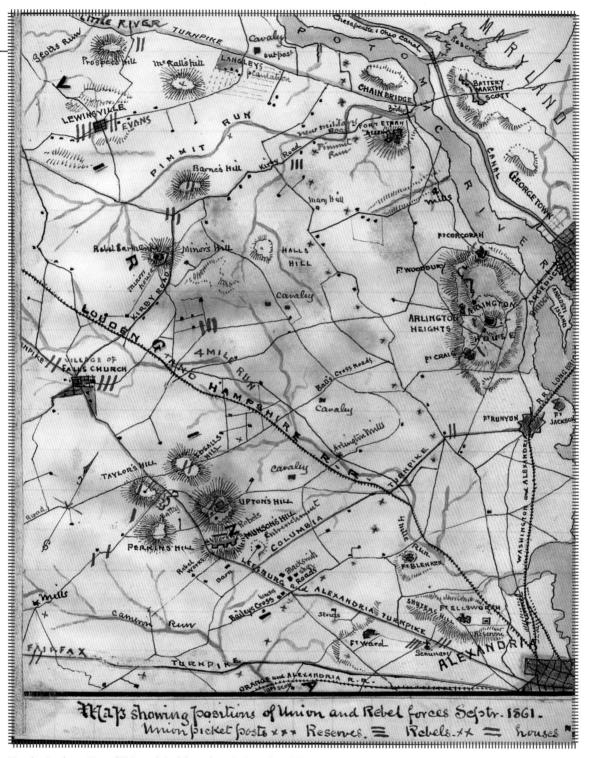

Map showing the positions of Union and Confederate forces in September 1861.

District of Columbia's Native Sons

Many the prominent men who grew up in the District of Columbia were divided by their loyalties. Some served the North and others served the South.

BRIGADIER GENERAL ALFRED PLEASONTON (1824–97)

Graduating seventh in the West Point class of 1844, Alfred Pleasonton was rapidly promoted during the Mexican War and served with distinction on the frontier. Raised to brigadier general on July 17, 1861, he had the chore of whipping the faltering, much-maligned, Cavalry Corps of the Army of the Potomac into shape. Pleasonton's cavalry battle at Brandy Station, Virginia, on June 9, 1863, against Major General James E. B. Stuart's Confederates marked the turning point of the Union Army's cavalry and Pleasonton also played a major part in the Battle of Gettysburg by preventing Stuart from joining General Robert E. Lee early in the three-day fight.

THE BROTHERS GOLDSBOROUGH

The Goldsborough brothers had accrued years of valuable experience before the Civil War broke out, by which time both men had become captains, the highest rating in the Navy. Louis Goldsborough commanded the North Blockading Squadron, and John Goldsborough became the senior officer of the blockading squadron of Charleston, South Carolina, and later the squadron at Mobile Bay. Louis experienced the most action. He commanded the squadron that attacked Port Royal and rendered valuable support during the Peninsula Campaign. He attained the rank of rear admiral, retiring in the District of Columbia, while his brother eventually became a commodore, retiring in Philadelphia.

Brigadier General Alfred Pleasonton.

Born in the District of Columbia, Louis Malesherbes Goldsborough (1805–73) *above left* and John Rodgers Goldsborough (1809–77) *above right* both joined the navy as midshipmen while in their mid-teens.

JAMES MURRAY MASON (1798–1871)

A Virginia aristocrat born in the District of Columbia, James Murray Mason served in the Senate from 1847 to 1861. A strict and domineering states' rights Democrat, he drafted the Fugitive Slave Act and part of the Compromise of 1850 – two laws guaranteeing the protection of slavery. When war broke out, Mason offered his services to Jefferson Davis, a close friend from their years together in the Senate, and when Davis wanted an envoy in England to raise money and lobby for Southern recognition, he sent Mason. The voyage resulted in the Trent Affair, during which Captain Charles Wilkes physically removed Mason and John Slidell from a British vessel and transported them to Boston's Fort Warren. The incident created a diplomatic crisis between the United States and England. After the war, Mason fled to Canada as a refugee and remained there until President Andrew Johnson's 1868 proclamation of amnesty allowed his return.

James Murray Mason.

LIEUTENANT GENERAL RICHARD STODDART EWELL (1817–72)

Born in the District of Columbia but raised after the age of nine in Virginia, Richard Ewell graduated from West Point in 1840 and joined the Dragoons. After receiving brevets during the war with Mexico, Ewell resigned his captaincy in the U. S. Army on May 7, 1861, and joined the Confederate army as lieutenant colonel. One month later Ewell became a brigadier general and, on January 24, 1862, a major general. In August 1862, while serving under Lieutenant General Thomas "Stonewall" Jackson during 2nd Bull Run (Second Manassas), Ewell lost his leg during the fighting at Groveton. Equipped with a wooden limb, Ewell returned to the Army of Northern Virginia to command the II Corps after the death of Jackson at Chancellorsville. Affectionately known to his men as "Old Bald Head", losing a leg took some of the fight out of Ewell and he could no longer ride a horse without the risk of falling. Although he was wounded twice more, Ewell lived out the balance of his life accused by many veterans as the cause of General Lee's defeat at Gettysburg.

Lieutenant General Richard Stoddart Ewell.

After the disaster at First Bull Run (First Manassas), President Lincoln took General Scott's advice and, on July 27, 1861, summoned thirty-four-year-old Major General George Brinton McClellan to Washington to take command of the army. McClellan had won two minor battles in western Virginia as opposed to McDowell's defeat at First Bull Run. Hailed as the "Young Napoleon" and called "Little Mac" by his friends, McClellan quickly performed a masterful task of building and organizing the Army of the Potomac while strengthening fortifications around the capital.

With everything working smoothly, McClellan now showed the other side of his personality by refusing to fight, blaming delay on his superior, the venerable General Scott. With reservations, Lincoln let Scott retire and made McClellan general-in-chief of the armies. Months passed and still McClellan continued to stall until Lincoln ordered him to attack General Johnston's army at Manassas. However, McClellan – who always claimed to have a better plan than his superiors – said he should capture Richmond instead. Lincoln had doubts but let the general have his way, resulting in McClellan's disastrous 1862 Peninsula Campaign and his recall to Washington.

After Major General John Pope bungled the Battle of Second Bull Run (Second Manassas), McClellan resumed command of the Army of the Potomac and fought General Lee to a draw at Antietam (Battle of Sharpsburg). Lincoln diagnosed McClellan's problem as the "slows" and replaced him with Major General Ambrose Burnside, a general willing to fight but unable to do so with competence.

CARE FOR THE WOUNDED

Soldiers were transported from the front lines to hospitals in safer, quieter areas. Washington, Georgetown, and Alexandria (about six miles down the Potomac in Virginia) became an important locations for such services. Among the most important hospitals providing help to the wounded were the Armory Square Hospital, Finley Hospital, and the Campbell Hospital.

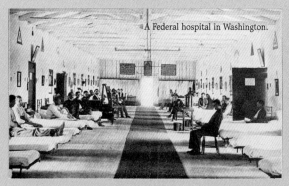

A Federal hospital in Washington.

A train of ambulances at City Point.

Major General George Brinton McClellan (1826–85) graduated from West Point second in a class of fifty-nine. Most of his friends at West Point were Southerners and when the Civil War began he held different views to those of most Northerners about how the war should be fought. He seldom listened to good advice and insisted on following his own misguided notions. In addition, he privately bad-mouthed Lincoln as an "incompetent gorilla," and ran against him as a Democrat in the 1864 presidential election. He lost by a huge majority.

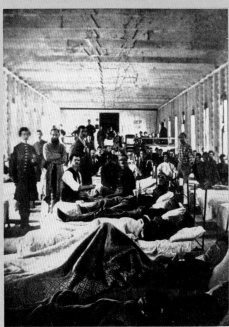

A hospital ward in Alexandria.

MAJOR GENERAL HENRY WAGER HALLECK (1815–72)

Known in the army before the war as "Old Brains", Halleck graduated third in a class of thirty-one at West Point and went on to write *Elements of Military Art and Science* in 1846. Lincoln put him in charge of the armies in the Western Theater, in which role Halleck distinguished himself by doing nothing.

Meanwhile, McClellan had lost his title as commander-in-chief during the Peninsula Campaign. Because Lincoln left it vacant, the responsibility for managing the war had devolved on Secretary of War Edwin McMasters Stanton, who replaced the ineffective Simon Cameron in January 1862. The war quickly became too much for Stanton to manage without help, however, so Lincoln brought Old Brains to Washington as general-in-chief in July 1862. Lincoln had never met Halleck, who Gideon Welles described as "pop-eyed, flabby, surly, and crafty" and within a month Halleck proved to be no more effective as general-in-chief than he had been in the field. Nevertheless, Lincoln needed a military man to communicate with the armies in military terms and retained Halleck as unofficial chief clerk. When Lieutenant General Ulysses S. Grant assumed command of the armies in March 1864, Halleck remained in Washington and became one of Grant's two chiefs of staff.

The War and Mr. Stanton

Before the war, Edwin McMasters Stanton earned $50,000 a year as a lawyer and had crossed paths with Lincoln when they both worked on the International Harvester patent case, during which Stanton had muscled Lincoln onto the sidelines. Lincoln never carried a grudge, however, and after maneuvering Simon Cameron out of the War Department, he brought in Stanton at $8,000 a year. Previously, Stanton had been President Buchanan's attorney general and had enjoyed the power of a cabinet post. Now, behind the scenes, he cleverly aided in Cameron's ousting by informing other cabinet members of his interest in the War Department. Although Stanton had many enemies, he also had a great deal of support in Congress and the war had, thus far, gone badly. By offering the post to Stanton, Lincoln improved his own damaged relationship with Congress.

Stanton roared into the War Department on January 15, 1862, like a man on fire. He quickly cleared out the dead wood, brought an end to the days of champagne and oysters in the Army of the Potomac, and joined the president in pressing McClellan for action. He also put pressure on Lincoln to fire bad generals, while at the same time giving the president full support. In fact, though he believed the president needed to be nudged at times, Stanton became immensely loyal. During the 1864 presidential battle, for example, Stanton went to extra effort to make sure that soldiers' ballots for Lincoln were counted without worrying too much about McClellan's ballots.

Lincoln called Stanton "Mars", and the nickname fitted him well. Nobody stormed about the War Department and the White House more than Stanton. And few grieved more when Lincoln passed away. After John Booth assassinated the president on April 14, 1865, during a performance at Ford's Theatre, it was Stanton who hunted down the plotters relentlessly and brought them to justice.

Secretary of War Edwin McMasters Stanton (1814–69)

A brilliant and wealthy lawyer, Stanton enjoyed power and, as secretary of war, brought energy, competence, and loyalty to an administration fumbling with the problems of Civil War. See also page 302.

Although he remained the secretary of war after Vice-President Andrew Johnson took the oath of office in a private room at Willard's Hotel, Stanton disliked the new president and worked surreptitiously with radicals in Congress to have him impeached.

Stanton hunted down Lincoln's assassins and brought them to justice.
Here John F. Hartranft reads the death warrant to the conspirators –
Mary Surratt, Lewis Powell, David Herold, and George Atzerodt – on the
scaffold on July 7, 1865.

THE MEDAL OF HONOR

The highest decoration for valor given by the United States, the Medal of Honor was authorized for navy enlisted personnel in December 1861, and for army enlisted men in July 1862. On March 3, 1863, Congress extended the award retroactively to include army officers to the beginning of the Civil War, but ignoring naval and marine officers (until 1915) because the commandant believed marines should only serve as guards on ships. There were few decorations available during the Civil War, and standards were lower, but 1,200 awards were eventually authorized, some being given decades later.

District of Columbia Union Units Furnished

Infantry regiments	2
Infantry battalions (3 mos.)	8
Cavalry regiment	1
Owen's Independent cavalry	1
Unassigned colored	1
Unassigned volunteers	1
Sailors/marines personnel	1,353
Colored troops	3,269

DISTRICT OF COLUMBIA UNION ARMY DEATHS

Troops Furnished	Killed/Mortally Wounded	Died of Disease	Died of Other Causes	Total
11,912	41	150	99	290

Florida

> I hereby authorize and empower you to raise a company of picked men and proceed to the Apalachicola River and seize and possess the arsenal, arms, ammunition, buildings and other property now in the possession of the General Government [at Chattahoochee], and retain the same subject to my orders.

GOVERNOR MADISON S. PERRY TO COLONEL WILLIAM GUNN,
7TH REGIMENT, FLORIDA MILITIA, JANUARY 5, 1861

During the 18th and 19th centuries Florida had been first a colony of Great Britain, then a colony of Spain, and, in 1822, a colony of the United States. Twenty-three years later, on March 3, 1845, Congress admitted it to the Union as the 27th state.

As the years passed, Florida grew slowly. By January 10, 1861, when it became the third state to announce secession, it had a population of only 140,000, almost half of which were slaves. With the state's economy heavily dependent on slave labor, delegates to the secession convention in Tallahassee voted sixty-two to seven for independence.

While avoiding publicity, Florida had already prepared for war by recruiting and training militia during the latter months of 1860. Governor Madison S. Perry put the troops to work on January 5, 1861, ordering them to seize the Chattahoochee arsenal. On January 7, he sent the militia to St. Augustine to take possession of Fort Marion. When he learned that the

St. Augustine, Florida. Interior view of Fort Marion, 1861.

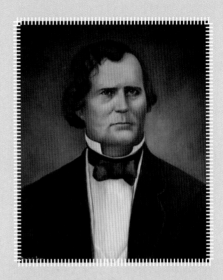

GOVERNOR MADISON STARKE PERRY (1814–65)

Madison Perry, Florida's fourth governor, served from October 5, 1857, to October 7, 1861. A South Carolinian by birth, and an outspoken secessionist, Perry began expanding the state militia immediately after John Brown's attack on Harpers Ferry armory in October 1859. Twenty days after Abraham Lincoln's election, and weeks before South Carolina's secession, he asked the state legislature to convene and declare Florida independent of the Union. Five days before the legislature met, Perry dispatched state troops to take over the arsenal at Chattahoochee and Fort Morgan at St. Augustine. The legislature met in Tallahassee on January 10, 1861, and voted sixty-two to seven for secession. Two days later a combined force of 550 Florida and Alabama troops captured the Pensacola Navy Yard. The governor's quick and decisive action provided arms and equipment for Florida's first infantry regiments, ordnance to fortify the state's ports across 13,000 miles of coastline, and a well-equipped navy yard for building Confederate ships. After leaving office on October 7, 1861, Perry attempted to take command of the 7th Alabama Infantry, but poor health forced his resignation and led to his death in 1865.

Federal government intended to reinforce the forts at Pensacola Bay, the governor called for help from the Alabama militia and, on January 12th, 550 troops captured the Pensacola Navy Yard. The small Federal garrisons at forts McRee and Barrancas retired across the channel to Santa Rosa Island and occupied Fort Pickens – a rundown compound with a few rusty cannon at the entrance to Pensacola Bay. Instead of attacking Pickens, however, Confederate Brigadier General Braxton Bragg hesitated, and by the time he took action, Union vessels had arrived with troops and reinforced the fort.

THE IMPASSE AT PENSACOLA

The fighting in western Florida would eventually become a part of the fighting in Alabama and many of the later problems for the South could have been avoided had General Bragg, in charge of the militia at Pensacola in early 1861, driven the Federals completely out of the area by capturing Fort Pickens. Instead, Bragg negotiated a *détente* with Captain Henry A. Adams, commanding the U.S.S. *Brooklyn*, and in February agreed to not attack Fort Pickens as long as Adams, who had eighty reinforcements on board, did not put the men ashore. A weak Federal force under the command of Lieutenant Adam J. Slemmer occupied the ramshackle fort, which Bragg could have occupied with little or no loss. The eighty men on the *Brooklyn* under Captain Israel Vogdes would have made little difference.

The situation continued until Bragg found that he had waited too long. Lieutenant David Dixon Porter arrived in mid-April with the U.S.S. *Powhatan* and fresh reinforcements under the command of Major Montgomery Meigs. Vogdes and Meigs went ashore with 500 men, reinforced Fort Pickens, and beat off an amphibious attack by Bragg's militia. The Federals held Fort Pickens until May 9, 1862, when Confederates burned part of the navy yard and abandoned Pensacola Bay. Much to the chagrin of former Florida Governor Perry, the Federals then reoccupied the navy yard and Pensacola became headquarters for the U. S. Navy's West Gulf Blockading Squadron.

First Florida Infantry Regiment Flag, 1863. Many units designed their own regimental flags. Organized at the Chattahoochee Arsenal during March 1861, the 1st Florida Infantry fought long and hard throughout the war and was involved in nearly every major battle fought by the Confederacy's Army of Tennessee. Even before suffering heavy casualties at Shiloh, the 1st Florida Infantry Regiment was reduced to battalion size through losses and providing staffing for other regiments. As a battalion and part of Major General Braxton Bragg's II Corps, the unit had the distinction of capturing the "Hornet's Nest" on April 6, 1862, during the Battle of Shiloh.

GENERAL BRAXTON BRAGG (1817–76)

After fumbling the defense of Pensacola Bay, Braxton Bragg became a full general in the Confederate army and between 1862 and 1863 commanded the Army of Tennessee. His friendship with Jefferson Davis, rather than his effectiveness as a commanding general, led to his promotion. See also page 294.

AFRICAN-AMERICAN POPULATION

In 1861, Floridians owned 61,000 slaves, eighty-five percent of whom engaged in the state's cotton production. After Richmond authorities placed an embargo on cotton, slaves became teamsters or earthwork builders for the Confederacy. Others labored in the state's important salt works and in the beef or fisheries industry. (When Federal forces reoccupied Pensacola, one Confederate said the destruction of the nearby salt-works "hurt the South more than would have the loss of Charleston.") As the war progressed, Florida's slaves began to desert and become part of the Union war effort. Thousands fled to parts of eastern and western Florida controlled by Union forces. African-Americans found employment on Union ships and more than a thousand former plantation slaves enlisted as soldiers and sailors. Slaves seeking freedom also became a reliable source of intelligence on Confederate troop movements, and many returned to their homes to have their families pack belongings and prepare to fall in behind a Union advance. During the latter years of war, the fear of slave uprisings was a constant thorn in the side of plantation owners.

Pensacola Bay and Fort Pickens. The navy yard in Pensacola Bay rated as one of the best in the South and the Confederacy lost an excellent opportunity by failing to capture Fort Pickens. Without the fort, Confederate troops could neither protect the navy yard nor defend Pensacola Bay.

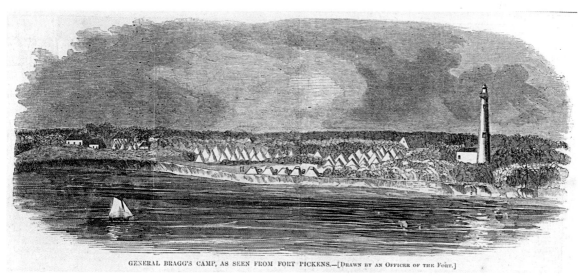

GENERAL BRAGG'S CAMP, AS SEEN FROM FORT PICKENS.—[DRAWN BY AN OFFICER OF THE FORT.]

Battle of Olustee

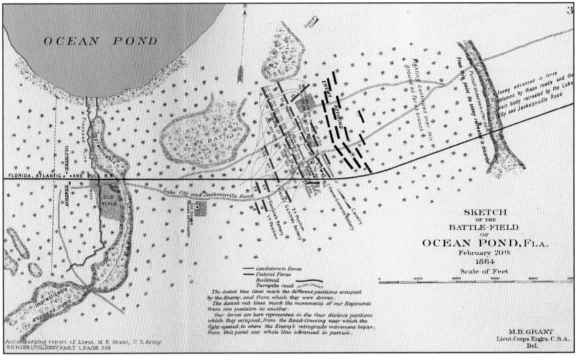

Battle of Olustee or Ocean Pond (February 20, 1864). The Confederate troops are in red; Union in blue.

Most of the battles in Florida rank as skirmishes, the exception being the frantic Battle of Olustee (Ocean Pond), which took place on February 20, 1864. President Lincoln's Emancipation Proclamation had gone into effect on January 1, 1863, and since that time the war had not gone well for Floridians.

BATTLE OF OLUSTEE CASUALTIES

	Killed	Wounded	Missing	Total
Union	203	1,152	506	1,861
Confederate	93	847	6	946

In early 1864, Union Major General Quincy A. Gilmore conceived a plan from his headquarters in South Carolina for an expedition into eastern Florida to secure Union enclaves, disrupt Confederate supply routes, and recruit slaves working on plantations. Gilmore assigned the mission to Brigadier General Truman Seymour, whose 5,500-man column disembarked at Jacksonville and moved westward toward the Suwannee River. Seymour pushed deep into Florida's interior until February 20th, when he collided with 6,500 Confederates under the command of Brigadier General Joseph Finegan near Olustee Station and a large lake known as Ocean Pond.

Seymour made the mistake of assuming the force he faced was the same Florida militia he had whipped before, so he piecemealed his troops forward. During an afternoon battle that took place on an open patch of ground flanked by pine trees, Union forces attacked but were repulsed by heavy cannon and rifle fire. As Seymour brought forward reinforcements, Finegan countered with Brigadier General Alfred H. Colquitt's brigade. Colquitt rushed into action with two regiments, which Seymour repulsed with heavy loss. The battle seesawed back and forth throughout the afternoon, neither general realizing until well into the fight that their troops were facing veterans, not militia. After nearly three hours of fierce fighting, Finegan committed his last reserves. The Union line, running short of ammunition, broke and began a retreat. Too exhausted to pursue, Finegan allowed most of the retiring Federals to reach Jacksonville. A few Confederates attempted to engage Seymour's rear echelon at dusk but were repulsed by two Federal regiments composed of African-Americans.

The ratio of Union casualties to the number of troops involved made Olustee the third bloodiest battle of the war for the Union. Soldiers on both sides later said they had never seen such furious fighting. Throughout the night, African-Americans from the 54th Massachusetts manually pulled carts filled with the wounded until horses could be obtained. Strong anecdotal evidence suggests the high number of Union casualties resulted from Confederate troops murdering wounded and captured African-American troops.

Union losses at Olustee prompted the War Department to question whether anything could be gained by further military involvement in eastern Florida, and after Olustee no major campaigns were fought in the region, only a few scattered skirmishes.

Sanderson, Florida, was occupied by advancing Federal troops before the battle of Olustee. *Harper's Weekly*, March 12, 1864.

BRIGADIER GENERAL JOSEPH FINEGAN (1814–85)

Born in Ireland, Finegan settled in Jacksonville, Florida, studied law, and moved to Fernandina. He served as a member of the secession convention before being designated by Governor Perry to handle all of Florida's military affairs. For repulsing the Federals at the Battle of Olustee, he received the thanks of the Confederate Congress and when General Robert E. Lee needed fighting generals, he brought Finegan to Virginia and placed him in charge of the Florida Brigade. As war began to wind down in the Petersburg trenches, Lee sent him back to Florida to keep the war-weary state in the fight. Finegan later returned to the practice of law and died in Savannah, Georgia, in 1885.

SANDERSON, FLORIDA, OCCUPIED BY OUR ADVANCE BEFORE THE BATTLE OF OLUSTEE.

SECRETARY OF THE NAVY STEPHEN R. MALLORY (1813–73)

Born in British Trinidad, Stephen R. Mallory grew up in Key West, studied law, and, in 1851, Floridians sent him to the U. S. Senate. By 1855, he had become the powerful chairman of the Senate's Committee on Naval Affairs and when he resigned in 1861 Jefferson Davis made him secretary of the Confederate Navy. Unlike other members of Davis's cabinet, Mallory came well-prepared for the job. He knew the financial limitations of the Confederacy's ability to build warships and sent talented men like James Dunwoody Bulloch to Europe to buy fast ships that could operate effectively on the high seas. Instead of trying to build a large navy, Mallory concentrated on constructing a small force of rugged ironclad ships to defend the ports and inland waters of the South. After the Virginia militia captured the Gosport Navy Yard at Norfolk in 1861, for instance, Mallory set men to work building the ironclad ram C.S.S. *Virginia* from the remains of the U.S.S. *Merrimack*. He also organized the Confederate Torpedo Bureau, which built floating and underwater mines and the torpedo boat/submarine *H.L. Hunley*.

Mallory received much criticism from the public for not providing the Confederacy with a more powerful navy, but in the final analysis the secretary accomplished more, with less, than any of his peers and, unlike other cabinet members, never lost the confidence of President Davis. Arrested after the war, Mallory spent ten months in prison before returning to the practice of law in Florida.

Secretary of the Navy Stephen R. Mallory.

Florida Units Furnished	
Confederate	
Infantry regiments	11
Infantry battalions	1
Infantry reserves	1
Home Guards	5
Misc. infantry units	13
Cavalry regiments	2
Cavalry battalions	3
Misc. cavalry units	3
Light artillery units	6
Engineer unit	1
Union	
Cavalry regiments	2

FLORIDA CONFEDERATE ARMY DEATHS

	Killed	Died of Wounds	Died of Disease	Total
Officers	47	16	17	80
Enlisted	746	490	1,030	2,266
Total	793	506	1,047	2,346

The Confederate Monument in St. Augustine was erected by the Ladies Memorial Association in 1872.

Epilog

During the war more than 1,200 white Floridians and about the same number of African-Americans served in the Union army. From those Florida volunteers came two Federal cavalry regiments. As the war came to an end, in January 1865, Union General William T. Sherman issued special orders setting aside a portion of Florida as a designated home for former slaves who had accompanied his command during its March to the Sea. The orders were never enforced and later revoked by President Andrew Johnson.

By May 1865, Edward M. McCook's Union division had arrived in Florida to re-establish Federal control of the state. Governor John Milton shot himself in the head rather than submit to Union occupation. On May 13th, Colonel George Washington Scott surrendered the last remaining Confederate troops in Florida and seven days later General McCook read Lincoln's Emancipation Proclamation during a ceremony in the state capitol at Tallahassee, ending slavery in Florida. Tallahassee thus had the distinction of being the second last Confederate capital to officially surrender to the Union. Austin, Texas, fell a month later. Another three years passed before Florida, on June 25, 1868, received readmission to the Union.

THEY DIED FAR FROM THE HOME THAT GAVE THEM BIRTH
BY COMRADES HONORED AND BY COMRADES MOURNED.

Battles in Florida

Battle of Fort Brooke	October 16–18, 1863
Battle of Fort Myers	February 25, 1865
Battle of Gainesville	August 17, 1864
Battle of Marianna	September 27, 1864
Battle of Natural Bridge	March 6, 1865
Battle of Olustee	February 20, 1864
Battle of Saint John's Bluff	October 1–3, 1862
Battle of Santa Rosa Island	October 9, 1861
Battle of Tampa	June 30–July 1, 1862

Florida Union Army Deaths

Troops Furnished	Killed/Mortally Wounded	Died of Disease	Died of Other Causes	Total
1,290	18	189	8	215

Georgia

" . . . we are not only fighting hostile armies, but a hostile people, and must make old and young, rich and poor, feel the hard hand of war, as well as their organized armies. I know that this recent movement of mine through Georgia has had a wonderful effect in this respect. Thousands who had been deceived by their lying newspapers to believe that we were being whipped all the time now realize the truth, and have no appetite for a repetition of the same experience . . . "

WILLIAM T. SHERMAN, IN A LETTER TO MAJOR GENERAL H. W. HALLECK, CHIEF-OF-STAFF, WASHINGTON, D.C., DECEMBER 24, 1864

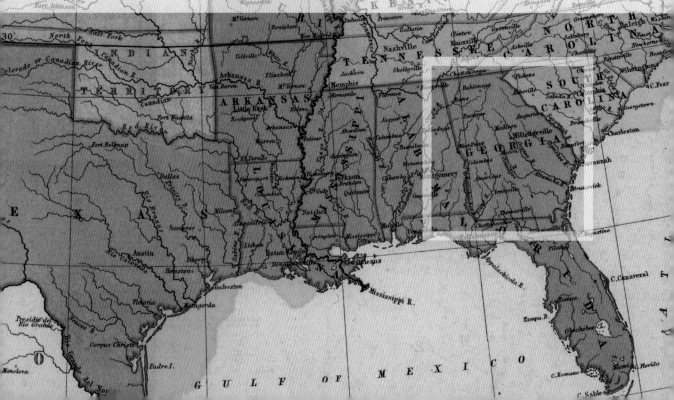

Georgia unofficial flag before 1879.

Georgia, one of the seven "Deep South" states that formed the original Confederate States of America, was very much at the heartland of the "Great Rebellion", (as the North called it), and a key bastion against "Northern Aggression", as it was seen in the South.

Early in the war, the "Empire State of the South" was geographically distant from the main fighting and, because of that secure position, became an important manufacturing center for munitions. Furthermore, when cotton plantations within the state switched to the production of food, Georgia helped to sustain the Southern war effort. The extensive transportation network linking the state with its neighbors enabled these resources to be quickly distributed. Later in the war, however, from late 1863, Georgia witnessed some of the most bitterly fought battles of the conflict. Indeed, the Atlanta Campaign brought the war to Georgia with a vengeance, and much of the state was laid to waste during Sherman's infamous "March to the Sea". Twenty-seven battles of importance were fought on Georgian soil, and the state provided 133,486 men for the Southern cause. Nearly 11,000 of them were lost in fighting.

SOCIETY, ECONOMY, AND POLITICS

Like all the Deep Southern states, the economy of Georgia in 1860 was heavily dependent on the production of cotton. The cotton plantations were concentrated in the middle of the state, the so-called

The chimney of the Confederate States Powder Works, Goodrich Street, Augusta, Richmond, Georgia. The only permanent edifice constructed by the Confederate States of America, the works was demolished in the 1870s save for the smokestack, which was left standing as a memorial to those who fought for the Confederacy.

POWDER WORKS FACTORY

Several munitions factories were established in Georgia to manufacture ordnance for the Confederate Army. The Powder Works Factory in Augusta was one of the largest and most important, as it supplied the Southern states with most of its badly needed explosive powder. The factory also produced cannons, cartridges, percussion caps, grenades, and signal rockets with much of the raw materials coming from donations – churches gave their bells and local women handed over lead window weights to be melted into bullets.

In July 1861, President Jefferson Davis ordered West Point-trained engineer, Colonel George Washington Rains to select a place for a gunpowder plant. Rains selected Augusta due to its canal, water power, railroad facilities, and secure position. When finished, the Powder Works Factory was the second largest munitions factory in the world at that time, comprising twenty-six buildings, which stretched two miles down the first level of the Augusta Canal. It operated under Rains from 1862 until April 18, 1865, manufacturing 2,750,000 pounds of gunpowder of the highest quality (then made from saltpeter smuggled through the Federal blockade from India via England). In fact, Rains was known to boast that no battle was lost for want of gunpowder.

"Black Belt" and were totally reliant on slave labor. In 1860, of a total population of 1,057,286, 462,198, or about forty-four percent, were slaves. Although only about forty percent of white families in Georgia held slaves, this represents a considerably higher percentage than in the South as a whole.

Although cotton was undoubtedly king in Georgia, the railroad fever that swept the nation in the 1830s had helped spur the development of other industries, including iron foundries, rolling mills, and machine shops; all of which shaped and prepared iron and steel for the railroad business. During the war, many of these facilities were turned over to the production of war materiel. In Atlanta, Augusta, Columbus, Macon, and Savannah, Confederate government arsenals manufactured weapons, along with other essential military equipment. And because so many of the white workforce was under arms, the workshops and factories were often dependent on slave labor. By 1863, around half the workforce at both the Macon Armory and the Augusta Powder Works were African-American slaves. Slaves were also used to maintain the state's vital rail network by constructing bridges, grading, and laying new track.

In the pre-war years, as in most other Deep South states, the free white population in Georgia supported either the Democratic Party, or the Whig Party. In broad terms, Democrat voters favored immediate secession, and were strongest in the coastal counties. Whig supporters favored a conciliatory, or "cooperationist" approach, and were dominant in the mountain counties. In the Black Belt, opinions were less clearly delineated, and varied from one place to the next.

GOVERNOR JOSEPH E. BROWN AND SECESSION

In December 1850, with the nation threatening to fall apart over the passage of the Compromise, delegates from across Georgia convened to debate the issue of secession. The voting demonstrated an overwhelming support for the pro-Union position. In fact, of the 264 delegates, 240 were Unionists.

Together, these delegates drafted the "Georgia Platform", an official response to the crisis. In effect, the proclamation accepted the measures of the Compromise, though Georgia's acceptance of the measures was conditional on Northern compliance with the Fugitive Slave Act and curtailment of efforts by Northern politicians to prevent expansion of slavery into new territories and states.

Although the Georgia Platform undermined the position of secessionists throughout the South, in the ensuing years tensions between North and South began to simmer again. Slavery was most often cited "as the most compelling reason for southern independence," but other issues also fueled the dispute, including questions involving free speech, runaway slaves, expansion into Cuba, and states' rights. The final catalyst for secession was the election of Abraham Lincoln in the 1860 elections. For many Southerners, the scale of the Republican victory in the North – where Lincoln won more than sixty percent of the vote – was ominous. It meant that Congress would be dominated by "Yankee" and antislavery factions.

In the wake of Lincoln's election victory, a secession convention was called for 1861, with delegates from each Georgia county chosen by popular ballot on January 1st. In the campaign for the election of these delegates, the secessionist faction – mostly former Democrats headed by Governor Joseph E. Brown – argued for the immediate severing of ties with the Union. The cooperationists were led by Alexander Stephens and included former Whig Party members as well as some conservative Democrats. They argued that if Georgia remained in the Union the Republican administration would be forced to make major concessions, which would protect slavery and Southern rights. In the January election, the immediate secessionists won, though, in reality, the result was probably much closer than officially declared. The Georgia state convention duly opened in Milledgeville on January 16th, and, after two days of debate, on January 19th the delegates voted 208-89 to break with the Union. On January 21st, secession ordinance was publicly signed. Georgia had become the fifth state to secede.

The Georgia Militia and Volunteers

At the outbreak of war, Georgia began to call up its militia and to organize volunteers for service with the Confederate Army. The state had a considerable body of manpower on which to draw. In fact, at the beginning of the Civil War, Georgia ranked third among the Confederate states in terms of human resources, behind only Virginia and Tennessee. Somewhere between 120,000 and 130,000 white males were nominally available to take up arms. This resource was destined to become an object of a great struggle between Governor Joseph Brown and Jefferson Davis, president of the Confederacy. Brown advocated keeping men back to provide a strong state defense but, as the war dragged on, Davis demanded more soldiers from Georgia.

Fort Pulaski and Fort McAllister

The first significant military event to took place in Georgia during the Civil War was the seizure of Fort Pulaski, a strategically important Federal post on Cockspur Island at the mouth of the Savannah River. On January 3, 1861, Georgia militia under orders from Governor Brown boarded the steamship *Ida,* moved downriver, and took the fort without a shot being fired. The only occupants were an ordinance sergeant and a civilian. Thereafter, the fort defenses were strengthened by the addition of five companies of infantry and its static armament upgraded to include forty-eight artillery pieces. During this time, Fort Pulaski was frequently targeted by Union naval forces that were operating off the coast of the Confederacy.

In December 1861, a Union force landed on neighboring Tybee Island and began to build siege batteries along the north coast. On April 10, 1862, the bombardment began. This was the first time the new "Parrot Gun" had been used in battle. Its longer range, together with greater accuracy, soon reduced the fort, and thirty hours later the garrison surrendered.

Governor Joseph Emerson Brown (1821–94)

As a youth, Joseph E. Brown developed a lifelong political philosophy around the egalitarian policies of Andrew Jackson and the states' rights doctrine of John C. Calhoun. Brown studied law before going into politics, earned a reputation for intellectual shrewdness, and, in 1857, became Georgia's governor, a position he held until 1865. Long before Georgia seceded, Brown began building the state's militia, and after Georgia seceded he used the militia to confiscate all the Federal property in the state, including the Augusta arsenal and Fort Pulaski near Savannah.

Despite strongly promoting secession and becoming deeply involved in putting some 100,000 men under arms, Brown had an early falling out with Jefferson Davis over the president's autocratic war measures. He fiercely scorned the Confederate government for infringing on the very states' rights Brown sought by seceding. He opposed the Conscription Act of 1862, as it applied to Georgia, and called government-imposed tax laws illegal. On the one hand, nothing annoyed him more than raising dozens of regiments for the defense of Georgia and having them called away to defend Richmond. On the other hand, he kept the Confederacy in the war by converting all Georgia's cotton plantations to raising food for the armies. Some critics said the governor's attacks on President Davis harmed the Confederacy, but Brown parried by claiming that Davis's dangerous policies would not have survived even if the government had won its independence. After the war, Brown urged Georgians to accept the government's reconstruction policies and eventually finished his life as a two-term senator to the U. S. Senate.

Winfield Scott's "Anaconda Plan" resulted from the realization by Union strategists that the war would be a long, drawn out affair and, in essence, was an attempt at the slow strangulation of the South by cutting off lines of communication. One of the plan's goals was the city of Savannah and with the fall of Pulaski in April, 1862, Union commanders decided to try and push up the Ogeechee River, threatening the city and several vital lifelines to the Confederacy – The King's Road, via which the harvests of southwestern Georgia were shipped by cart to Savannah then moved north on rail cars to the Army of Northern Virginia; the Ogeechee Road, which led to the great plantations of the coastal islands; and the Atlantic and Gulf railroad bridge which brought the harvest, supplies, and men from Florida to Georgia's port.

In July, 1861, the 1st Georgia Infantry was ordered to build an earthwork fort to protect Savannah from amphibious assault. Named Fort McAllister, it would come under attack on a number of occasions during the course of the war. Gunboats, under Admiral Samuel Dupont, commander of the expeditionary force that had taken Fort Pulaski, began the Union efforts at the beginning of July, 1862, when the *Potomska* sailed into the Ogeechee and approached the fort. After a short exchange of fire, the outgunned *Potomska* moved back down the river.

At the end of the month, Fort McAllister came under Union attack for the second time. The Confederate vessel *Nashville*, which had previously been successfully turned away from Charleston and Savannah by the Union naval blockade, finally broke through and headed up the Ogeechee to the protection of the guns of Fort McAllister. A small flotilla was sent in pursuit but, after fighting an artillery duel with the batteries at the fort, the Union ships retreated to safety down the river. Following this attack, the fort was reinforced and over the following months came under attack on several further occasions, including by the Union ironclad, *Montauk*.

Vice President Alexander Hamilton Stephens.   Howell Cobb.

VICE-PRESIDENT ALEXANDER HAMILTON STEPHENS (1812–83)

Because of his physical stature, his constituents called him "Little Aleck", and while serving in the House of Representatives during 1847–48, he became a close friend of Abraham Lincoln. In the early 1850s, he attempted to form a party with fellow Georgians Howell Cobb and Robert A. Toombs based on states' rights and slavery, but in opposition to secession. When Cobb and Howell later embraced secession, Stephens broke with his two political friends, argued against disunion, but eventually signed the ordinance on January 19, 1861, which removed Georgia from the Union.

On the formation of the Confederate government in the weeks ahead, Stephens became vice-president. A year later he broke with President Jefferson Davis over the latter's policies on conscription, *habeas corpus*, and establishing military governments within the South. Instead of holding office in Richmond, Stephens moved back to Georgia and waited out the war. Although imprisoned briefly after the war, Stephens returned home, resumed his legal practice, and eventually returned to the U.S. House of Representatives. After winning a term as Governor of Georgia in 1882, he died in Atlanta on March 4, 1883, shortly after his inauguration.

HOWELL COBB (1815–1868)

A former Governor of Georgia, Howell Cobb also became a personal friend of President James Buchanan and his secretary of the treasury. Cobb advocated compromise until the election of Abraham Lincoln, immediately after which he urged fellow Georgians to secede. He hoped to be named president of the Confederacy but had to settle for

Robert Augustus Toombs.

Commander James Dunwoody Bulloch.

serving as speaker of the Provisional Congress. This did not satisfy Cobb, so he organized the 16th Georgia Infantry and as its colonel took his regiment to Virginia in 1861. Elevated to brigadier general in 1862, Cobb participated in every major battle of the Army of Northern Virginia in 1862 from the Peninsula Campaign to Antietam.

Cobb returned home in late 1862 and became a major general in command of the District of Georgia and Florida. During the Atlanta Campaign in 1864, he led the Georgia reserve corps. Being a professional lawyer and politician, Cobb never particularly distinguished himself as a military commander, but after the war ended he used his well-honed political skills to unsuccessfully oppose the Reconstruction policies of his former enemies.

ROBERT AUGUSTUS TOOMBS (1810–85)

A long-time political ally of Alexander Stephens and Howell Cobb, "Bob" Toombs was also a very wealthy plantation and slave owner. After Abraham Lincoln's election, Toombs resigned from the U.S. Senate and returned home to lobby for Georgia's secession. Like Howell Cobb, he sought the presidency of the Confederacy and took the loss hard with the election of Jefferson Davis. Although Davis named Toombs secretary of state, the Georgian disliked the post almost as much as he grew to dislike Davis, who he considered an inferior.

Like Howell Cobb, Toombs became a brigadier general in the Army of Northern Virginia, fought in the Peninsula Campaign, and suffered a serious wound at Antietam. Throughout his short military career, Toombs retained his seat in the Confederate Congress and became a passionate critic of Davis's military policy. He resigned his commission in 1863 and never stopped disparaging Davis's management of the war. When Union forces invaded Georgia in 1864, Toombs led the state's militia without much success. After the defeat of the Confederacy in 1865, Toombs never applied for a pardon, which prevented him from ever again holding political office.

COMMANDER JAMES DUNWOODY BULLOCH (1823–1901)

On the day Georgia seceded, James Bulloch commanded a commercial mail steamer for the Federal government. When authorities at New Orleans attempted to seize his ship, he refused and returned her to New York. There he resigned and offered his services to the Confederacy. Aware of Bulloch's resourcefulness and integrity, Secretary of the Navy Mallory sent him to England to secretly build and equip a pair of Confederate commerce destroyers, which in 1862 became the C.S.S. *Alabama* and the C.S.S. *Florida*. Bulloch cleverly used England's own neutrality laws to man the ships and get them to sea. In 1864, he commissioned a third, the C.S.S. *Shenandoah*.

Bulloch wasted no time in England. In addition to three Confederate cruisers, he purchased several blockade runners and began building two high-seas ironclad rams to cross the Atlantic and tear apart the Union blockade. When England threatened to stop the work, Bulloch took the project to France and completed the C.S.S. *Stonewall*. The ironclad somewhat resembled the first naval destroyers but did not reach American waters in time to see action. Of all the efforts by Secretary Mallory to build a Confederate navy, only those implemented by Bulloch achieved any success.

Bombardment of Fort Pulaski, Cockspur Island, Georgia, April 10-11, 1862.

At the end of February, 1863, Union Navy Admiral Dupont ordered the *Montauk*, the *Passsaic*, the *Nahant*, and the *Patapsco* ironclads from Port Royal, South Carolina, to invest Fort McAllister. After steaming up the river, the vessels bombarded the fort for eight hours, opening large gaps in its walls. In the aftermath of that attack, however, the Union ironclads were redeployed to attack Charleston, South Carolina, and, as attacks on the fort became less likely, the garrison was reduced in size.

Finally, in mid December, 1864, General William Sherman's advancing forces arrived at Fort McAllister, now the only obstacle separating Sherman from the Union supply fleet lying off the Georgia coast. After a brief exchange, the fort was taken.

THE LIGHTNING MULE BRIGADE

The actions that took place in the first two years of the war on Georgia's Atlantic coast were of relatively minor importance and it was not until 1863 that the first significant land action occurred on Georgia soil. This was the attack on Rome, in northwest Georgia, by Colonel Abel Streight's "Lightning Mule Brigade".

In advance of the Tullahoma Campaign, General William Rosecrans ordered Streight to proceed up the Tennessee River to a landing point east of Memphis, from where his force would move overland at Rome. The Independent Provisional Brigade, popularly known as the "Lightning Mule Brigade" and comprising four regiments of infantry, two companies of cavalry, two mountain howitzers, plus over 700 mules, set sail in a small flotilla

of boats on April 10, 1863. By the beginning of May, Streight's force had landed and marched to within twenty-five miles of Rome. Rome's citizens quickly threw up barricades across the main entry points on the Coosa and Etowah rivers, and on approaching roads. The militia was mustered out, armed with what weapons could be found, and ordered to take up defensive position. An urgent request for reinforcements was sent to neighboring Kingston.

Although the residents did not know it, Streight's column had been harangued since landing by Confederate troops under Nathaniel Forrest. Consequently, by the time they arrived on the outskirts of Rome, the men were close to exhaustion. Unable to do much except some limited damage to a local iron foundry, the exhausted Yankee brigade, numbering some 1,700 men, were captured on May 3, 1863. Nevertheless, Union cavalry would arrive a year later, to capture the town as Sherman made his way toward Atlanta.

MARTELLO TOWER ON TYBEE ISLAND.[3]

Fort McAllister, Georgia, from the flagstaff, looking up the Ogeechee River, December 1864.

The Battle of Chickamauga

During the summer of 1863, Major General William S. Rosecrans's Army of the Cumberland advanced through Middle Tennessee, forcing Braxton Bragg to abandon Tullahoma and fall back on Chattanooga. After the Tullahoma Campaign, Rosecrans regrouped at Stevenson, Alabama, on the Nashville and Chattanooga Railroad, to be resupplied. Then, in September, he split his men into three corps with the intention of forcing the Confederates out of Chattanooga. Accordingly, his troops advanced on separate routes and, in early September, Bragg's army withdrew from Chattanooga, heading south toward LaFayette, Georgia. On September 10th, however, Union troops under Major General George Thomas, which were closing on LaFayette from the northeast, were forced to withdraw by Confederate attack at the Davis Cross Roads.

Rosecrans, realizing he was overextended, began a complex movement north in an effort to concentrate his forces. Meanwhile, in LaFayette, Bragg began planning an offensive that would allow the Army of the Tennessee to reoccupy Chattanooga. It was directed at Crittenden's XXI Corps concentrated at Lee and Gordon Mill on West Chickamauga Creek.

Bragg's army moved north toward the points at which he had specified that it was to cross the creek on the 17th. By nightfall of the 18th, all three of his corps (Hood, Walker, and Polk) were across. In the meantime, the Union XXI Corps had been reinforced on their left by Thomas's XIV Corps.

The next morning, the Battle of Chickamauga began in earnest. Bragg's men hammered but did not break the Union line and the next day, Bragg continued his assault on the left of the Union line. During the late morning, Rosecrans was informed that he had a gap in his line. In moving units to shore up this supposed gap, he created a new one, and James Longstreet's men promptly exploited it, driving one-third of the Union army, including Rosecrans himself, from the field. George H. Thomas now took over command and began consolidating forces on Horseshoe Ridge and Snodgrass Hill. Although the Confederates launched determined assaults on these positions, they held until after dark. Thomas, the "Rock of Chickamauga", now ordered his men to withdraw, and joined the Union Army in pulling back to Chattanooga. Bragg occupied the surrounding high ground on Lookout Mountain and Missionary Ridge, to the east of the city.

Bragg is generally attributed with a victory at Chickamauga. He handed the Army of the Cumberland the worst defeat suffered by any Union corps during the war, resulting in over 16,000 Union casualties. However, the cost to his own army was enormous, at nearly 18,500 killed or wounded. Either way, Chickamauga was the bloodiest two days of American history.

By late 1863, Rosecrans was besieged in Chattanooga by Bragg's Army of the Tennessee from its positions atop Lookout Mountain, on Missionary Ridge, and along the Tennessee River. In November, Ulysses S. Grant arrived and began to raise the siege. Lookout Mountain was captured by Joe Hooker on November 24th, in the so-called "Battle Above the Clouds". Two days later, three Union armies (Sherman, Hooker, Thomas) struck at Missionary Ridge. Thomas achieved a breakthrough and Bragg ordered his heavily outnumbered army to retreat. Two days after that, Hooker's pursuing Union forces were halted by the rearguard action of Patrick Cleburne at Ringold Gap, allowing Bragg to fall back in good order to Dalton, Georgia. There, Bragg resigned his command and was replaced at the end of the year as commander of the Confederate Army of Tennessee by Joseph Johnston.

With Chattanooga, the "Gateway to the South", now secure, Grant was in a position to strike into Georgia, a task which would be prosecuted with ruthless, but brilliant, skill by William Sherman the following year.

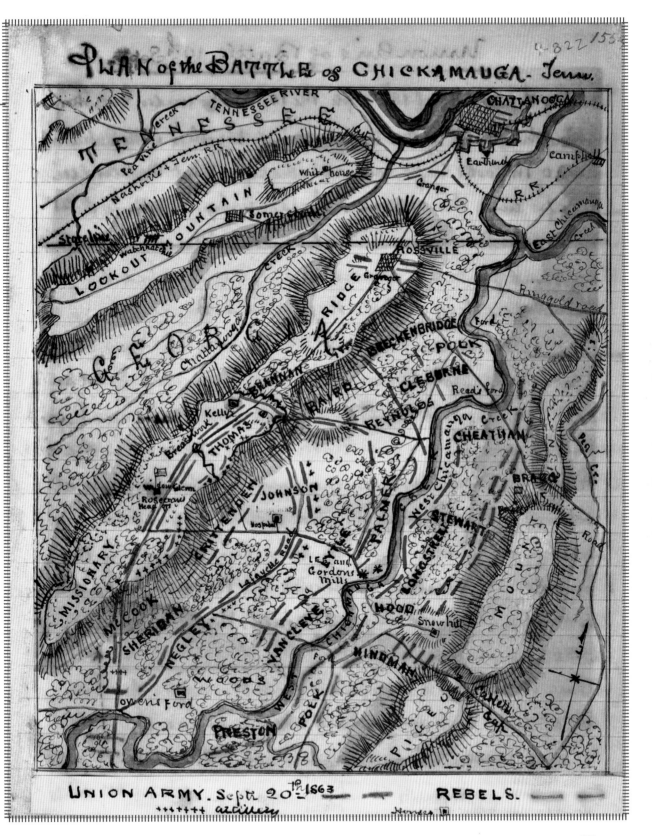

PLAN of the BATTLE of CHICKAMAUGA. Tenn.

THE GREAT LOCOMOTIVE CHASE

An interesting sideshow took place just two days after the fall of Fort Pulaski when a group of twenty Union saboteurs, led by James Andrews, stole "The General" – a fifty-seven ton Western and Atlantic Railroad locomotive – from the depot at Big Shanty (now Kennesaw), Georgia. A ninety-mile chase ensued, later made famous as the "The Great Locomotive Chase". It ended two miles north of Ringgold Gap when, with wood and water running out, the locomotive blew a valve. Andrews and his men fled west toward the mountains south of Chattanooga, but a massive search netted all the participants. In early June, Andrews escaped from the Swims Jail in Chattanooga, but was recaptured and hanged on June 6, 1862. Six other men convicted of spying met the same fate. Of the rest, six men escaped and eight were exchanged for prisoners. All the men except Andrews, who had never enlisted, were awarded the Medal of Honor.

THE ATLANTA CAMPAIGN

The best-known military action to take place in Georgia during the Civil War was a series of seventeen battles and maneuvers collectively known as the Atlanta Campaign. The Union aim was to capture the strategically important city of Atlanta, which sat at the point where four rail lines converged, and it was planned to coincide with Grant's own offensive against Virginia. The campaign began in May, 1864, and was led by General William T. Sherman who built his enduring reputation as the "Father of Modern Warfare" in battles against Johnston and Hood on a line of advance that extended from Ringgold to Atlanta and Jonesborough. Sherman's army consisted of 100,000 men, 254 guns, and 35,000 horses. Johnston's army had 63,000 men and 187 guns. In the course of the fighting over 67,000 soldiers would be killed, wounded, or captured.

From February 1864, Union General George Thomas began probing the defensive Confederate line that had been established at Dalton. The main thrust of the advance began in May, however. The Union armies of the Tennessee (McPherson) and Cumberland (Thomas) moved across the state line into Georgia from Chattanooga, heading for Dalton, while the Army of the Ohio (Schofield) moved toward the city on the Union left. Advancing southward down the Western and Atlantic Railroad through the flat, easy terrain of Georgia's Great Valley, during mid to late May these armies forced Johnston to fall back steadily southwards through a succession of defensive lines at Rocky Face Ridge (May 7th to 13th), Resaca (May 13th to 15th), and southeast of Cassville.

From this position, Sherman knew that to continue closing on Atlanta along the railroad route, he would have to overcome the strong Confederate defenses sited at the Allatoona Pass – a deep cutting through a high ridge in the rugged mountains east of Cartersville, and the gateway to Atlanta. He had seen the pass in 1844, while serving in the U.S. Army and recognized that it presented a significant obstacle to the attacker. Seeking to avoid the costly losses that were inevitable should he try a direct attack on Allatoona, he chose instead to leave the security of the railroad and bypass Allatoona in a wide arc to west. After resting and regrouping at Adairsville, Sherman's three armies marched on. Progress through the hilly, brush-covered terrain was slow, and became a crawl as wagons, horses, and men battled along red clay roads.

Meanwhile Johnston's Army of the Tennessee had been forced by these maneuvers to withdraw from

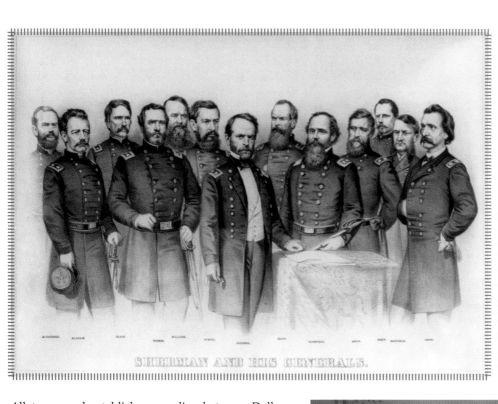

Sherman and his generals: the distinguished commanders of the Atlanta and Georgia campaigns. *From left to right*: McPherson, Slocum, Blair, Thomas, Williams, Howard, Sherman, Geary, Schofield, Davis, Buer, Kilpatrick, Logan.

Allatoona and establish a new line between Dallas and Lost Mountain, east of Marietta.

On May 25th, on the right of Sherman's line, "Fighting Joe" Hooker's XX Corps, in the vanguard of the Army of the Tennessee, came up against Confederate troops under John Bell Hood at the New Hope Church crossroads to the northeast of Dallas, while Schofield engaged at Picketts Mill, where the Army of the Cumberland ran headlong into the battle-hardened division led by Patrick Cleburne and was savagely repulsed.

Since taking the railhead at Kingston, Sherman had been trying to move supplies to his front lines twenty miles south and had hoped also to forage what could not be transported. However, the barren and rugged countryside was playing havoc

Sherman at the siege of Atlanta. A painting by Thure de Thulstrup published in *Prang's War Pictures*.

GEORGIA CONFEDERATE ARMY DEATHS

	Killed	Died of Wounds	Died of Disease	Total
Officers	172	140	107	419
Enlisted	5,381	1,579	3,595	10,555
Total	5,553	1,719	3,702	10,974

General Joseph E. Johnston.

with his logistical efforts and the general realized that he needed to regain a position on the railroad south of Allatoona Pass. Accordingly, he began to extend the left wing of the army to the east.

In the opposite camp, Johnston interpreted these maneuvers as a opportunity for an attack on the western flank of the Union line. In one of the few Confederate offensive moves during the Atlanta Campaign, Johnston engaged the entrenched Union Army at the Dallas crossroads on May 28th. The Union defenses were, however, considerably stronger than Johnston had anticipated, and the attack failed. This would be the final battle in the fighting west of Marietta. Union cavalry took Allatoona Pass on June 1, 1864, and, three days later, Johnston began to withdraw from the Dallas-New Hope line to a new positions on Lost Mountain, Pine Mountain, and Brush Mountain, located to the northwest of Marietta.

Until this time, the fighting in the Atlanta campaign had been characterized by complex maneuvering as Sherman tried to outflank Johnston, who, in turn, had withdrawn through successive lines of defense. Casualties on both sides had been light. All that changed during two weeks of fighting at Kennesaw Mountain, a steep, heavily fortified, 1,808-ft peak overlooking Marietta from the north, dominating the vital railroad. The battles commenced on June 22nd, when John Bell Hood launched an unsuccessful attack on Schofield's positions to the south of Kennesaw, at Kolb's

Farm. On June 27th, Thomas struck at the center of the Confederate line but was driven off after suffering heavy losses. Nonetheless, a flanking maneuver, on July 2nd, by McPherson's Army of the Tennessee on the Union left forced Johnston to withdraw to new positions at Smyrna. Just under a week later, Schofield's troops crossed the Chattahoochee River, the last natural barrier in front of Atlanta.

HOOD SUCCEEDS AS COMMANDER OF THE ARMY OF THE TENNESSEE

"General Johnston has failed, and there are strong indications that he will abandon Atlanta. He urges that prisoners should be removed immediately from Andersonville. It seems necessary to relieve him at once. Who should succeed him? What think you of Hood for the position?"

PRESIDENT JEFFERSON DAVIS'S COMMUNIQUÉ TO GENERAL ROBERT E. LEE ON JULY 12, 1864

The Confederate president was, by this time, becoming increasingly frustrated by what he viewed as Johnston's failures. When Johnston requested support for an offensive at Peach Tree Creek, none was offered. He had received all the help Richmond could afford to send, and his days as commander were numbered.

Lee, however, seems to have been less convinced of the wisdom of Davis's plan to relieve Johnston and replace him with Hood. His reply to the president's message read, "It is a bad time to release the commander of an army situated as that of Tennessee. We may lose Atlanta and the army too. Hood is a bold fighter. I am doubtful as to the other qualities necessary."

On July 16th, Davis sent a urgent telegram to Atlanta, demanding to know Johnston's plans. Johnston indicated that, once again, he planned to stay on the defensive, and "watch for an opportunity to fight to advantage." The next day a telegram arrived at his Atlanta headquarters, ordering him to turn command of the Army of Tennessee over to John Bell Hood.

THE BATTLE OF ATLANTA

In his new role as commander of the Army of Tennessee, Hood would soon be sorely tested. In the last week of July, Sherman began the final determined push to capture the prize – the city of Atlanta.

Before the battle of Peach Tree Creek, north of the city of Atlanta, Sherman ordered his men to advance toward the city. He arrayed the Union forces in a semi-circle around the north and east of Atlanta, and began to pressure Hood. To the east, General Francis Blair was able to dislodge Patrick Cleburne's troops from the ridgeline known as Bald Hill. Blair's Union troops immediately dug in, and began moving artillery to the top of hill. Although Union heavy artillery had already bombarded the outskirts of Atlanta, from the position on Bald Hill, gunners could now put their shells directly into the town center. So advantaged, Sherman was not alone in believing that the battle for Atlanta was over.

His sentiments seemed to be confirmed when frontline Union posts began to observe troop and civilian movements within the city, suggesting a withdrawal was underway. In fact, what the Union observers were seeing were preparations for a Confederate attack against Major General James B. McPherson's Army of the Tennessee. In preparation for the attack, Hood abandoned his outer defenses and fell back on inner line.

In the meantime, General William "Old Reliable" Hardee began a wide swing around the Union flank with his corps, planning to hit the vulnerable Union left and rear, east of the city. As this attack was launched, it was planned that Wheeler's cavalry would harass Sherman's supply lines while General Frank Cheatham's corps attacked the Union front. Hardee had not been given enough time for his forced march and turned north too early, running headlong into XVI Corps (Granville Dodge), which McPherson had repositioned on the left flank of the Army of the Tennessee. Nevertheless, XVI Corps recoiled from the withering attack of General Hardee's forces and, for a brief time, it appeared that the Confederates might win the battle. However, XVI Corps finally formed and held a line.

General John B. Hood.

Unaware that XVI Corps had successfully stabilized their line, Hood launched a secondary attack to the north, in the vicinity of the Decatur Road. At about 4:00 pm Cheatham's corps broke through the Union front at the Hurt House, but were turned back by precise artillery fire, directed by Sherman himself. General John A. "Blackjack" Logan's XV Army Corps then led a counterattack to retake the hill near the Troup-Hurt House. With the line stabilized and losses mounting to an unacceptable level, Hood called off the attack. During these actions the estimated casualties were 12,140 (3,641 Union, 8,499 Confederate).

On September 2, 1864, the Atlanta Campaign ended when Union troops entered Atlanta and the national flag was unfurled over the courthouse. Sherman wired Washington, D.C. with the message, "Atlanta is ours, and fairly won..." Expecting a counterattack, two days afterward, Sherman issued an order for the inhabitants to leave the town within five days, so that the place might be appropriated to military purposes. Within a few days it had been evacuated by civilians.

HOOD'S NASHVILLE CAMPAIGN

Hood's defeated Confederate Army sat on the Macon Road in the vicinity of Palmetto until late September, 1864. Then, in early October, Hood began the Nashville Campaign – the last great Confederate offensive of the Civil War – during which he drove north from Palmetto toward Rome, before turning northeast toward Dalton and then southwest into Alabama.

Georgia's Generals

Lieutenant General James Longstreet.

Lieutenant General William J. "Old Reliable" Hardee.

LIEUTENANT GENERAL JAMES LONGSTREET (1821–1904)

James Longstreet graduated from West Point in 1842, fifty-fourth in a class of sixty two. Brevetted major during the Mexican War, Longstreet retained that rank until June 1, 1861, when he resigned to join the Confederate army as a brigadier general. At First Bull Run (First Manassas) he proved to be a skillful leader and on October 7, 1861, earned promotion to major general. His masterful defensive actions during the Peninsula Campaign impressed General Robert E. Lee, who later divided the Army of Northern Virginia into two corps with Longstreet, now a lieutenant general, commanding I Corps. Not until later did Lee discover Longstreet's flaws – a penchant to act slowly on orders if he did not agree with them and an inability to function effectively as an independent commander. He died in 1904 and is buried at Alta Vista Cemetery in Gainesville, Georgia. Lee affectionately called Longstreet "My Old War Horse," and his men called him "Old Pete." After Longstreet's misstep at Gettysburg during "Pickett's Charge", Lee used the general's defensive skills to great advantage and always credited his "Old War Horse" as a superior corps commander.

LIEUTENANT GENERAL WILLIAM J. "OLD RELIABLE" HARDEE (1816–73)

At the outbreak of war, William Hardee was already a distinguished soldier in the U.S. Army, the veteran of more than two decades of service. He was born in Camden County, Georgia, in 1815 and his lifetime of soldiering began when he enrolled at West Point, graduating in 1838. Commissioned into the U.S. Army as a 2nd lieutenant (2nd U.S. Dragoons), he fought in both the Seminole War and the Mexican War. Hardee was awarded two brevets while serving with the Army of Occupation in Mexico, but was wounded at La Rosia, Mexico. Somewhat later,

in 1853, he returned to West Point as a tactics instructor and served as commandant of cadets. During this time he wrote *Rifle and Light Infantry Tactics (Hardee's Tactics)*, which was for many years the authoritative textbook on the subject and was used by both sides during the Civil War.

On January 31, 1861, as the nation teetered on the brink of war, Hardee resigned his commission as lieutenant colonel, 1st Cavalry. He was then commissioned into the C.S.A. as a colonel of cavalry, and was quickly promoted to brigadier general, commanding the Upper District of Arkansas. Promoted to major general and assigned to central Kentucky, he commanded a corps in the Confederate attacks at Shiloh (April 1862), where he was again wounded. He led his corps during the defense of Corinth, Mississippi, and was with Bragg's Army of Mississippi during the advance into Kentucky. Hardee subsequently fought at Perryville (October, 1862), was promoted to lieutenant general, and fought at the second Murfreesboro battle and during the Tullahoma Campaign.

By this time Hardee had developed a deep and lasting dislike for the Bragg. He therefore sought and was granted a transfer to Joseph E. Johnston's command. However, when Leonidas Polk was killed at Pine Mountain, during the Atlanta Campaign, Hardee was quickly recalled to the Army of Tennessee to take over Polk's III Corps. He led the corps (Hardee's Corps of the Army of Tennessee) through the Atlanta Campaign. At Jonesboro, the final act of that campaign, he led two corps in the Confederate attacks. Chafing under Hood's leadership, he was sent to command the Atlantic coast and served there for the remainder of the war. He oversaw the successful evacuation of Savannah and withdrew into North Carolina with the remnants of his corps. His last engagement was at Bentonville.

Lieutenant General Joseph "Fightin' Joe" Wheeler.

Major General John Brown Gordon.

Hardee surrendered along with Johnston's command on April 26, 1865. He is considered by some to be the best lieutenant general to have served in the Confederate Army of Tennessee. After the war he retired to Alabama, where he died in 1873.

LIEUTENANT GENERAL JOSEPH "FIGHTIN' JOE" WHEELER (1836–1906)

Small in stature, but with the heart of a lion, "Little Joe" or "Fightin Joe" Wheeler, as he was popularly known, was a native of Augusta, Georgia. During the Civil War, he made a name as an outstanding cavalry commander, rising from the rank of first lieutenant to corps commander in just four years.

After graduating West Point in 1859, Wheeler was commissioned as a second lieutenant in the Regiment of Mounted Riflemen. At the outbreak of war he resigned from this post to fight for the South. His first assignment was as a lieutenant of artillery and in September he was promoted to colonel. At the Battle of Shiloh, Wheeler was in command of an infantry regiment, which he thereafter led during operations around Corinth, Mississippi. In the summer of 1862, Bragg chose him to lead the cavalry for the Army of the Mississippi. He led a mounted brigade at Perryville and a division at Murfreesboro. Given command of a corps of mounted troopers, he led it in the Tullahoma Campaign and at Chickamauga was in charge of one of the two cavalry corps. He came into conflict with the other great Confederate cavalry leader, Nathan Bedford Forrest, which led to Forrest's reassignment.

Wheeler subsequently gained charge of all the cavalry with the Army of Tennessee, and led them at Chattanooga and during Sherman's Atlanta Campaign. During this campaign he led raids on the Sherman's supply lines. Following the fall of Atlanta, Wheeler remained to defend Georgia, while Hood launched his invasion of middle Tennessee. Greatly outnumbered, however, he could do little to hinder Sherman's March to the Sea.

Fightin' Joe's final actions of the war were during the Carolinas Campaign. He was taken prisoner in Georgia in May 1865, but was quickly released and moved to Alabama. There he became a congressman in the postwar years, and was commissioned into the U.S. Army as a major general of volunteers in the Spanish-American War. In 1900, he was retired with the regular army rank of brigadier general. He is one of the few Confederate commanders to be buried in Arlington National Cemetery, earning that honor because of his postbellum military service.

MAJOR GENERAL JOHN BROWN GORDON (1832–1904)

"A more gallant, generous, and fearless gentleman and soldier has not been seen by our country."

PRESIDENT THEODORE ROOSEVELT UPON THE DEATH OF JOHN BROWN GORDON

Born in Upson City, Georgia, in February, 1832, Gordon attended the University of Georgia but dropped out to study law and was admitted to the Atlanta Bar. The law practice he subsequently established was not a success, however, and instead he turned his hand to journalism in the state capital, Milledgeville. Thereafter he and his father established a coal mining company in Dade Country. Gordon also became involved in politics, earning skills as orator that would later help him to inspire troops in battle.

At the outbreak of war, Gordon raised a company of volunteers (the Raccoon Roughs), which was incorporated into the 6th Alabama Regiment. Commissioned into the C.S.A. as a captain, he was quickly promoted to major and fought with the 6th Alabama at the First Battle of Bull Run (First Manassas), being promoted regimental colonel upon the regiment's reorganization. At the Seven Pines battle he distinguished himself in temporary command of Rodes' brigade, D. H. Hill's Division, Department of the Virginia. He also fought through the Seven Days, part of the time in brigade command.

While advancing to Rome, Hood detached General Alexander P. Stewart's Third Corps from the main body of his Army of Tennessee and ordered it to advance from the hills of west Cobb County to gain the Western and Atlantic Railroad. Moving northwest, Stewart's troops skirmished with Union garrisons established by Sherman to protect his vital rail supply line and, on October 3rd, quickly defeated the small Union garrisons stationed at Big Shanty (now Kennesaw), Moon's Station, and Acworth. The men then set to work tearing up the track for eight miles north of Big Shanty. The following day General Samuel French (of Stewart's corps) was ordered to advance on Allatoona Pass and barricade it, and thereafter destroy the Etowah Bridge.

At Allatoona, the Union Army had a major supply depot with tons of rations for the Union Army in Atlanta. For the Confederate Army capturing these stores would represent a major coup. Sherman therefore ordered 1,000 reinforcements to move from Rome to Allatoona. Once there, the men worked quickly to strengthen the two small forts at the top of the ridge both east and west of the railroad tracks for the looming attack. As the Confederate division began to deploy to the west of the Star Fort, frantic dispatches were signaled to Kennesaw Mountain asking, "Where is General Sherman?" It was at this time that General Sherman is reputed to have made the statement, "Hold the fort for I am coming," as later popularized in a hymn by that name. The actual communication was, in fact, rather less theatrical. Sherman indicated that help was on the way but that until it arrived the garrison would have to hold out.

Having received no reply to his surrender demand, at 10:30 am French gave the order to begin the assault. Withering fire halted the initial Confederate advance, but was followed up by a second attack on the Federal left which overran the Union first line of defense. On the north side of the mountain, another attack forced Corse to withdraw to the Star Fort. Over the next two and a half hours, Confederate forces attacked four times with the final assault at 1:30 pm. Then, believing a large Federal force was

advancing on his position, French retreated from Allatoona. Casualties of the battle are estimated at 1,505 Union and Confederates 799.

After the Allatoona battle, Hood continued to move to the northwest and crossed the Coosa River west of Rome, Georgia, near the Alabama state line. He then turned northeast toward Resaca, Georgia, but bypassed the city, moving north, and continued to destroy the railroad. On October 13th, Lieutenant General Alexander P. Stewart captured the Federal garrison at Dalton, Georgia, which included 600 African-American soldiers. These men were stripped of their shoes and some clothing and marched to the railroad, where they were forced to tear up about two miles of track in brutal conditions. (Some of these soldiers were afterward returned to their slave masters.) From Resaca, Hood withdrew to the west toward Gadsden, Alabama.

SHERMAN'S "MARCH TO THE SEA"

In the fall of 1864, in what would be the final major military action in Georgia, Sherman drove through the heart of the state on his famous "March to the Sea", leaving a trail of devastation in his wake.

In the aftermath of the Atlanta Campaign, Sherman began making plans to move against Savannah, Georgia – the "Jewel of the South". The scheme he devised was inspired by the belief that to defeat the Confederacy it would be necessary to destroy the South's economic capacity and psychological will to resist, and to eliminate resources that could be used by the Confederate Army (a strategy that is synonymous with later concepts of total war). He ordered that as his men pushed southeast toward Savannah, they should systematically destroy all manufacturing plants, agricultural infrastructure, and the railroads. Furthermore, because the army would be cut off from its supply lines, the troops were told to forage off the land wherever possible. The last factor would inflict further depredations upon the civilian population.

The 300-mile "March to the Sea" began on November 15, 1864, two days after Lincoln's reelection. Sherman started by destroying the city

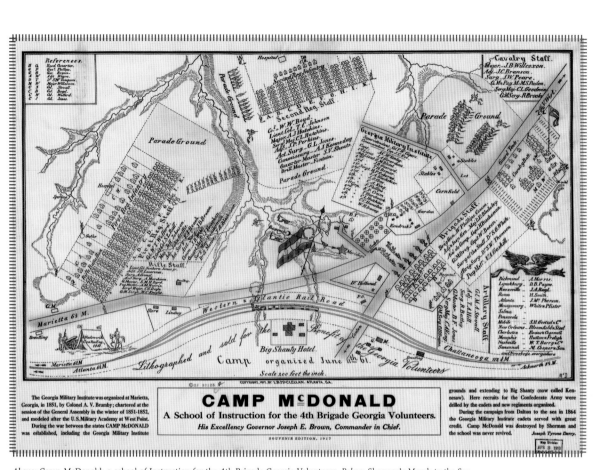

CAMP McDONALD

A School of Instruction for the 4th Brigade Georgia Volunteers.

His Excellency Governor Joseph E. Brown, Commander in Chief.

The Georgia Military Institute was organized at Marietta, Georgia, in 1851, by Colonel A. V. Brumby; chartered at the session of the General Assembly in the winter of 1851-1852, and modeled after the U.S. Military Academy at West Point. During the war between the states CAMP McDONALD was established, including the Georgia Military Institute grounds and extending to Big Shanty (now called Kennesaw). Here recruits for the Confederate Army were drilled by the cadets and new regiments organized.

During the campaign from Dalton to the sea in 1864 the Georgia Military Institute cadets served with great credit. Camp McDonald was destroyed by Sherman and the school was never revived.

Joseph Tyrone Derry.

Above: Camp McDonald; a school of Instruction for the 4th Brigade Georgia Volunteers. *Below:* Sherman's March to the Sea.

of Rome and tearing up railway track between Dalton and Allatoona Pass. He then sent messages from the Cartersville Depot, the last communication the Union Army would have with the North for six weeks. Sherman's troops then advanced along two major routes with Major General Oliver O. Howard's Army of Tennessee on the right and Major General Henry Slocum's Army of Georgia on the left – a strategy that Sherman hoped would confuse Hardee as to his ultimate objective. As Howard pushed south he forced Confederate troops out of Lovejoy's Station, before pressing on toward Macon. To the north, Slocum's two corps moved east then wheeled southeast towards the state capital at Milledgeville.

To oppose Sherman's 62,000 men, Lieutenant General William J. Hardee had forces totaling approximately 13,000 troops. When he became aware that Savannah was Sherman's goal, he began concentrating his troops to defend the city, while ordering Major General Joseph Wheeler's cavalry to attack the Union flanks and rear.

The first significant action of the march occurred on November 22nd, when Wheeler's cavalry and Georgia militia attacked Howard's Army of Tennessee at Griswoldville. This assault was driven away with heavy casualties and the march resumed.

During the remainder of November, and in early December, a number of small skirmishes were fought, including those at Buck Head Creek and Waynesboro, but the vastly outnumbered Confederate troops could do little to hold up the relentless push toward Savannah. Consequently, on December 10th, a little over a month after departing from Rome, Sherman arrived outside Savannah. Forewarned of his approach, Hardee had ordered his engineers to inundate the open ground in front of the city, a tactic which he hoped would force Sherman to approach via a few narrow and exposed causeways. In this relatively strong, defensible position, Hardee refused all surrender pleas and signaled his intention to hold out.

Meanwhile, having stripped Georgia of all they could find, Sherman's troops were in urgent need of supplies. The general knew that a Union fleet under

Rear Admiral John Dahlgren was lying off the coast with tons of much needed food and ammunition, and therefore dispatched Brigadier General William Hazen's division to try and link up with the fleet. On December 13th, after capturing Fort McAllister on the Ogeechee River, communications were opened with Dahlgren's ships.

The March to the Sea was complete. During the six-week campaign through Georgia, Sherman's scorched earth strategy had effectively eliminated the region's economic usefulness to the Confederate cause. Nevertheless, although he had achieved his objective, Sherman was not yet finished with Georgia. He now turned his attention back to Savannah, where the garrison was still holding out. On December 17th, an ultimatum was sent to Hardee, asking him to surrender the city and warning that if he refused shelling would begin. Three days later, defiant to the last, Hardee escaped over the Savannah River. On the morning of December 21st, the mayor of Savannah formally surrendered the city to Sherman.

With the city secured, the general then made his famous signal to President Abraham Lincoln: "I beg to present you as a Christmas gift the City of Savannah, with one hundred and fifty guns and plenty of ammunition, also about twenty-five thousand bales of cotton."

As the final acts of the war were played out, Federal troops captured Confederate President Jefferson Davis near Irwindale, Georgia, on May 10, 1865. Two days later General William Wofford surrendered his men in Kingston, Georgia.

Andersonville Prison, Georgia.

Georgia Units Furnished	
Infantry regiments	64
Infantry battalions	12
Sharpshooter battalions	4
State Guard regiments	7
State Guard battalions	12
Militia infantry regiments	15
Militia infantry battalions	3
Reserve regiments	11
Reserve infantry battalions	2
Local defense units	24
Misc. infantry units	66
Cavalry regiments	11
Cavalry battalions	7
Cavalry State Guard units	18
Misc. cavalry units	30
Heavy artillery battalion	1
Heavy artillery batteries	1
Light artillery regiment	1
Light artillery battalions	9
Misc. light artillery units	38

ANDERSONVILLE PRISON (CAMP SUMTER)

At least a dozen Confederate prisoner-of-war camps were established in Georgia but none is more notorious than the camp at Andersonville. Otherwise known as Camp Sumter, it was one of the largest military prisons established by the Confederacy during the Civil War and during its fourteen-month existence over 45,000 Union soldiers were confined there. The largest number held in the twenty-six-acre stockade at any one time was more than 32,000, during August of 1864.

Conditions in the camp were appalling, exacerbated by the fact that the South was itself suffering grievously from shortages by this time. Of the men who were incarcerated, almost 13,000 died from disease, poor sanitation, malnutrition, overcrowding, and exposure to the elements. After the war, the camp commandant was tried and executed, becoming the only Confederate officer to suffer this punishment. However, some historians have argued that he was used as a scapegoat by vengeful Northern politicians, and that the brutality of Camp Sumter was also commonplace in Union prisons.

Bird's-eye view of Andersonville Prison from the southeast.

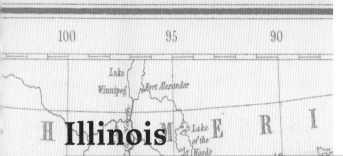

Illinois

ILLINOIS

"Nearly 80 years ago we began by declaring that all men are created equal; but now from that beginning we have run down to the other declaration, that for some men to enslave others is a 'sacred right of self-government.' These principals cannot stand together."

EXTRACT FROM A SPEECH GIVEN BY ABRAHAM LINCOLN IN PEORIA, ILLINOIS, ON OCTOBER 16, 1854

Illinois achieved statehood in 1818, when it became the twenty-first state of the Union. Although it was mostly a non-slave-owing state, a few people were kept in bondage at that time. In the decades leading up to the Civil War, the state developed into an economic force of great political importance and its population grew from around 50,000 on statehood to more than 1.7 million by 1860.

Throughout the war, Illinois served the Union well, supplying roughly a quarter of a million men (the fourth largest amount of any state) to the military, as well as providing food, clothing, and equipment to the troops. The state was also an important transport hub, with access to both rivers and railways that were used intensively to move Union troops. Perhaps the greatest contribution that Illinois made, however, was the man who led the Union through years of bloody war to eventual victory: President Abraham Lincoln (1809–65).

ILLINOIS IN THE ANTEBELLUM

During the early to mid 19th century "The Prairie State" of the Midwest transformed from an under populated and underdeveloped frontier territory into a prosperous agricultural state, with a rapidly growing urban population and expanding industrial base. By 1860, Illinois had grown to be a major producer of cereals including grain and corn, livestock, and commercial lumber. The development, in turn, had encouraged improved transportation. The Illinois and Michigan Canal, linking the Illinois River with Lake Michigan was finally completed in 1848 and gave Illinois a direct water route from Chicago to the Mississippi and the Gulf of Mexico. In the 1850s, the expanding railroad network began to link many areas of the state, and drove the growth of towns and cities. Chicago, at the center of this transport network, enjoyed the most spectacular growth. Illinois' agricultural and urbanization also

GOVERNOR RICHARD YATES (1815–73)

Yates was a staunch Republican who served as Illinois' thirteenth governor throughout the war. He was keenly pro-Union and anti-slavery, and, accordingly, backed fully Lincoln's drive to preserve the Union. Quickly moving to raise troops at the outbreak of war, he made Illinois a major provider of manpower, and, with the seizure of the strategically important town of Cairo at Illionois' southern tip, provided a key staging point for future operations. He also recognized the talents of the future General Ulysses S. Grant and gave him his first wartime work, that of state mustering officer. In addition, Yates secured Federal funds so that Illinois could contribute even more to the war effort. Some of the money went to building Camp Douglas in Chicago, the largest prisoner of war camp in the North.

encouraged other development, including lead and coal mining.

Attracted by Illinois' peacetime prosperity, large numbers of immigrants came from Germany, Scandinavia, Ireland, France, and Scotland. The southern part of the state, known as "Egypt", was settled by migrants from the South. In the two decades before the war, the population more than tripled, from 476,183 to 1,711,951. This number was swelled during the war by those who were uprooted by the fighting.

Although it was ostensibly a "free" state, insofar as slavery was outlawed in the state constitution, in the early 19th century, slaves were brought in

SPRINGFIELD

Lincoln's home from 1837 until 1861 was settled in the late 1810s – most likely by transient trappers and traders attracted by the Sangamon River – and the first permanent cabin was built there in 1821. The fledgling town was originally named Calhoun in honor of Senator John C. Calhoun of South Carolina and soon began to attract settlers from Kentucky, North Carolina, and Virginia. Over time, it was transformed from a sleepy backwater into a center of enterprise, and one with growing political prominence within the state. By the early 1830s Senator Calhoun's star was on the wane but Springfield's growing influence was recognized when it became the state capital in 1839, a transformation largely brought about by a group of prominent residents, including Lincoln, known as the "Long Nine".

Abraham Lincoln with his son Tad (Thomas) photographed in 1865 by Alexander Gardner.

for seasonal harvest work or to work as domestic servants. However, Illinois citizens were opposed to allowing African-Americans as permanent residents. For this reason, they voted against an effort to permit slavery in 1822, but also tried to discourage African-American settlement by implementing so-called "black codes". Under these codes African-American residents had to have a certificate proving they were free. If they couldn't produce the correct document, they were presumed to be a slave. The codes also outlawed African-American residents from voting, testifying against or suing a white person, gathering in groups, serving in the militia, or even owning a weapon. In 1853, a law was passed that prohibited all African-Americans, including freedmen, from settling in the state.

Nevertheless, despite these measures, and the fact that the state vigorously enforced the Fugitive Slave Law, Illinois was a favorite destination for African-American slaves fleeing from bondage in the South via the Underground Railroad. This trend continued through the war as freed slaves made their way north to Chicago, Rock Island, and other urban centers. During the war this influx became a major source of unrest among the white population, leading to efforts to halt African-American migration.

THE RACE TO POWER

The 1860 presidential race was contested by four candidates, two of whom had Illinois connections, though neither was originally from the state. Abraham Lincoln had been born in Kentucky, but moved to Illinois in 1830 and settled in Springfield seven years later. The other figure was Vermont-born Stephen A. Douglas, who had been active in the state's politics since moving there in 1833. Douglas was originally a Democrat but became the Northern Democratic Party's candidate after the party split along factional lines in early 1860, while Lincoln had been a member of the Republican Party since 1856. The two men differed on their views of slavery – Lincoln wanted no expansion of it, and Douglas felt that the local voters in new territories and states should decide the issue.

DOUGLAS AND LINCOLN

Stephen A. Douglas (1813–61) began his political career in Illinois, where he became a key figure in the state's Democratic Party. As the issue of slavery became ever more divisive, he advocated territories and states voting individually on the issue of prohibiting or adopting slavery. During the 1858 Senate elections, Douglas engaged in seven debates with Lincoln. The latter was relatively unknown outside Illinois but their debates – in which Lincoln argued that Douglas's stance on slavery threatened the republic and that the Founding Fathers would have had had no truck with the institution – drew large crowds and received widespread newspaper coverage. Douglas won that race but Lincoln became national figure with his chances of securing the Republican Party's presidential candidature in 1860 much enhanced.

THE 1864 ELECTION

The war had decisively turned in the North's favor by 1864, but no-one knew when it might actually end in victory. War-weariness had set in and the sometimes bad news from the battlefields lowered the spirits of ordinary people. Both Lincoln and other Republicans felt there was a real possibility that he might lose the election. Lincoln, in fact, wrote that he would stay on to defeat the Confederacy whatever the outcome. More practically, he also sent more troops to Grant and was cheered by the capture of Atlanta, Georgia, and Mobile, Alabama, during the election campaign. As things turned out, Lincoln won a landslide victory, securing all but three states, and seventy-eight percent of soldiers voted for him.

Lincoln outside the house on the corner of Eighth and Jackson streets, Springfield, as they appeared on his return at the close of the campaign with Senator Douglas. Today, the house is a National Historic Site.

LINCOLN AND MCCLERNAND

General John A. McClernand (1812–1900) was a lawyer, newspaper editor, and Democrat politician from Lincoln's home state. In 1861, Lincoln made him a brigadier general as a sop to Northern Democrats. Unfortunately for the new president, McClernand was politically ambitious, insubordinate, and a rarely effective commander. His main problems were with superiors, particularly General Ulysses S. Grant whom McClernand complained about to the president in 1862. Matters came to a head during the Second Vicksburg Campaign in 1863. Grant accused him of tardiness at Champion's Hill in May and McClernand responded by publicly criticizing Grant and two other officers. He was immediately dismissed.

Allan Pinkerton, President Lincoln, and Major General John A. McClernand at Antietam, 1862.

In the event, the contest between the two in Illinois was close. Lincoln secured some 172,171 votes, roughly 50.7 percent of the total cast, while Douglas secured 160,215 in all, or 47.2 percent. Thus Lincoln secured a narrow victory in his resident state. Nevertheless, Illinois was broadly supportive of Lincoln throughout the war, though *The Chicago Times* – a staunch supporter of the Democrats – was critical of both him and his emancipation of the slaves.

ABRAHAM LINCOLN AS PRESIDENT

Lincoln's anti-slavery stance was deeply unpopular in the South and when he became president in 1860, South Carolina became the first state to leave the Union, on December 20th. The new president refused to recognize the right of a state to secede and believed that his foremost duty as the country's leader was to preserve the Union. He was, to some extent, willing to give ground on the issue of slavery but rejected the Crittenden Compromise of December 18th that would have extended the Missouri Compromise, which divided slave-owning and free states, believing that it pandered to the South. However, he supported the Conwin Amendment of March, 1861, which permitted slavery to continue where it was already practiced. In reality, the South was in no mood to compromise and Lincoln had little choice but to contemplate war in order to preserve the Union.

In selecting a cabinet, Lincoln was forced to walk a tightrope. He needed to take a conciliatory line with senior figures of the defeated North Democratic Party to gain their support for the prosecution of the war and also had to deal with the more radical wing of the Republican Party, which wanted the slaves freed as soon as possible. Nevertheless, Lincoln's cabinet was largely filled by able men. Secretary of state William H. Seward (Republican) proved to be a talented diplomat while Edwin M. Stanton (Democrat), secretary for war from 1862, overhauled a corrupt and inefficient war department (though his abrasiveness made him few friends). Salmon P. Chase (Republican) was an outstanding secretary of the

Statue erected in 1886 by 21st Illinois Regiment veterans, commemorating the spot where Ulysses S. Grant was commissioned a general in 1861.

treasury but became the key figure in an anti-Lincoln faction that believed the president's direction of the war was flawed. Accused of disloyalty he resigned in 1864. One of the most outstanding, and perhaps unsung, figures in the cabinet was Gideon Welles (Republican). As secretary of the navy throughout the war, Wells increased its size seven-fold and defined the Union's naval strategy.

Between his election in November 1860 and the Confederate bombardment of Fort Sumter in Charleston Harbor in April 1861, Lincoln sought a political compromise to the crisis, even as the South was raising thousands of troops. He had always vowed not to be the first to shed blood but, equally, could not idly watch a Union garrison starved into submission and a Union military facility taken over by the Confederacy. So, when the garrison's commander made a request for supplies, Lincoln agreed. The Confederate leadership saw this as an act of war against their sovereign territory and opened fire on April 12th, effectively shedding the first blood of the war. The president was left with no other option but war to preserve the Union.

Lincoln had little military experience but, when Civil War came, effectively made himself the Army's commander-in-chief. In an effort to overcome his inexperience, he immersed himself in books on war matters from the Library of Congress and digested telegraphed reports from the war fronts. He recognized two important points – firstly, that Washington, D.C. had to be protected at all cost (the Union's main field force, the Army of the Potomac, was created to do just that), and, secondly, that the South's Army of Northern Virginia protecting its capital, Richmond, had to be destroyed.

The president selected his main field commanders on the basis of their recent performance, though many failed to live up to his expectations. In fact, he faced endless problems with generals. Some were military lightweights, while others were political schemers. A few were both. General George B. McClellan was a superb organizer but a dilatory fighter. General Ambrose E. Burnside, who replaced McClellan as head of the Army of the Potomac, knew he was not

Soldier of the 12th Illinois Volunteers, "The First Scotch Regiment", in greatcoat and tam o' shanter cap.

up to the job and did not want to command the army at all. Next came Joseph Hooker, a general of similar abilities and shortcomings to McClellan, who was wholly out-thought by General Robert E. Lee. From the military talent on offer, Lincoln wisely selected General Ulysses S. Grant for ever higher command.

As commander-in-chief, Lincoln took a meticulous interest on the way the war was fought and also had to fulfill the more usual political role associated with any president. Both roles were never less than taxing and, as the war progressed, Lincoln took more and more powers for himself. He suspended *habeas corpus*, newspapers were suppressed, and those merely suspected of disloyalty imprisoned. For the first time in U.S. history, unpopular conscription was introduced. Lincoln was also obliged to deal with disloyalty among senior military and political colleagues. Indeed, some members of his own cabinet wanted him replaced and Congress was often difficult to deal with. Yet Lincoln, the consummate politician, outmaneuvered them all and steadfastly stuck to his belief that above all else the Union should be preserved.

WARTIME POLITICS AND OPPOSITION

During the war itself, the Republican Party continued to draw support from the northern part of the state, while the Democrats were dominant in the southern counties. Central Illinois vacillated between the two parties. The state's political leadership, including the office of the governor, was firmly Republican territory. Control of the state legislature, on the other had, was hotly contested between Republicans and their Democrat rivals.

With attack on Fort Sumter, Illinois' Republican political leaders rallied around the Union flag. Democrat Stephen Douglas, who had been an advocate of a compromise solution with the South during the run-up to the war, also immediately declared his support for the Union. Likewise, Governor Richard Yates declared in his inaugural address that "the whole material of the government, moral, political and physical, if need be, must be employed to preserve, protect and defend the constitution of the United States."

Although, on balance, Illinoisans favored emancipation, many felt that they were fighting to save the Union, not for the freedom of slaves. News of the preliminary Emancipation Proclamation, in September 1862, was received with hostility by Union troops from western and southern Illinois, many of whom were recent migrants from the Carolinas, Tennessee, and Kentucky. In southern Illinois, radical anti-war activists called for the secession of southern Illinois and encouraged draft resistance and desertion. For their vocal opposition to the war and pro-Southern sympathies, state officials imprisoned many Confederate supporters, including members of Congress, judges, and state legislators while, by 1864, as a Union victory came into sight, violent acts against those suspected of being sympathetic to the Confederacy or critical of the government became more frequent.

ILLINOIS AT WAR

In the aftermath of the firing upon Fort Sumter, thousands of men came from all over Illinois to

This contemporary photograph shows: Col. Paine's barracks (he was CO of the 9th Regiment of the Illinois Volunteer Militia), brigade hospital and headquarters, roof of State quartermasters office, U. S. Quartermasters Department, ice houses, and the Mississippi River in the distance.

volunteer for military service. To provide them with martial training, the state legislature provided funding for new training camps at Alton, Caseyville, and Cairo in southern Illinois. New military installations were also built at Cairo, Camp Butler, and Camp Douglas. From these points men and materiel were sent down the Mississippi to support Union troops.

By the summer of 1862, Illinois had sent over 130,000 men to war, and at the cessation of the conflict this number had risen to more than a quarter of a million. These troops predominantly fought in the Western Theater, though a few Illinois regiments played important roles in the East, particularly in the Army of the Potomac.

On the home front, as the war dragged on, demand for foodstuffs, both at home and abroad, fueled an agricultural boom. Illinois farmers benefited from rising crop prices, and many were able to expand their farms. Chicago merchants grew rich as the city became the Union's great grain port and rail hub. Illinois farms and the state's factories turned out considerable volumes of foodstuffs and war materiel for the Northern armies. The state was also a vital

node in the vast Union supply network, particularly for the armies fighting along the Mississippi – the great water highway to the South. Running into the Mississippi in southwestern Illinois is the Illinois River, which, with the Illinois and Michigan Canal, forms a link allowing shipping to travel uninterrupted from the North to the South.

GRANT'S OPERATIONS FROM CAIRO

In the great Union logistical network, the city of Cairo, which sits at the confluence of the Mississippi and Ohio rivers, was particularly important. During the war, it served for a time as General Grant's headquarters, and throughout as the base of operations for the Western armies. For this purpose Cairo was turned into a huge Union military camp and supply depot, a marshalling point for troops and war materiel from across the Northwest.

ILLINOIS REGIMENTS

Reflecting the ethnic and religious diversity of the Illinois population, among the regiments raised in Illinois were units of men with German, Irish, Scots, and Scandinavian origins, as well as others comprised

Generals of Illinois

Major General John Buford.

Brigadier General Benjamin H. Grierson.

Major General John H. Logan.

Major General James H. Wilson.

MAJOR GENERAL JOHN BUFORD (1826–63)

Raised in Illinois, Buford graduated from West Point in 1848. He was given command of a cavalry brigade during the Second Battle of Bull Run (Second Manassas) in 1862 and led a cavalry corps during the Gettysburg Campaign the following year. His decision to hold McPherson Ridge on the first day of the battle was a key factor in the Union victory. Buford was subsequently struck down by typhoid fever and died in December.

BRIGADIER GENERAL BENJAMIN H. GRIERSON (1826–1911)

Grierson was commissioned a major of cavalry in late 1861 and participated in several operations in Tennessee and Mississippi. His most spectacular action was a raid in support of the Second Vicksburg Campaign in 1863. He led some 1,700 cavalry from La Grange, Tennessee, on April 17th and took them through Mississippi before reaching Union-held Baton Rouge, Louisiana, on May 2nd. He traveled some 600 miles and destroyed fifty miles of railroad track as well as large quantities of supplies.

MAJOR GENERAL JOHN H. LOGAN (1826–86)

Logan gave up his seat in Congress to defend the Union. After fighting in the First Battle of Bull Run (First Manassas) in 1861, he raised a regiment and was wounded during the capture of Fort Donelson in 1862. Promoted to major general, he served with the Army of the Tennessee in the Vicksburg and Atlanta campaigns, and took part in the March to the Sea as well as the final Carolinas Campaign.

MAJOR GENERAL JAMES H. WILSON (1837–1925)

Wilson graduated from West Point in 1860 and had reached the rank of major general by the end of the Civil War. He was particularly associated with the cavalry and, in the last two years of the conflict, commanded a mounted corps. He is best remembered for a number of spectacular raids he made through the Confederacy. In Wilson's final raid of the war he captured the Confederate president, Jefferson Davis.

Illinois Union Units Furnished	
Infantry regiments	150
Colored Infantry regiments	1
Cavalry regiments	17
Ind. cavalry battalion	1
Light artillery regiments	2
Independent light artillery	1
Sailors/marine personnel	2,224
Colored troops	1,811

solely of men of the Jewish faith. There were also units organized along vocational lines, in which, for example, the men were all railroad workers or schoolteachers. The "Temperance Regiment" was comprised mostly of men of the cloth.

The 45th Illinois, stands out because of its moniker – the "Washburne Lead Mine Regiment." The regiment was organized in July, 1861, by John E. Smith, who was commissioned as its first colonel. It recruited in northwest Illinois, an area where lead mining was an established industry. The regiment mustered at Camp Douglas on Christmas day, from where it moved to Cairo. In February, 1862, it was attached to 2nd Brigade, 1st Division, Army of the Tennessee, for operations against Fort Henry and Fort Donelson. It would remain attached to the Army of the Tennessee for the duration of the war. The regiment fought at Shiloh, the Siege of Corinth, and Grant's Central Mississippi Campaign. In 1863, it saw action in the siege of Vicksburg; in June 1864, the Atlanta Campaign; in 1864, against Hood in north Georgia and north Alabama, and to the sea with Sherman. After the siege of Savannah, it took part in the Carolinas Campaign, and fought its last actions of the war at Bentonville. The regiment mustered out on July 12, 1865.

The 34th Illinois Infantry, otherwise known as the "Rock River Rifles," was raised in Dixon County, and mustered into Federal service on September 7, 1861. It fought at Shiloh and was later assigned with McCook's Corps to the Army of the Cumberland, and took part in the Siege of Corinth, Stone River, Chickamauga, Rocky Face Ridge, Resaca, Rome, Lost Mountain, Kennesaw Mountain, Peach Tree Creek, the Siege of Atlanta, Jonesboro, the March to the Sea, Averasboro, Bentonville, North Carolina. The regiment was mustered out on July 12, 1865.

MARY ANN BALL BICKERDYKE (1817–1901)

Bickerdyke was a member of the Sanitary Commission and helped evacuate the wounded from Fort Donelson in 1862. She then ran various field hospitals and kitchens, first in Tennessee and Mississippi and then in the Chattanooga and Atlanta campaigns. Much admired by ordinary soldiers, who nicknamed her "Mother Bickerdyke", she also established field laundries and undertook fund raising tours. She was granted a Congressional pension in 1887.

ILLINOIS UNION ARMY DEATHS

Troops Furnished	Killed/Mortally Wounded	Died of Disease	Died of Other Causes	Total
255,057	9,884	21,065	3,875	34,834

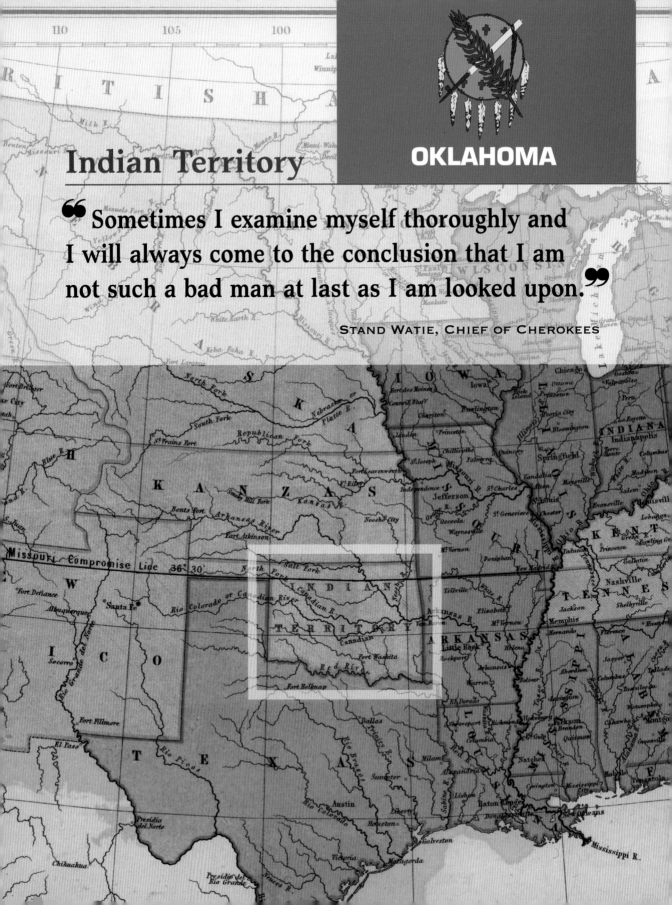

Indian Territory

OKLAHOMA

> ❝ Sometimes I examine myself thoroughly and I will always come to the conclusion that I am not such a bad man at last as I am looked upon. ❞
>
> Stand Watie, Chief of Cherokees

Following the Louisiana Purchase in 1803, the Mississippi River no longer served as the western border of the United States and Easterners formed the mistaken impression that much of the area known as the Great Plains was nothing more than uninhabitable desert.

Many, including Thomas Jefferson and those who followed him, envisioned a colonization zone for Native-Americans somewhere on the frontier as a way solving "the Indian problem." Having never seen the lands of the Louisiana Purchase, these self-fashioned experts decided a solution might be to have Indians relocated west of the Mississippi while leaving whites to live unmolested east of the river. This concept was briefly revived during the administration of John Quincy Adams, though the notion of leaving lands west of the Mississippi to Indians changed quickly after whites began crossing the river, leading to Arkansas becoming a territory in 1819 and Missouri a state in 1821.

When establishing a western border for Arkansas in 1824, surveyors included an area consisting of fourteen counties in present-day Oklahoma. Four years later, they adjusted Arkansas's border to as it is today and created a vast Indian territory to the west. In 1830, President Andrew Jackson signed into law the Indian Territory, a large area directly west of Arkansas and Missouri that encompassed the present states of Oklahoma, Kansas, Nebraska, and part of Iowa. Under the 1830 Indian Removal Act, the Federal army moved dozens of Northeastern, Midwestern, and Southeastern tribes into the territory. As more settlers moved into Kansas, Nebraska, and Iowa's fertile land, the southern part of the original Indian Territory – present-day Oklahoma – became the

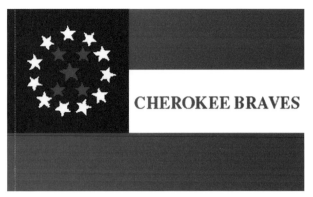

CHEROKEE BRAVES

The Cherokee Braves flag was replaced with the flag of Oklahoma on April 2, 1925, in recognition of the Native American heritage.

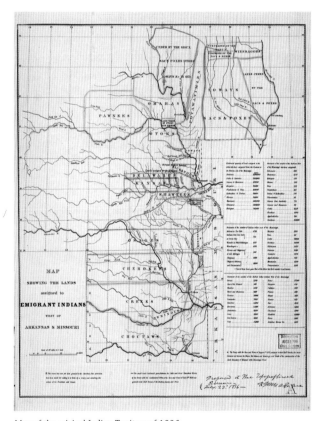

Map of the original Indian Territory of 1836.

official Indian Territory and, by the mid-1830s, this area had become the home of the Cherokee, Choctaw, Creeks, Chickasaws, and Seminoles – the "Five Civilized Tribes" from the Southern states.

THE FIVE NATIONS OF THE CONFEDERACY

Confederate President Jefferson Davis believed that the Five Civilized Tribes forced into the Indian Territory carried a grudge against the Federal government and Texas Governor Edward Clark suggested the Native-Americans could be recruited for the Confederacy. So, too, did Albert Pike, a lawyer and Mexican War veteran who had earned the trust of the tribes. In March 1861, Davis sent Pike as a commissioner to the Indian Territory to assess the possibilities of recruiting within the Five Nations on the pretext that they would be defending themselves from Federal invasion. Pike returned to Richmond with the news that he could raise 5,000 warriors.

Commissioned brigadier general on August 15, 1861, Pike returned to the Five Nations in command of the Department of Indian Territory. Washington had been violating its own treaties with the Native-Americans, making the tribes sympathetic to Pike's overtures and, on October 7, 1861, he negotiated a new treaty with Chief John Ross of the Cherokee Nation, the terms of which applied also to the Chickasaw, Choctaw, Creek, and Seminole tribes. The treaty gave the Five Nations generous new rights, such as being near equals to whites, which the Federal government had denied them.

Although Southern politicians voiced high expectations for Pike's Five Nations Army, for several decades the tribes had been concentrating on becoming "civilized" and had neither military training nor discipline. Indian company commanders could not keep their cavalry under control in the field and many of them left their posts and returned home whenever they pleased.

Similar problems had already been experienced by Colonel Douglas H. Cooper of Mississippi who had raised the 1st Choctaw and Chickasaw Mounted Rifles before Pike became Commissioner of Indian Affairs. Cooper commanded the regiment at Pea Ridge on March 7-8, 1862, where the mounted rifles fought well but could not be restrained from

Pike was a lawyer who represented the Creeks in a long court case against the Federal government. He won the $800,000 case, and became a trusted envoy in the Indian Territory. He raised three regiments of warriors for the Confederacy. See also page 38.

scalping and mutilating the battlefield dead. Raised to brigadier general, Cooper's command grew to two Indian regiments, a mixed Indian battalion, and two Texas cavalry regiments. At Newtonia, Missouri, on September 30, 1862, Lieutenant Colonel Tandy Walker's 1st Choctaw and Chickasaw Mounted Rifles and Major J. M. Bryant's 1st Cherokee Cavalry Battalion engaged three Federal volunteer regiments of the Indian Home Guard, made up of tribes in Kansas and Missouri. Cooper's command charged headlong into the Union line, posting a Confederate victory. The battle boosted Cooper's confidence in his mini-brigade's fighting ability.

DISASTER AT HONEY SPRINGS

In mid-July 1863, Cooper learned the Arkansas River had become fordable and that Brigadier General James G. Blunt was already advancing with 3,000 men, mostly Indian and black troops. Accordingly, Cooper decided to strike at Blunt's troops before they struck him. Skirmishing began on the 17th, and, though Cooper's Cherokee and Choctaws outnumbered Blunt's troops, they experienced problems with inferior gunpowder. Heavy fighting started around 10:30 a.m. and lasted about two hours. Cooper finally thought he had gained an advantage, but then a light rain turned into a downpour and rendered his defective gunpowder completely useless. The entire brigade began withdrawing and the best Cooper could do was to form a rearguard action.

The Honey Springs engagement involved 8,000 men and was the largest fought in the Indian Territory. Neither side suffered many casualties, though both were demoralized. After Honey Springs, Cooper did little more fighting and concerned himself instead with politics while Stand Watie continued the fight.

Chief John Ross (1790-1866) of the Cherokees, described as "Moses" by his people, led the tribe through some of the most tumultuous years of their existence.

BRIGADIER GENERAL DOUGLAS HANCOCK COOPER (1815–79)

Douglas Hancock Cooper, more than any other Confederate officer involved with the Five Nations, represented Jefferson Davis's hope of retaining control of the Indian Territory. He had been the Federal agent to the Chickasaw and Choctaw tribes for eight years and also exerted influence over the other three tribes. Unlike the 300-pound Albert Pike, Cooper was a leader who fought with his men rather than standing on the sidelines. He also had an understanding of the Native-American culture, and tried to capitalize on their skills as scouts, skirmishers, and raiders. However, he became discouraged when Confederate authorities failed to furnish his men with proper arms and supplies, and that discouragement infected his men, who deserted in large numbers.

Cooper felt a genuine concern for the Native Americans and eventually became the district commander of the Indian Territory in July 1864. After the war he remained in the Indian Territory, pressing prewar claims against the Federal government. In this he had little success, and in 1879 died impoverished at Old Fort Washita, Indian Territory.

Stand Watie's Cherokees

Flag of the Cherokee Nation.

In December 1863, General Maxey (below) was given command of the Indian Territory. He successfully tied down Union forces, thus stopping a Union invasion of Texas. His success led to a promotion to major general and in 1865 he took command of a division, passing the Indian Territory to the Indian General Stand Watie on February 21, 1865.

Of the Five Nations, the Cherokees were the most "civilized" in terms of adopting the customs and clothing of the whites. They lived in northern Georgia, on very productive land, and had assimilated with Southern whites better than most tribes. White plantation owners, however, wanted Cherokee land, which led to the "Trail of Tears", as the tribes were uprooted from their homeland in Georgia and forced to to the Indian Territory: thousands died along the route of the march. Since that time, almost thirty years had passed. Stand Watie remembered it well, being one of the signers of the removal treaty, but he also became a successful planter in his new home in the Indian Territory.

At the outbreak of the Civil War, the Cherokees divided politically. While a few listened to Albert Pike's recruiting overtures, others followed Watie's advice and attempted to remain neutral. The Confederate victory at Wilson's Creek, Missouri, on August 10, 1861, changed Watie's mind. He raised the Cherokee Mounted Rifles and was rewarded with a colonelcy from the Confederate government. Although Jefferson Davis wanted organized cavalry units for his Western armies, Watie thought about warfare differently. After losing men at the Battle of Pea Ridge on March 6-7, 1862, he abandoned conventional warfare, adopted hit-and-run tactics, and became a genius at guerrilla warfare. When two white and two Indian regiments from Kansas captured Tahlequah, the Cherokee capital, Watie returned with a vengeance and drove the intruders out of the Indian Territory. His success led to the creation of the Second Cherokee Mounted Rifles and companies made up of Indians from other tribes. They patrolled the Indian Territory, striking Federal outposts in Kansas and Arkansas.

A brigadier general from May 6, 1864, Watie caused more trouble with his guerrilla raids than his counterpart, General Cooper, achieved by leading his command in organized warfare. Prowling the Arkansas River, Watie's Cherokees upset traffic and captured enough steamers to keep his men supplied and fed. While Jefferson Davis disapproved of Cooper's plan to use Chickasaw's, Choctaws, and Creeks as guerrillas, he praised Watie's success. When the Eastern war ended in April 1865, Watie's Cherokees continued their raids. Even after General E. Kirby Smith surrendered all forces under his command in the West, Watie refused to apply the war ending capitulation to the Indian Territory. Two more months passed before Watie gave up his sword on June 23, 1865 – the last Confederate general to surrender his command.

EPILOG

On matters of slavery, the Cherokees could be regarded as more "civilized" than the plantation owners who ousted them from Georgia. When the tribes settled in the Indian Territory, many of them brought slaves to work their farms but, while Stand Watie and his command were still staging raids, in February 1863 the Cherokee Council voted to forsake their alliance with the Confederacy and rejoin the North. In making this pledge, the Cherokees freed all their slaves and granted part of their property to those they had emancipated. Neither the North nor the South demonstrated such generosity. Other tribes were not so munificent but during the Reconstruction period Union officials imposed land concessions upon the tribes, mandating that any former slaves be allowed to become either members of their respective tribes or be awarded Indian land.

INDIAN TERRITORY UNITS

BRIGADIER GENERAL STAND WATIE (1806–71)

At the age of fifty-five, Stand Watie organized the 1st Cherokee Mounted Rifles and became one of the most daring cavalry leaders in the West. After suffering heavy casualties at Pea Ridge, he picked his fights without ever engaging in another major battle. He understood the nature of his men and led them in doing what they did best, ambushes and raids. Neither Albert Pike nor Douglas Cooper could have controlled the Cherokees, so Watie fought his own war the way he knew best.

Brigadier General Douglas H. Cooper's Brigade
1st Choctaw and Chickasaw Mounted Rifles
Daniel McIntosh's Creek Regiment
Mixed Battalion Creeks and Seminoles
9th Texas Cavalry
4th Texas Cavalry (McCulloch)

Brigadier General Stand Watie's Indian Cavalry Brigade
1st Cherokee Mounted Rifles
2nd Cherokee Mounted Rifles
Creek Squadron Osage Battalion
Seminole Battalion

Indiana

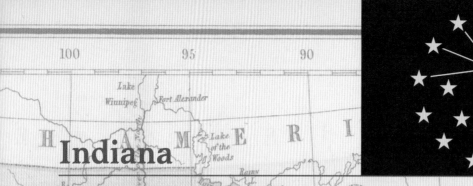

> **That on the first day of January, in the year of our Lord one thousand eight hundred and sixty-three, all persons held as slaves within any State or designated part of a State, the people whereof shall then be in rebellion against the United States, shall be then, thenceforward, and forever free . . .**

ABRAHAM LINCOLN, EMANCIPATION PROCLAMATION, JANUARY 1, 1863

Indiana played a crucial role during the Civil War, supplying between 190,000 and 210,000 soldiers to the Union cause (plus several thousand to the Confederates). Its regiments fought in every major engagement of the war.

Oliver P. Morton of Indiana.

What's more, despite a strong cadre of Southern sympathizers, its government, led by the indefatigable Governor Oliver H.P. Morton (1823–77), remained steadfast throughout the great conflict. Early in his gubernatorial tenure (1861–67), Morton prepared for a war which he believed was inevitable. He appointed strong Unionists to cabinet positions, established a state arsenal, and employed hundreds of men to produce ammunition and weapons, all without legislative consent.

When the telegraph brought news of Fort Sumter's fall in April, 1861, Indiana responded with mass meetings and immediate enlistments. Three days later, Morton telegraphed Lincoln that he had 10,000 soldiers under arms. Lincoln initially requested only 7,500 men from Indiana, but within weeks 22,000 men had volunteered.

The terrible legacy of such enthusiasm was that by war's end a third of Indiana's volunteers were casualties: more that 26,000 dead and 50,000 wounded. Although twice as many men were mustered in World War II, more than twice as many Hoosiers died in the Civil War.

SECRETARY OF THE INTERIOR CALEB BLOOD SMITH (1808–64)

A "machine politician," Caleb Smith was the first Indiana resident to serve in a president's cabinet. A Hoosier by way of Ohio, Smith studied law and fought through the political ranks – state legislator, U.S. congressman – to become a Whig power broker. It may have been his backing that gave Lincoln the Republican presidential nomination in 1860, and, as reward, Lincoln made Smith his secretary of the interior. Smith accepted unenthusiastically and, disagreeing with the Emancipation Proclamation, he resigned from the cabinet and returned to Indiana.

Without Morton's forceful leadership suppressing pro-slavery Democrats, Indiana may have provided the nail that secured the Union's coffin. On one occasion, Morton ushered Republican legislators into hiding, preventing a pro-Southern Democratic legislative majority, and preserving Indiana's place

GENERAL SOLOMON MEREDITH (1810–75)

Farmer, politician, and lawman, Solomon Meredith led the "Iron Brigade" at Gettysburg. This brigade suffered the highest percentage of casualties of any brigade in the war. On two occasions, Meredith had horses shot and killed while he rode into battle. Each time they fell on top of him breaking his ribs and crushing his legs. Coupled with a near-death experience from shrapnel on the second day of Gettysburg, the second fall from a horse left him unfit for field command. He spent the balance of the war in administrative positions along the Mississippi River as a brevet major general.

GENERAL JEFFERSON C. DAVIS (1828–79)

Indiana's Jeff Davis had the unfortunate distinction of sharing a name with the President of the Confederacy, though earlier in his life it was perceived as an honor. Both served ably in the Mexican-American War. A competent commander, Davis actually enlisted in the 1840s and worked his way up in rank. He was on duty at Fort Sumter the day the war began and ended the conflict as commander of Sherman's XIV Army Corps, sweeping through Georgia on the "March to the Sea". Davis's reputation is sullied by his murder of an officer during a quarrel in 1862 and for abandoning freed slaves to the mercy of Confederate Cavalry during the Ebenezer Creek Incident in Georgia in December 1864.

General Jefferson C. Davis.

as a leader among the Federal states. Then, realizing the state's power to tax would quickly lapse, he privately raised millions of dollars to support troops and the continuity of state government. When Kentucky Governor Beriah Magoffin refused to allow military mobilization, Morton called for loyal Kentuckians to enlist in Indiana regiments. Indeed, he became known briefly as the "Governor of Indiana and Kentucky." Morton not only provided recruiting and financial leadership, but he organized hospitals and an orphanage for the children of war veterans.

His efforts on behalf of the Union stand in vivid contrast to that of Indiana's U.S. Senator, Jesse Bright, a pro-slavery Democrat. In 1862, Bright became one of the few senators to ever be expelled from that body, having written to Confederate President Jefferson Davis offering weapons for "the cause."

Confederate raids into southern Indiana were prompted by the state's pro-slavery minority. Paradoxically, however, when Morgan's Confederate cavalry crossed the Ohio River into Indiana in 1863, they received little support. Indeed, their plundering and burning alienated many erstwhile supporters among the so-called "Knights of the Golden Circle" (or "Sons of Liberty") a secret club of Southern sympathizers.

Not only did 200,000 Indiana men serve with the Union Army, but they fought with valor in both the Eastern and Western theaters. In the manner of the day, men enlisted for various terms of service, but most Hoosier regiments mustered out and disbanded before the final shots were fired.

Indiana's contribution was highlighted at the Second Battle of Bull Run (Second Manassas) and

Detachment of 3d Indiana Cavalry Photograph from the main eastern theater of war, the siege of Petersburg, June 1864-April 1865.

Gettysburg. At Gettysburg, the 14th Indiana Infantry Regiment seized Cemetery Hill on the first day of that desperate three-day struggle. This tactical decision saved the Union position, giving the army time to concentrate its forces. The 19th Indiana Volunteer Infantry Regiment served in the Iron Brigade and was so decimated in battle that it eventually consolidated with the 20th Indiana Regiment. The remaining men from the 19th and the 20th fought with Ulysses S. Grant in Virginia and saw difficult duty during the siege of Petersburg. In early 1864, Indiana formed the 28th Indiana Colored Infantry Regiment. This group served with distinction losing 212 men during the war, many at the awful Battle of the Crater in Petersburg.

Indiana men served to the last and beyond. John Williams, officially the final casualty of the war died on May 13, 1865. He was a member of Indiana's 34th Regiment fighting in Texas. The 13th Regiment of Indiana Cavalry mustered out on November 10, 1865, and the 28th Colored Regiment followed eighteen days later.

It was not only in the category of active combatants that Indiana made enduring contributions to the Union. The state also became the granary for the Federal effort. Having lost the agricultural South, the Northern states needed more food to feed its hungry population and the people of Indiana responded.

The Civil War had lasting effects on Indiana, effects beyond the terrible toll of casualties. Cities along the Ohio River – New Albany, at one time Indiana's largest city, and Port Fulton – experienced a temporary boom from riverboat construction and war business (including smuggling). With fear of Confederate raiding and the construction of railroads through Indianapolis and Chicago, however, industry moved into the northern half of the state, leaving the southern half to agriculture and mining.

Although Indiana again supported Lincoln in 1864, this time in his electoral battle with former Major General George McClellan, it became, after the war, the first state to elect a Democrat, Thomas Hendricks, as governor. Staunch Unionist Morton became a U.S. Senator and voted in the minority for the impeachment of Andrew Johnson

GENERAL SILAS COLGROVE (1816–1907)

Attorney Silas Colgrove was appointed lieutenant colonel of the three-month 8th Indiana Volunteer Infantry in April 1861. The 8th saw service in what is now West Virginia until September when Colgrove was appointed colonel of the 27th Indiana Infantry. Infamous as a mean disciplinarian, the men pleaded in vain for his removal. Moved east they fought in the Shenandoah Valley (Virginia) Campaign, in engagements at Front Royal and Winchester, and at Cedar Mountain. In the bloody "Cornfield" at Antietam (Battle of Sharpsburg), Colgrove's men sustained casualties of nearly half their number. From Chancellorsville to Gettysburg, the 27th fought savagely, though Colgrove proved to be an erratic commander. Transferred west, the 27th fought their way into Atlanta where Colgrove was seriously wounded and ultimately forced to leave the army.

The Morgan Raid

When Confederate cavalry led by General John Hunt Morgan (1825–64) crossed the Ohio River and appeared in Indiana in 1863, a shock wave rippled through Northern states. From Tennessee to Kentucky and onward into Indiana and Ohio, where the raiders were finally captured six weeks after their adventure began, Morgan's horsemen covered more than a thousand miles.

Morgan himself grew up on a farm near Lexington, Kentucky, but was attracted to military life. He enlisted as a cavalryman to fight in the war against Mexico and was promoted to first lieutenant prior to the Battle of Buena Vista in 1847.

When the Civil War erupted, Morgan was a Lexington hemp manufacturer. A slave owner, he nevertheless spoke against secession yet raised a brigade of cavalry for the Confederate ranks. Morgan fought at Shiloh in Tennessee in April 1862, raided Federal supply lines and was promoted to brigadier general in December.

Entranced by the chivalric ideal, Morgan dreamed of cavalry adventures and convinced General Braxton Bragg to let him lead diversionary raids into occupied Kentucky. He insisted that he could tie down thousands of troops protecting the Union's lines of supply. Bragg consented, but ordered Morgan not to cross the Ohio River.

On June 11, 1863, Morgan and 2,460 cavalrymen left Tennessee with four artillery pieces. Their objective was to attack Union supply depots which stretched from the Ohio River to the forward lines of the Army of the Cumberland, even then massing to drive the Confederates out of Tennessee.

By July 2nd – the same day that Robert E. Lee's thrust into Pennsylvania foundered at Gettysburg – Morgan crossed into Kentucky. Meeting with widespread public support, Morgan impulsively disavowed his orders.

INDIANA UNION ARMY DEATHS

Troops Furnished	Killed/Mortally Wounded	Died of Disease	Died of Other Causes	Total
196,363	7,243	16,663	2,766	26,672

General John Hunt Morgan of the Confederate Army. This portrait was published in *Harper's Weekly* in 1864, announcing Morgan's death.

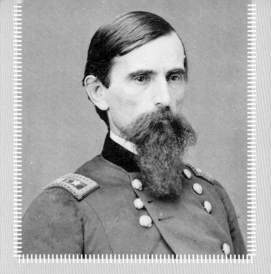

MAJOR GENERAL LEWIS "LEW" WALLACE (1827–1905)

Within a week he had crossed the Ohio River into Indiana although he had been warned by spies that little support would be forthcoming from the Hoosiers.

Indeed, Indiana quickly organized local militia and home guard units, and harassed Morgan's cavalry in farms and towns along their route to the Northeast: Corydon, Salem, Vienna, North Vernon. Along the way the cavalrymen burned and looted, often stealing personal valuables for their own families.

On July 13th, Morgan led what was left of his tattered command into Ohio at a point just north of Cincinnati where they burned bridges, railroads, and government stores. They had raced through southeastern Indiana in less than a week.

By this time though, harassed continually, Morgan's men and horses were exhausted. Their every attempt to return south was blocked. The Confederates had become hunted men and as the raid dwindled from continuing losses, they were trapped near West Point, Ohio. The spot is recognized as the northernmost point reached by an officially organized Confederate unit during the war.

Imprisoned, Morgan and several officers escaped after a few months. He made his way south to Bragg's command, but less than a year later, he was killed in Tennessee.

News of Morgan's Raid excited Southern partisans and frightened the citizens of the North. In six weeks he had plundered a thousand miles, caused the diversion of numerous bodies of Union troops, and destroyed hundreds of thousands of dollars worth of munitions. Southerners were heartened by his strike north and cheered by news accounts of his daring raid, yet the lasting results and effects on the war were of doubtful importance.

Indiana born and bred, Lewis Wallace was the scion of a political family, a lawyer, and an author (he published the novel *Ben Hur* in 1880.) As war with Mexico loomed, he raised troops and fought under Zachary Taylor. A lawyer between wars, Wallace was appointed state adjutant general when the Civil War broke out and quickly rose in responsibility. A year later, having shown fearless leadership in the capture of Confederate forts along the Mississippi and Cumberland rivers, he was promoted to major general. Wallace's military reputation was damaged at Shiloh, Tennessee, in April, 1862, when he was blamed for incompetence in moving his troops. Although he served in important subsequent posts, his standing never recovered.

Indiana Union Units Furnished	
Infantry regiments	152
Cavalry regiments	13
Misc. cavalry units	3
Heavy artillery regiments	1
Light artillery companies	26

Iowa

IOWA

❝ Once let the black man get upon his person the brass letter, U.S., let him get an eagle on his button, and a musket on his shoulder and bullets in his pocket, there is no power on earth that can deny that he has earned the right to citizenship. ❞

FREDERICK DOUGLASS

Thickly populated by Native-American tribes – the Arikara and the Fox, the Kickapoo and the Pawnee – the Iowa Territory saw settlers trickling in during the early 1800s.

In 1806, as the Lewis and Clark Expedition raced homeward on the Missouri River from the Pacific Ocean they met trappers, traders, and the occasional farm family blazing their own trails westward.

By 1846, the year of its statehood, Iowa was settled and farmed. During the next fifteen years railroads sliced across the rolling prairies and the original subsistence farming – often conducted from sod huts, hence the name "sod busters" applied to early prairie farmers – began to be replaced by commodity farming.

Deeply divided opinions and the absence of nearby law enforcement made the frontier state volatile. The Quakers of Iowa participated in what became known as the "Underground Railroad", funneling runaway slaves north and west to freedom. After fighting with the free state or anti-slavery partisans in "Bloody Kansas" (men referred to as Jayhawkers or Redlegs) militant abolitionist John Brown rested at the home of William Maxson near Springdale in east central Iowa. There he began planning his raid on the United States Arsenal at Harpers Ferry, Virginia. Indeed, he took two local young men with him on that ill-fated raid in October, 1859. Nevertheless, there was a vocal anti-war or "Copperhead" sentiment among recent settlers – predominantly Southerners and German immigrants – along the Mississippi River and in southern counties.

William Maxson House, State Highway No. 1, Springdale vicinity, Cedar, Iowas. After fighting in Kansas, John Brown rested here before departing for the famous raid on the arsenal at Harpers Ferry.

Governor Samuel J. Kirkwood

As war loomed, Iowa was predominantly abolitionist and Governor Samuel J. Kirkwood energetically raised and equipped volunteers for the Union cause. The state voted heavily for Lincoln and the Republican Party, the Iowa Democrats having split into numerous feuding factions.

Despite its strong pro-Southern minority, Iowa contributed a disproportionate number of young men to the Union armies – 76,242, or more than ten percent of its entire population. Iowa men fought from the beginning of the war, when it was believed that the conflict would be short and relatively bloodless, to its bitter end, chasing stray Confederate units through the Texas scrub and into Mexico. They fought in the Western and Cumberland theatres, from Fort Donelson through the prolonged and bloody siege of Vicksburg. Iowa regiments were essential in slicing the western states of the Confederacy away from that renegade nation's heartland and confirming General Winfield Scott's Anaconda Plan for dismembering and defeating the South.

On its border with Missouri, however, many Iowans were pro-slavery, anti-Lincoln Confederate sympathizers and they provided safe haven for raiding irregulars. These men, dedicated to the Southern cause and often called "bushwhackers" for their tendency to attack isolated farm houses, occasionally raided into Iowa. A typical incursion took place in the fall of 1864 and was designed to disrupt Lincoln's reelection. On October 12th, a dozen raiders disguised themselves as Union soldiers and terrorized Davis County, where they looted, burned buildings, and kidnapped three men, eventually murdering them.

Although no battles between uniformed troops ever took place in the state, it was by no means certain at the time that this would be the case. In 1864, for example, a strong and mobile army of Confederate raiders under Sterling Price – 12,000 cavalry with fourteen artillery pieces – swung through Missouri and eastern Kansas. Price had determined to save Missouri for the Confederacy, but his men were defeated in every significant encounter – especially at Westport, Missouri, called the "Gettysburg of the West" – and ultimately, dragging captured wagons and material possessions, moved too slowly to prevent the massing of opposing Union troops. Price eventually led what remained of his men into Texas, offering their services in the Mexican wars and elsewhere.

BRIGADIER GENERAL JAMES M. TUTTLE (1823–92)

Like so many Americans, James Tuttle's family moved west for greater opportunities. A Democrat, he was a sometime farmer, sheriff, and small-town elected official who raised a company of Iowa volunteers in April, 1861. Assigned to the 2nd Iowa Infantry Regiment, Tuttle was elected regiment lieutenant colonel and fought with distinction at Fort Donelson and Shiloh. Thereafter, he was promoted to brigadier general and fought at Vicksburg. Although Tuttle served well, his order to the Catholic Bishop of Natchez to recite prayers for Abraham Lincoln was overturned and soon after he resigned his commission, returning to Iowa. Following the war, he served in the Iowa legislature, switched to the Republican Party, and was active in business.

Distinguished Generals

Brigadier General James M. Tuttle.

Major General Grenville M. Dodge.

Major General Samuel R. Curtis.

Major General Francis J. Herron.

MAJOR GENERAL GRENVILLE M. DODGE (1831–1916)

A civil engineer and railroad surveyor by training, Grenville Dodge saw opportunity when Fort Sumter was shelled. He was appointed colonel of the 4th Iowa Volunteer Infantry Regiment and fought with it at the battle of Pea Ridge after which he was appointed brigadier general. His appointment as commander of the District of the Mississippi involved protecting and building railroads. In 1864, he was appointed major general and served with Sherman's army in Georgia. He led the XVI Corps at the Battle of Ezra Church and was shot in the head during the battle of Atlanta. Dodge ended the war commanding the Department of the Missouri. His service record was, however, sullied by his association with Thomas Durant, a shady businessman who profited by smuggling contraband cotton. In 1865, Dodge resigned from the army to become chief engineer of the Union Pacific Railroad and a leading figure in the construction of the Transcontinental Railroad.

MAJOR GENERAL SAMUEL R. CURTIS (1805–66)

An opportunistic graduate of West Point, Samuel Curtis was a regular army officer who became a lawyer and was appointed military governor of several occupied cities during the Mexican-American War. A staunch Republican and supporter of Abraham Lincoln, he was elected to the U.S. House of Representatives from Iowa, but resigned that seat when war broke out. Curtis was appointed colonel of the 2nd Iowa Infantry in 1861 and was subsequently promoted to brigadier general. During his command Curtis was involved in actions west of the Mississippi River, including halting the northward advance of Confederate General Sterling Price at the small but decisive Battle of Westport in what is now Missouri.

MAJOR GENERAL FRANCIS J. HERRON (1837–1902)

A bank clerk, Francis Herron organized the "Governor's Grays" militia even before Lincoln's inauguration. In April 1861, he was appointed captain of the 1st Iowa Volunteer Regiment. Wounded and taken prisoner at Pea Ridge, he was exchanged and eventually promoted to brigadier general. His efforts at Pea Ridge resulted in the award of a Medal of Honor for rallying men "to repeated acts of daring." As a result of his actions at Prairie Grove, Herron was appointed major general, the youngest on either side at the time. At Vicksburg with Ulysses S. Grant, he commanded the extreme left of the Union lines and ended the war leading the XIII Army Corps on the coast of Texas. After the war, he remained in Louisiana and then traveled to New York City where he worked in the law and in banking. Sadly, however, Herron died a pauper living in a tenement.

General Belknap and Staff. Seated (from left to right): Captain Oliver D. Kinsman, General William Worth Belknap, Major Alonzo J. Pope, 13th Iowa Infantry. Standing (left to right): Captain Charles W. Keppler, 13th Iowa Brt., Major William H. Goodrell, 13th Iowa Brt., Major Henry Clay McArthur, 15th Iowa Lieut., Wyatt Buckner Pomeroy, 11th Iowa. In 1861, Belknap was commissioned major in the 15th Iowa Infantry and participated in the battles of Shiloh, Corinth, and Vicksburg. In 1864, he was promoted to brigadier general and given command of the 4th Division, XVII Corps, and participated in General Sherman's operations in Georgia and the Carolinas. He was mustered out of service as a major general in 1865.

THE 1ST IOWA CAVALRY REGIMENT

The 1st Iowa Cavalry Regiment was typical of Federal units from Iowa. Organized at Davenport, troopers mustered in for three years of service, the first three-year cavalry regiment accepted for Federal service during the war. Unusually for Union cavalry, members provided their own horses and equipment. The regiment mustered out on February 15, 1866, while on Reconstruction duty in Austin, Texas. A total of 2,115 men served in the 1st Iowa and it suffered two officers and fifty-six enlisted men killed in action or who died of their wounds. Another two officers and 233 enlisted men died of disease – dysentery, measles, pneumonia, malaria tuberculosis, typhoid fever, and a host of other maladies that are curable or preventable today – for a total of 293 fatalities.

Lieutenant Colonel W.H. Merritt, commanding first officer of the 1st Iowa Infantry.

IOWA UNION ARMY DEATHS

Troops Furnished	Killed/Mortally Wounded	Died of Disease	Died of Other Causes	Total
76,242	3,540	8,498	963	13,001

Congressman Rush Clark helped organize of volunteer regiments in Iowa.

A corporal from Camp McClellan, Iowa.

Iowa Union Units Furnished	
Infantry regiments	51
Light artillery companies	4
Cavalry regiments	9

THE 1ST REGIMENT IOWA VOLUNTEER INFANTRY (AFRICAN DESCENT)

Organized in Keokuk, six companies of the 1st African-American Regiment mustered into Federal service for a term of three years beginning in October, 1863. At the time there were scarcely fifteen hundred African-Americans living in Iowa, but four additional companies were added before the end of the year. Altogether, 1,153 men served with the regiment before it was mustered-out of the Army two years later.

This regiment of black troops took part in numerous scouting and foraging expeditions. Its lone engagement with Confederate troops took place at Wallace's Ferry, Big Creek, Arkansas on July 26,

1864. Attacked by a larger force of cavalry at dawn, and with its commanders killed or wounded, the black troops formed lines and fought for four hours until help arrived.

The regiment primarily performed garrison duties in the Department of Arkansas, guarding leased plantations which grew food and saleable materials for the Union, and was re-designated the 60th Infantry Regiment U.S. Colored Troops in March, 1864. It suffered 344 fatalities: one officer and eleven enlisted men killed in action or who died of their wounds, plus 332 enlisted men who died of disease.

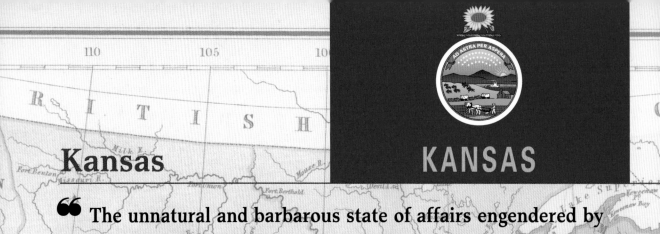

Kansas

> The unnatural and barbarous state of affairs engendered by war was terribly emphasized on Kansas soil, where the anti-slavery people were exposed to the malignant hate of an enemy in the throes of defeat, whose schemes of revenge took form in arson, robbery, pillage and murder wherever defenceless bordertowns promised hope of success to these murderous marauders.

FROM *GUN AND THE GOSPEL* BY THE REV. H.D. FISHER, D.D.

Europeans were traders in Kansas long before the fledgling United States purchased the Louisiana Territory from France in 1803. That act, however, opened the floodgates for settlers who brought their plows and, in some cases, black slaves onto the prairie.

COL FREMONT'S LAST GRAND EXPLORING EXPEDITION IN 1856.

The issue of slave ownership soon created strife among the new neighbors and a long, sometimes bloody, struggle ensued between pro-slavery and "Free Soil" factions.

Both pro-slavery and abolitionist influence in Kansas was the result of mixed emigration, from the North – as far as Massachusetts – and from the Southern border states of Missouri and Arkansas. Friction often became violent and resulted in the formation of gangs called "bushwhackers" or "Jayhawkers" who burned property and murdered those who held opposing views.

Pre-war violence reached its peak in the mid-1850s when sentiments were stoked by the passage of the Kansas-Nebraska Act in 1854. The act allowed settlers in those territories to determine by vote whether they would allow slavery within their boundaries. Typical of the violence of the "Bleeding Kansas" days was the attack on the town of Lawrence and the "Pottawatomie Massacre." Lawrence was founded in 1854 as a center for anti-slavery agitation. Barely two years later, on May 21, 1856, a pro-slavery posse led by Sheriff Samuel J. Jones attacked the town destroying the newspapers, looting businesses, and burning the Free-State Hotel. In response, John Brown launched the nearby Pottawatomie Massacre on the night of May 24th, during which five

In this cartoon, titled "Colonel Fremont's last grand exploring expedition in 1856," Frémont and his abolitionist supporters are ridiculed. In particular, the artist condemns the Republican candidate's alliance with *New York Tribune* editor Horace Greeley and Henry Ward Beecher and Beecher's role in the Kansas-Nebraska conflict. Frémont (center) rides a scrawny "Abolition nag" with the head of Greeley. The horse is led toward the left and "Salt River" (i.e. political doom) by prominent New York politician William Seward. Fremont muses hopefully, "This is pretty hard riding but if he only carries me to the White house in safety I will forgive my friends for putting me astride of such a crazy Old Hack." Greeley, meanwhile, says, "Seward it seems to me we are going the same Road we did in 'fifty two' but as long as you lead I'll follow if I go it blind." Seward: "Which ever road I travel always brings me to this confounded river, I thought we had a sure thing this time on the Bleeding Kansas dodge." On the right stands radical abolitionist minister Henry Ward Beecher, laden with rifles. He preaches in verse, "Be heavenly minded my bretheren all / But if you fall out at trifles; / Settle the matter with powder and ball / And I will furnish the rifles." Beecher was linked to the New England Emigrant Aid Society, and was known to have furnished anti-slavery emigrants with arms to participate in the struggle between pro-slavery and anti-slavery settlers in Kansas. A frontiersman (far right), a figure from Frémont's exploring past, leans on his rifle and comments, "Ah! Colonel! – you've got into a bad crowd – you'll find that dead Horse on the prarie, is better for the Constitution, than Abolition Soup or Wooly head stew in the White House."

pro-Southern sympathizers (three of them known slave catchers) were murdered in cold blood.

Kansas became the 34th state of the United States – a state free of the stain of slavery – on January 29, 1861, just months before the assault on Fort Sumter. Having resolved its status on slavery already, the state had allowed its militia to fall into disuse.

SENATOR JAMES HENRY LANE (1814–66)

Born in Indiana, James Lane inherited a political disposition from his father. Following service in the Mexican War, he was elected lieutenant governor of Indiana, then sent to Congress as a Democrat. He voted in favor of the Kansas-Nebraska Act of 1854, which created new territories, repealed the Missouri Compromise, and allowed those territories to determine whether they would permit slavery. His vote ruined him in Indiana and he emigrated to Kansas in 1855 where he allied with Free State forces and joined the Republican Party.

Lane took an active part in the domestic strife known as "Bleeding Kansas". Energetic, unscrupulous, and an emotional orator, he was elected U.S. Senator and when South Carolina fired on Fort Sumter in 1861 he immediately organized a company of Kansans to guard President Lincoln. Exploiting his political contacts, Lane served the Union in Kansas and Missouri, raising troops and taking part in several battles. He even planned to launch an expedition to invade New Mexico, though it came to nothing. A year after the war, accused of financial irregularities and in questionable health, he committed suicide.

Thus, unlike neighboring Iowa, it had no organized state militia, and no supplies or structure, with which to defend the Union.

Kansas' free soil spirit was, however, exemplified by Senator James Henry Lane. A lawyer, politician, and fiery orator, Lane immediately organized Kansans in Washington, D.C., to provide protection for President Lincoln. Back on the prairie, distant from the killing fields of Virginia, the war seemed far away. Still, Kansas men – both white and black – rushed to enlist. Altogether more than 20,000 men served the Federal cause and at least thirteen percent died in service, ranking Kansas high in the list of states that contributed "more than their fair share" toward the preservation of the Union.

Over the course of the war, Kansas troops fought in hundreds of engagements west of the Mississippi. The regiments' duties were to protect America's grain lands and railroads, to keep rivers open for commerce in compliance with Winfield Scott's Anaconda Plan, to strangle the rebellious slave states, and to bring those states west of the Mississippi out of the Confederacy. Battles were often fought against irregular troops: guerrilla bushwhackers such as those commanded by the William Quantrill. Such fighting took place in a land that was still considered a frontier and in the absence of the law and the strong Federal forces of the East. The bushwhackers' miserable work often took the form of night time raids; small actions designed to burn

Lawrence burns during the attack by William Quantrill and his Confederate raiders. As seen in *Harper's Weekly*, September 19, 1863.

After the raid Lawrence was in ruins. Image from *Harper's Weekly*, September 5, 1863.

the farmstead and crops of an opposition figure and perhaps even to kill him and his family. By allowing their undisciplined raiders to steal anything of value including livestock, Southern border ruffians like Quantrill or his successor, "Bloody Bill" Anderson, gave their men incentive to act outside the law.

Small battles, such as Baxter Springs in October, 1863, pitted Quantrill's men with units from Kansas. However, because the irregulars usually lived off the land and traveled fast, their units were difficult for infantry to fully engage. Thus Quantrill surprised the Federal troops during this engagement, killing more than a hundred before galloping away.

On August 21, 1863, Quantrill sacked the city of Lawrence in an action that became known as the "Lawrence Massacre". Abolitionist Kansas Senator James Henry Lane was the target of the raid, though he managed to escape through a cornfield in his nightshirt. Nevertheless, the bushwhackers, on Quantrill's orders, murdered 183 men and boys "old enough to carry a rifle." Quantrill carried out several executions personally, dragging men from their homes and killing them before their families. The ages of those killed ranged from fourteen years to ninety. By the time Quantrill's men rode away, most of Lawrence was in flames. His raiders looted indiscriminately and robbed the town's bank.

Troops from Kansas were also involved in halting the ill-fated Missouri Campaign of Confederate General Sterling Price in the fall of 1864. During his campaign, Price led 12,000 cavalrymen from Arkansas into Missouri, hoping to smash Federal troops there and return the state to the Confederacy. His unsupported troops won several small battles, such as Pine Knob, but were ultimately defeated with thousands of casualties. Price escaped with the remains of his exhausted troopers into Oklahoma and finally into Texas.

In late 1865, most troops from Kansas were mustered out of service and returned home. Except for the thousands of dead and wounded, and despite the civil strife, their state was relatively untouched by the war.

Kansas Union Units Furnished	
Infantry regiments (two failed to complete organization)	11
Militia regiments	25
Sharpshooter companies	0
Sharpshooter battalions	0
Misc. infantry units	0
Cavalry regiments	9
Heavy artillery battalions	0
Light artillery batteries	7
Garrison artillery units	0

BRIGADIER GENERAL ALBERT LINDLEY LEE (1834–1907)

Lee joined the Union Army at the start of the war and became a major in the 7th Kansas Cavalry in October 1861. Promoted to colonel of the regiment, he was with Halleck at the capture of Corinth, Mississippi, and then commanded the 2nd Brigade in the Cavalry Division of the Army of the Mississippi. On November 29, 1862, he was promoted to brigadier general and became chief-of-staff to the XIII Corps under Major General John A. McClernand. He served through much of the Vicksburg campaign, commanding 9th Division's 1st Brigade before being wounded in the assault on Vicksburg. In August 1864, he commanded the Cavalry Division of the Department of the Gulf and led the cavalry forces during the Red River campaign. He resigned his commission in 1865.

1ST KANSAS COLORED VOLUNTEERS (79TH U.S. COLORED TROOPS)

This troop was mustered in as a battalion on January 13, 1863, though their designation was changed to the 79th U.S. Colored Infantry a year later. Survivors were mustered out on October 1, 1865. Throughout their service, the men of the 1st Kansas served on the rugged frontier of Kansas, Missouri, and Arkansas.

Senator James Lane, something of a self-appointed general in the Kansas militia, ordered recruiting officers to enlist black volunteers in August, 1862, months ahead of Lincoln's Emancipation Proclamation of January 1, 1863. The regimental commander was Colonel James M. Williams and his men were said to be mostly fugitive slaves from Arkansas and Missouri. Dressed in make-shift uniforms for half of their service, they skirmished with Confederate guerrillas at Island Mound, Missouri on October 29, 1862. This small engagement, taking place months before their official mustering-in, was the first in which black troops engaged Confederates in battle and resulted in the first combat death of a black soldier in the Civil War.

Once in Federal service, the 1st Kansas, now officially the 79th U.S. Colored Infantry, engaged uniformed Confederate forces and Southern partisans in Missouri, Arkansas, and the Indian Nations throughout 1863 and 1864. The regiment lost at least 344 men during wartime service, more than any other Kansas regiment. Many of the men were murdered during the battle of Poison Springs, Arkansas, on April 18, 1864, by Confederates commanded by Nathan Bedford Forrest who became, following the war, the original leader (the first "Grand Wizard") of the racist terrorist group known as the Ku Klux Klan.

The 2nd Kansas Colored Infantry Regiment avenged the slaughter of its sister regiment during the battle at Jenkins' Ferry, Arkansas, on May 4, 1864, charging the enemy and screaming "Remember Poison Spring."

KANSAS UNION ARMY DEATHS

Troops Furnished	Killed/Mortally Wounded	Died of Disease	Died of Other Causes	Total
20,149	737	1,638	255	2,630

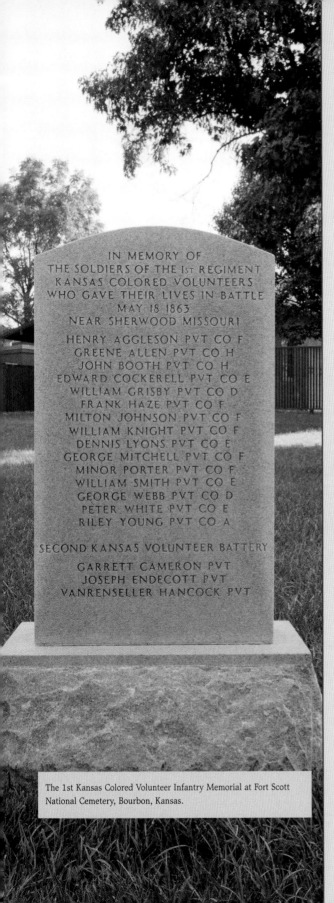

IN MEMORY OF
THE SOLDIERS OF THE 1st REGIMENT
KANSAS COLORED VOLUNTEERS
WHO GAVE THEIR LIVES IN BATTLE
MAY 18 1863
NEAR SHERWOOD MISSOURI

HENRY AGGLESON PVT CO F
GREENE ALLEN PVT CO H
JOHN BOOTH PVT CO H
EDWARD COCKERELL PVT CO E
WILLIAM GRISBY PVT CO D
FRANK HAZE PVT CO F
MILTON JOHNSON PVT CO F
WILLIAM KNIGHT PVT CO F
DENNIS LYONS PVT CO E
GEORGE MITCHELL PVT CO F
MINOR PORTER PVT CO F
WILLIAM SMITH PVT CO E
GEORGE WEBB PVT CO D
PETER WHITE PVT CO E
RILEY YOUNG PVT CO A

SECOND KANSAS VOLUNTEER BATTERY

GARRETT CAMERON PVT
JOSEPH ENDECOTT PVT
VANRENSELLER HANCOCK PVT

The 1st Kansas Colored Volunteer Infantry Memorial at Fort Scott National Cemetery, Bourbon, Kansas.

MAJOR GENERAL JAMES G. BLUNT (1826–81)

Blunt grew up on a farm in Maine and began practicing medicine in 1849, by which time he had already earned his certificate as a sea captain. However, an urge to move west landed him in Kansas where he allied himself with abolitionist John Brown and James Lane. When war broke out, Blunt was appointed to command troops and became the only major general from Kansas. He fought, with varying degrees of success, throughout the war – at the outbreak he was appointed lieutenant colonel of the 2nd Kansas Volunteer Regiment, and later appointed brigadier general of volunteers and given command of the Department and Army of Kansas, and later of the District of the Frontier. However, following the debacle of Quantrill's raid on Lawrence, he lost his position, but later performed with distinction in 1864 in command of the 1st Division of Army of the Border.

After the war, Blunt resumed the practice of medicine and also studied law. In 1869, he moved to Washington, D.C., but within ten years had become erratic in behavior and was committed to the mental asylum where he died two years later.

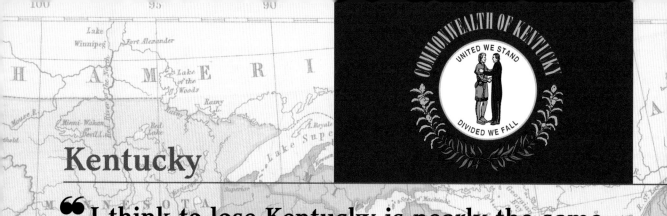

Kentucky

"I think to lose Kentucky is nearly the same as to lose the whole game . . . we would as well consent to separation at once, including the surrender of the capital."

PRESIDENT ABRAHAM LINCOLN IN A SEPTEMBER, 1861, LETTER TO ORVILLE BROWNING

Both Abraham Lincoln and Jefferson Davis were born in Kentucky and the residents of the state itself were split in their support of either side. There was a shadow Confederate government of Kentucky, but Kentucky officially remained "neutral" throughout the war.

Lincoln needed the Kentucky Commonwealth. It was his home state and that of his wife, Mary Todd. Jefferson Davis needed it too. After all, its northern border was the Ohio River – deep and wide and therefore defensible. Kentucky, however, was not sure who or what it needed. Unlike "Deep South" states such as Louisiana, which held almost as many slaves as free men, slaves were barely one-fifth of the population, though the census still numbered them at 225,483. Kentucky also bound to the South by the Ohio and Cumberland and Mississippi rivers, waterways that transported its produce – tobacco, corn, wheat, hemp, and flax – as well as people, though the new railroads were pushing through the state in all directions.

As war closed in, Kentucky seemed to lack a center. It was mostly Democrat, not altogether opposed to Lincoln and the Republicans but certainly not fully in accord. It was no surprise then that Governor Beriah Magoffin, who personally favored black slavery and secession if necessary, sought to keep Kentucky neutral. At this juncture, he was not supported by the General Assembly which favored the Union, but voted for compromise. By 1861, however, events were running out of control.

Three days after South Carolina Confederates led by P.G.T. Beauregard bombarded Fort Sumter on April 12, 1861, Abraham Lincoln called for troops. His April 15th telegram to Governor Magoffin was rebuffed, Magoffin responding: "President Lincoln, Washington, D.C. I will send not a man nor a dollar for the wicked purpose of subduing my sister Southern states." A month later, Kentucky declared its neutrality and if the war had been relatively short and bloodless as many believed it

Beriah Magoffin (1815–85) ensured Kentucky stayed neutral and, in face of a hostile legislature, only resigned if he could name his successor. He nominated James Fisher Robinson who was also a moderate and earned criticism from the Lincoln administration for opposing the Emancipation Proclamation.

would, that policy might have succeeded. Even then though, both the Union and the Confederacy had established recruiting stations and fortresses on Kentucky's borders and thousands of Kentuckians left the Commonwealth to take sides.

In fact, the Kentucky militia was as divided as its leaders. Simon Buckner's State Guard favored the Confederacy. The Home Guard was primarily Unionist. Thus Kentucky spent the early months of the war on the fence. The turning point came in the 1861 elections. Union candidates won overwhelmingly, dealing a body blow to pro-slavery advocates. The state house and the senate suddenly had veto-proof Unionist majorities and quickly overturned Magoffin's policy. Almost immediately, Union General William "Bull" Nelson, supported by the Lincoln administration, established a recruiting camp in Garrard County. Confederate volunteers streamed across the border to a camp south of Guthrie. After a fit of political intrigue that brought moderate James Robinson to the statehouse, Magoffin resigned. Kentucky's neutrality was over.

THE 5TH KENTUCKY AND GENERAL LOVELL ROUSSEAU (1818–69)

Lawyer and politician, Lovell H. Rousseau was a self-made man who served in high office in both Indiana and Kentucky. Commissioned as a captain in the Mexican-American War, he raised a company of volunteers and led them at the Battle of Battle of Buena Vista, fighting at a key point in that battle.

When war approached in 1861, he resigned his seat in the Kentucky senate and raised two regiments composed entirely of Kentuckians at the Union's Camp Joe Holt, across the Ohio River from Louisville in Indiana. They became the 5th Kentucky Infantry, known informally as the "Louisville Legion". Aided by a battalion of the Louisville Home Guard, the men saved Louisville from Bragg's advance in 1862.

The Louisville Legion fought in virtually every significant battle of the Western campaign: Shiloh, Perryville, Corinth, Stone's River, Chattanooga, Missionary Ridge, Kennesaw Mountain, Atlanta, and more, losing a total of 302 men during service.

By the war's end, Rousseau had become a major general commanding a division.

THE RACE FOR KENTUCKY

By September 1861, both sides were trying to take control of the Commonwealth. Confederate General Gideon Pillow occupied and fortified Columbus, a railroad terminus on the Mississippi River. On its high bluffs the Southerners constructed Fort DuRussey to control river traffic. They equipped the fortress with 143 cannon, dubbing it "The Gibraltar of the West". For his part, Union General Ulysses S. Grant marched into Paducah, a railroad nexus and a strategic intersection of the navigable Tennessee and Ohio rivers. During the same month, the General Assembly finally ordered the Stars and Stripes to be raised over the state capitol in Frankfort. Kentucky was officially Union.

This did not, however, end Southern hopes in Kentucky. In the days that followed, General Albert Sidney Johnston fortified Bowling Green as part of a Confederate line that stretched from Columbus to the Cumberland Gap and onward through the Appalachian Mountains. A splinter group of Southern sympathizers met in October to form a Confederate state government. It elected George Johnson, a lawyer and farmer, as governor and nominated Bowling Green, now occupied by Confederate troops, as the new state capital. Although it was effectively powerless, this government of Kentucky was admitted to the Confederacy in December. Governor Johnson was killed at Shiloh the following year.

In fact, Kentucky seethed with small, but deadly, encounters in the run-up to major troop movements. In January 1862, for example, Union General George Thomas advanced on the Confederate position at Mill Springs. In the ensuing fight and under terrible conditions of rain and fog, the rebel forces under George Crittenden were forced to retreat across the rain-swollen Cumberland River. Many men were drowned.

The Confederates reinforced their defenses on the Mississippi River with Leonidas Polk concentrating his forces around Columbus. Nevertheless, Grant won victory across the Mississippi at Belmont, Missouri, then advanced; not against Columbus but, instead, up the Cumberland and Tennessee rivers toward forts Henry and Donelson. The Union troops were supported by ironclad steamers fresh from success at the Battle of Lucas Bend on the Mississippi where they had smashed wooden Confederate warships. Because most of his troops had been withdrawn to defend Columbus, Fort Henry's General Lloyd Tilghman was unable to mount an effective defense and surrendered after a single day of fighting.

Johnston sent troops to defend Fort Donelson, but his failure to clarify the command situation between generals Pillow, Buckner, and Floyd was to prove disastrous. Disagreements delayed the Confederate commanders and gave Grant time to receive reinforcements. Buckner – left in charge when Pillow and Floyd escaped – was forced to surrender.

Overnight, Grant became a Union hero and, more importantly, the fall of the two key forts forced the Confederates to abandon Columbus, their "Gibraltar of the West". Johnston forfeited Kentucky on February 11, 1862, retreating into Mississippi.

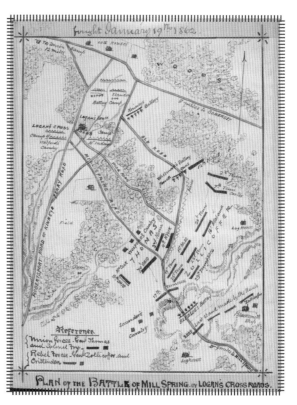

Above: Sneden's plan of the battle of Mill Spring or Logan's Cross Roads, fought on January 19, 1862.

Below: Map of the rebel fortifications at Columbus surveyed under the direction of Brigadier General George W. Cullum.

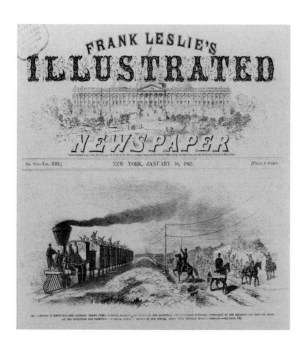

The campaign in Kentucky. Troops under General Johnston advancing on the Louisville and Nashville Turnpike are overtaken by their baggage on the Louisville and Nashville Railroad.

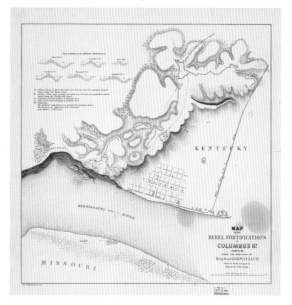

Morgan's Raids Spark Invasion

While the Union had temporarily rid Kentucky of Confederate armies, another scourge soon presented itself in the form of John Hunt Morgan. By May 1862, Morgan was successfully harassing Union supply lines and over the following months, his mounted raiders struck in small towns across the Commonwealth – Tompkinsville, Harrodsburg, Lebanon, Cynthiana.

A showman as well as a fighter, Morgan telegraphed confusing and taunting messages to Union foes. When his force left Kentucky, he claimed to have captured and paroled 1,200 Union soldiers, recruited 300 men, acquired hundreds of cavalry mounts, used or destroyed supplies in seventeen towns, and incurred fewer than 100 casualties. As well as vexing the enemy, his success also encouraged Confederate generals Braxton Bragg and Edmund Kirby Smith to plan an invasion of Kentucky via Nashville where they expected to defeat Union Major General Don Carlos Buell and recruit many Kentuckians to the Southern cause. Their forces entered Kentucky on August 28th, and soon found that while Southern sympathy was strong, the number of recruits was small. In response to the incursion, Indiana Governor Oliver Morton sent reinforcing regiments from his state across the Ohio into Louisville.

Although Smith and Bragg won several partial victories, they never successfully joined forces to bring the weight of their experienced troops to bear at any significant battle. Smith set upon a small group of Bull Nelson's troops at Richmond and inflicted heavy casualties, wounding

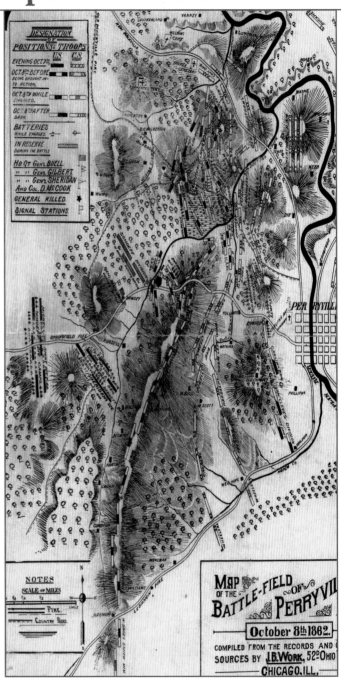

Map of the battlefield of Perryville, October 8, 1862, compiled from the records by J. B. Work, 52nd Ohio Volunteer Infantry.

Nelson in the process. Bragg's men inflicted heavy losses on a group of Union regiments guarding the railroad nexus of Munfordville, but the delay developing the Munfordville siege allowed Union forces to concentrate against them.

At the Battle of Perryville on October 8th, Bragg engaged a smaller division of Union soldiers. Hard fought and bloody, the battle was tactically indecisive but halted the Confederate invasion and forced a withdrawal into Tennessee. Because he failed to pursue the fleeing enemy, Buell was replaced by Major General William S. Rosecrans but for the remainder of the war there were no concerted efforts by the Confederacy to retake Kentucky.

THE ORPHAN BRIGADE AND JOHN CABELL BRECKINRIDGE (1821–75)

The largest Confederate unit recruited in the state, the 1st Kentucky was nicknamed the "Orphan Brigade." Its original commander was Major General John C. Breckinridge, former U.S. vice President. The brigade fought throughout the war, from mere skirmishes to pitched and bloody battles, such as Shiloh in 1862 and Stones River the following year. Indeed, it was at Stones River on January 2, 1863, that the brigade received its nickname.

Over Breckenridge's objections, General Braxton Bragg ordered a bloody, unsuccessful, and – as it turned out – near suicidal assault on the Federal lines. The 1st Kentucky's commander, Brigadier General Roger Hanson, was killed along with many of his men. As survivors straggled back to the Confederate lines, the dismayed Breckinridge, who had since been promoted to division command, rode among them crying out, "My poor orphans!"

The term "orphan" was, however, generally applied to Kentuckians who fought for the Confederacy; Kentucky officially being a Union state. The term became popular after the war among unit veterans,

Brigadier General Roger Hanson (1827–63).

especially after the 1868 publication of Ed Porter Thompson's brigade history in which he used the term "Orphan Brigade".

The brigade lost a second commander at the Battle of Chickamauga in September 1863, when Brigadier General Benjamin Hardin Helm (brother-in-law to Abraham Lincoln) was killed, and fought throughout the Atlanta Campaign of 1864, whereupon it was converted to mounted infantry to oppose Sherman's March to the Sea. The Orphans ended the war in South Carolina in April 1865, and surrendered.

A lawyer and veteran of the war with Mexico, Breckenridge was the youngest vice-president in U.S. history, inaugurated at age thirty-six. When war erupted he joined the Confederacy and served with distinction, eventually becoming an advisor to Jefferson Davis and the last Confederate Secretary of War. After the war he eventually returned to Kentucky where he again practiced law and spoke out against the depredations of the Ku Klux Klan.

LIEUTENANT GENERAL SIMON BOLIVAR BUCKNER, SR. (1823–1914)

Like many of the officers in the Civil War, Simon Bolivar Buckner gained valuable, if deadly, experience in America's War with Mexico. A graduate of the U.S. Military Academy, he was serving as adjutant general of Kentucky when the Civil War erupted. In this position, he enforced Governor Beriah Magoffin's policy of neutrality. Declining a commission in the Union Army, Buckner threw his lot with the Confederates, becoming the first Confederate general to surrender an army in the war – capitulating to Ulysses S. Grant at Fort Donelson on February 16, 1862, and practically the last – surrendering again on May 26, 1865, in New Orleans. After the war he became active in politics and was elected Governor of Kentucky.

GENERAL JOHN BELL HOOD (1831–79)

A West Point graduate, Kentucky-born John Bell Hood had a reputation as an aggressive commander. His personal bravery was an asset to the Confederacy and he directed units as large as a division. Fighting for Lee's Army of Northern Virginia, Hood often placed himself at the front and was promoted first to brigadier and then to major general in 1862. At Gettysburg, Hood was wounded and lost the use of his left arm. Transferred to the West he then lost his right leg at the Battle of Chickamauga. Despite these injuries, he was promoted to full general and given command of the Army of Tennessee, defending against Sherman. Hood frittered away thousands of men that the South could not afford to lose in daring, but fruitless, attacks and was relieved. After the war, he settled in New Orleans and made a living in insurance and as a cotton broker. He died during an epidemic of yellow fever leaving ten destitute orphans.

GENERAL ALBERT SIDNEY JOHNSTON (1803–62)

Born in Kentucky, Johnston was a career military officer whom Jefferson Davis considered the finest general officer in the Confederacy. Johnston left the U.S. Army in 1834 to care for his wife, who was dying of tuberculosis, and ended up as a general in the Army of Texas. In Texas, he developed a plantation, fought a duel, fought Indians, and served in the Mexican-American War. When Texas seceded, Johnston was serving in California and with a small group of would-be Confederates made a remarkable four-month journey by horse and foot to Virginia where Jefferson Davis appointed him a full general. While leading his soldiers at the Battle of Shiloh in April, 1862, Johnston was shot in the leg and died, the bullet probably having been fired by one of his own men. He was the highest ranking officer, Union or Confederate, killed during the entire war and Davis believed the loss of Johnston "was the turning point of our fate."

MAJOR GENERAL GEORGE BIBB CRITTENDEN (1812–80)

A career officer with a checkered record, George Crittenden fought in the Black Hawk War of 1832, resigned his commission, and then served in the army of the Republic of Texas. Captured by the Mexicans, Crittenden was exchanged and rejoined the U.S. Army to fight in the Mexican-American War. Released following that conflict, he was restored the next year. Crittenden threw his lot with the Confederacy and was promoted to major general, but on January 18, 1862, he was soundly defeated by the Union's General George Thomas at the Mill Springs, the first important Confederate defeat of the war. The loss broke the Southern hold on eastern Kentucky. Crittenden briefly commanded the 2nd Division of the Army of Central Kentucky, but was relieved on March 31, 1862. Arrested for drunkenness, he was restored only to face a court of inquiry. In July, Crittenden resigned as a general officer, reverting to Colonel in October. After the war he served as the state librarian of Kentucky.

Fort Anderson, Paducah, Kentucky, and the camp of the 6th Illinois Cavalry, in April 1862. Sketched by A.E. Mathews, 31st Regtiment Ohio Volunteers.

MORGAN RETURNS

In December 1862, John Hunt Morgan again led his cavalry raiders into Kentucky. On Christmas day they rode northward, cutting the lines of supply to Rosecrans' army in Nashville, then continued through Elizabethtown and, in a cold, drenching rain, swarmed toward Campbellsville for New Year's Eve. They returned to Tennessee on January 3, 1863.

It was nearly six months before any significant action again took place in Kentucky and then it was Morgan who led the action once again. Instructed to raid throughout the Commonwealth, Morgan disobeyed his orders, leading his men across the Ohio River on July 8th. In Indiana, his cavalry was attacked on all sides and prevented from returning to the Confederacy. Although they burned and looted for hundreds of miles, Morgan finally surrendered on July 26th. He had ridden a thousand miles but had only 363 men left from a force that originally numbered 2,460 plus four horse-drawn howitzers.

LAST DAYS OF THE WAR AND BEYOND

Except for sporadic engagements by small units, there were no significant battles in Kentucky for nearly a year. In the spring of 1864, however, Confederate Lieutenant General Nathan Bedford Forrest organized a raid to obtain fresh horses and provisions, disrupt Union supply lines, and discourage the enlistment of blacks in the Union army. On March 25th, he attacked the small garrison at Fort Anderson at Paducah where his cavalrymen were met with heavy fire from the fort and the sheltering gunboats on the Ohio River. After plundering in the town, he departed the following day. Irritated by Union newspaper coverage, which denigrated his effort, Forrest then sent Brigadier General Abraham Buford back to Kentucky where his fast-moving troops seized additional horses and supplies.

As the war drew toward conclusion, intense partisan activities escalated. In June 1864, Union Major General Stephen G. Burbridge was sent to

Kentucky Units Furnished	
Confederate	
Infantry regiments	9
Infantry battalions	7
Infantry mounted	7
Partisan battalions	4
Sharpshooter units	0
Cavalry brigade	1
Cavalry regiments	19
Cavalry battalions	9
Mounted rifles	7
Other	8
Artillery batteries	8
Artillery horse	1
Union	
Infantry regiments	34
(11 failed to complete organization)	
Mounted infantry regiments	10
Cavalry regiments	17
Cavalry battalions	1
Light artillery batteries	5
(2 failed to complete organization)	
Engineer companies	1

A plan of Fort Anderson by Captain John Rziha, acting engineering officer 19th U.S. Infantry.

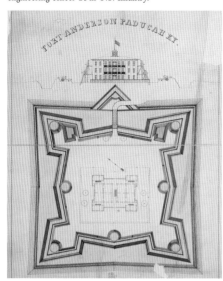

Major General William "Bull" Nelson.

Major General Thomas Leonidas Crittenden.

MAJOR GENERAL WILLIAM "BULL" NELSON (1824–62)

The remarkable career of Kentucky's William Nelson was cut short when he was murdered by fellow Union General Jefferson Davis in 1862. Nelson was both a naval officer and an army major general. In the navy, he commanded a battery at the Siege of Veracruz, Mexico (1847), and in 1858, as commander of the *Niagara*, returned to Africa the men and women rescued from the slave ship *Echo*. A family friend of Abraham Lincoln, Nelson served as a brave and effective commander at Shiloh but his subsequent command, a small unit called the "Army of Kentucky," was routed and Nelson wounded in action. While recovering Nelson was shot by Davis whom he had insulted and even slapped on a prior occasion. Davis was never tried for the murder.

MAJOR GENERAL THOMAS LEONIDAS CRITTENDEN (1819–93)

Thomas L. Crittenden was the brother of George B. Crittenden. A lawyer and the son of a U.S. Senator, he was lieutenant colonel of the 3rd Kentucky Volunteer Infantry during the war with Mexico. In 1861, Crittenden, who was, by then, a major general in the Kentucky militia, was appointed brigadier general and given command of the 5th Division of the Army of the Ohio. He led his men at Shiloh in 1862 and was promoted to major general and commander of II Corps during the Perryville Campaign. He led troops in the Army of the Cumberland under Rosecrans and fought at Stones River, then through the Tullahoma Campaign and at Chickamauga. Initially blamed for that defeat and relieved of command, Crittenden and fellow corps commander Alexander McCook were later exonerated. At Spotsylvania Court House, Crittenden stepped in to command the 1st Division, IX Corps and led it through Cold Harbor before resigning from the army in December, 1864. After the war Crittenden served as the state treasurer of Kentucky.

occupy the state, beginning a period of military martial law that would last through early 1865. In an effort to stamp out the guerrilla activities, Burbridge quickly became a tyrant earning the nickname "Butcher of Kentucky". On July 16, 1864, he issued Order No. 59, which declared: "Whenever an unarmed Union citizen is murdered, four guerrillas will be selected from the prison and publicly shot to death at the most convenient place near the scene of the outrages." Burbridge had been a successful Union field commander, but was dismissed from his post in Kentucky in 1865.

Although many Confederate archives were saved by Secretary of State Judah Benjamin, no exact accounting exists for the devastation in Confederate lives and property during the war. Nevertheless, this rich border state paid a heavy price during and after the conflict, brother fighting brother, and both scars and hope for healing persist to this day.

Night action on Island No. 10. The siege of this island, so-called because it was the tenth island on the Mississippi south of its junction with the Ohio, took place between the end of February and early April 1862. Brigadier General John Pope needed naval support for his attack on the island and persuaded Flag Officer Andrew Hull Foote to send a gunboat past the batteries. U.S.S. *Carondelet* and U.S.S. *Pittsburg* made the perilous journey on the moonless nights of April 4th and 5th. Before they did, Colonel George W. Roberts organized a raid (pictured here) by sailors in the flotilla and soldiers from the 42nd Illinois Infantry. This raid spiked the guns of Battery No. 1 on the night of April 1st to smooth the passage of the gunboats.

KENTUCKY UNION ARMY DEATHS

Troops Furnished	Killed/Mortally Wounded	Died of Disease	Died of Other Causes	Total
75,760	2,478	6,383	1,913	10,774

The Confederate monument in Louisville was completed in 1895. Funded by the Kentucky Women's Confederate Monument Association, it was dedicated on May 6, 1895, and coincided with the 29th Grand Army of the Republic annual reunion.

Louisiana

❝This accession of territory affirms forever the power of the United States, and I have given England a maritime rival who sooner or later will humble her pride.❞

NAPOLEON BONAPARTE, COMMENTING ON THE LOUISIANA PURCHASE, 1803

In 1812, when Louisiana was admitted to statehood, New Orleans was the principal international shipping facility on the lower Mississippi. The state was a primary exporter of cotton and sugar and an importer of slaves.

Rear Admiral David Dixon Porter.

Admiral Farragut.

By 1840, the city had the largest slave market in the U.S. and sold both captured slaves from Africa and slaves moved around the U.S. as a result of changing agricultural practices. According to the U.S. Census, by 1860 nearly half of the population of Louisiana was enslaved and white interest in maintaining the slave system contributed overwhelmingly to Louisiana's decision to secede from the union, which it did on January 26, 1861.

Because of the state's strategic position, the Federal plan to dismember the Confederacy began with Louisiana and early in the war troops fought their way down and up the vital Mississippi River, quickly severing the state from its allies. To seize New Orleans itself, Union forces either had to march overland through hellish swamps or fight toward the city along the Mississippi. Downstream, the river was protected by heavily fortified earthworks: forts Jackson and St. Philip. Threatened from two directions, the Confederates guessed the Union supreme thrust would come down the river from Memphis and troops and armaments were positioned accordingly. They would be proved wrong. In April, 1862, Admiral David G. Farragut brought his combined command of 18,000 troops under General Benjamin Butler and a flotilla of mortar schooners and support vessels under Commander David Dixon Porter up the river. Bombardment of the forts began on April 18th.

The battle lasted a week and was concluded when Farragut's fleet ran the passage during a spectacular engagement on the night of April 24th, destroying Confederate gunboats, fighting off fire barges, smashing massive chains placed across the river,

and dealing with the Confederate ironclad rams *Manassas* and *Louisiana*.

The next day, Federal troops captured New Orleans. Nevertheless, the forts remained unconquered. It would take another week of bombardment by Porter's mortar schooners before the sick, hungry, and demoralized men in Fort Jackson mutinied and forced surrender.

Important as it was, New Orleans was not the final Union effort in Louisiana. Indeed, fighting continued sporadically until the end of the war. Upstream, in March 1863, General Nathaniel Banks led an army on Port Hudson (which was less a port than fortified heights at a sharp bend in the Mississippi) while Farragut bombarded the fortress from the river. Farragut, however, impetuously moved his fleet before Banks' men were in position and his ships sustained immense damage. The admiral's battle group was forced to retreat with only two ships able to pass the heavy cannon of the Confederate bastion, and the navy played no further part in the battle for Port Hudson.

Assaults on the heights subsequently failed and, instead, Banks laid siege to Port Hudson, which was capably defended by General Franklin Gardner. Although the defenders suffered from disease and starvation, without advantage of significant naval support and fighting uphill through deep ravines Banks' men suffered enormous casualties. The siege lasted forty-eight days, the Confederates surrendering only after hearing of the fall of Vicksburg. Nevertheless, clearing the heights of Confederates opened the Mississippi River to Union navigation from its source to the Gulf of Mexico.

The Red River Campaign

The question of whether the Federal Red River Campaign to drive up the Red River and capture Shreveport, seize valuable stores of raw cotton, and continue into East Texas was a brilliant plan or an idiotic expedition may never be settled. It was, however, a massive undertaking settled from April 8th to the 10th, 1864, at the battles of Mansfield and Pleasant Hill in Northwest Louisiana.

Although the effective fighting forces available to Union General Nathaniel Banks and Confederate General Richard Taylor, the son of former President Zachary Taylor, were vastly unequal – the Union forces, supported by Rear Admiral David Dixon Porter's gunboats on the Red River, numbered about twice those of the Confederates – Banks was unable to concentrate his men. Thus, on the days the armies fought, the sides were roughly equal, about 12,000 men each.

Banks had expected to engage the Southern forces near Shreveport but at Mansfield, on April 8th, Taylor surprised the Union advance, which was strung out across miles, interwoven with the slow-moving baggage train and far from the sheltering fire of the navy gunboats. The result was a fiasco for the Federals who could not stand their ground long enough to develop a defense, much less seize the initiative.

The next day the Confederates once again attacked but Banks had gathered sufficient forces to hold his ground at Pleasant Hill, though barely, and he withdrew under cover of night.

The result of the battles was the end of the Red River Campaign. Casualties, though small compared to battles in the Eastern Theater, were several thousand on each side. In addition, more than two thousand Union soldiers were captured and sent to prison camp in Texas. Following the campaign, Banks was removed from command in the field while Taylor was promoted to lieutenant general.

Lieutenant General Richard Taylor.

Benjamin F. Butler and the Occupation of New Orleans and Louisiana

He was called "Beast Butler" by the white people of New Orleans – even by some in the North – and a century after his death, Ben Butler's leadership abilities and his qualities of character are still hotly debated. An excellent lawyer and subtle politician, he represented his state in the U.S. Congress and eventually served as its governor. Nevertheless, his reputation was tainted by his rule of occupied New Orleans, the debacle of his attack on Fort Fisher, North Carolina, and his ineffectual leadership in the Bermuda Hundred Campaign (Virginia) where he was dramatically out-performed by Confederate General P.G.T. Beauregard who had far fewer troops. He was, however, also the first Union general to refuse to return runaway slaves to their Southern masters, though he was inconsistent in the application of this sentiment.

Major General Benjamin F. Butler hailed from Massachusetts. Although he had little practical military experience, his political connections meant that President Lincoln promoted him to major general in May, 1861. When New Orleans was taken by Union forces, it was Butler who commanded the force of occupation. In this role he was often forceful, sometimes restrained, and occasionally outrageous in dealing with the city's inhabitants (he closed newspapers, hanged a private citizen, and imprisoned ministers who refused to pray for Lincoln), but it was his General Order No. 28 of May 15, 1862, that forever marked him as a "beast" to those who favored the Lost Cause.

Butler's order, doubtless driven by continuing provocation, was extreme in its particulars. It stated that if any woman insulted or showed contempt for any officer or soldier of the United States, she would be regarded as and held liable to be treated as a "woman of the town plying her avocation": in other words, a prostitute. In striking back at the infuriating animosity shown to Federal troops, Butler earned the eternal enmity of Southerners and caused protests both in the North and the South. He was removed from his Department of the Gulf command in December.

During his time in command, he had also earned another nickname, "Spoons Butler", because it was alleged that he stole silverware from the Southern mansions in which he was housed. Although no witness proved that he actually pilfered knives, forks, or spoons, it was later discovered that he was certainly guilty of colossal graft in his administration of Southern territories.

Major General Mansfield Lovell was tasked with the defense of New Orleans and was roundly condemned for its fall to the Union.

GENERAL PIERRE GUSTAVE TOUTANT BEAUREGARD (1818–93)

If one individual symbolized the Renaissance Man of his times it was P.G.T. Beauregard. Born in Louisiana, he was a military officer, politician, inventor, writer, civil servant, and businessman. A West Point graduate, Beauregard served capably as an engineer in the Mexican-American War, where he was wounded in action. He became the first brigadier general of the Confederacy, commanding at the assault on Fort Sumter and shortly afterward routing the Union army at the First Battle of Bull Run (First Manassas). An able, though inconsistent, general, he also led his men at Shiloh and Corinth, then defended Charleston and Petersburg against superior Federal forces. His contentious relationship with Confederate President Davis ultimately meant that he was denied major commands, however, though during the war he served in every Southern state.

Louisiana's Politicians

JOHN SLIDELL (1793–1871)

Originally from New York City, John Slidell moved to New Orleans where he took up the practice of law, became a pro-slavery proponent of states' rights, and employed his engaging personality to win elections. He served as a state representative and district attorney, as a U.S. representative and senator, and even internationally as special presidential ambassador to Mexico.

With war pending, Slidell resigned from the Senate and was appointed Confederate States ambassador to France. On the journey to Europe he was aboard the British mail carrier *Trent*, which was intercepted by the U.S.S. *San Jacinto*. Slidell and Confederate delegate to Britain James Mason were both seized, creating an international incident during which the Lincoln administration narrowly avoided war with Britain. Slidell's mission to France, and that of Mason to Britain, ultimately failed, however, and following the war Slidell remained in Europe.

GOVERNOR THOMAS OVERTON MOORE (1804–76)

Originally from North Carolina, Moore moved to Louisiana to become a cotton planter. He also practiced law and became engaged in politics. A democrat and slave owner, he was elected Governor of Louisiana in 1860 and served in that role from 1860 to1864. He had a volatile temperament, which did not seem to blemish his effectiveness. After Abraham Lincoln's election, Moore led the state out of the Union. Before the legislature met, he sent the Louisiana militia to take possession of all Federal buildings, the Baton Rouge arsenal, and to occupy forts Jackson,

John Slidell.

St. Philip, and Pike. The ordinance of secession passed two weeks later and Moore placed Braxton Bragg in command of the state military. Recognizing the commercial and strategic value of New Orleans near the mouth of the Mississippi River, he raised troops and petitioned the Confederacy to strengthen river defenses. When his term of office expired in 1864, he attempted to return to his plantation, but Federal troops burned it and liberated his slaves. Moore fled to Cuba, where he lived until pardoned by President Andrew Johnson. He returned to Louisiana and rebuilt his plantation.

Governor Thomas Overton Moore.

JUDAH P. BENJAMIN (1811–84)

The well-traveled Judah P. Benjamin was born in the West Indies, moved to Charleston, then to Connecticut where he studied at Yale, and then to Louisiana to practice law. Along the way, he shifted his allegiance from Britain, to the U.S., to the C.S.A and, ultimately, back to Britain. In Louisiana, he purchased slaves and a plantation, becoming one of the few Jews to attain high political office in that era, though when Louisiana seceded he resigned his seat in the U.S. Senate. Eloquent and witty, he once challenged Jefferson Davis to a duel, though the two ultimately became friends and Davis later appointed Benjamin to his Confederate cabinet. It was Benjamin who, in 1864, suggested that if slaves would enlist in the army they would be given their freedom. Although conservatives blocked this proposal for many months several thousand black men eventually joined the South. At war's end, Benjamin fled to Britain where he became a counsellor to Queen Victoria.

Benjamin Franklin Jonas, Senator of Louisiana, served in the Washington Artillery until 1863.

Thousands od Louisiana's men died during the war: these, from the Louisiana regiment were killed at Antietam.

The Washington Artillery

The official date listed for organization of the Washington Artillery of New Orleans is September 7, 1838. Louisiana researchers believe, however, that the antecedents of this fighting unit go much further back, perhaps even to the founding of the city of New Orleans by the French in 1718.

When Louisiana seceded from the Union and war erupted, the four New Orleans companies of the Washington Artillery – two companies of artillery and two of infantry – immediately volunteered. Wearing blue militia uniforms and preceded by a marching band, they mustered into Confederate service on May 26, 1861 – not for three months or a year, but for the "duration of the war." Major (later colonel) J.B. Walton was the artillery commander.

By train, the Washington Artillery traveled to integrate with the Army of Northern Virginia while, at home, additional recruiting brought in two more additional companies that were sent north to the to the Confederate Army of Tennessee. Ultimately units of the artillery were engaged in more than sixty battles and skirmishes including every important battle of the Civil War – Antietam (Sharpsburg), Chancellorsville, Gettysburg, Shiloh, Cold Harbor, Atlanta, and many more. It was distinguished by such moments as the intense hand-to-hand fighting on Henry Hill at First Manasses (First Bull Run) where the tide of the battle turned from Union success to a decisive Confederate victory and its doomed defense of Fort Gregg in the defense of Petersburg.

Today, the Washington Artillery is officially the 141st Field Artillery, part of the Louisiana Army National Guard headquartered in New Orleans. The 141st has deployed to Iraq, but retains its snarling tiger head logo and its motto: "Try Us".

Louisiana Confederate Army Deaths

	Killed	Died of Wounds	Died of Disease	Total
Officers	70	42	32	144
Enlisted	2,548	826	3,027	6,401
Total	2,618	868	3,059	6,545

LOUISIANA UNION ARMY DEATHS

Troops Furnished	Killed/Mortally Wounded	Died of Disease	Died of Other Causes	Total
5,224*	214	624	107	945

MAJOR GENERAL BENJAMIN F. BUTLER (1818-93)

Butler hailed from Massachusetts. Although he had little practical military experience, his political connections meant that President Lincoln promoted him to major general in May, 1861. When New Orleans was taken by Union forces, it was Butler who commanded the force of occupation. In this role he was often forceful, sometimes restrained, and occasionally outrageous in dealing with the city's inhabitants (he closed newspapers, hanged a private citizen, and imprisoned ministers who refused to pray for Lincoln), but it was his General Order No. 28 of May 15, 1862, that forever marked him as a "beast" to those who favored the Lost Cause.

Butler's order, doubtless driven by continuing provocation, was extreme in its particulars. It stated that if any woman insulted or showed contempt for any officer or soldier of the United States, she would be regarded as and held liable to be treated as a "woman of the town plying her avocation:" in other words, a prostitute. In striking back at the infuriating animosity shown to Federal troops, Butler earned the eternal enmity of Southerners and caused protests both in the North and the South. He was removed from his Department of the Gulf command in December.

During his time in command, he had also earned another nickname, "Spoons Butler", because it was alleged that he stole silverware from the Southern mansions in which he was housed. Although no witness proved that he actually pilfered knives, forks, or spoons, it was later discovered that he was certainly guilty of colossal graft in his administration of Southern territories.

Louisiana Units Furnished

Confederate

Infantry regiments	33
Infantry battalions	9
Militia battalions	45
Sharpshooter battalions	3
Cavalry battalions	5
Cavalry regiments	18
Other	17
Heavy artillery battalions	3
Light artillery batteries	5
Field artillery batteries	2
Partisan Ranger battalions	1

Union

Infantry regiments	11
New Orleans/ Native Guard regiments	6
Cavalry regiments	2
Heavy artillery regiments	1
Light artillery batteries	3

Maine

" Every pioneer and musician who could carry a musket went into the ranks. Even the sick and foot-sore, who could not keep up in the march, came up as soon as they could find their regiments, and took their places in line of battle, while it was battle, indeed. "

JOSHUA CHAMBERLAIN

Maine was strongly for the Union and provided more men in proportion to its population than any other state. These included more than two dozen generals and many brigade leaders.

Winters of ice and summers of insects made Maine a difficult place for Europeans to gain a foothold and early colonies languished. It was only as the population slowly grew during the early 19th century that Maine was separated from Massachusetts to become the 23rd state on March 15, 1820. At that time, Federal legislation known as the Missouri Compromise allowed Maine to join the Union as a free state. Missouri joined as a slave state, thus balancing regional interests that would, two generations later, collapse into bloody civil war.

Prior to the Civil War, the new state was a frontier for loggers and fishermen. Life was hard and evangelical Christianity flourished. It was a land of small isolated hamlets with short summers and rocky soils, where the people were early converts to the new Republican Party, especially the "free soil" plank in its platform. Hardy individualists, Mainers opposed slavery, believing that free men on free soil comprised a morally and economically superior system to slavery.

When news of the siege of Fort Sumter reached the state, its men flocked to the Union colors. Unlike those of Virginia or Georgia, the state's towns were physically untouched by war but Maine nevertheless paid a

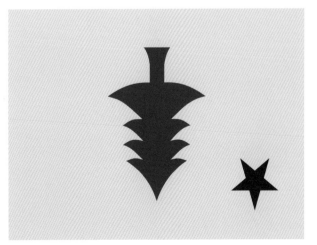

Flag of Maine in 1901.

HARRIET BEECHER STOWE (1811–96)

Abolitionist and author, Harriet Beecher Stowe wrote the novel "Uncle Tom's Cabin" while her husband, Calvin Stowe, taught at Bowdoin College in Brunswick, Maine. Stowe's novel depicts the lives of African-Americans as slaves and, when published in 1852, it exploded on the American cultural scene. Abolitionists praised the work. Those who supported slavery damned it. When she met Abraham Lincoln in November, 1862, he is reported to have remarked, "So you are the little woman who wrote the book that started this great war." The quotation may not be accurate, but the book certainly represented the attitudes and arguments of millions of people. Before the war ended, Beecher Stowe moved to Mandarin, Florida, on the banks of the St. Johns River where she was instrumental in promoting education among former slaves.

desperate price for the conflict. Ten percent of its men entered the Union Army and Navy during the war, a larger number of combatants in proportion to its population than any other Union state.

BOWDOIN'S CONTRIBUTION

Three years before Civil War broke out, former secretary of war and current U.S. Senator, Mississippi's Jefferson Davis had spent the summer in Maine, recovering from an illness that threatened his eyesight. Although he was a slave owner and would soon become President of the Confederate States of America, he had spoken against secession and was awarded an honorary degree by Maine's famous Bowdoin College where he made many friends. The college would later become even more intimately connected to the war, hosting Harriet Beecher Stowe who wrote the incendiary novel *Uncle Tom's Cabin* on campus.

Bowdoin's greatest moment, however, came at the most decisive moment of the war. On July 2, 1863, former Bowdoin professor – and future president – Joshua Chamberlain led the 20th Maine Volunteer Infantry Regiment in defense of a hill at the extreme

left of the Union line at Gettysburg. The hill was Little Round Top and Chamberlain's desperate order to fix bayonets and charge the advancing Alabama Confederates arguably saved the Union.

The 20th Maine served from the initial and disastrous battle of Manassas (First Bull Run) in 1861 until the surrender of Confederate troops at Appomattox Court House, Virginia. The men fought in terrible battles including Chancellorsville, Gettysburg, the Wilderness, Spotsylvania, Cold Harbor, and Petersburg. Of an initial enrolment of 1,621 men, 150 were killed in action, 146 died from disease, 381 were wounded, and fifteen taken prisoner.

THE 1ST MAINE HEAVY ARTILLERY REGIMENT

The 20th Maine was not the only unit from the Pine Tree State to serve with distinction. The 1st Maine Heavy Artillery Regiment lost more men in a single charge during the siege of Petersburg, Virginia, than any Union regiment in the war. On June 18, 1864, the regiment was ordered to take heavily defended fortifications by their commander, Colonel Daniel

In 1889 veterans of the 20th Maine Volunteer Infantry gathered at Gettysburg with General Joshua L. Chamberlain, the officer who commanded them in battle. Chamberlain is seated at center right, bracketed by the unit's regimental flag. The upright object on the left is a monument to the unit erected by its veterans.

Chaplin, a former merchant who was later killed by a Confederate sharpshooter. During the action, the unit lost seven officers and 108 men killed, while another twenty-five officers and 464 men were wounded: 67 percent of the 900-man force. In fact, over the course of the war, the 1st Maine sustained one of the highest casualty rates of any regiment.

Maine Union Units Furnished

Infantry regiments	33
Infantry battalions	1
Sharpshooter companies	1
Sharpshooter battalions	1
Misc. infantry units	1
Cavalry regiments	2
Heavy artillery battalions	1
Light artillery batteries	7
Garrison artillery units	1

Above Right: Corporal John A. Hartshorn of Company A, 19th Maine Infantry, sitting with bayoneted musket. He volunteered to enlist in the army as a substitute for John W. Crane in August 1863. Hartshorn died on May 23, 1864, of wounds received at Cold Harbor.

Below: "1st Maine Cavalry Skirmishing", by Alfred Waud, published in *Harper's Weekly*, September 5, 1863.

MAINE UNION ARMY DEATHS

Troops Furnished	Killed/Mortally Wounded	Died of Disease	Died of Other Causes	Total
70,107	3,184	5,257	957	9,398

Politicians and Generals

U.S. Vice-President Hannibal Hamlin.

Governor Israel Washburn.

Secretary of the Treasury William Pitt Fessenden.

Secretary of the Treasury Hugh McCulloch.

SECRETARY OF THE TREASURY
WILLIAM PITT FESSENDEN (1806–69)

An anti-slavery lawyer and founding member of the Maine Temperance Society, William Pitt Fessenden was socially well-connected. He was elected to the State Assembly as well as the U.S. House of Representatives, and three times to the U.S. Senate. As war approached, Fessenden switched from the Whig to the Republican Party and his eloquent rhetoric was often quoted in Lincoln's presidential campaigns. In the Senate, he became a master of public finance and from 1864 to 1865 served as secretary of the treasury. Fessenden thought of himself as a moderate, supervised congressional oversight of Southern reconstruction, and voted to acquit impeached president Andrew Johnson. He died while serving in the senate.

SECRETARY OF THE TREASURY
HUGH McCULLOCH (1808–95)

Born in Kennebunk, Hugh McCulloch became a lawyer and an influential Indiana banker. As novice cashier and manager of the Fort Wayne branch of the fledgling Bank of Indiana, it is said that he was appointed to the institution's presidency because "he was the most qualified person willing to take the position." Eventually, he was appointed treasury secretary on two separate occasions, first by Lincoln shortly before his assassination. McCulloch's greatest contribution was managing the Federal war debt and reintroducing a system of taxation into the former Confederate states.

U.S. VICE PRESIDENT HANNIBAL HAMLIN (1809–91)

Hannibal Hamlin was a farm boy from Paris, Maine, who spent his early years as a farmhand, schoolmaster, woodcutter, surveyor, and newspaper editor. Eventually, he gravitated to law and then into politics. Elected to the state legislature, the U.S. House of Representatives, and the U.S. Senate, he served briefly as governor and, eventually, as vice president during Lincoln's first administration. Although Hamlin opposed slavery and supported Lincoln's Emancipation Proclamation as well as the arming of black troops, Lincoln rarely consulted him, replacing him with Tennessee's Andrew Johnson for the second term. After the war, Hamlin was once again elected U.S. Senator and served as Ambassador to Spain.

GOVERNOR ISRAEL WASHBURN (1813–83)

A principal founder of the Republican Party, attorney Israel Washburn may have been the first nationally-recognized politician to use the term "Republican" in 1854. At that time he was incensed by passage of the Kansas-Nebraska Act, which allowed territorial settlers to determine whether new states would allow slavery. Washburn served as a U.S. Congressman and as governor of Maine during the early stages of the rebellion. He recruited troops – although he did not serve himself – and upon its publication in 1863 supported Lincoln's Emancipation Proclamation.

GENERAL ADELBERT AMES (1835–1933)

Adelbert Ames began life as a sailor but entered West Point, receiving his commission as a lieutenant of artillery in 1861. Severely wounded during the First Battle of Bull Run (First Battle of Manassas), he refused to leave his post and was promoted to major and nominated for a Medal of Honor, which he received thirty years later. Ames then lobbied for an infantry assignment and led Union troops throughout the war from Virginia to Florida, often abandoning safe rear echelon command posts to accompany his men at the front. After the war, Congress appointed Ames, a radical Republican who believed in immediate enfranchisement for former slaves, provisional Governor of Mississippi, for which he was labeled a "carpetbagger." In 1898, he served as an army general during the Spanish-American War.

MAJOR GENERAL OLIVER OTIS HOWARD (1830–1909)

A deeply religious farm boy, Oliver Howard graduated from West Point and fought against the Seminole Indians in Florida before the Civil War broke out. Under George McClellan in the Army of the Potomac he was promoted to general and suffered wounds to his right arm that made amputation of the limb necessary. For his courage, he ultimately received the Medal of Honor. He also led the Union's XI Corps through the battles of Chancellorsville and Gettysburg, with mixed results, and was transferred to the Army of the Cumberland in Tennessee. He led troops during Sherman's battle of Atlanta and the March to the Sea. Following the war, Howard served as commissioner of the Freedmen's Bureau, as founding president of Howard University in Washington, D.C., and held various commands fighting Native-Americans in the West.

BRIGADIER GENERAL JOSHUA L. CHAMBERLAIN (1828–1914)

Joshua Chamberlain was a college professor who spoke a remarkable ten languages. He was promoted to brevet major general in the Union army and won the Medal of Honor for "daring heroism and great tenacity," and leadership "above and beyond the call of duty." Chamberlain's moment came on July 2, 1863 when he and the 20th Maine saved Little Round Top at Gettysburg. Nearly outflanked, low on ammunition, and having taken many casualties, his troops fixed bayonets and charged the onrushing Confederates. His initiative was the pivotal moment in the battle. At Appomattox Court House, Virginia, in 1865, Chamberlain presided over the formal surrender of Confederate infantry. Wounded on six occasions, he was nevertheless elected governor four times before returning to college life. Chamberlain was probably the last Civil War veteran to die as a result of his wounds.

General Adelbert Ames.

Major General Oliver Otis Howard.

Brigadier General Joshua L. Chamberlain.

Maryland

> "I would fight for my liberty so long as my strength lasted, and if the time came for me to go, the Lord would let them take me."

HARRIET TUBMAN

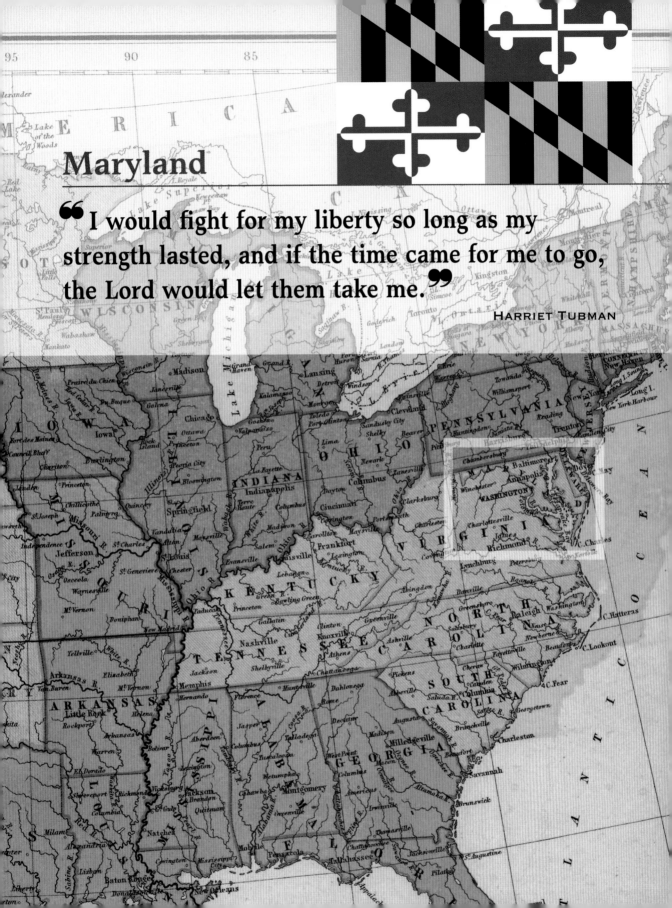

Maryland

> "I would fight for my liberty so long as my strength lasted, and if the time came for me to go, the Lord would let them take me."

HARRIET TUBMAN

General Adelbert Ames.

Major General Oliver Otis Howard.

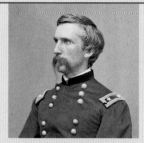
Brigadier General Joshua L. Chamberlain.

GENERAL ADELBERT AMES (1835–1933)

Adelbert Ames began life as a sailor but entered West Point, receiving his commission as a lieutenant of artillery in 1861. Severely wounded during the First Battle of Bull Run (First Battle of Manassas), he refused to leave his post and was promoted to major and nominated for a Medal of Honor, which he received thirty years later. Ames then lobbied for an infantry assignment and led Union troops throughout the war from Virginia to Florida, often abandoning safe rear echelon command posts to accompany his men at the front. After the war, Congress appointed Ames, a radical Republican who believed in immediate enfranchisement for former slaves, provisional Governor of Mississippi, for which he was labeled a "carpetbagger." In 1898, he served as an army general during the Spanish-American War.

MAJOR GENERAL OLIVER OTIS HOWARD (1830–1909)

A deeply religious farm boy, Oliver Howard graduated from West Point and fought against the Seminole Indians in Florida before the Civil War broke out. Under George McClellan in the Army of the Potomac he was promoted to general and suffered wounds to his right arm that made amputation of the limb necessary. For his courage, he ultimately received the Medal of Honor. He also led the Union's XI Corps through the battles of Chancellorsville and Gettysburg, with mixed results, and was transferred to the Army of the Cumberland in Tennessee. He led troops during Sherman's battle of Atlanta and the March to the Sea. Following the war, Howard served as commissioner of the Freedmen's Bureau, as founding president of Howard University in Washington, D.C., and held various commands fighting Native-Americans in the West.

BRIGADIER GENERAL JOSHUA L. CHAMBERLAIN (1828–1914)

Joshua Chamberlain was a college professor who spoke a remarkable ten languages. He was promoted to brevet major general in the Union army and won the Medal of Honor for "daring heroism and great tenacity," and leadership "above and beyond the call of duty." Chamberlain's moment came on July 2, 1863 when he and the 20th Maine saved Little Round Top at Gettysburg. Nearly outflanked, low on ammunition, and having taken many casualties, his troops fixed bayonets and charged the onrushing Confederates. His initiative was the pivotal moment in the battle. At Appomattox Court House, Virginia, in 1865, Chamberlain presided over the formal surrender of Confederate infantry. Wounded on six occasions, he was nevertheless elected governor four times before returning to college life. Chamberlain was probably the last Civil War veteran to die as a result of his wounds.

The Maryland flag contains elements form the secessionist flag (above) and the black and yellow chequered union flag.

Maryland held an ambivalent position prior to the outbreak of the Civil War. It was a slave state, though divided geographically between the slave-holding southern tobacco areas and the northern region where there were few slaves.

Political lines were drawn in a similar manner, with the state legislature controlled by Democrats in favor of the Southern states while the governor was a staunch Unionist. The stance of the state in relation to the war was, however, of particular significance as it surrounded the nation's capital, Washington, D.C., on three sides. Maryland's decision on secession could have been a deciding factor in the fate of the city. In the end, its close economic links with the North, combined with the political machinations of the governor, led to Maryland siding with the Union, though with a strong undercurrent of support for the South. Of roughly 85,000 Marylanders who fought during the Civil War, some 25,000 served with Confederate forces. Nevertheless, despite the incursions of the Army of North Virginia into Maryland, and Lee's calls for the state to secede, Maryland remained part of the Union throughout the war.

GOVERNOR THOMAS HOLLIDAY HICKS (1798–1865)

One of the principal reasons for Maryland remaining part of the Union was its governor of the time, Thomas H. Hicks. In many ways, Hicks represented the split nature of Maryland politics in the antebellum period. He was no abolitionist and supported the slave-holding status quo. However, he was unwilling to see his state secede from the Union, and, in an effort to influence a vital vote being taken on the subject, moved it from the state capital, Annapolis – a southern Democrat stronghold, to the northern city of Frederick, which was much more favorably inclined toward the Union. The vote on April 26, 1861, went for Maryland to remain part of the Union as a neutral state. Following his term as governor, Hicks served as one of the U.S. senators for Maryland and it was in Washington that he died in 1865.

A Civil War-era envelope showing Columbia, the American flag, and the state seal of Maryland.

THE BALTIMORE RIOTS

Another reason behind Governor Hicks' decision to move the vote to Frederick was the civil unrest boiling elsewhere in the state, notably in Baltimore. The city, which held a third of the state's population, had considerable Confederate sympathies and when the 6th Massachusetts Regiment, *en route* to Washington, D.C. in response to Lincoln's call for troops, was forced to cross the city from its eastern side to catch a train to the capital on April 19th, a riot broke out.

A mob surrounded the soldiers, attacking them with bricks, paving stones, and even pistols. Panicked, the soldiers returned fire and the riot grew in size, with four soldiers and twelve locals eventually killed, along with numerous wounded. These are considered as the first casualties of the Civil War. The riot also destroyed a number

of newspaper offices in the town and there were further outbreaks of violence over the following month. Although Governor Hicks asked Lincoln to avoid sending any more troops through Baltimore it was unavoidable.

The next wave of troops to arrive in Maryland from Massachusetts came under the command of General Benjamin Butler, a wily politician who would later gain notoriety for his role in the capture and administration of New Orleans. His force arrived by ship at Annapolis on April 20, 1861 and, despite protestations from Governor Hicks, Butler persuaded him to permit his troops to land and move to Washington by rail via Annapolis Junction.

Butler, having been reinforced by more troops from New York, decided to move on Baltimore on his own authority and sent troops into the city on

May 13th, declaring martial law and imprisoning a number of Southern-leaning notables in Fort McHenry. This impromptu advance led to General Winfield Scott relieving Butler of his command, though he was rapidly appointed as a major general of U.S. volunteers by a grateful Abraham Lincoln.

LINCOLN SUSPENDS HABEAS CORPUS

Another by product of the unrest in Baltimore, and throughout Maryland, was the suspension of *habeas corpus* by President Lincoln. The fallout of Lincoln's decision to send Union troops through Maryland had led to Hicks authorizing the destruction of railroad bridges into Baltimore on April 20th to prevent the arrival of further troops and thus more unrest and bloodshed. One of the militia captains who was ordered to carry out this attack was John Merryman, a noted Southern sympathizer. Among the first arrested following Lincoln's suspension of *habeas corpus* on April 27th, Merryman was just one of many swept up in this process, which was immediately challenged by the local judiciary.

Merryman's case was heard in the U.S. circuit court in Maryland. Its president was Roger B. Taney, who also happened to be the Chief Justice of the Supreme Court. He had risen to prominence in the administration of President Andrew Jackson, serving as attorney general before being appointed to the Supreme Court in 1836 following a protracted political battle. In his role as chief justice he was a strong supporter of states' rights and had come into conflict with the Lincoln administration on a number of occasions. In the Merryman case he ruled that only Congress had the authority to suspend the writ of *habeas corpus* and that Lincoln's actions were, therefore, illegal. Taney expected to be arrested himself for his decision but Lincoln ignored the judgment and continued to make arrests as he pleased. Merryman was later released without charge.

Attack on the Massachusetts 6th at Baltimore, April 19, 1861 – a steel engraving by O. Pelton.

MARYLAND'S REACTION TO FIRST BULL RUN

The Battle of First Bull Run, otherwise known as First Manassas, was the first significant encounter of the Civil War and the Confederacy's first victory in the field. In the summer of 1861, both sides were busy forming armies of newly recruited officers and men, principally in the area of northeastern Virginia. These untried forces, under Beauregard and Johnston for the Confederates and McDowell and Patterson for the Union side, met near Manassas Junction on July 21st, along the River Bull Run. Expectations were high on the Union side. In the event, however, the battle developed into a rout for the Union forces, with McDowell's army pouring back toward Washington, D.C. in disarray. Fortunately for the Union, Confederate forces were too tired and disorganized to affect a pursuit and the opportunity to push into Maryland, or even on to the capital itself was lost.

Throughout that summer the Lincoln administration had been increasingly asserting its authority over Maryland, and Baltimore in particular.

The suspension of *habeas corpus* enabled the Union generals Nathaniel Banks and John A. Dix to arrest known Confederate sympathizers without recourse to law and they used their power widely, with Banks arresting the entire Baltimore police board, including the police chief, on July 1st.

Following the Battle of First Bull Run such measures became even more extensive. A meeting of the state legislature from September 12th to the 17th provoked the arrest of those representatives and other influential figures suspected of having Southern sympathies. The state elections of November 1861 provided an opportunity for the Union forces to consolidate the state. Provost marshals stood guard at the polls and a special three-day furlough was granted to Maryland troops in the Union Army so they could go home and vote. This led to the election of a group of solidly pro-Union representatives.

Arrest of George Proctor Kane, Marshal of Police in Baltimore during the riot. Arrested at his house at 3:00 am on Thursday, June 27, 1862, by order of Major General Banks on a charge of treason, he was incarcerated without benefit of *habeas corpus*.

Maryland's Contribution to the Confederacy

Admiral Franklin Buchanan.

Rear Admiral Raphael Semmes.

Brigadier General James J. Archer.

Despite the fact that the majority of combatants from Maryland fought on the side of the Union, there were a number of important Confederate commanders from the state, notably in the field of naval warfare.

ADMIRAL FRANKLIN BUCHANAN (1800–74)

Buchanan joined the U.S. Navy in 1815 as a midshipman, rising to the rank of captain and becoming commandant of the Washington Navy Yard. At the outset of the Civil War, he joined the Confederate side and was given command of the C.S.S. *Virginia,* a vessel he commanded on March 8, 1862: the first day of the Battle of Hampton roads. He was, however, wounded that day and took no part in the second day's fighting when the *Virginia* participated in her famous duel with the U.S.S. *Monitor*.

Following the battle, Buchanan was promoted admiral and commander of Confederate naval forces in Mobile Bay. It was in this role that he was defeated in the Battle of Mobile Bay, August 5, 1864. Wounded again, and captured, this proved to be his last active involvement in the Civil War.

REAR ADMIRAL RAPHAEL SEMMES (1809–77)

Semmes was another prominent Confederate naval officer. He commanded was the C.S.S. *Alabama*, an English-built commerce raider that terrorized Union shipping between August 1862 and June 1864, capturing some fifty-five prizes. See also page 18.

BRIGADIER GENERAL JAMES J. ARCHER (1817–64)

The most prominent Confederate officer from Maryland during the Civil War, Archer served in the U.S. Army from 1855, but resigned his commission in 1861 to join the Confederate Army as a captain. He was appointed colonel of the 5th Texas Regiment in October 1861 and served with this regiment in the Peninsula Campaign, including the Battle of Seven Pines, following which he was promoted brigadier general. His brigade served with the Army of Northern Virginia during its major campaigns, including Second Bull Run (Second Manassas), Antietam (Battle of Sharpsburg), Fredericksburg, and Chancellorsville. At the Battle of Gettysburg, Archer was captured and was exchanged in August, 1864. He rejoined the Army of Northern Virginia, taking command of his old brigade but died of illness in Richmond having fought in the Petersburg Campaign.

SECOND BULL RUN AND THE CONFEDERATE INVASION OF MARYLAND

Also known as Second Manassas, on August 29–30, 1862, Union and Confederate forces clashed once more around Manassas Junction. The commanders were different, with Robert E. Lee now in charge of the Army of North Virginia while John Pope commanded the Union Army of Virginia, but the outcome was same as the previous battle. Lee cleverly divided forces until they were in a position to concentrate against Pope's men and drive them back (Second Bull Run has been described as his greatest campaign). Unlike the battle of First Bull Run, however, this time a pursuit was planned, with Lee and his 55,000-strong Army of Northern Virginia poised to invade the North.

Resisting the temptation of going for the Union capital of Washington, D.C., Lee decided to take the war across the Potomac into Maryland, reasoning that the presence of a large body of Confederate troops on the soil of Maryland might convince the state to declare for the Confederacy. He also hoped that a major Confederate victory in the state might lead to European recognition of the Confederacy.

Lee crossed the Potomac on September 5, 1862. At the town of Frederick he issued his Special Order No. 191, which divided his army once again. Jackson's corps advanced on Harpers Ferry while Longstreet's corps moved on Hagerstown. This risky strategy was largely based on the belief that, following defeat, Union forces would be slow to reorganize and advance against him. However, the Union armies – consolidated under the command of George McClellan – moved away from Washington, D.C. in pursuit on September 7th with some 87,000 men. They arrived in Frederick on September 12, 1862.

General George B. McClellan passing through Frederick at the head of the Army of the Potomac in pursuit of General Lee, September 12, 1862, as sketched by Edwin Forbes.

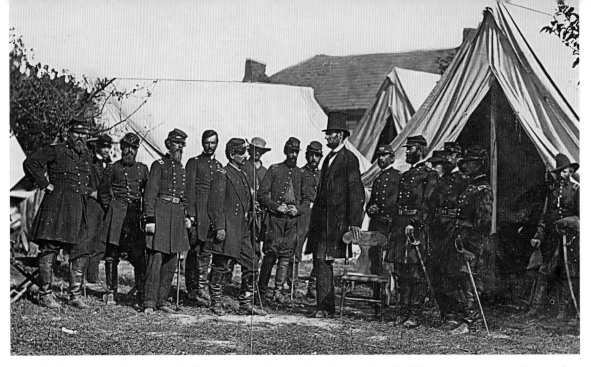

Two weeks after the Battle of Antietam, President Lincoln experienced immense frustration over General McClellan's reluctance to pursue the Army of the Northern Virginia and made a personal visit to the commanding general's headquarters at Antietam (Sharpsville, Maryland). McClellan promised to promptly send his army after the retreating Confederates but never did.

THE BATTLE OF ANTIETAM: LEE'S LOST SPECIAL ORDERS AND McCLELLAN'S REACTION

When McClellan entered Frederick, either by luck or design he found a copy of Lee's Special Order No. 191 wrapping a packet of cigars. The document gave him full knowledge of Lee's dispositions, most importantly the fact that he had divided his forces. McClellan telegraphed President Lincoln stating that Lee had made a gross mistake would be severely punished for it.

By the evening of September 13th, Lee had been informed that McClellan was aware of his intentions and ordered a withdrawal south of the Potomac. He also ordered Longstreet's corps to support D. H. Hill's division, which was covering the passes to the right of the Confederate advance around South Mountain.

Union forces advanced against Hill's South Mountain position on September 14th, and three separate engagements took place: the battles of Crampton's Gap, Fox's Gap, and Turner's Gap. The aim was to force the passes and place the Union army between Jackson's corps at Harper's Ferry and Longstreet's position. Thanks to D. H. Hill's delaying action at South Mountain, however, Union forces were unable to break through on the 14th, and this – along with Jackson's reduction of Harper's Ferry on the 15th – meant that Lee was able to concentrate his army once again. The immediate danger of the Confederates being defeated piecemeal in separate actions had passed.

Accordingly, Lee now elected to stand and fight at Sharpsburg Creek rather than retire across the Potomac. On September 17, 1862, the Battle of Antietam (known to the Confederacy as the Battle of Sharpsburg) took place. It was the single bloodiest day of the Civil War, yet by the end of it the Confederate position still held and Confederate troops were able to withdraw across the Potomac River on the 18th and 19th, with the Union Army of the Potomac offering no effective pursuit. McClellan had squandered his advantage through a combination of his innate caution and poor maneuvering. Nevertheless, the threat to the North from the Confederacy was much diminished.

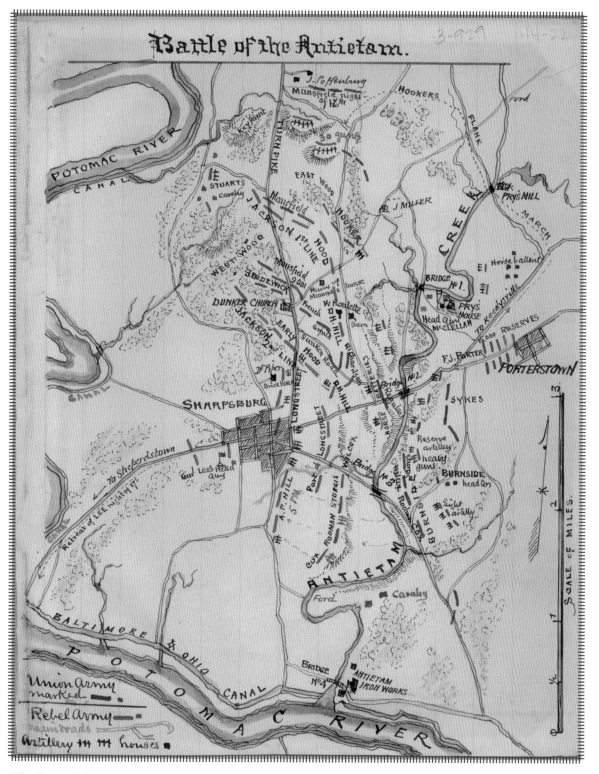

Robert Knox Sneden's map of the Battle of Antietam.

Alfred R. Waud's sketch of the bridge over Monocacy
—the "Scene of Lew Wallace battle with Early, 1864."

LEE'S INVASION OF MARYLAND: JUNE 1863

Despite the Union success in forcing the Army of Northern Virginia south of the Potomac, 1863, saw the Confederate position reinforced as Union advances in Virginia were rebuffed at the battles of Fredericksburg and Chancellorsville. Lee was once more ready to go on the offensive: taking the war away from Virginia, relieving the pressure on Vicksburg in the east, and, once again, influencing European opinion in favor of the Confederacy.

Having reorganized the Army of Northern Virginia into three corps following the death of Stonewall Jackson, Lee began to move his troops westward on June 3rd, and then brought his corps northward up the Shenandoah Valley into West Virginia, having taken the town of Winchester on June 14th. The next day Ewell's corps crossed the Potomac into Maryland near Hagerstown, with Longstreet and Hill following on June 24th and 25th. The Confederate forces did not dwell here, pressing on to Pennsylvania as quickly as possible, though Stuart's cavalry spent some time in the state in late June as part of his circuitous route to Gettysburg.

Montgomery Blair was an abolitionist and a loyal member of Lincoln's administration, serving as postmaster general from 1861 to 1864 and campaigning strongly for Lincoln in 1860 and 1864. His house at Silver Spring in Maryland was burned by the Confederates during their advance on Washington.

MARYLAND UNION ARMY DEATHS

Troops Furnished	Killed/Mortally Wounded	Died of Disease	Died of Other Causes	Total
33,995	909	1,160	913	2,982

Maryland Units Furnished	
Confederate	
Infantry regiments	1
Infantry battalions	3
Walter's Zouaves	1
Maryland Line	1
Cavalry regiments	1
Union	
Infantry regiments	15
100-day infantry regiments	2
Six-month infantry regiments	2
Patapsco Guards	1
Purnell Legions	2
Baltimore Light Infantry	1
Cavalry regiments	3
Six-month cavalry regiments	1
Independent cavalry	1
Heavy Artillery regiments	1
Light artillery regiments	1
Six-month light artillery	2
Baltimore Light Artillery	1
Unassigned units	1
Sailors/marine personnel	3,925
Colored troops	8,718

EARLY'S INVASION OF MARYLAND AND RAID ON WASHINGTON: 1864

The final incursion into Maryland came with Jubal Early's raid in the summer of 1864. In an action designed by Lee to reduce the Union pressure on his front and the Confederate lines around Richmond, Early marched with the 18,000 men of his II Corps. Evading the Union garrison at Harpers Ferry, he crossed the Potomac into Maryland near Sharpsburg on July 5th, moving on to Frederick by July 7th.

On July 9th, Early's forces were brought to battle by a makeshift Union force under Major General Lew Wallace and a division under Brigadier General James Ricketts. Wallace's forces were comprehensively defeated at the Battle of Monocacy along the Monocacy River, but the delay imposed on Early allowed Grant to reinforce Washington's defenses. Subsequently, when Early resumed his advance upon the city he found it too heavily defended to attempt. Having put the fortifications under some desultory long-range shelling, he withdrew once more to the Potomac.

Edwin Forbes' sketch shows the charge of Burnside's 9th Corps on the right flank of the Confederate Army during the Battle of Antietam.

Massachusetts

> **❝I know not what record of sin awaits me in the other world, but this I know, that I was never mean enough to despise any man because he was black.❞**
>
> <small>JOHN ALBION ANDREWS, GOVERNOR OF MASSACHUSETTS</small>

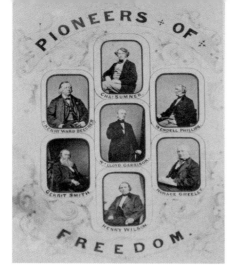

"Pioneers of Freedom" – portraits of Charles Sumner, Henry Ward Beecher, Wendell Phillips, William Lloyd Garrison, Gerrit Smith, Horace Greeley, and Henry Wilson.

Massachusetts was one of the most steadfast of the Northern states in its position on slavery in the years leading up to the outbreak of the Civil War. A source of funding and inspiration for abolitionists, it was among Lincoln's staunchest supporters. When the president called for troops, Massachusetts responded admirably, providing some of the Union's most famous units.

MASSACHUSETTS' ABOLITIONIST RADICALS

By far the most famous of the pre-war abolitionists was John Brown, who launched his abortive raid on the Federal armory at Harpers Ferry in October 1859. Brown could not have carried out his raid without extensive financial support, and most of this came from a group of wealthy and influential figures in the abolitionist movement known as the "Secret Six". They were Thomas Wentworth Higginson, Samuel Gridley Howe, Theodore Parker, Franklin Benjamin Sanborn, Gerrit Smith, and George Luther Stearns. Their names were exposed during Brown's trial and three fled to Canada, while Smith confined himself to an insane asylum. Only Higginson remained in America and publicly declared his support for Brown during his trial.

CHARLES FRANCIS ADAMS, JR. (1835–1915), MINISTER TO ENGLAND

One of the most prominent political figures from Massachusetts during the Civil War, Adams was the son and grandson of former presidents and a notable state politician. He stood (unsuccessfully) as a candidate for the vice-presidency in 1848 and was elected to the House of Representatives in 1858.

From 1861 to 1868 he served as the U.S. minister to Great Britain, where he was vital in pressing the cause of the Union. His efforts helped stop Great Britain from recognizing the Confederacy and possibly even entering the war on the side of the Southern states. He developed a strong relationship with the British foreign secretary, Lord John Russell, and managed to smooth over affairs such as the *Trent* incident that threatened to lead to war between Great Britain and the U.S.

Julia Ward Howe from a photograph by J.J. Hawes.

Julia Ward Howe, the wife of Samuel Gridley Howe, later became intrinsically linked with the memory of John Brown when she wrote the "Battle Hymn of the Republic" in November 1861 to the tune of the popular marching song "John Brown's Body." The hymn was published in the *Atlantic* magazine in February 1862 (for which Julia Ward Howe was paid five dollars), and gained rapid popularity in the North, being adopted by the Union Army as a marching song. It remains a central part of the American patriotic canon to this day.

The state was the birthplace and home of many other notable abolitionists. William Lloyd Garrison was born in the state in 1805 and, in 1831, founded the anti-slavery weekly newspaper the *Liberator*, which ran until the end of the Civil War. He was also deeply involved with the founding of the New-England Anti-Slavery Society and the American Anti-Slavery Society. Charles Sumner was another prominent anti-slavery campaigner, and served as a U.S. senator from 1851 through to 1874. In this role, he was actively involved in calling for the abolition of slavery and was famously attacked by Preston Brooks, a congressman from South Carolina following a speech made by Sumner attacking the Kansas–Nebraska Act of 1856. Following the assault Sumner was unable to take up his post in the Senate for three years.

LINCOLN'S CALL FOR TROOPS

With the outbreak of the Civil War heralded by the fighting at Fort Sumter, President Lincoln made an appeal for 75,000 volunteers to form a militia, with

BATTLE HYMN OF THE REPUBLIC

Mine eyes have seen the glory of the coming of the Lord:
He is trampling out the vintage where the grapes of wrath are stored;
He hath loosed the fateful lightning of His terrible swift sword:
His truth is marching on.
(Chorus)
Glory, glory, hallelujah!
Glory, glory, hallelujah!
Glory, glory, hallelujah!
His truth is marching on.
I have seen Him in the watch-fires of a hundred circling camps,
They have builded Him an altar in the evening dews and damps;
I can read His righteous sentence by the dim and flaring lamps:
His day is marching on.
(Chorus)
I have read a fiery gospel writ in burnished rows of steel:
"As ye deal with my contemners, so with you my grace shall deal;
Let the Hero, born of woman, crush the serpent with his heel,
Since God is marching on."
(Chorus)
He has sounded forth the trumpet that shall never call retreat;
He is sifting out the hearts of men before His judgment-seat:
Oh, be swift, my soul, to answer Him! be jubilant, my feet!
Our God is marching on.
(Chorus)
In the beauty of the lilies Christ was born across the sea,
With a glory in His bosom that transfigures you and me:
As He died to make men holy, let us die to make men free,
While God is marching on.
(Chorus)
He is coming like the glory of the morning on the wave,
He is Wisdom to the mighty, He is Succour to the brave,
So the world shall be His footstool, and the soul of Time His slave,
Our God is marching on.
(Chorus)

William Lloyd Garrison.

a term of enlistment of three months. Each state was asked to provide a set number of men for this force, and the border states all declared that they would not send men for an army of Northern oppression of their Southern neighbors. Other states in the North were more enthusiastic, and none more so than Massachusetts.

The Governor of Massachusetts, John A. Andrew – a pre-war supporter of Lincoln and staunch opponent of slavery – had already been making preparations for war and organizing the militia in the immediate pre-war period, so when Lincoln requested some 1,560 men in two regiments from Massachusetts he was able to dispatch the first regiment, the 6th Massachusetts Volunteer Militia Regiment, to the nation's capital within forty-eight hours.

THE BALTIMORE RIOTS

When the 6th Massachusetts Volunteer Militia Regiment set off to Washington, D.C., to defend the capital against Southern attack, it had to travel through Baltimore, crossing the city by foot to get from one railroad to the other on April 19, 1861. In the course of the journey, a pro-Southern mob set upon the soldiers, throwing missiles and provoking a lethal response. The inexperienced soldiers opened fire and in the fracas four soldiers and twelve locals were killed, and many more wounded, in what were the first casualties of the Civil War.

Continued on page 201

GOVERNOR JOHN ALBION ANDREW (1818–67)

Andrew joined the abolitionists and before the war helped to raise funds for John Brown's followers who raided the Harpers Ferry armory in 1859. He supported Abraham Lincoln during the 1860 presidential nominating convention in Chicago. When the War Department called for troops in April 1861, Andrew was the first to respond and hurried the first of two militia regiments to Washington. He also raised the state's first African-American regiment and never faltered in his support of the Union.

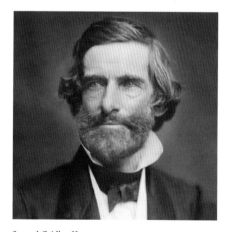

Samuel Gridley Howe.

Famous Corps Commanders

As a major contributor to the Union cause, Massachusetts provided some of the senior commanders of Union forces in the Civil War, including three notable corps commanders.

along Marye's Heights, suffering heavy casualties. Couch remained in command of II Corps for the Chancellorsville Campaign of 1863, but following a quarrel with the army commander, Joe Hooker, he asked to be reassigned and was placed in charge of the newly created Department of the Susquehanna during the Gettysburg Campaign. His final active military service came in December 1864, when he was assigned a divisional command in the Army of the Ohio during the Franklin-Nashville Campaign.

MAJOR GENERAL DARIUS N. COUCH (1822–97)

Although he was not born in Massachusetts, Crouch lived in the state during the years immediately preceding the Civil War. Having served in the regular army in the 1840s and 50s – when he saw service in the Mexican-American War – he was immediately appointed commander of the 7th Massachusetts Infantry on the outbreak of war. Later promoted to brigadier general, he was given a divisional command in the Army of the Potomac during the Peninsula Campaign of 1862, before being promoted major general in July 1862.

In November the same year, he was placed in command of II Corps and commanded it during the Battle of Fredericksburg in December, where his corps was hurled headlong at the Confederate defenses

Major General Joseph Hooker.

MAJOR GENERAL JOSEPH HOOKER (1814–79)

The highest-ranking general from Massachusetts, Hooker ended up in command of the Army of the Potomac during the Chancellorsville Campaign and the early stages of the Gettysburg Campaign.

As a pre-war regular artillery officer, Hooker served in both the Second Seminole and Mexican-American wars, though he later left the army following a disagreement with General Winfield Scott. With the outbreak of the Civil War, he obtained a commission as a brigadier general of volunteers, commanding a brigade, and then a division, in the Army of Potomac. Having been promoted to major general, he was transferred to the Army of Virginia where he took over III Corps during the Second Battle of Bull Run (Second Manassas). His corps, now renamed I Corps, was then transferred back to the Army of the Potomac and he served with distinction at Antietam (Battle of Sharpsburg).

In the Fredericksburg Campaign, Hooker was placed in charge of both III and V Corps. Following the disaster of Fredericksburg and the debacle of the "mud march" that followed, he took overall command of the Army of the Potomac on January 26, 1863, and succeeded in re-establishing the organization and morale of his army. However, in battle against Lee he fared as badly as the previous commanders, losing heavily at Chancellorsville, following which he lost Lincoln's confidence. His resignation was accepted three days before the battle of Gettysburg. Nevertheless, Hooker continued to serve as a corps commander under Grant in the Western Theater, before eventually commanding the Northern Department.

MAJOR GENERAL NATHANIEL P. BANKS (1816–94)

Banks had a distinguished pre-war career as a Massachusetts politician, serving in the state House of Representatives, as well as being elected to Congress in 1849 and serving as speaker of the house from 1851 to 1852. He later became Governor of Massachusetts from 1858 to 1860. With the outbreak of the Civil War, President Lincoln appointed him a major general of volunteers. In this role he served throughout the Peninsula Campaign, defending Washington, D.C. from the Confederate forces of Stonewall Jackson.

Despite being bested by Jackson at Winchester on May 25, 1862, Banks managed to hold his ground at Cedar Mountain on August 9th. Having commanded the Washington Garrison he was dispatched to New Orleans as commander of the Department of the Gulf, where he supported Ulysses S. Grant during his Vicksburg Campaign. His Red River Campaign of March–May, 1864, however, was a complete disaster and led to him being relived of his command. Following the war he resumed his political career, serving once more in Congress.

DOROTHEA LYNDE DIX
(1802–87)

Dorothea Lynde Dix was one of the nursing heroes of the Civil War. Famed for her pre-war efforts to improve conditions in jails and mental asylums, when the Civil War started she offered her services to the Union Army and became Superintendent of Union Army Nurses, recruiting some 2,000 female nurses. Despite her many successes in the role, she fell out with the army bureaucracy and was known as "Dragon Dix" for her autocratic style and many clashes with authority.

List of killed, wounded, and missing in battle of July 1, 1862, from the 10th Massachusetts Volunteers.

MASSACHUSETTS UNION ARMY DEATHS

Troops Furnished	Killed/Mortally Wounded	Died of Disease	Died of Other Causes	Total
122,781	6,115	5,530	2,297	13,942

A Massachusetts 13th Regiment Rifles Civil War-era envelope showing Lady Justice dressed in an American flag.

To prevent the same thing happening again, Governor Andrew sent the next wave of Massachusetts troops – the 8th Massachusetts Infantry Regiment under the command of General Ben Butler – to Annapolis rather than Baltimore. Here, Butler managed to politically best Governor Hicks of Maryland and, having repaired the railroads around Baltimore, took control of the city itself on May 13th, thus securing Washington's vital lifeline.

This impromptu action, along with Butler's somewhat rash appropriation of other Union forces, led to his immediate dismissal by an irate Winfield Scott, though Lincoln almost immediately reinstated him, appointing him a major general of volunteers from May 16th onward. Although much of his later Civil War military service was less than successful, Butler gained notoriety when he was put in charge of the Union occupation of New Orleans. His strict administration caused a great deal of controversy at the time and led to him being called "Beast Butler" by Confederates.

Massachusetts Union Units Furnished	
Infantry regiments	75
Colored infantry regiments	2
Infantry battalions	3
3-month militia regiments	5
9-month militia regiments	5
100-day infantry regiments	3
Sharpshooter units	2
Cadet infantry units	2
Cavalry regiments	5
Cavalry battalions	3
Heavy artillery regiments	4
Heavy artillery battalion	1
Light artillery batteries	18
Unassigned infantry units	26
Sailors/marine personnel	19,983
Colored troops	2,966

Massachusetts Regiments

THE 2ND MASSACHUSETTS VOLUNTEER INFANTRY

Raised in May 1861, the 2nd Massachusetts was originally commanded by Colonel George H. Gordon and served throughout the Shenandoah Valley campaign of 1862, before moving to the Army of Virginia for the Peninsula Campaign.

Having been transferred once again to the Army of the Potomac in August 1862, the 2nd Massachusetts took part in most of the significant battles in the Eastern Theater in 1862 and 1863, fighting at Antietam (Battle of Sharpsburg), Chancellorsville, and Gettysburg.

Having been sent back to New York to deal with riots, the regiment was transferred to the Army of the Cumberland in late 1863, and took part in the battle of Chattanooga as well as the Atlanta Campaign and the later March to the Sea. In total the 2nd Massachusetts Regiment lost 288 officers and men during the Civil War.

THE 15TH MASSACHUSETTS VOLUNTEER INFANTRY

The 15th Massachusetts was raised in July, 1861, and consisted almost entirely of men from Worcester County. It suffered heavy casualties at Balls Bluff on October 21, 1861, losing more men than any other Union regiment, and went on to take part in most of the major campaigns of the Eastern Theater, losing over half its men at Antietam (Battle of Sharpsburg), before fighting at both Fredericksburg and Gettysburg. The fighting of 1864 further reduced the regiment's numbers and the remnants were captured by the Confederates during the Petersburg Campaign, leading to the disbanding of the regiment.

The regiment's first colonel was Charles Devens, a pre-war state senator and U.S. marshall. Following his appointment, he became a brigadier general and commanded a brigade in the Maryland campaign, following which he was given command of a division.

Charles Devens.

Devens served as a divisional commander for the rest of the war, taking part in the Siege of Petersburg and occupying Richmond.

THE 22ND MASSACHUSETTS VOLUNTEER INFANTRY

The unexpected defeat suffered by Union forces at the First Battle of Bull Run (First Manassas) in July, 1861, led to a realization that more troops would be needed above and beyond Lincoln's initial call for 75,000, and a second wave of regiments were raised. One of the largest of these was the 22nd Massachusetts, originally intended as a brigade but rushed to the front as a regiment when the need for troops became dire. As such it had an attached battery of artillery and a company of sharpshooters.

The regiment served throughout McClellan's Peninsula Campaign, taking heavy casualties at the battle of Gaine's Mill. It remained with the Army of the Potomac through the Maryland Campaign, and was involved in the assault on Marye's Heights at

Fredericksburg, again taking heavy casualties. The regiment served at Gettysburg and remained in the East throughout Grant's Overland Campaign, fighting at the Siege of Petersburg until it was withdrawn from the line and mustered out, having completed its three-year term of service.

The foundation of the 22nd Massachusetts was the brainchild of Henry Wilson, a senator from Massachusetts and chairman of the Senate's Committee on Military Affairs. He was inspired to found the regiment after witnessing the First Battle of Bull Run (First Manassas) and served as its first colonel. Wilson had been active in the anti-slavery movement in the pre-war years and, after the Civil War, served as President Ulysses Grant's vice-president from 1873 until his death in November 1875.

Senator Henry Wilson.

THE 57TH MASSACHUSETTS INFANTRY

The 57th Massachusetts was a veteran regiment, formed from men who had already served at least nine months service with another regiment, and was founded in late 1863. It set off for war in April 1864, and joined the Army of the Potomac in time for the Battle of the Wilderness, where it took heavy casualties. It also took part in the Battle for Spotsylvania Courthouse and the Siege of Petersburg.

William Francis Bartlett, who was responsible for raising the 57th, enlisted as a private at the beginning of the Civil War. He originally served in the 4th Battalion Massachusetts Infantry for ninety days before being commissioned a captain in the 20th Massachusetts Infantry, with whom he served at the battle of Ball's Bluff and throughout the Peninsula Campaign until he was severely wounded, requiring the amputation of his leg. Following his recovery he became the colonel of the newly formed 49th Massachusetts, until he was again wounded. He then founded the 57th, and served with them until another wounding and his promotion to brigadier general in 1864.

William Francis Bartlett.

Storming Fort Wagner.

THE 54TH MASSACHUSETTS COLORED REGIMENT

Probably the most famous of the regiments supplied by Massachusetts to the Union forces during the Civil War, the 54th Massachusetts was one of the first colored regiments organized in the North and, as such, attracted a great deal of attention and publicity.

The foundation of the regiment was authorized by Governor John A. Andrew in March 1863, and Colonel Robert Gould Shaw was appointed as its commanding officer. (The 54th's officers were all white, while its enlisted men were free blacks – mainly from Massachusetts itself.) Shaw came from a prominent Massachusetts abolitionist family and had already served with the 7th New York Infantry Regiment and the 2nd Massachusetts Infantry before being offered the command of the new regiment by his father. He was promoted from lieutenant to colonel following his appointment.

The regiment underwent training and left for the front on May 28, 1863. Having spent a period on manual tasks it saw its first combat on July 16th. Two days later its men had gained fresh fame for their role in the assault on Battery Wagner on July 18th. The 54th was in the vanguard of the assault on this heavily defended Confederate position and suffered extremely heavy casualties – 281, of whom fifty-four were killed and forty-eight unaccounted for. Among those who were killed during the assault was Colonel Shaw.

The 54th also played a prominent role in the battle of Olustee on February 20, 1863, when, in order to delay a Confederate attack and prevent a Union collapse, the regiment deployed as a rearguard alongside the 35th United States Colored Troops as part of Montgomery's Brigade. They succeeded in delaying the Confederate advance long enough for the rest of the Union forces to retreat, but suffered heavy casualties in the process.

Colonel Robert Shaw.

From 1777, the Springfield Armory was the United States' main center for the manufacture of military small arms. It was also important in the development of precision manufacturing, assembly line production, and modern business practice. The most important infantry weapon of the Civil War – the Springfield 1861 rifled musket firing the .58 Minie ball – was developed and produced here.

CENTER OF INDUSTRY AND THE MILITARY

One of the major reasons for the North's eventual success in the Civil War was its industrial superiority over the mainly agricultural Southern states. This superiority was clearly demonstrated at facilities such as the Springfield Armory, located in Massachusetts, and one of only two Federal armories at the start of the Civil War. Most famous as the home and main production facility of the Springfield rifle, the principal weapon of the Union infantryman, it produced almost one and a half million of the guns during the course of the war.

Another important military installation in Massachusetts was the Boston, or, more correctly, Charleston, Navy Yard. Founded in 1799, and famous for its production of the U.S. Navy's first ship-of-the-line, the seventy-four-gun *Independence* during the War of 1812, the Civil War gave the navy yard a new lease of life and saw it expand rapidly to become a vital repair and supply base for the squadrons of U.S. Navy ships blockading Southern ports and harbors. It was also responsible for the construction of a number of small vessels including the monitor U.S.S. *Monadnock*.

Michigan

" Thank God for Michigan! "

PRESIDENT ABRAHAM LINCOLN

Michigan adopted its first state flag in 1911. Although distant from the central issues that brought about the Civil War, the state was steadfast in its support for the Union, with the strength of reaction to the fall of Fort Sumter demonstrated by the *Detroit Free Press* in its unusual headline: "War! War! War!"

Michigan had shown strongly for Lincoln during the election of 1860, with 88,445 votes compared to 64,958 for his closest challenger, the Northern Democrat candidate. This support was reflected in the speedy response to Lincoln's call for troops. The governor, Austin Blair, had already made preparations and Michigan was the first Western state to send troops to Washington, D.C. – in mid-May 1861 – with the 1st Michigan Volunteer Regiment being formed from ten independent militia companies that already existed in the state. At the same time, Michigan raised considerably more troops than were originally asked for by Lincoln. This was despite its poor economic situation and overall lack or resource. In fact, the condition of the state treasury was such that the governor was compelled to take on loans from the city of Detroit, among others, and even spent a considerable part of his own fortune on raising and equipping units.

JOHN LINCOLN "JOHNNY" CLEM (1851–1937): FROM DRUMMER BOY TO BRIGADIER GENERAL

John Clem was born as John Joseph Klem in Ohio in 1851, served as a drummer boy in the Union Army, and finished his career as a major general in the U.S. Army in 1916, the last surviving soldier of the Civil War on active service.

Having run away from home at the age of ten, Clem attempted to enlist in the 3rd Ohio, but

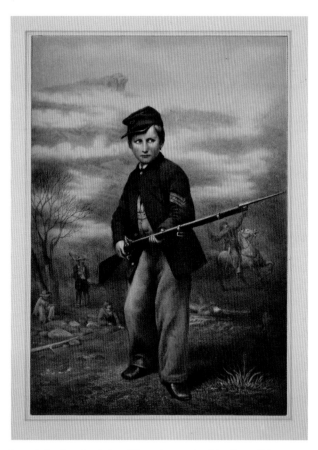

James Fuller Queen's painting of Union drummer boy John Clem at Point Lookout, Tennessee.

was rejected. Instead, he followed the 22nd Michigan until they accepted him as a mascot and drummer boy. He first achieved fame during the Battle of Chickamauga in September 1863, when, while riding an artillery caisson during the Union retreat, he shot a Confederate colonel who demanded his surrender. This was widely reported in the press and Clem was referred to as the "Drummer Boy of Chickamauga" and promoted to sergeant. Despite being captured in October 1863, he was paroled and discharged from service in 1864 having been wounded twice.

Clem returned to the army in 1871, having appealed to President Ulysses S. Grant following his failure to get into the U.S. Military Academy. He rose eventually to the rank of brigadier general in the quartermaster department before being promoted major general on his retirement in 1916.

Michigan's Courageous Women

SARAH EMMA EDMONDS
(1841–98)

A native of Canada, Sarah Edmonds settled in Flint, Michigan, where she passed herself off as a man, in part to evade her abusive father. It was in this role that she enlisted in the 2nd Michigan Infantry as Franklin Flint Thompson, initially serving as a male nurse. Through a strange sequence of events Edmonds became a spy for the Union Army, using her abilities at disguise to infiltrate Confederate positions in the Peninsula, and later in the Shenandoah Valley. Transferred west, she undertook the same role in Kentucky before reverting to her old role of nurse for Grant's Vicksburg campaign. Falling ill with malaria, she went into a private hospital to avoid discovery and was listed as a deserter, following which she went to Washington D.C. and worked as a nurse, though this time as a woman. Following the war she published her memoirs and eventually obtained a Congressional discharge for her desertion as well as an army pension.

JULIA SUSAN WHEELOCK
(1833–1900)

A native of Ohio, Julia Wheelock became known as the "Florence Nightingale of Michigan" for her efforts in nursing wounded soldiers. Her Civil War experiences started when her brother, Orville, was wounded at the Battle of Chantilly in September 1862. Julia went to Virginia to nurse him and, finding that he had died, decided to remain. She was soon appointed an agent of the Michigan Relief Association and, in this role, spent the rest of the war administering to sick, wounded, and dying soldiers, while at the same time trying to improve unsanitary conditions. She married Porter C. Freeman, of Middleville, Michigan, on May 18, 1873.

Sarah Edmonds in 1887.

Above: In 1890, Mary A. Livermore's *My Story of the War* included an engraving "A Woman in Battle – Michigan Bridget Carrying the Flag." It showed Bridget Divers or Deavers who rode with the First Michigan Cavalry, and was said to have been present at various battles including that of Fair Oaks in May 1862. After General Grant banished women from operations in 1864, Bridget worked with the United States Sanitary Commission.
Below: Annie Etheridge.

LORINDA ANNA "ANNIE" BLAIR ETHERIDGE (1839–1913)

Annie Blair served as a "Daughter of the Regiment" with the 2nd Michigan Infantry throughout the Civil War, helping out with chores and tending the wounded. She followed the regiment wherever it went and was almost captured at Second Bull Run (Second Manassas), before she transferred to the 3rd Michigan when the 2nd Michigan was sent west. Anna was wounded at the Battle of Chancellorsville and, when Ulysses S. Grant ordered all women to leave the camps, she served as a nurse at City Point, Virginia. For her service, she was awarded the Kearney Cross for noble sacrifice and heroic service to the Union Army.

Michigan's Distinguished Generals

MAJOR GENERAL GEORGE ARMSTRONG CUSTER (1839–76)

Most famous today for his defeat at the hands of the Sioux at the Battle of Little Big Horn in 1876, Custer's career as a soldier during the Civil War was a splendid one, during which he proved himself one of the most successful – not to mention one of the youngest – major generals.

Though he was born in Ohio, he spent most of his early years in Monroe, Michigan, and having attended the U.S. Military Academy at West Point his class was graduated a year early in attempt to make up a shortage of officers caused by the onset of war. Custer became a lieutenant in the 5th Cavalry and served as aide-de-camp to General Phil Kearney at the Battle of First Bull Run (First Manassas). He was promoted temporarily to captain by General McClellan during the Peninsula Campaign, and also became McClellan's aide-de-camp. With the general's fall from office in November 1862, Custer reverted to his previous rank of lieutenant and became an aide to General Alfred Pleasonton who commanded a cavalry division. Thanks to his new patron, Custer, by now a captain again, was promoted to brigadier general of volunteers and put in charge of the Michigan Brigade of cavalry, part of Pleasonton's Cavalry Corps, just prior to the Battle of Gettysburg.

Custer's brigade fought aggressively in the Gettysburg Campaign, highlighting a style of command that he would continue throughout the Civil War and beyond. His brigade took part in screening and scouting operations for the Army of Potomac, coming into conflict with J.E.B. Stuart's Confederate forces while carrying out these tasks. Promoted to divisional command in September 1864, Custer was heavily involved in the victory over Jubal Early at Cedar Creek and, in 1865, while under the command of General Sheridan, his division fought in the battles of Waynesboro, Dinwiddie Court House, and Five Forks, before finally blocking off Lee's retreat at Appomattox Court House.

MAJOR GENERAL ORLANDO B. WILLCOX (1823–1907)

Also born in Detroit, Willcox was another pre-war regular soldier who served in the Mexican-American War and the Third Seminole War. At the outset of the Civil War he became colonel of the 1st Michigan Infantry, being captured and winning the Medal of Honor at the First Battle of Bull Run (First Manassas). He later fought at Antietam (Battle of Sharpsburg) and Fredericksburg and ended the war a major general.

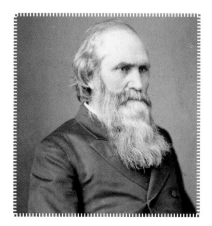

BRIGADIER GENERAL ELON JOHN FARNSWORTH (1837–63)

Hailing from Green Oaks, Michigan, Farnsworth served as a cavalry officer in the Union Army throughout the Civil War. Rapidly promoted through the ranks from lieutenant at the outbreak of the war to brigadier general on June 29, 1863, he was killed leading his brigade in a charge at the Battle of Gettysburg.

BREVET MAJOR GENERAL HENRY J. HUNT (1819–89)

Chief of Artillery in the Army of the Potomac for most of the Civil War, Hunt was born and raised in Detroit, Michigan. He served in the pre-war army and was responsible for artillery drill and tactics. Hunt was steadily promoted in the early days of the Civil War until he became chief of artillery under McClellan, a position he would maintain to the end of the war.

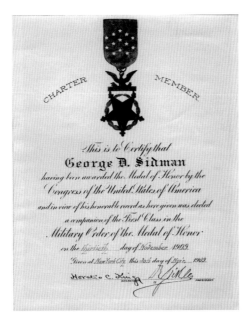

Discharge certificate of William Collins dated May 12, 1865.

THE 4TH MICHIGAN VOLUNTEER INFANTRY

Organized at Adrian, Michigan, the 4th Michigan was mustered into Federal service for a three-year enlistment on June 20, 1861, mustering out at Detroit in June 1864. In between, the regiment served with the Army of the Potomac in the Eastern Theater, fighting at every major campaign from the Peninsula, through Antietam (Battle of Sharpsburg), Fredericksburg, Chancellorsville, and Gettysburg, to the Wilderness Campaign of 1864. Following its mustering out in 1864, it was reorganized and sent to the Western Theater.

THE 5TH MICHIGAN VOLUNTEER INFANTRY

The 5th Michigan was organized in Detroit in August 1861 and, like the 4th, served with the Army of the Potomac, taking part in McClellan's Peninsula Campaign, then Fredericksburg, where it lost over 100 killed and wounded. It went on to participate in the Chancellorsville and Gettysburg campaigns, and, having been diverted to New York to help put down the draft riots, served again with the Army of the Potomac at the Siege of Petersburg and during Grant's Overland Campaign right up until the final battle of Appomattox Courthouse.

THE 7TH MICHIGAN VOLUNTEER INFANTRY

The 7th Michigan also served with the Army of Potomac throughout the war, having been mustered in Monroe in August 1861. It took part in all the major battles, with one of its members winning the Medal of Honor at the Battle of Fair Oaks, part of the Peninsula Campaign. It was reorganized back at Monroe in January 1864, following which the regiment returned to the Army of the Potomac and served out the rest of the war until Appomattox Courthouse, following which it took part in the grand review in Washington, D.C. before being disbanded.

THE 24TH MICHIGAN VOLUNTEER INFANTRY

Mustered in Detroit in August, 1862, the 24th also joined the Army of the Potomac. It first saw combat at the Battle of Fredericksburg, before going on to serve in the Gettysburg Campaign – taking heavy casualties with the famous "Iron Brigade" during the battle. It then took part in the Wilderness Campaign and the Siege of Petersburg. Having been withdrawn from the line for special duties, it was one of the regiments to have the honor of escorting the funeral procession of President Lincoln following his assassination.

THE 27TH MICHIGAN VOLUNTEER INFANTRY

The 27th Michigan was founded in April 1863 and sent to the Western Theater, serving first in Kentucky before being dispatched to support Ulysses S. Grant's Siege of Vicksburg. It served with Grant till the fall of Vicksburg, and then advanced on Jackson, which fell on July 11, 1863. It then fought in Tennessee and took part in the defence of Knoxville. Following this, the 27th was transferred to the Army of the Potomac in the Eastern Theater, where it served in the Wilderness Campaign, the Siege of Petersburg, and the pursuit of Lee.

The gallant charge of the 6th Michigan Cavalry near Falling Waters, Maryland.

Michigan Union Units Furnished

Infantry regiments	33
Colored infantry regiments	1
3-month infantry regiments	1
Sharpshooter units	8
Cavalry regiments	11
U.S. Lancers	1
Horse Guard	1
Light artillery batteries	15
Engineer units	2
Provost/Stanton Guards	2
Sailors/marine personnel	498
Colored troops	1,387

Serving as the state's thirteenth governor, Austin Blair made strong statements against Southern secession and set the stage for Michigan's participation in the Civil War. Blair immediately called for troops after Fort Sumter, only to find that all the funds in the state's treasury had been stolen. Although Michigan was still a sparsely settled state, he raised money through public donations, formed and equipped the first regiments, and had the first Michigan unit in Washington ahead of schedule.

MICHIGAN UNION ARMY DEATHS

Troops Furnished	Killed/Mortally Wounded	Died of Disease	Died of Other Causes	Total
85,479	4,448	8,269	2,036	14,753

Minnesota

❝We are gathered from all the States of the Union and almost all civilized nations of the world. We can have no narrow or sectional feeling. We are a young State, not yet very numerous or powerful, but we are for the Union as it is. We hope, we expect no fraternal war.❞

GOVERNOR ALEXANDER RAMSEY, JANUARY 9, 1861

At the outbreak of the Civil War Minnesota was a new state, only admitted to the Union in 1858, and a small one, with a population of less than 200,000.

The years leading up to Minnesota's admission to the Union had seen turmoil between the slave-owning states of the South and the free states of the North and the admission of new territories as states had proved a controversial part of this: neither side wanted the balance of power in the U.S. House of Representatives to be changed by the admission of new members who would enable the opposite side to decisively win the argument. Minnesota's rise to statehood had, indeed, taken much longer than had been hoped while the thorny situation over the admission of Kansas to the Union was

GOVERNOR ALEXANDER RAMSEY (1815–1903)

Alexander Ramsey had served as a member of Congress for the state of Pennsylvania in the 1840s and was appointed as the Territorial Governor of Minnesota following its establishment as an official territory in 1849. He became mayor of St. Paul in 1855, and the second Governor of Minnesota from 1860 to 1963, leading the state during the early years of the Civil War. Following his term as governor, Ramsey was elected to the U.S. Senate and went on to serve as secretary of war in the administration of President Rutherford B. Hayes.

Brothers Private Hiram J. and Private William H. Gripman of Company I, 3rd Minnesota Infantry Regiment, two of some 25,000 men of Minnesota who fought for the Union cause.

decided. Meanwhile, the division between the two sides widened and by 1861 it was clear to many that conflict was inevitable. The dramatic events at Fort Sumter finally edged the country into war, and Minnesota was one of the first states to offer troops for the Union. By chance the governor, Alexander Ramsey, was in Washington, D.C. at the time and, on hearing of the fall of Fort Sumter, immediately offered to send 1,000 troops from Minnesota to help the government. His offer was gratefully accepted and those 1,000 men would be the first of some 25,000 from the new state who would serve during the Civil War.

The 1st Minnesota Volunteer Infantry

The 1st Minnesota was one of the first bodies of troops to be promised to the Union at the start of the Civil War. Organized on April 14, 1861, for three months service, this was extended to three years in May. Its first colonel was Willis A. Gorman, a former governor of the territory and a veteran of the Mexican-American War. The regiment became part of the Army of the Potomac and received its baptism of fire at the First Battle of Bull Run (First Manassas), where it lost some twenty percent of its men in casualties. The 1st Minnesota went on to serve throughout the war in the East with the Army of the Potomac, fighting in the Peninsula Campaign, at Antietam (Battle of Sharpsburg) and Fredericksburg, and was seriously under strength by the time of the Gettysburg campaign of 1863, having only 262 men left out of the original 1,000. Nevertheless, it won great renown at Gettysburg, launching a desperate headlong charge in an effort to stop the Confederates breaking through the Union line. The charge had the desired effect, but came at the price of 215 casualties out of the 262 men committed, a rate of eighty-two percent. The 1st Minnesota continued to serve with the Army of the Potomac until mustered out in April 1864.

The 2nd Minnesota Volunteer Infantry

Formed during the summer of 1861, the 2nd Minnesota was kept in the state for garrison duty until October, when it moved to Washington, D.C. and then joined the Army of the Ohio. It marched through Kentucky and Tennessee, narrowly missing the Battle of Shiloh, but took part in the Siege of

1st Minnesota Infantry.

Corinth in April 1862. In the fall of that year, the 2nd Minnesota was involved in the race to Louisville to stop the Confederate counteroffensive, culminating in the Battle of Perryville.

Having spent nearly five moths stationery, the regiment moved again in June 1863, taking part in the Battle of Chickamauga, where it lost a third of its strength. The 2nd Minnesota then fought at Chattanooga in November 1864, before re-enlisting *en masse* in 1864 and, following a period of leave, participating in Sherman's Atlanta Campaign and the March to the Sea.

The 4th Minnesota Volunteer Infantry

The 4th Minnesota fought in many of the same campaigns as the 2nd, having been mustered at Fort Snelling in October, 1861, and then sent west in May 1862 to take part in the Siege of Corinth as part of the Army of the Mississippi. It

2nd Minnesota Infantry.

Battle of Nashville.

remained there until August before being detached and participating in the Battle of Iuka. Returning to Corinth, the 4th Minnesota was next sent toward Vicksburg in November. It took part in the siege and was present when the city fell in July 1863.

Following the end of the term of the regiment's enlistment, around three-quarters of the men re-enlisted in January 1864, and the 4th was sent to join Sherman's forces in June. It missed the Battle for Atlanta, but was part of the March to the Sea. At the end of the war, the 4th took part in the grand review at Washington, D.C., where it was at the head of the column of Sherman's army. It was mustered out at Louisville, July 19, 1865.

THE 5TH MINNESOTA VOLUNTEER INFANTRY

The 5th Minnesota also saw action in the Western Theater, though three companies took part in the Indian fighting of the Dakota War of 1862. The remaining seven saw action at the Siege of Corinth as part of the Army of the Mississippi, before going on to take part in the Battle of Iuka and fighting once more around Corinth in October, 1862, winning praise from the divisional commander for driving Confederates back from a breach they had made.

Following the 5th's heroics in Corinth, the regiment took part in the other actions in central Mississippi and western Tennessee before joining the Siege of Vicksburg in spring, 1863. It remained there until the fall of the city in July. Having re-enlisted as a group, the regiment later fought in the battles of Tupelo and, later, Nashville in December 1864. The last year of the Civil War saw it participate in the Siege of Mobile and the assault on Fort Blakely.

THE 7TH, 9TH, AND 10TH VOLUNTEER INFANTRY REGIMENTS

The 7th, 9th, and 10th Minnesota regiments all had similar histories. They were all raised in the summer of 1862 and all took part in the efforts to put down the Sioux uprising that became known as the Dakota War of 1862. When this conflict ended with the mass hanging of thirty-eight Sioux convicted of massacring settlers, the three regiments were sent west in mid-1864 to take part in the final campaigns of the Civil War in Tennessee. All three regiments took part in the Battle of Nashville that decided the campaign, when the Union Army under George H. Thomas crushed John Bell Wood's Confederate forces on December 15th and 16th.

Generals from Minnesota

MAJOR GENERAL NAPOLEON J. T. DANA (1822–1905)

A pre-war regular officer who had served in the Mexican-American War, Dana was originally from Maine, but settled in Minnesota after leaving the army in 1855. Between then and the outbreak of the Civil War, he worked as a banker while also acting as a brigadier general of militia. After the conflict erupted, Dana volunteered for the Union cause and became colonel of the 1st Minnesota Regiment in October 1861. Promoted to brigadier general in February 1862, he commanded the 3rd Brigade at the battles of the Peninsula Campaign and then at Antietam (Battle of Sharpsburg), where he was severely wounded. Although promoted to major general in November 1862, Dana was still recuperating and unable to take up any command until the summer of 1863, when he commanded the defenses of Philadelphia during the Gettysburg Campaign.

Sent to the Department of the Gulf, Dana commanded XIII Corps throughout 1863 and 1864, before moving to the Army of the Tennessee where he commanded Vicksburg and then XVI Corps. His final major post was the Department of Mississippi, which he led from 1864 to 1865.

BRIGADIER GENERAL WILLIS A. GORMAN (1816–76)

Gorman came to the war from a political background, though he also had a substantial amount of military experience. A native of Kentucky, he studied law in Indiana and set up practice there while going into state politics. He volunteered for the army during the Mexican-American War, and became the civil and military governor of Puebla before returning to Indiana where he was elected congressman in the late 1840s. Gorman was appointed the territorial governor of Minnesota from 1853 to 1857, and later practiced law in St. Paul.

With the outbreak of war he became colonel of the 1st Minnesota Infantry, leading them at the First Battle of Bull Run (First Manassas) before taking over a brigade of the Army of the Potomac during the Peninsula Campaign. He continued to command this brigade through to the end of the Antietam Campaign, after which he was placed in command of the District of Eastern Arkansas. This was his final command as he left the army in 1864 and returned to his law practice in St Paul.

Minnesota Union Units Furnished	
Infantry regiments	11
Sharpshooter units	2
Cavalry regiments	2
Cavalry battalions	2
Heavy artillery regiments	1
Light artillery batteries	3
Sailors/marine personnel	3
Colored troops	104

MINNESOTA UNION ARMY DEATHS

Troops Furnished	Killed/Mortally Wounded	Died of Disease	Died of Other Causes	Total
23,913	626	1,677	281	2,584

Mississippi

Republic of Mississippi Flag.

❝ . . . the Southern states battling in defense of property, honor, life, all for which freemen should wish to live, cannot abandon the conflict no matter what sacrifices may be required to be made in its continuance. We must triumph or perish! ❞

EXTRACT FROM GOVERNOR JOHN J. PETTUS' SPEECH TO THE LEGISLATURE OF MISSISSIPPI, NOVEMBER 5, 1861

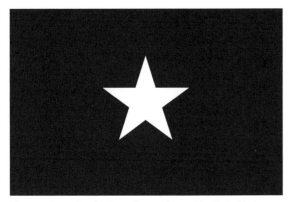

The state also produced a flag and a song forever identified with the Confederacy. On the day of secession a new, temporary flag – a central white star on a blue background – was raised over the state capitol. This was subsequently incorporated into a new official state flag that was first raised on January 21, 1861. The first flag raising was witnessed by Harry McCarthy and he penned some lyrics to commemorate the event. The song's title was "Bonnie Blue Flag". It became a popular tune throughout the South, while the first flag became the unofficial flag of the Confederacy. See also page 222.

GOVERNOR JOHN J. PETTUS (1813–67)

Pettus was Mississippi's governor for just five days in January 1854, but was elected to a full term in 1859 and served until 1863, after winning re-election in late 1861. As a so-called "Fire-Eater", he was staunchly secessionist and did much to facilitate and encourage the state's breakaway from the Union in January 1861. In the months following secession, Pettus was active in raising, clothing, and arming many militia units across the state and he would later see them enlisted in the Confederate Army, making Mississippi the second biggest contributor of manpower to the Southern cause. When his second term came to an end, he himself served in the army for the duration of the war.

Mississippi seceded from the Union, the second state to do so, on January 9, 1861, briefly became a republic, and then formally founded the Confederacy with six other states in February.

It is, perhaps, not surprising that the state was a frontrunner in seceding as it had a long tradition of slave owning, anti-abolitionist sentiment, and dogged support for states' rights. Slaves, who comprised fifty-five percent of its population, were the cornerstone of its economy and its voters were overwhelmingly Democrat.

In 1860, the Southern Democrat contender, John C. Breckinridge, took fifty-nine percent of the vote, while the national winner, Lincoln, did not even appear on the state's ballot paper.

Thus Mississippi fully embraced the Southern cause. In a speech published on the day of secession, its political leaders published a statement entitled "A Declaration of the Immediate Causes which Induce and Justify the Secession of the State of Mississippi from the Federal Union," which included the line "our position is thoroughly identified with the institution of slavery – the greatest material interest of the world." During the conflict, scores of thousands of its menfolk fought in the Confederate Army and one of its pre-war leading lights on the national political stage, Jefferson Davis, became the first and only President of the Confederate States of America.

"THE BONNIE BLUE FLAG"

We are a band of brothers and native to the soil
Fighting for our Liberty, With treasure, blood and toil
And when our rights were threatened, the cry rose near
*   and far*
Hurrah for the Bonnie Blue Flag that bears a single star!
Chorus
Hurrah! Hurrah!
For Southern rights, hurrah!
Hurrah for the Bonnie Blue Flag that bears a single star.
2. As long as the Union was faithful to her trust
Like friends and like brethren, kind were we, and just
But now, when Northern treachery attempts our rights
*   to mar*
We hoist on high the Bonnie Blue Flag that bears a single star.
Chorus
3. First gallant South Carolina nobly made the stand
Then came Alabama and took her by the hand
Next, quickly Mississippi, Georgia, and Florida
All raised on high the Bonnie Blue Flag that bears a
*   single star.*
Chorus
4. Ye men of valor gather round the banner of the right
Texas and fair Louisiana join us in the fight
Davis, our loved President, and Stephens statesmen rare
Now rally round the Bonnie Blue Flag that bears a single star.
Chorus
5. Now here's to brave Virginia, the old Dominion State,
With the young Confederacy at last has sealed her fate,
And spurred by her example, now other states prepare
To hoist high the bonnie blue flag that bears a single star.
Chorus
6. Then cheer, boys, cheer, raise a joyous shout
For Arkansas and North Carolina now have both gone out,
And let another rousing cheer for Tennessee be given,
The single star of the Bonnie Blue Flag has grown to
*   be eleven.*
Chorus
7. Then here's to our Confederacy, strong we are and brave,
Like patriots of old we'll fight, our heritage to save;
And rather than submit to shame, to die we would prefer,
So cheer for the Bonnie Blue Flag that bears a single star.
Chorus

President Jefferson Davis (1808–89)

Davis was born in Kentucky but raised in Mississippi, where his family gradually grew in social importance. He attended West Point and subsequently served in the Black Hawk War of 1832. After resigning from the military, he returned to his small plantation and in his leisure time read widely on political issues, developing a firm belief in the slave system and states' rights. This period of self-imposed isolation ended in 1845, when he remarried and secured a seat in Congress, only to resign after a few months to take part in the American-Mexican War. He returned to Washington, D.C. as a senator in 1847 and became well known for his political views. Participating in various debates over slavery and abolition in the 1850s, he opposed secession until Lincoln declared that he would not allow slavery to be expanded into new territories.

Davis resigned in January 1861, hoping to become the Confederacy's commander-in-chief, but was actually inaugurated Provisional President of the Confederate States of America on February 18th. The new president took control of a new country that was in no way prepared for war and lacked the resources to match the North. He was not a man of the caliber needed to overcome the many problems the Confederacy faced. Often badly-tempered, irascible, and inflexible (and plagued by poor health), Davis clashed with many of his senior political and military figures, frequently overruling their better advice. Few in the Confederate Congress supported him by 1863 and he was not much liked by the wider population.

From 1864 to 1865, Davis provoked outrage by suggesting that some 40,000 slaves should be armed and then freed when the fighting was over. He rejected all calls for the South to seek a negotiated peace and thus probably prolonged the war, heaping unnecessary misery on the South. He was captured near Irwinville, Georgia, on May 10, 1865, and held prisoner for two years. However, Davis never stood trial and was released in May 1877, whereupon he returned to Mississippi before settling in the Gulf of Mexico to write his memoirs.

THE BATTLE OF CORINTH
OCTOBER 3 AND 4, 1862

Before Major General Henry Halleck, commander of the Union's Department of the Mississippi, was recalled to Washington in July 1862, he split his force in two and sent them in different directions – Major General Don Carlos Buell's Army of the Ohio went east into Tennessee, while Brigadier General Ulysses S. Grant's Army of the Tennessee conducted small-scale operations along the Mississippi River. Grant was, however, concerned that his 45,000-strong force was spread too thinly between Memphis and Corinth, Mississippi, and that his lines of communications back to the distant base at Cairo, Illinois, were over-extended.

The Confederates knew that Grant was at Corinth with 25,000 men and decided to combine the forces of major generals Sterling Price and Earl van Dorn against him. Grant tried to prevent the two from linking up but narrowly failed to do so at Iuka on September 19th and 20th, largely due to the poor showing of one of his subordinates, Brigadier General William S. Rosecrans. The combined Southern force was attacked at Corinth on October 3rd and fighting lasted until the next day. Although Grant won the victory, it was not as overwhelming as it could have been, again due to Rosecrans. Nevertheless, Grant remained in control of Memphis and Corinth and began preparing for the First Vicksburg Campaign.

THE FIRST VICKSBURG CAMPAIGN

After the Battle of Corinth in early October 1862, Brigadier General Ulysses S. Grant concentrated his Army of the Tennessee around Grand Junction, Tennessee, prior to moving south against Vicksburg. He advanced on November 13th, with his troops brushing aside any opposition from the forces of Lieutenant General John C. Pemberton. Some 40,000 men under Major General William T. Sherman were simultaneously sent on an amphibious operation toward Vicksburg with the Mississippi River Squadron under Rear Admiral David D. Porter.

As the two forces advanced, Grant's movement was dislocated by a raid against his supply and communications lines in northwest Tennessee, by Major General Nathan B. Forrest, as well as the loss of a key supply dump at Holly Springs, Mississippi, to Southern troops under Major General Earl van Dorn on December 20th. The Sherman-Porter operation faired little better. Entering the Yazoo River, they attempted to capture the Chickasaw Bluffs north of Vicksburg on December 27th to the 29th but were rebuffed. Thus, at the year's end, the South still controlled the Mississippi from Vicksburg to Baton Rouge, Louisiana.

THE SECOND VICKSBURG CAMPAIGN

After the fiasco of his First Vicksburg Campaign, Ulysses S. Grant spent the first months of 1863 preparing for a second attack on the key city. He moved in April. Leaving one corps under Major General William T. Sherman above Vicksburg, Grant marched the rest of his 50,000-strong force to Hard Times on the west bank of the Mississippi River below Vicksburg. At the same time a flotilla of gunboats and transports braved its batteries and sailed down to rendezvous with him, while, between April 18th and May 3rd, a cavalry raid by Colonel Benjamin H. Grierson rampaged through much of the state in a damaging diversion before reaching safety at Baton Rouge, Louisiana.

Grant crossed the Mississippi on April 30th, drove off the Confederate garrison at Port Gibson the next day, and linked up with Sherman on May 3rd. He next struck fifty-five miles eastward, making for Jackson, where he defeated some 9,000 Southern troops on the 14th. Grant now turned westward for Vicksburg and a victory at Champion's Hill two days later allowed his force to cross the Big Black River, the last physical obstacle before the city.

Two attempts to storm Vicksburg were made – on the 19th and 22nd – but both were bloody failures and, subsequently, a formal siege was begun. With his troops short of food and ammunition, the Confederate Lieutenant General John C. Pemberton, surrendered on July 4th. Mississippi was in Union hands and the Confederacy fatally split in two.

CAVE LIFE IN VICKSBURG

The Siege of Vicksburg commenced on May 19, 1863, and ended on July 4th. In that time, the city was under almost constant bombardment from gunboats and mortar barges on the Mississippi and by siege artillery on its landward sides. Tens of thousands of shells badly damaged houses and civilians sought protection elsewhere. Many chose a ridge between the main city and its perimeter defenses, excavating caves and more elaborate dugouts fitted with furniture and carpets from its clay soil. Something like 500 were built and the area became so pitted that Union troops nicknamed it "Prairie Dog Village" after the burrowing rodent. The caves were largely effective, however, as only a dozen or so of Vicksburg's citizens are known to have died during the siege.

THE MISSISSIPPI RIVER SQUADRON AT VICKSBURG

During October 1862, Rear Admiral David D. Porter took charge of what had been the Union Army's Western Gunboat Flotilla. It was transferred to naval control and renamed the Mississippi River Squadron. This collection of gunboats, ironclads, mortar barges, and transports would play an important role in Grant's Vicksburg Campaign.

A Kurz & Allison lithograph of the Siege of Vicksburg by the 13th, 15th, and 17th corps. It shows the Confederates on their way to surrender to Grant, July 4, 1863.

During the campaign, a major problem for Grant was moving his Army of the Tennessee from the west to the east bank of the Mississippi at a point south of Vicksburg so that he could lay siege to the city. While his troops took an overland route down the west bank to Hard Times, Porter ran the gauntlet of Vicksburg defenses. This was brilliantly accomplished in mid-April 1863, and the flotilla ferried the army across at end of the month. Porter was next tasked with various shore bombardments, culminating in a ferocious pounding of the city before Grant launched an assault on May 22nd. This was rebuffed and the squadron settled down to siege operations, firing some 22,000 shells into Vicksburg before the city surrendered in early July. Porter received the thanks of Congress for his efforts.

The levee at Vicksburg, with the Mississippi in the background. February 1864.

LIEUTENANT GENERAL JOHN C. PEMBERTON (1814–81)

A Pennsylvanian by birth, Pemberton attended West Point and subsequently fought in the American-Mexican War. Married to a Virginian, he refused a Union commission at the outbreak of the Civil War and joined the Confederate Army in April 1861. Despite his limited abilities, Pemberton was promoted to lieutenant general the next year and took charge of the Department of Mississippi, Tennessee, and East Florida. He was in command of Vicksburg during the siege of 1863, and was forced to surrender unconditionally on July 4th in what was a humiliating and strategically devastating defeat for the South. Because of his Northern origins, some wrongly suspected him of treachery. Pemberton was subsequently exchanged but resigned his command in 1864. He served in minor posts for the remainder of the war

BRIGADIER GENERAL WILLIAM E. BALDWIN (1827–64)

Baldwin joined the Confederate Army after his home state seceded in 1861, and was made colonel of the 17th Mississippi Infantry Regiment. After service in Florida, he transferred to Tennessee and then Kentucky, but was captured at the fall of Fort Donelson in 1862. Subsequently exchanged, Baldwin was made brigadier general and served in the Second Vicksburg Campaign in 1863. Captured and exchanged again, he was assigned to the District of Mobile but died in a riding accident.

Brigadier General Joseph R. Davis.

Mississippi Generals

Brigadier General Benjamin G. Humphreys.

BRIGADIER GENERAL JOSEPH R. DAVIS (1825–96)

Nephew of the Confederate president, Davis entered Southern service in spring 1861, and served as his uncle's aide-de-camp. He was promoted to brigadier general the following year despite murmurs of nepotism and, in late spring 1863, was attached to the Army of Northern Virginia. His brigade was the second to be committed on the first day of Gettysburg, but was rested on the second after suffering heavy losses and then took part in Pickett's Charge on the last day of battle. Thereafter he fought at Spotsylvania Court House, Cold Harbor, and the Siege of Petersburg before surrendering.

BRIGADIER GENERAL BENJAMIN G. HUMPHREYS (1808–82)

Expelled from West Point for riotous behavior, Humphreys returned to Mississippi where he became a senator in the state legislature. He joined the army in 1861 and was promoted to brigadier general. His regiment, the 21st Mississippi, fought at Gettysburg in 1863, and helped push Union troops out of the Peach Orchard and back to Cemetery Ridge on July 2nd. When Humphreys' brigade commander was killed, he took charge and led it for the remainder of the war.

MAJOR GENERAL EARL VAN DORN (1820–63)

Van Dorn graduated from West Point in 1842 and went on to serve in the American-Mexican War as well as various Native-American campaigns. After the Civil War broke out, he was given command of the South's Trans-Mississippi Department in 1862, but was defeated at Pea Ridge, Arkansas, in March and at Corinth, Mississippi, the following October. Exonerated of any blame for the latter by a formal commission, he went on to serve as a cavalry commander at Holly Springs in December. He was shot and killed by a man who accused him of having an affair with his wife in May 1863.

Major General Earl van Dorn.

THE C.S.S. ARKANSAS

This 165-foot Confederate ironclad ram was laid down at Fort Pickering below Memphis, Tennessee, in October 1861, and was towed up the Yazoo River half-finished shortly before Union troops captured the city in early July 1862. The eight-gun vessel, protected by wood-backed two-inch thick iron, was finally completed at Greenwood, Mississippi, and commissioned into the Confederate Navy on May 26, 1863, though its engines were far from ideal.

Arkansas and its 230-strong crew under Lieutenant Commanding Isaac N. Brown steamed back down the Yazoo on July 14th and skirmished with the ironclad U.S.S. *Carondelet* and two wooden gunboats the next day. The Union ironclad was battered into submission and Brown pursued the other vessels into the Mississippi River. *Arkansas* now ran into a flotilla of thirty Union vessels but fought its way through in thirty minutes to reach the relative safety of Vicksburg. After running repairs, *Arkansas* sailed on to Baton Rouge, Louisiana, to aid a land attack on the city's Union defenders. However, its patched-up engines failed on August 6th as it tried to ram the U.S.S. *Essex*. *Arkansas* was run aground and destroyed by its own crew after just twenty-three days in service.

Combat between the Confederate iron-plated ram *Arkansas* and the Federal gunboat *Carondelet*, at the mouth of the Yazoo River, Tuesday, July 15, 1862.

There are 1,340 memorials and monuments in the Vicksburg National Military Park. This one remembers the Rhode Island Infantry.

THE ARMY OF MISSISSIPPI (CONFEDERATE)

Three distinct armies of this name served the Southern cause during the Civil War. The first, sometimes known as the Army of the West or Army of the Mississippi, was activated in March 1862, under General P.G.T. Beauregard and was commanded in quick succession by famous generals such as Albert S. Johnston, Braxton Bragg, and Leonidas Polk. It saw action at Shiloh, where Johnson was killed, and Perryville, but was renamed the Army of Tennessee in November. The second was sometimes referred to as the Army of Vicksburg and its sole task was to defend that key city. It was organized in December 1862 and contained troops from the Department of Mississippi and East Louisiana. It had two commanders – Lieutenant General John C. Pemberton and Major General Earl van Dorn – but ceased to exist when Vicksburg surrendered in July 1863. The third army was commonly known as III Corps of the Army of Tennessee. It was activated in 1863 and served in the Atlanta Campaign before surrendering in 1865.

THE ARMY OF THE MISSISSIPPI (UNION)

There were two Union forces designated the Army of the Mississippi. The first was created in February 1862 under the command of Major General John Pope. It initially comprised just two divisions but other infantry and cavalry units were soon added to its strength, along with a gunboat flotilla. The army saw action at Island Number Ten and the Siege of Corinth between February and May. After Pope was transferred to the Army of Virginia in June, Brigadier

MISSISSIPPI CONFEDERATE ARMY DEATHS

	Killed	Died of Wounds	Died of Disease	Total
Officers	122	75	103	300
Enlisted	5,687	2,576	6,704	14,967
Total	5,809	2,651	6,807	15,267

OF 545 MISSISSIPPI TROOPS FIGHTING FOR THE UNION, 78 LOST THEIR LIVES FROM SIMILAR CAUSES.

General William S. Rosecrans took charge for the battles of Iuka and Corinth in September and October. He, in turn, was moved to take over the Army of the Ohio that month and his previous command was deactivated.

The second army, formerly two corps from the Army of the Tennessee, emerged on January 4, 1863, under Major General John A. McClernand, who led it during the capture of Arkansas Post. He was effectively sacked shortly thereafter and the two corps returned to their old command.

THE 10TH MISSISSIPPI INFANTRY REGIMENT

The first regiment was organized in March, 1861, with recruits enlisting for a year. After traveling to Mobile, Alabama, it undertook coastal garrison duties and fought in the Battle of Santa Rosa Island in October. It returned to its home state in 1862 and disbanded in March. A new regiment was, however, activated on the 15th and went on to fight at Shiloh in April, Perryville in October, and at Stones River (December 1862 to January 1863). The 10th Mississippi went on to see action at Chickamauga in September and was present at the subsequent Siege of Chattanooga. In the spring and summer of 1864, the regiment served in the Atlanta Campaign as well as the Franklin-Nashville Campaign in the final months of the year. Spring 1865 saw the unit participating in the Carolinas Campaign and it surrendered in April.

Mississippi Confederate Units Furnished	
Infantry regiments	49
Infantry battalions	6
Cavalry regiments	7
Cavalry battalions	4
Partisan Ranger regiments	2
Light artillery batteries	20

The original Surrender Monument from the battlefield of Vicksburg. It was moved after being vandalized and is now on show in the museum.

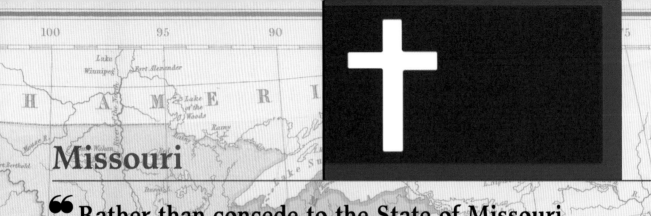

Missouri

"Rather than concede to the State of Missouri . . . the right to dictate to my Government ... I would see . . . every man woman and child in the State dead and buried."

CAPTAIN NATHANIEL LYON, U.S. ARMY, TO GOVERNOR CLAIBORNE JACKSON, 1861

Missouri played a pivotal role in the developments that brought about the Civil War and its territory became one of the most bitterly contested regions during the conflict.

According to the Official Records of the war only Virginia and Tennessee saw more battles. Missouri is situated in territory that became part of the United States with the Louisiana Purchase of 1803. After the establishment of the state of Louisiana in 1812, the remainder of the purchase land became the Missouri Territory, covering a much larger area than the modern state. As part of the Missouri Compromise, Missouri (with its present-day boundaries) was carved out of this territory in 1821 and admitted to the Union as a slave state, balancing the number of free and slave states. By 1860, almost ten percent of its population were slaves.

Through the 1850s, the state was at the center of developments that heightened the divisions between North and South. The 1854 Kansas-Nebraska Act increased the area of the nation in which slavery might be permitted and inspired pro-slavery Missourians, known as "Border Ruffians", to intervene fraudulently in Kansas elections to bring that state over to slavery. Although ultimately unsuccessful, this provoked retaliation from abolitionists, with murders and other atrocities being committed by both sides. Events in "Bleeding Kansas" outraged supporters of respective points of view everywhere in the nation. The state was also the focus of a crucial Supreme Court decision, in the Dred Scott case. Scott, who lived in St. Louis, was ruled by the court to be a slave even though he had been taken to a free state at an earlier point in his life. This was seen as an important assertion of slave owners' property rights. Again, abolitionists were furious.

From 1803 to the outbreak of the Civil War, Missouri's population rocketed, multiplying some sixty times from the census of 1810 to that of 1860, and its economy developed at a similar rate.

FRÉMONT AND EMANCIPATION

When the Civil War began, freeing the South's slaves was not a war aim for President Lincoln or most of his supporters in the North. For some time the president tried to keep it that way, fearing that any such move would send the various "border states," including Missouri, solidly into the Southern camp. In September 1861, however, Major General John Frémont, commanding the Union Army's Department of the West, made a controversial proclamation from his headquarters in St. Louis. Worried by the Union defeat a few weeks previously at Wilson's Creek, Frémont imposed martial law on Missouri and announced that all the property of rebels in the state would be confiscated and their slaves set free.

President Lincoln was faced with a dilemma. Radical abolitionists hailed Frémont's actions, and Lincoln needed their support, but for many Unionists it was a step too far. Lincoln first tried to persuade Frémont to withdraw the measure and then ordered him to cancel it. In November, after he had sought and received unfavorable reports, he fired Frémont for incompetence. Nevertheless, for Lincoln the whole affair was instructive. Before he issued his Emancipation Proclamation in January 1863, he prepared the ground carefully and made sure that he did so in a manner that would be difficult to challenge legally.

Frémont, a prewar national hero for his exploration expeditions in the West and his role in taking California from Mexico, briefly held an active command in Virginia in 1862 but was removed after being defeated in the Battle of Cross Keys. He played no further significant part in the war.

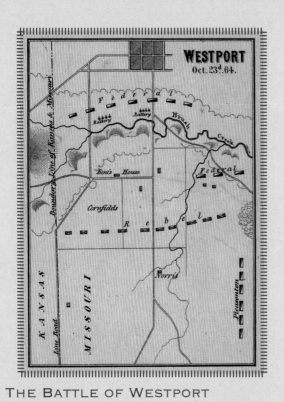

THE BATTLE OF WESTPORT

Sometimes called the "Gettysburg of the West", more troops were engaged at Westport than in any other battle of the war west of the Mississippi.

By October 23, 1864, Major General Price knew that his Confederate Army of Missouri, some 9,000 strong, was heavily outnumbered by potential enemies. Ahead of him, to the west, was Major General Alfred Curtis's Army of the Border while closing in from the east was Major General William Rosecrans's Department of Missouri, led by a cavalry division commanded by Major General Alfred Pleasonton. Despite the odds, Price decided to try to beat his opponents separately, starting with Curtis.

Curtis had deployed his forces in a strong defensive position north of Brush Creek when Price attacked. In a series of attacks and counterattacks, first one side then the other seemed to gain the upper hand. The Union side, however, gradually made its superior numbers tell while Pleasonton's cavalry were, all the time, approaching from the east. After several hours of fierce combat, and some 1,500 casualties on each side, Price ordered his battered army to retreat.

Above: Missouri's Governor Claiborne Fox Jackson (1806–62) was a fiery secessionist who tried to raise his own army. In 1861, he ordered the state militia to report for six days training in a plan to take control of the St. Louis arsenal, which contained 60,000 muskets, forty artillery pieces, and 90,000 pounds of powder. To hedge his efforts, he also asked Jefferson Davis for two cannon to be shipped to him in boxes marked "marble." Captain Nathaniel Lyon anticipated the plot, took control of the arsenal, and, in a daring attack, captured Jackson's camp. Jackson fled from the state's capital at Jefferson City to Neosho, where he established a rump legislature that voted to secede. Jackson eventually escaped to Little Rock, Arkansas, where he died in 1862.

Poor deluded Miss-Souri takes a Secession bath, and finds it much hotter than she expected!

Earlier in the period, settlers from the South were predominant, but the number of Irish and German immigrants as well as incomers from Northern states later outstripped them. Perhaps the best measure of the balance of Northern and Southern support in the state is that some three-quarters of Missourians who fought in the war did so for the Union.

Despite such heavy Union leanings, in 1861, as war began, Governor Claiborne Jackson strongly favored the South and did all he could to swing the state to the Confederacy's side. His principal opponent was Captain Nathaniel Lyon, who commanded the U.S. Army arsenal at St. Louis. Relying heavily on troops recruited mainly from among German immigrants, Lyon gained the upper hand in their initial confrontation. Jackson and the pro-Southern militia force – the Missouri State Guard, led by Sterling Price – retreated to the south of the state. Lyon's troops followed, captured the state capital of Jefferson City, and established a new pro-Union government there in July, 1861. In October, Jackson and his allies established a competing state government at Neosho. Although it was recognized by the Confederacy, its members soon left the state for good and, indeed, it never controlled any significant part of Missouri.

The tide seemed to turn somewhat when Confederate troops defeated Union forces at the Battle of Wilson's Creek, near Springfield, on August 10, 1861, and Lyon was killed in the battle. The Confederates were unable to follow up their success, however, and, in March 1862, a Union victory at Pea Ridge in northern Arkansas effectively ensured that Missouri would remain under Union control.

Nevertheless, fighting in the state was far from over. The remainder of the war saw a bitter partisan struggle raging in many parts, especially in the south and the areas bordering Kansas. The legacy of Bleeding Kansas meant that irregular forces on both sides – usually

Rebel prisoners in the dungeon of the State House at Jefferson City, Missouri, 1961.

QUANTRILL, ANDERSON, JENNISON, AND LANE

This quartet were the most notorious leaders of the ferocious guerrilla war that devastated much of eastern Kansas and western Missouri in the Civil War years and left a legacy of lawlessness that troubled the region for many years afterward.

William C. Quantrill and W.T. "Bloody Bill" Anderson were Bushwhackers, fighting, at least nominally, for the Confederacy, while C.R. "Doc" Jennison and J.H. "Jim" Lane were Jayhawkers, on the Union side. Their actions remain controversial even today, with some people seeing one or the other pair as striving to serve an honorable cause in difficult circumstances. Others see them as brutal, terrorist killers and thieves whose increasingly reckless love for violence brought misery and devastation to the areas they fought over. The latter would probably be closer to the truth.

Quantrill and Anderson led massacres at Lawrence (Kansas) and Centralia (Missouri) and Anderson's men were noted for hanging scalps of their victims from their horses' bridles. Lane, for his part, commanded the murderous Union sacking and burning of Osceola (Missouri) in 1861, while Jennison's plundering was so outrageous that he was eventually court-martialled and dismissed from the Union Army. Quantrill and Anderson were both killed later in the war; Lane died in 1866. Jennison survived until 1884 and enjoyed a postwar career in Kansas politics.

called "Jayhawkers" or "Redlegs" on the Union side and "Bushwhackers" on the Confederate side – soon sprang into action. They carried out raids and counter-raids on areas they judged supported the other section; looting, burning, and killing indiscriminately. Yet, for all the devastation their actions caused, neither Jayhawkers or Bushwhackers affected the course of the war.

The most notorious incidents that took place in Missouri (those involved also fought in Kansas) were the September 23, 1861, Jayhawker attack on Osceola and the September 27, 1864, Centralia massacre by Bushwhackers. The real toll of the partisan conflict, however, was not in these major attacks but in the huge mass of smaller-scale killings and robberies that occurred throughout the contested rural areas. Horror at the devastation caused is best exemplified by General Order No. 11 issued by Union Major General Thomas Ewing in August, 1863 (in response to the Bushwhacker massacre at Lawrence, Kansas, a few days before). Union leaders believed that Bushwhackers operating on both sides of the state border gained most of their supplies and support from sympathizers in four counties in the west of Missouri – Bates, Cass, Jackson, and Vernon. Ewing's order forced all civilians living outside a few towns in these counties to evacuate their homes, whether they were Union supporters or not. Thousands were forced from their homes. Then the Army burned all buildings and property.

Many of Ewing's troops were volunteers from Kansas who saw this as a license to loot and, by the time the soldiers had finished, the entire area was so devastated that it was many years after the war before the local economy recovered. Whether the Bushwhackers were greatly hindered is a matter of speculation. How much they depended on supplies from the area is uncertain and, in any case, after the destruction, farm animals and other resources were left behind for the taking.

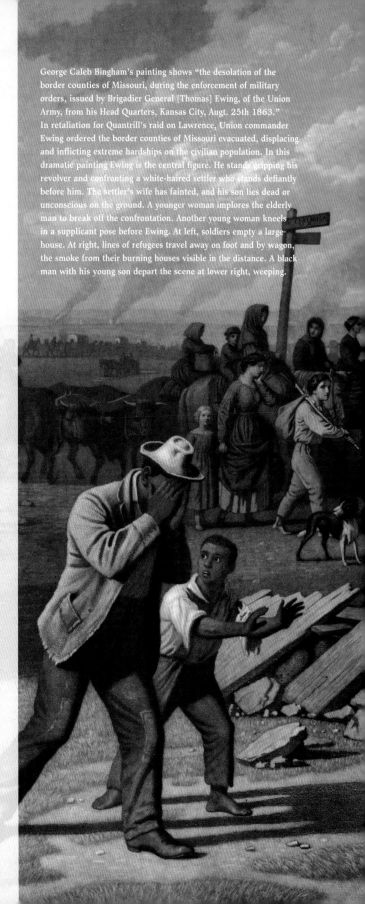

George Caleb Bingham's painting shows "the desolation of the border counties of Missouri, during the enforcement of military orders, issued by Brigadier General [Thomas] Ewing, of the Union Army, from his Head Quarters, Kansas City, Augt. 25th 1863."
In retaliation for Quantrill's raid on Lawrence, Union commander Ewing ordered the border counties of Missouri evacuated, displacing and inflicting extreme hardships on the civilian population. In this dramatic painting Ewing is the central figure. He stands gripping his revolver and confronting a white-haired settler who stands defiantly before him. The settler's wife has fainted, and his son lies dead or unconscious on the ground. A younger woman implores the elderly man to break off the confrontation. Another young woman kneels in a supplicant pose before Ewing. At left, soldiers empty a large house. At right, lines of refugees travel away on foot and by wagon, the smoke from their burning houses visible in the distance. A black man with his young son depart the scene at lower right, weeping.

The battlefield of Lexington, showing the plan of the earthwork defended by Federal troops under command of Colonel James A. Mulligan, September 18–20, 1861.

Ewing's part in the war the next year would be less controversial. By 1864, Confederate fortunes were clearly on the wane. One of the final serious attempts to turn the tide of war – and perhaps derail Lincoln's likely re-election in the fall – was an invasion of Missouri led by Major General Sterling Price. Price's aim was to recapture the state for the South and, failing that, to take significant supplies of food, horses, and draft animals, as well as military materials.

Price and his 12,000 men crossed into Missouri from Arkansas in mid-September. Their first target was Fort Davidson, commanded by Ewing, which they attacked on the 27th. Heavily outnumbered, Ewing withdrew after performing his delaying mission well. Price moved on toward St. Louis, but Federal reinforcements now arrived and the attackers swerved west toward Jefferson City. Once again the area was strongly defended by Union forces and Price moved further west toward Kansas City, Missouri.

In a series of minor clashes at places like Glasgow, Lexington, and Independence, the Southern force held off Federal attacks through the middle part of October. However, Price and his men were now menaced from both east and west by converging enemy forces. On October 23rd, the armies clashed at Westport (now part of Kansas City, Missouri) in what would prove to be the largest battle of the war fought west of the Mississippi. The Union armies won a decisive victory and the remnants of Price's force retreated south by a roundabout route through Indian Territory and into Texas, harried as they went by pursuing Federals. This was the last major action of the war in this theater.

Missouri Units Furnished	
Confederate	
Infantry regiments	36
Infantry battalions	4
Infantry brigades	3
Sharpshooter units	3
Misc. infantry units	41
Cavalry regiments	23
Cavalry brigades	1
Cavalry battalions	5
Misc. cavalry units	62
Light artillery batteries	7
Misc. artillery units	19
State Guards units	92
Provost Guards	1
Union	
Infantry regiments	73
Colored infantry regiments	4
Infantry battalions	13
3-month regiments	8
Sharpshooter units	1
Home Guard units	56
Militia regiments	127
Misc. infantry units	4
Cavalry regiments	16
Cavalry battalions	8
Cavalry militia regiments	20
Misc. cavalry units	14
Light artillery regiments	2
Light artillery battalions	2
Light artillery batteries	17
Horse artillery	1
Engineering regiments	2
Misc. units	4
Sailors/marine personnel	151
Colored troops	8,344

MISSOURI UNION ARMY DEATHS

Troops Furnished	Killed/Mortally Wounded	Died of Disease	Died of Other Causes	Total
100,616	3,317	9,243	1,325	13,885

Nebraska

"That guerrilla warfare is a horrible business . . . when it comes for men to watch from behind trees and bushes and shoot one another down in cold blood like wild beasts it is terrible to think of."

THOMAS KEEN, 1ST NEBRASKA VOLUNTEER CAVALRY, MARCH 31, 1864,
DESCRIBING THE WAR IN SOUTHERN MISSOURI

The territory that is now Nebraska first became part of the United States with the Louisiana Purchase of 1803, having previously been claimed by France and, before that, by Spain.

Thereafter "Nebraska" became, for a time, part of the Missouri Territory but reverted to an unorganized status when the state of Missouri was admitted to the Union in 1821. The region was home to various Native-American tribes, including Arapahoe, Pawnee, and Siouan groups.

By the mid-19th century, settlers were streaming west in ever-increasing numbers and Native-Americans were steadily being dispossessed of their lands. America's victory in the war with Mexico, the opening up of California, and the massive mineral finds there and elsewhere, helped incorporate the Nebraska area into the expanding settlement frontier and made it important as a route to points further west.

The Nebraska Territory was therefore established and organized by Congress under the Kansas-Nebraska Act of 1854. Nebraska then was considerably larger than the modern state, including parts of present-day Colorado, Idaho, and South Dakota which passed to these areas when they became territories in 1861–63. Crucial to Nebraska's future was the question of whether it would be a free or slave territory; a question that was left to be decided locally under the doctrine of popular sovereignty. Only a very few slaves lived in Nebraska in this early period (the 1860 U.S. Census recorded the territory's population as just under 29,000 of whom only fifteen were slaves) and slavery was finally prohibited by large majorities in the state legislature in 1861.

Most citizens in the state were strongly opposed to secession and large numbers answered President Lincoln's call for volunteers for the Union Army. In fact, the territory's contribution to the Union forces during the war was substantial when compared to its population. In all, 3,157 saw military service, or at least one-third of all men of military age. The first men to volunteer may have initially believed that they

were enlisting for service within the territory only and expected to be involved in operations against Indians, rather than fighting the South. At the start of the war, however, most regular troops in the territory were withdrawn east, leaving only minimal numbers watching the emigrant and supply trails to the West. Fort Kearny, with some 125 men, was, for a time, Nebraska's only significant garrison.

Although no Confederate forces entered Nebraska and no battles were fought there, some former Confederate soldiers did see active service against Indians in Nebraska in the Civil War period. These were so-called "galvanized Yankees", former Southern soldiers made prisoners of war who had offered allegiance to the Union and were released into military duty far from the war's battlefields.

BREVET MAJOR GENERAL JOHN M. THAYER (1820–1906)

Thayer, a native of Massachusetts, came to Nebraska in 1854. Soon active in local politics as a Republican he also became commander of the territory militia and when the Civil War began he played a leading part in raising the 1st Nebraska Infantry, resigning from the state legislature to become its first colonel. He also played a leading role in having the regiment sent east. As he later commented, "We were tired of fighting Indians, and since it had to be, we wanted a try at fighting white men." Thayer commanded a brigade at Fort Donelson and afterward participated in the Vicksburg Campaign and then the later stages of the fighting in Arkansas.

After the war, Thayer returned to Nebraska politics and was active in the negotiations that led to Nebraska's statehood in 1867. He later became one of the new state's first U.S. senators alongside Thomas Tipton, who had been the chaplain of the 1st Nebraska throughout the war. Thayer was not re-elected in 1871 but, later in the 1870s, became Governor of the Wyoming Territory before returning to become Nebraska's governor in from 1887 to 1892.

THE 1ST NEBRASKA VOLUNTEER INFANTRY REGIMENT

Nebraska's initial military contribution to the Union forces was the 1st Nebraska Volunteer Infantry Regiment, which was mustered in June 1861 and left Omaha in July. It was sent to the southern Missouri area where it remained until early 1862, trying to hunt down various bands of rebels.

In February 1862, the 1st Nebraska saw more significant service as part of Grant's force in northwestern Tennessee. On February 15th, it helped beat back a breakout attempt by the Confederate garrison of Fort Donelson, leading to the fort's surrender the next day. The 1st Nebraska also played a significant part in the second day of the Battle of Shiloh, April 7, 1862. The Nebraskans arrived at the end of the first day's fighting and joined in the successful Union advance the next day.

These were the only major battles fought by Nebraskan troops, but the 1st Nebraska – redesignated as the 1st Nebraska Cavalry in 1863 – continued to serve in the bitter and demanding guerrilla and partisan struggle in southern Missouri and northern Arkansas until mid-1864. This was a demanding assignment in various ways. The climate and terrain were often challenging while poor leadership exacerbated a lack of supplies, leading to much hardship for the men. Malaria and other severe illnesses were common. There were threats of mutiny at various times and even clashes, including fatalities, with a Ohio regiment that the Nebraskans claimed had left them in the lurch by a cowardly retreat during the Shiloh fighting. At times some Nebraskans also felt that their efforts were overlooked; as the sole regiment from their sparsely populated and distant territory they attracted little attention in the press.

As the Civil War began, conflict with various groups of Plains Indians also escalated, though this did not at first effect Nebraska to a substantial extent, with most of the significant fighting occurring in present-day Colorado, the Dakotas, and Minnesota. (The 2nd Nebraska Cavalry, raised in fall 1862, participated

The Civil War memorial outside the Dawson County courthouse, Nebraska.

in some of these actions, serving in Brigadier Alfred Sully's expedition against the Sioux in North Dakota in 1863, and losing a small number of men killed in the action at Whitestone Hill that September.) In the summer of 1864, the enlistments of the original members of the 1st Nebraska expired and the troops were given a furlough in Nebraska. On their return to service they were not sent back to Arkansas as they expected but, instead, remained in Nebraska. The clashes between Native-Americans and whites were increasingly threatening the overland routes along the Platte River across Nebraska and the men were needed to help protect them. From that summer to the next there were numerous Indian raids on wagon trains, supply stations, and ranches

all along the North and South Platte, both within Nebraska and farther west.

For the soldiers this duty mostly involved months of hardship and boredom, guarding and patrolling in difficult conditions, and rarely, if ever, meeting a hostile Indian. Nevertheless, at times, especially in 1864, Indian attacks did succeed in effectively closing the trails for short periods, with ranches and stagecoach stations being destroyed and cattle and horses taken. Even so, the mass of goods and people flowing west scarcely slackened and in the end the outcome was never truly in doubt. This phase of the Indian Wars came to an end with the U.S. Army's successful Powder River Campaign in the Dakotas in 1865.

NEBRASKA UNION ARMY DEATHS

Troops Furnished	Killed/Mortally Wounded	Died of Disease	Died of Other Causes	Total
3,157*	35	159	45	239

* NEBRASKA FURNISHED TWO CAVALRY REGIMENTS AND ONE BATTALION.

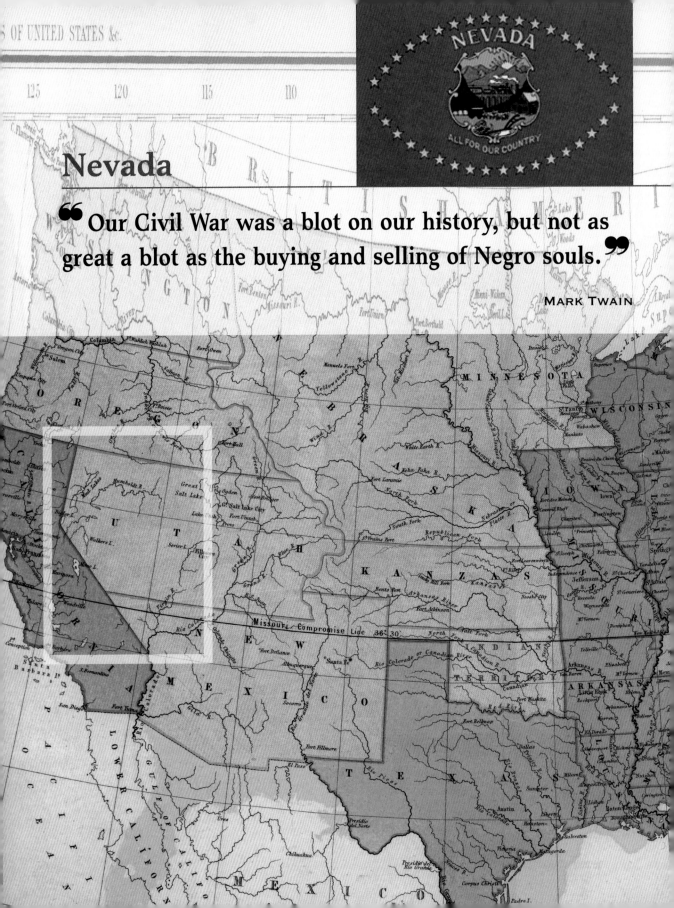

Nevada

ALL FOR OUR COUNTRY

> " Our Civil War was a blot on our history, but not as great a blot as the buying and selling of Negro souls. "

MARK TWAIN

The first flag flown in Nevada appeared in 1905 (above) and then changed in 1915 to include the coat of arms.

The area including the modern state of Nevada became a part of the United States when it was acquired from Mexico under the terms of the Treaty of Guadalupe Hidalgo at the end of the Mexican–American War.

Spanish travelers from Mexico had first come to the region during the 18th century and various American "mountain men" are known to have visited the area from the 1820s onward. It had, of course, long been the home of Native-Americans, notably groups of Shoshone and Paiute.

"Nevada" became an organized part of the United States in 1850, when the Utah Territory was established, covering an area much larger than the modern state of Utah. Initially, the largest group of settlers were Mormons, but non-Mormon fortune-seekers soon began making modest gold finds in the far west of the territory. Their relations with the Mormon communities to the east were troubled and, consequently, they began moves to establish a separate jurisdiction. This was recognized in March, 1861, with the establishment of the Nevada Territory. At that time the territory did not include a significant area in the east of the modern state, which was taken from Utah and added to Nevada in 1863. A smaller area in the south was acquired from Arizona in 1867.

To complete the sequence of political changes, Nevada was admitted to the Union as the 36th state on October 31, 1864. This followed the usual preliminary stages of

MARK TWAIN IN VIRGINIA CITY

The writer Samuel Langhorne Clemens (1835–1910) was a Civil War era resident of Virginia City and it was there that he first used his more famous pen-name: Mark Twain.

Clemens was born and brought up in Missouri and, as a young man, worked as a printer and journalist before training as a riverboat pilot on the Mississippi. When the Civil War began, river traffic on the Mississippi was greatly reduced and Clemens served briefly in a volunteer unit of the Confederate forces. He soon resigned, however, and set off for Nevada, accompanying his older brother Orion who had been appointed secretary to Governor Nye of Nevada. (Their journey west provided material for his 1872 novel *Roughing It*.) Here, Clemens worked for a time as a miner along the California–Nevada border, with little success, and began contributing articles to local newspapers. From 1862 to 1863, he lived in Virginia City, working as a journalist for the *Territorial Enterprise*. During this time he used a number of pen-names, including Mark Twain. In 1864, he moved on to California, where fame soon found him.

Nevada Union Units Furnished	
Infantry battalions	1
Cavalry battalions	1

In March 1861, Abraham Lincoln appointed James Nye (1815–76) Territorial Governor of Nevada. Nye served until 1864, when the territory received statehood and the governor switched hats and became a U. S. senator. During his period in office, Nye raised two battalions: one infantry to serve as garrison and one cavalry for Indian control. For a brief period of time Mark Twain served as his secretary and left an account of their relationship in *Sketches Old and New.*

a territorial convention (held in the territorial capital, Carson City, in July that year) and then approval by a public vote. The process was rushed through before the November presidential election, with the state constitution being sent to Washington, D.C. by telegraph in what is claimed to be the longest telegram ever sent. The new state, as anticipated, provided Lincoln with its two electoral college votes.

One of the new state's first U.S. senators, William M. Stewart, is credited with drafting the 15th Amendment to the U.S. Constitution, in 1869, stating that the right to vote was not to be denied "on account of race, color, or previous condition of servitude." Nevada was the first state to ratify the amendment, but only after Stewart had reassured his constituents that they could still prohibit Chinese and Irish immigrants from voting. The amendment came into force in 1870.

Nevada's population on admission was far lower than was usual for a territory achieving statehood. The 1860 Census reported a total of 6,857 people (and no slaves), and some 16,400 votes were cast in the 1864 election. But Nevada's importance to the country far exceeded the size of its population. Throughout the 1850s, a few hundred prospectors had found modest amounts of gold in the area around what is now Virginia City. In 1859, however, the outside world learned of a much larger find: the so-called Comstock Lode, an enormous strike of silver and gold. Precisely who found the lode and exactly when is uncertain but it is named after one Henry Comstock, and Virginia City is said to take its name from another of those who were initially involved, James Finney, nicknamed "Old Virginny". As news of the strike spread, new settlers flocked to Nevada and Virginia City became a boom town, home to over 15,000 people (roughly three-quarters of them men) by 1863.

Neither the original finders or most of the new arrivals ever made their fortunes. Comstock and his associates mostly sold their interests for no more than a few thousand dollars and, while miners could make a large income by the standards of the time, living costs in the area were proportionately high and money was easily frittered away in the saloons, gambling dens, and brothels of the boom towns. Mining also quickly became industrial in scale, requiring investment in materials and machinery, and knowledge of advanced techniques of extracting metal from the ore.

Each year through the 1860s the Comstock Lode yielded silver and gold worth tens of millions of dollars, contributing greatly to the Union's economy. Other finds in the state, notably around Austin and Eureka, were quickly exploited, inspiring further settlement and exploration. In fact, Nevada's wealth was its only great contribution to the Union cause during the Civil War; there were no military engagements with Confederate forces in the territory or state in the course of the war and no units from Nevada participated in any of the war's battles. In the course of the war the territory did, however, raise two battalions of troops, the 1st Nevada Volunteer Cavalry and the 1st Nevada Volunteer Infantry to participate in local defence. Also important, however, was the first transcontinental telegraph line, completed in the fall of 1861. The work involved extending the line from the previous terminus at Carson City, in western Nevada, across the territory to Salt Lake City.

Nevertheless, Nevada was not entirely peaceful. In the lead-up to the war, the influx of prospectors had led to disputes with local Native-Americans over land and water and there were also clashes between Indians and the many wagon trains of settlers and supplies heading across the territory for California, with allegations of thefts and atrocities on both sides. In 1860, the so-called Pyramid Lake War had broken out, in which Northern Paiutes were defeated by a U.S. Army and California militia force. One of the results of the war was the establishment of Fort Churchill, which became the main military base in the territory in the Civil War years, though its garrison was always small (usually no more than 200 men). As in other Western territories, the outbreak of the Civil War led to a reduction in the U.S. military force stationed in the region. The main duty of those that remained was to protect the settler and supply trails passing across the territory.

In the summer of 1862, parts of the 3rd California Infantry under the command of Colonel Patrick

Patrick Connor ended up as a general, receiving his promotion in 1863 after leading the Bear River Massacre of Soshoni Indians.

Connor entered Nevada – though most of the men continued on to Utah, both to overawe the Mormon population – suspected of disloyalty – and to engage in operations there against the Indians. Nevada's own regiments were not formed until 1863: the 1st Cavalry in the summer and the 1st Infantry shortly before the end of the year. Both were mustered at Fort Churchill. Several companies of the 1st Cavalry served in Utah through the summer of 1864 and the remainder of the battalion and of the 1st Infantry was involved in patrolling and scouting along the emigrant trails and in expeditions to more distant parts of the state, including the northerly Humboldt County area. The 1st Infantry was disbanded in December 1865 and the 1st Cavalry in summer 1866. As the casualty figures show, Nevada troops saw little combat.

NEVADA UNION ARMY DEATHS

Troops Furnished	Killed/Mortally Wounded	Died of Disease	Died of Other Causes	Total
1,080	2	29	2	33

New Hampshire

> **We shall speak against slavery as we have hitherto done. We can find no language that has the power to express the hatred we have towards so vile and so wicked an institution.**

MOSES CHANEY, EDITORIAL IN *THE MORNING STAR*, DOVER,
NEW HAMPSHIRE, 1853

No Civil War battle took place in New Hampshire but, like all the states of the Northeast, large numbers of its citizens served in the Union forces while its industries provided a variety of raw materials and goods to the Union military.

New Hampshire's population expanded considerably in the first half of the 19th century, from 214,000 in 1800 to 326,000 in 1860 on the eve of the Civil War and some 33,000 men from the state served in the course of the war, a typical proportion of roughly one in ten of the population. Perhaps surprisingly, slaves in New Hampshire were never formally freed, though the 1860 census found none in the state and there had been none as far back as 1810 (though eight were reported in 1830 and one in 1840). Although slavery itself was thus almost unknown in New Hampshire throughout the 19th century, other forms of discrimination continued. In an autobiographical novel called *Our Nig: Sketches from the Life of a Free Black*, Harriet Wilson of Milford wrote a critical account of the indenture system. Her book, published in 1859, is regarded as the first novel published by an African-American, male or female.

In the early 19th century, New Hampshire's traditional industries were lumber inland, and shipbuilding and related trades in coastal areas. These continued to be important during the Civil War but had by then been joined by a range of other activities. As in other areas of New England, water power provided by the state's rivers led to the development of mill towns, working mainly in the textile industries. Manchester was the largest center of this Industrial Revolution, producing cotton goods in particular but also rifles, general machinery, and railroad locomotives. Among other towns, Rochester became one of the nation's largest

Soldiers' Monument, Merrimack Common, Manchester, New Hampshire.

PRESIDENT FRANKLIN PIERCE (1804–69)

The fourteenth President of the United States, serving between 1853 and 1857, Pierce is the only president to date to come from New Hampshire. In retrospect, he is generally seen as an unsuccessful leader whose actions and policies helped bring about the Civil War.

Pierce supported the idea of Manifest Destiny – that the United States ought to expand into new territories – but did so in ways that were seen as leading to the expansion of slavery and which, therefore, provoked antagonism and further strife. Pierce also favored proposals for the annexation of Cuba, though he soon had to back-track from these. He did, however, succeed in carrying out the Gadsen Purchase, buying land from Mexico to add to the Territory of New Mexico. This was controversial enough, but his support for the 1854 Kansas-Nebraska Act and its repudiation of the Compromise of 1850 was even more strongly resented. As violence escalated, Pierce recognized the fraudulently elected pro-slavery Kansas legislature. Worse troubles would soon follow.

THADDEUS LOWE (1832–1913)

Thaddeus Lowe earned Civil War fame was as the Union Army's first chief aeronaut, pioneering the use of balloons in military reconnaissance. In later life he became a celebrated inventor in chemistry and other fields.

Born in Jefferson Mills, New Hampshire, Lowe was mainly self-taught and, by the late 1850s, described himself as a professor of chemistry. Despite his lack of formal education he had, in fact, developed considerable expertise in making and using hydrogen and other lighter-than-air gases. He built his first balloon in 1857 and was soon planning giant balloons with which he hoped to make a trans-Atlantic flight. After various setbacks, his first major rehearsal was in April 1861. Intended to be a flight from Cincinnati to the East Coast he came down in South Carolina after a 900-mile trip just days after Fort Sumter and was nearly executed as a Union spy.

Summoned to Washington, D.C. on his return home, Lowe quickly found himself in the service of the Union Army. He provided some useful reports to General McDowell during the First Bull Run Campaign and later had some success during the 1862 Peninsula battles. Nevertheless, there were always difficulties. Lowe crashed behind enemy lines at Bull Run, for example, and met repeated problems with his gas-generating equipment. He resigned in May 1863 and balloons featured little in the war thereafter.

Thaddeus S. Lowe replenishes the balloon *Intrepid* from the balloon *Constitution* during the Battle of Fair Oaks, Virginia, May 1862.

makers of boots and shoes, and especially of blankets for the Army. As might be expected of such a industrially developed state, New Hampshire's communications and transportation facilities were also excellent. In the pre-war period, railroads had been extensively developed to link the state's industries with their markets and suppliers, with Nashua, for example, standing at the intersection of six different rail lines.

In politics, New Hampshire and its leaders played a particularly influential role in the events of the period leading up to the Civil War, and arguably had a major role in widening the divisions that caused the conflict. From the 1840s, New Hampshire became one of the strongholds of abolitionism, though the importance of cotton milling – with its dependence on supplies from the South – meant that such views were never universally held. Places like Milford,

Canaan, and Thornton were significant "stops" on the Underground Railroad transporting escaped slaves to Canada. Moses Cheney of Thornton, a friend of Stephen Douglass, was one important figure. Working in Dover, Cheney printed and later edited the abolitionist newspaper *The Morning Star* from 1833 until after the Civil War.

Two candidates in the 1852 presidential election hailed from New Hampshire and they epitomized the disagreements that would shortly lead the nation into Civil War. The successful candidate, Franklin Pierce, had Southern sympathies, whereas John P. Hale was the nominee of the antislavery Free Soil Party. Hale began his political life as a Democrat but quarreled with his party over the slavery issue and had spells in and out of office through the 1840s and 1850s as opinion in the state swung back and forth. He was elected as a Free Soil candidate to the U.S.

Senate in 1846 and strongly opposed the Mexican War because he believed it would increase the number of slave states and territories in the Union. Another important leader of the Free Soil Party, and later Lincoln's highly effective treasury secretary, Salmon P. Chase, was also a New Hampshire native. However, the Free Soil Party lost all significance after Hale's poor showing in the 1852 election, when he won only five percent of the popular vote. Nevertheless, members of the party were important early recruits to the Republican Party which began forming in 1854 in response to the Kansas-Nebraska Act.

In the 1860 election, whatever divisions there may have been previously, Lincoln comfortably carried New Hampshire and as war preparations began in the spring of 1861 Governor Ichabod Goodwin played a notable part in getting the state's military potential mobilized. Indeed, with the state legislature out of session at the time, he borrowed money in his own name to begin arming two infantry regiments. The legislature supported his actions when it reconvened and New Hampshire took its place in the Union ranks for the remainder of the war.

ICHABOD GOODWIN (1794–1882)

Goodwin was an ambitious man who wanted a political career, though this remained elusive until 1860 when he was elected Governor of New Hampshire. He served one term of two years during which he became a good friend of Abraham Lincoln. When the president called for volunteers, the New Hampshire legislature was on recess but Goodwin ignored protocol and borrowed $680,000 from banks to supply and arm two regiments. Despite performing several other extra-legal activities to get the state on a war footing, Goodwin received the backing of the legislature, which later approved all his actions.

New Hampshire Units Furnished	
Infantry regiments	18
Sharpshooter units	3
Cavalry regiments	2
Heavy artillery regiments	1
Heavy artillery companies	2
Light artillery batteries	1
Militia companies	2
Sailors/marine personnel	882
Colored troops	125

NEW HAMPSHIRE UNION ARMY DEATHS

Troops Furnished	Killed/Mortally Wounded	Died of Disease	Died of Other Causes	Total
32,930	1,903	2,427	552	4,882

SERGEANT MAJOR ABRAHAM COHN (1832–97)

Sergeant Major (later first lieutenant) Abraham Cohn of the 6th New Hampshire Infantry was one of the 1,522 Civil War recipients of the Medal of Honor. Like many others who fought in the war, he had only been in America for a small part of his life before he fought so bravely for his new country. Originally from Prussia, he did not arrive in the U.S.A. until he was twenty-eight years old and may, therefore, have had some military experience. Although relatively little is known about his earlier life, the fact that he did not enlist until January 1864 and was quickly promoted to sergeant major in March demonstrates a degree of character and maturity. He was also a man of some education as his pre-war occupation was given as "teacher."

Cohn's Medal of Honor was awarded for his actions in two major battles. On May 6, 1864, during the Battle of the Wilderness, the 6th New Hampshire was with Hancock's Corps when it was driven back in some disorder by a surprise assault by Longstreet's Rebels. Cohn rallied fleeing soldiers from a number of regiments and led them back into battle in what must have been an amazing display of natural authority and determination. Then in July, during the hideous carnage of the Battle of the Crater at Petersburg, Cohn, according to his citation, "bravely and coolly carried orders to the advanced line under severe fire," a rather bald description of what was clearly astonishing bravery.

NEW HAMPSHIRE'S REGIMENTS

New Hampshire's infantry regiments and sharpshooter units were typical of formations from the Northeast. The majority of their service was with the Army of the Potomac and included participation in all the war's major battles in that theater. Additionally, some regiments spent significant periods in operations on the coast of the Carolinas, especially later in the war in the Army of the James. The 1st New Hampshire Cavalry, for example, fought in this area in 1864–65 while

WALTER HARRIMAN (1817–84)

Harriman served two terms as the Governor of New Hampshire. He ended the war as a brevet brigadier general in the Union Army. Appointed colonel of the 11th New Hampshires, he was captured at the Battle of the Wilderness and sent south as a prisoner of war. He was exchanged in September 1864.

other units, including the 6th Infantry, also served in the Western Theater, participating successfully in the Vicksburg Campaign. The regiment's colonel in 1863, Simon G. Griffin, became a major general and division commander later in the war.

Several New Hampshire regiments fought with distinction at Gettysburg. The 2nd, 5th, and 12th Infantry all fought on the Union left flank on July 2nd, the second day of the battle, helping repulse the rebel attacks that, in retrospect, can be seen as the last chance Lee's men had to gain victory. Indeed, the 2nd and 12th took dreadful casualties with the 2nd reporting 219 killed, wounded, and missing out of an initial strength of only 353 men while the 12th lost over 100 out of 224. The 5th's losses, meanwhile, included its noted colonel, Edward E. Cross. In the war as a whole the 5th New Hampshire had the highest combat casualties of any Union regiment with over a thousand killed and wounded.

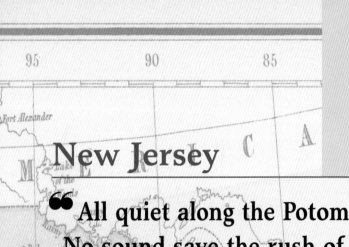

New Jersey

“All quiet along the Potomac to-night;
No sound save the rush of the river;
While soft falls the dew on the face of the dead-
The picket's off duty forever!”

NEW JERSEY POET ETHEL LYNN BEERS (1827–79)

New Jersey is often described as the cradle of the Industrial Revolution in America. Its population more than tripled between 1800 and 1860 – from 211,000 to 672,000 – and its industrial output and transportation infrastructure were transformed in line with this expansion.

It was in precisely these areas that the South could not hope to compete with the North during the Civil War and, while no fighting took place in New Jersey, the state, its people, and its industries played a vital role in the war effort of the North.

In the 18th century New Jersey's economy depended principally on farming, with obvious major markets nearby in New York and Philadelphia. In the years leading up to the Civil War transportation of agricultural products was an important driver in the expansion of the region's infrastructure. First canals – like the 107-mile Morris Canal that linked the Delaware River and the Hudson – and, later, railroads, moved agricultural products and at the same time created demand for industrial products like steel for railroad track or locomotives or barges.

The development of Paterson epitomized the industrial development of the state as a whole. Paterson was not formally incorporated as a city until March, 1861, but by then it had been long established as one of the greatest industrial centers in the nation. Initially, its main interests were connected to cotton milling but by the time of the Civil War iron and steel and related trades were dominant. Other New Jersey municipalities were also booming. Newark, for example, was the nation's leading leather-manufacturing center

GENERAL SAMUEL COOPER (1798–76)

Samuel Cooper served as the most senior officer in the Confederate Army throughout the war but his work in an administrative role gained him none of the fame that came to the likes of Robert E. Lee or Stonewall Jackson.

He was born in Bergen County, New Jersey, and entered West Point as a teenager, graduating thirty-sixth in a class of forty students in 1815 and being commissioned into the artillery. From the mid-1830s most of his service was in Washington, D.C. apart from a brief and successful period of active duty in the Seminole War of 1841–42. In 1852, now a colonel, he became the army's adjutant general and held that post until 1861.

Cooper had married in 1827. His wife (née Maria Mason) was from Virginia and had connections to various prominent Southern families. In the 1850s, Cooper also became friendly with Jefferson Davis, then U.S. Secretary of War. These relationships fostered strong Southern sympathies although Cooper was, himself, a Northerner, and he resigned from the U.S. Army in March 1861. Within days he was commissioned into the Confederate forces and appointed as adjutant and inspector general. He served in this post throughout the war, reporting directly to President Davis. Later in 1861 he was appointed a full general, the most senior of seven officers who would hold that rank in the South.

At the end of the war Cooper was instrumental in preserving the South's military records from destruction, a vital contribution to modern knowledge of the period's history. After the war he lived in Virginia, working as a small farmer in comparative poverty up to his death in 1876.

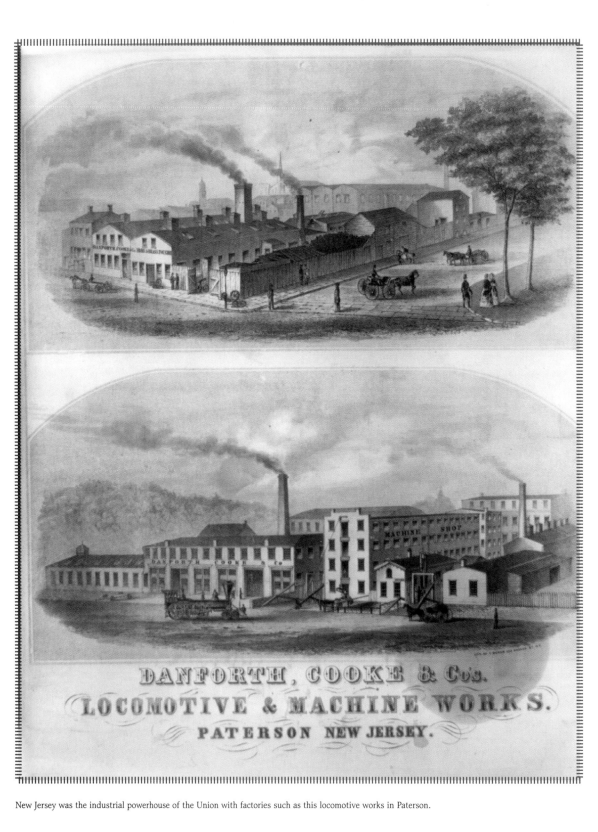

DANFORTH, COOKE & Co's.
LOCOMOTIVE & MACHINE WORKS.
PATERSON NEW JERSEY.

New Jersey was the industrial powerhouse of the Union with factories such as this locomotive works in Paterson.

(and leather, of course, was a vital part in much military equipment as well as footwear).

If New Jersey's industries stood firm for the Union, the state's political position and its attitudes toward slavery were more ambiguous. The two wartime governors, Charles Olden (Republican, in office 1860–63) and Joel Parker (Democrat, in office 1863–66) both strongly backed the Union cause and were generally supported by the legislature. However, New Jersey was the only free state that did not support Lincoln in either the election of 1860 or in 1864. In 1860, Stephen Douglas received four of the state's electoral college votes and Lincoln three. In 1864, General George McClellan gained a narrow majority (McClellan did well in the election in New Jersey but he was not a native of the state, though he became its governor later in the 1870s).

In elections through the 1850s, in the run-up to the war, New Jersey citizens generally favored candidates who opposed any move to extend the territories where slave-holding was legal but during the conflict itself so-called "Copperheads" or "Peace Democrats" held significant influence, mostly in rural areas in the northern parts of the state. New Jersey was also the last Northern state to enact laws leading to the abolition of slavery, and the measure passed in 1804 made this a gradual process. Existing slaves, and their children, were often compelled to enter long-lasting or even permanent "apprenticeships." At the close of the Civil War, a small number of African-Americans in New Jersey were still apprentices under this system and, in effect, remained in bondage until the ratification of the Thirteenth Amendment in 1865. New Jersey itself was slow to ratify the amendment, not doing so until early in 1866.

Some of the state's uncertain attitudes toward slavery probably stemmed from the pre-war ties of its industries to markets and raw material suppliers in the South. On the other side, there was a strong Quaker tradition in the state, which vigorously opposed slavery. The Underground Railroad was active in New Jersey, passing escaped slaves across the state to safer locations further north.

Charles Smith Olden (1799–1876) served as New Jersey's Republican governor from 1860 to 1863. Although of Quaker background, Olden did not espouse abolition and would have preferred compromise with the South. Once secession began, however, he became a staunch Unionist and raised $500,000 from state banks to finance mobilization. He disagreed with some of Abraham Lincoln's policies on civil rights but fully cooperated with the president on supporting the war effort.

Judson Kilpatrick – nicknamed "Kilcavalry" for his complete disregard for the lives his men – was a hard-living Union general whose indiscretions could not hide the ability that made Sherman say "I know that Kilpatrick is a hell of a damned fool, but I want just that sort of man to command my cavalry."

Waud's brilliant sketch of Kearny at Williamsburg, where he is said to have rallied his men with the cry, "I'm a one-armed Jersey son-of-a-gun, follow me!"

PHILIP KEARNY AND THE 1ST NEW JERSEY BRIGADE

Major General Philip Kearny (1815–62) had one of the most colorful lives of any Civil War officer. He was born into a wealthy New York family whose members included several notable soldiers and, after initially studying law, joined the army himself in 1837. He saw active service in the Mexican War, losing an arm while leading a cavalry charge, but left the army in 1851 and settled in New Jersey. Ever adventurous, however, he saw combat again in the French cavalry, being decorated for bravery at the Battle of Solferino (the bloodbath that inspired the creation of the Red Cross) in 1859.

In 1861, he rejoined the U.S. Army as a brigadier general and was given command of the 1st New Jersey Brigade, which he trained very effectively. He was soon promoted to a divisional command but in September, 1862, during the Battle of Chantilly, he accidentally rode into the Confederate lines and was shot and killed. The town in New Jersey where he lived was later renamed Kearny in his honor.

To the end of the war, the 1st New Jersey Brigade had the unusual distinction of being composed entirely of New Jersey units. It initially included the 1st, 2nd, and 3rd New Jersey Volunteer Infantry regiments, all of which were raised in the late spring and early summer of 1861, and these were soon joined by the 4th Regiment. The brigade saw its first important actions during the Peninsula Campaign of June 1862. The 4th Infantry suffered badly at Gaines' Mill in an earlier phase of that campaign but the brigade played a notable role in stemming Confederate attacks during the Battle of Glendale three days later. After these actions Kearny was vociferous in his condemnation of General McClellan's timid retreat.

Later in the war, the 1st New Jersey Brigade also saw combat at many of the most vicious battles, including Fredericksburg, Gettysburg, and the 1864 Overland Campaign. The 15th New Jersey Volunteer Infantry, which joined the brigade in late September 1862, had the heaviest losses of its units with some 370 men killed in action or dying of other causes.

When the war began, in common with almost all parts of the nation New Jersey experienced a wave of enthusiastic enlistment and units began training at camps at such places as Hoboken, Newark, Trenton, and various others. Figures in sources vary, but at least 67,500, and perhaps as many as 74,300, citizens of New Jersey served in total, roughly one in ten of the population of the state as recorded in the 1860 census. Military personnel included some 8,000 serving in the navy or marines and almost 3,000 "colored troops," slightly more than ten percent of the state's pre-war African-American population. The figures for war casualties are also slightly uncertain, with figures for deaths ranging from 5,700 to 6,300, slightly under ten percent of those serving, or about one percent of the state's population. More than half of those died from non-combat causes, including over 400 who died while prisoners of war in Confederate hands.

As might be expected, New Jersey regiments fought mainly in the Eastern Theater and played a significant part in many of the major battles from first to last. Perhaps the most famous New Jersey military formation was the 1st New Jersey Brigade, commanded for a time by General Phil Kearny. The brigade's service is commemorated by a notable memorial on the Gettysburg battlefield. Other significant New Jersey units and commanders included the 12th and 15th Volunteer Infantry, Judson Kilpatrick, George Bayard, Charles Harker, and – on the Southern side – Samuel Cooper. The Union Navy's Samuel F. Du Pont was an influential New Jersey naval officer.

THE 12TH NEW JERSEY VOLUNTEER INFANTRY REGIMENT

This regiment was formally accepted into service in September 1862 and joined the Army of the Potomac at the end of the year, taking its place in Hays' brigade of the 3rd Division, II Corps. It was the only New Jersey regiment assigned to that corps. The 12th's first major battle was Chancellorsville in May 1863, in which it lost 179 men, killed, wounded, and missing.

Samuel Gibbs French was born in New Jersey on November 22, 1818, and graduated from West Point in 1843. As a major general in the Confederate army, he commanded a division in the Army of Tennessee in the Western Theater and served with distinction. He died in 1910.

The regiment's most famous exploits came at Gettysburg, however. On the second day of the battle, July 2, 1863, four companies from the 12th captured a farm in no-man's land between the armies' lines that was being used by Confederate sharpshooters, taking about 100 of them prisoner. On the third day, the regiment also participated in the repulse of Pickett's Charge.

In 1864, the 12th was heavily engaged during in the Wilderness Campaign and in the fighting around the Siege of Petersburg. It began these battles with some 425 men but by early 1865 had only ninety left. It fought finally in the Appomattox Campaign and was present at Lee's surrender.

REAR ADMIRAL SAMUEL FRANCIS DU PONT (1803–65)

One of the most important commanders of the U.S. Navy in the earlier stages of the Civil War, Samuel was born in New Jersey and belonged to the noted du Pont family, whose gunpowder business in nearby Delaware was the nation's largest supplier during the Civil War and the forerunner of the modern du Pont chemical corporation. His father had not met the same business success as his uncle, however, and Samuel was accordingly sent to take up a naval career.

He entered the navy in 1815, aged twelve, and by the outbreak of the Mexican War was a commander serving off California. With his sloop *Cyane* he played a notable part in the capture from the Mexicans of San Diego and then in the subsequent blockade and landing operations off the Mexican coast. Most of his career to that point had been afloat but there then followed a brief spell on shore as superintendent of the U.S. Naval Academy and involvement in various measures to modernize the navy as a whole.

At the outbreak of the Civil War, du Pont was commandant of the Philadelphia Navy Yard and soon became a leader in the navy's planning for the war against the Confederacy. In 1861, he took command of the South Atlantic Blockading Squadron with the rank of flag officer. One of his first acts, and an important stage in the development of the blockade, was the capture of Port Royal in November 1861. However, in April 1863, now a rear admiral, Du Pont led a naval attack on Charleston that proved a dismal failure. Du Pont had argued against carrying out the attack with a solely naval force but was nonetheless blamed for the outcome and was relieved of his command three months later. He died in 1865.

Rear Admiral Samuel Francis Du Pont.

New Jersey Union Units Furnished	
Infantry regiments	40
Three-month infantry regiments	4
Cavalry regiments	3
Light artillery batteries	5
Sailors/marine personnel	8,129
Colored troops	c.3,000

NEW JERSEY UNION ARMY DEATHS

Troops Furnished	Killed/Mortally Wounded	Died of Disease	Died of Other Causes	Total
67,500	2,578	2,415	761	5,754

This monument to the 14th Regiment New Jersey Volunteer Infantry stands off Urbana Pike near Frederick, Maryland. The 14th New Jersey Infantry mustered in for three years service on August 26, 1862, commanded by Colonel William Snyder Truex. They fought in many battles including that of Monocacy, near Frederick, on July 9, 1864. The regiment lost a total of 257 men in its years of service: 8 officers and 139 enlisted men killed or mortally wounded, 110 enlisted men died of disease.

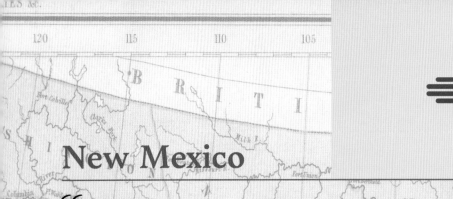

New Mexico

" Citizens of New Mexico, your Territory has been invaded, the integrity of your soil has been attacked . . . and the enemy is already at your doors. "

U.S. Territorial Governor Henry Connelly's call to arms,
September 9, 1861

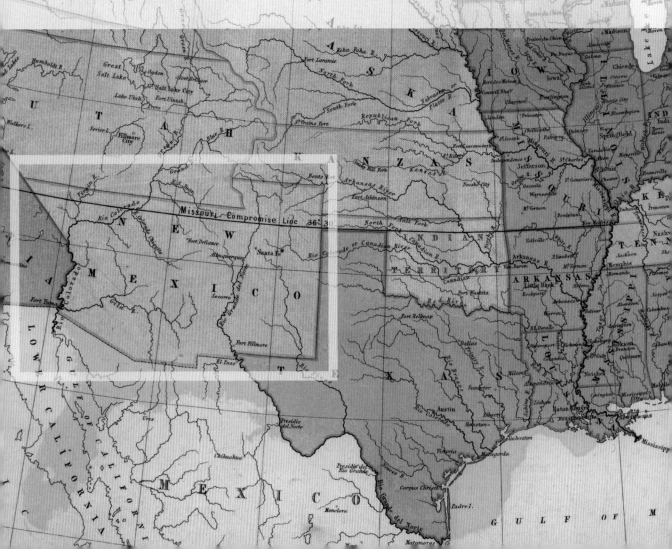

When New Mexico was admitted to the Union as the 47th state in January, 1912, it had substantially different boundaries than when it first became part of the United States in the aftermath of the Mexican–American War.

Under the 1848 Treaty of Guadalupe Hidalgo its borders were uncertain, with the region east of the Rio Grande being claimed by Texas. This issue was resolved as part of the Compromise of 1850, a wide-ranging series of agreements on various issues between the slave and free states. The New Mexico Territory was thus formally organized in September, 1850, and included the area previously disputed. At this point in its history, it covered most of the present-day states of New Mexico and Arizona as well as small parts of modern Colorado and Nevada. It was enlarged further in 1853, by the Gadsen Purchase in which the United States bought land from Mexico in what is now southern New Mexico and Arizona.

In 1850, the U.S. Census recorded the non-Indian population of New Mexico as some 61,500. These people were largely of Hispanic origin and generally cared little about the issues that were already dividing the states. By 1860, however, the population had increased by more than half and attitudes had changed. In the northern parts of the territory new settlers had ties stretching back to the Missouri Valley and mainly held antislavery views; in the southern areas connections were to Texas and the South. In fact, Southerners had been active in promoting the Gadsen Purchase and had hoped the land acquired would be added to the Union as "Arizona" and be used as the route of a transcontinental railroad linking the South with California.

Through the 1850s, southern New Mexicans made various proposals to divide the territory, creating "Arizona" in roughly the southern half of the two modern states. All of these were blocked in the U.S. Congress. In March 1861, as the Civil War loomed, conventions meeting in Mesilla (modern New Mexico) and Tucson (Arizona) declared the secession from New Mexico of the southern areas as the Territory of Arizona and immediately began seeking admission to the Confederacy.

From 1861 to 1866, Henry Connelly (1800–66) served as the Republican Governor of the New Mexico Territory. During his term, New Mexico broke into half with the establishment of the Arizona Territory to the west. Connelly had many problems early in the Civil War because of Confederate incursions out of Texas, brought on – in part – by his successful efforts in 1861 to repeal the New Mexico Slave Act.

At that time, various U.S. Army garrisons were present in New Mexico serving in the ongoing conflicts with the territory's Apache and Navajo peoples. These took a turn for the worse in early 1861, when a clash between soldiers and Chiricahua Apaches led by Cochise began what was later called the Apache Uprising. It took place exactly as the Civil War was beginning and, as a consequence, the army was abandoning various forts so that soldiers could be sent east to help deal with the crisis in Missouri and other parts of that region. At the same time, about one-third of army officers in the Department of New Mexico resigned and set off to join the South.

Together, these developments weakened the Union position, giving the South a chance to intervene. As the Civil War began, Texas troops under Colonel John Baylor occupied Fort Bliss and other abandoned U.S. Army positions in the northwest corner of that state and in July 1861, Baylor moved into New Mexico. He occupied Mesilla on the 24th and, the next day, his 2nd Texas Mounted Rifles won an engagement with troops from the nearby Fort Fillmore, whose garrison was either killed or captured over the next few days. Baylor then proclaimed the incorporation of Arizona into the Confederacy. (In response, during 1862–63 the U.S. Congress passed laws establishing the Arizona Territory as a free soil area having the modern north–south boundary with New Mexico, not the east–west one recognized by the Confederacy.)

By now, the South had developed an ambitious scheme for the region, planning an attempt to gain control of the whole Southwest. In December 1861, Brigadier Henry Sibley, commanding the Confederate Army of New Mexico, announced the territory's annexation and, in February, began an advance from Mesilla north up the Rio Grande with some 2,500 men. His objective was not just to take control of New Mexico but to reach the Colorado goldfields and then strike west to capture Nevada and California, with all their mineral resources.

The Union force at this stage included some 3,000 men, two-thirds of them volunteers and militia, under the command of Colonel E.R.S. Canby, who concentrated his troops at Fort Craig, about 100 miles north of Mesilla. On February 20th, Sibley's army arrived and began bypassing the fort to cut its communications. The next day, the two armies fought an indecisive battle at Valverde just to the north. The Union force suffered heavier casualties – around 400 killed, wounded, and captured – and lost several artillery guns, but retired to the fort, which was too strong for Sibley to attack.

In 1861, John R. Baylor drove Union troops from the Southwest. Victory at the Battle of Mesilla saw the surrender of Federal forces and Baylor proclaimed himself the military Governor of Arizona Territory – the modern states of New Mexico and Arizona.

Although he knew that Fort Craig would be a threat to his communications, Sibley decided to continue his advance north toward Albuquerque and Santa Fe. In effect, he was abandoning his supply line and relying on what he and his men could capture from the Federals as they moved forward. Sibley's men reached Albuquerque at the beginning of March and Santa Fe on the 13th, but captured few supplies. Meanwhile, Union troops under Colonel Gabriel Paul were assembling at Fort Union, east of Santa Fe across the Sangre de Cristo range. They were joined there by reinforcements from Colorado under Colonel John Slough.

In the last days of March, 1861, parts of both armies met in and around Glorieta Pass in the Sangre de Cristo range. Paul's 1,200 men slightly outnumbered the rebel force under Lieutenant Colonel William Scurry but, even so, on March 28th, the Confederates forced the enemy army to retreat. However, while the main battle was going on, a Union detachment led by Major John Chivington came across the Confederate supply train and

NEW MEXICO UNION ARMY DEATHS

Troops Furnished	Killed/Mortally Wounded	Died of Disease	Died of Other Causes	Total
6,561	78	144	60	277

New Mexico Union Units Furnished	
Infantry regiments	5
Infantry battalions	1
Militia regiments	1
Independent militia units	4
Cavalry regiments	1
Cavalry battalions	1
Independent cavalry units	5

burned ninety wagons as well as killing 800 draft animals. The Confederates thus lost most of their supplies and ammunition and had little option but to retreat to Albuquerque.

General Canby, still in overall command of the Union forces, now began to assemble his units close by. Sibley withdrew toward Texas, hurried on his way by an engagement at Peralta on April 14th. A small detachment of his force remained at Fort Thorn, northwest of Mesilla, until July, but after they retreated to Texas no Confederate troops ever entered New Mexico again.

Although losses on each side had been in the region of 150–200 men – trivial when compared to any major battle in the Eastern Theater – the fighting at Glorieta Pass had been decisive. Sometimes called the "Gettysburg of the West", it marked the high point of the South's advance in that theater and an end to Sibley's hopes of a triumphant sweep across the Western territories. Nevertheless, the Confederates continued to make plans for a return to "their" Arizona Territory – some secessionists had retreated to Texas with Sibley's troops and set up an Arizona government there – but, instead, Union forces moved into west Texas and captured some Confederate positions as the war continued. These Union troops were chiefly from Colonel James Carleton's California Column which had advanced across Arizona, pushing the Confederates out as they came.

Carleton's men were also involved in hostilities against the Apache and Navajo as they advanced,

MAJOR GENERAL EDWARD R.S. CANBY (1817–73)

A Kentuckian, Canby was a pre-war regular soldier who saw action in the Mexican War and, afterward, had assignments in California and the Utah Territory. By 1860, he was in New Mexico and fighting the Navajo. In the New Mexico Campaign of 1861–62, his cautious defensive strategy contributed greatly to the defeat of Sibley's invasion. He then served in administrative posts in the East before returning to combat commands in 1864. After the war he held various assignments in the South during the Reconstruction era but was moved to the Pacific Northwest in 1870. In 1873, he was killed at an abortive peace conference during the Modoc War, the most senior officer to die in the Indian Wars.

CHRISTOPHER H. "KIT" CARSON (1809–68)

An iconic figure of the American frontier and famed long before his involvement in the Civil War, Carson was born in Kentucky and mostly raised in Missouri by his widowed mother. He ran away from an apprenticeship to join a wagon train bound for Santa Fe in 1826, and worked as a trapper for the next decade and more, traveling widely throughout the Southwest. He later guided John C. Frémont on his exploration expeditions and was also involved in California's rebellion against Mexico.

By the late 1850s, Carson was an Indian agent in northern New Mexico where, unlike many others, he tried to treat the Indians honestly and fairly. Commissioned into the Union Army at the start of the Civil War, he fought at Valverde and, thereafter, was principally involved in fighting the Apache and Navajo. He carried out these tasks with ruthless efficiency but retained a degree of respect for his enemies. Carson moved to Colorado with his family after the war and died there in May 1868.

and for the remainder of the Civil War Union troops in New Mexico concentrated on Native-American affairs rather than seeking new battles with the Confederacy. Carleton replaced Canby in command of the New Mexico Department in September, 1862, and took overall charge of this struggle. His most prominent subordinate was Christopher "Kit" Carson, famed "mountain man" and explorer, who served as colonel of the 1st New Mexico Volunteer Cavalry.

Following the so-called "Bascom Affair" that led to U.S. forces hanging the brother and nephews of Cochise, chief of the Chiricahua Apache, the Apache began raiding local settlers and fighting both Union and Confederate troops as they encountered them. They were initially encouraged by the Union Army's abandonment of various positions, thinking this was in fear of their attacks rather than a consequence of the Civil War. In January 1863, the Apache chief Mangas Coloradas agreed to talks with a Union officer but, instead, was imprisoned and murdered shortly after. This event and Carleton's relentless attacks demoralized them and through 1863 many Apache accepted removal to the Bosque Redondo reservation, near Fort Sumner in southeastern New Mexico.

The Navajo were also involved in hostilities with U.S. forces in the Civil War period. In September 1861, a drunken dispute over a horse race at Fort Fauntleroy, near modern Gallup, New Mexico, led to troops killing a number of Navajo, an outcome that put paid to a peace treaty negotiated earlier in the year. A typical frontier sequence of raids and counter-raids followed but, by 1863, Union forces were able to turn against the Navajo in strength. Kit Carson led a "scorched earth" campaign that summer, destroying Navajo fields and orchards and capturing livestock. As fall turned to winter, more and more Navajo surrendered and began the infamous "Long Walk" to poverty and despair in the Bosque Redondo reservation.

Navajo at Fort Defiance, New Mexico. Following Kit Carson's scorched earth campaign the Navajo were forced to walk from their lands in eastern Arizona Territory and western New Mexico Territory to the Bosque Redondo area.

New York

> **The two systems [slave and free-labor] are . . . incompatible. They have never permanently existed together in one country, and they never can.**

REPUBLICAN SENATOR WILLIAM H. SEWARD, FROM A SPEECH ENTITLED "ON THE IRREPRESSIBLE CONFLICT," DELIVERED IN NEW YORK, 1858

During the American Civil War, New York State was the major provider of manpower and materiel to the Union Army. More than 200 regiments of men from New York served the Union cause, while much of its economy was turned over to the war effort.

The state's extensive manufacturing base turned out vast quantities of supplies to provision the Union Army. Also, the New York Navy Yard in Brooklyn was an important facility for the manufacturing and repairing of Union Navy ships.

By the middle of the 19th century, New York City was already the major hub for trade and finance on the American continent and the Southern cotton trade was hugely important for the city economy. While cotton flowed in through New York's ports, Northern goods and capital went South, garnering healthy profits for New York's merchants and bankers, and creating employment for the working classes.

At the outbreak of the war, New York was the nation's most populous and culturally diverse state. The major metropolis, New York City, was home to a colorful mix of Europeans, Asians, and African-Americans, some of whom were established residents and others newly arrived immigrants. The city's residents were sharply stratified in social and economic terms. During the war, this complex socio-economic profile meant New York City remained ambivalent in its political loyalties. Personal sympathies were influenced in different degrees by economic self-interest, sense of loyalty to the Federation, by questions over the extent of Federal authority and the rights of individual states, by moral indignation over the slavery issue, and by family ties. In very general terms, while the middle and upper classes tended to support the Republican Party, and the Union war effort, working class New Yorkers were traditionally aligned with the Democrat Party, and were less sympathetic to the Union cause. Throughout the war, in fact, New York City

MAYOR FERNANDO WOOD
(1812–81)

In the mid-19th century, the New York City political scene was to a large degree controlled by Tammany Hall, an organization that since 1845 had become powerful through the loyal support of immigrant Irish. Tammany Hall exercised a powerful influence over the New York Democratic Party, which at the outbreak of war was led by Democratic Mayor Fernando Wood. Like many of his fellow New York Democrats he was a so-called "Copperhead," a nickname used by Republicans for those sympathetic to the Confederacy. In January 1861, Wood even suggested that New York City should secede from the Union and declare itself a free city, in order to continue trading with the Confederacy. On the subject of New York's secession, in January, 1861, Mayor Wood said: "Amid the gloom which the present and prospective condition of things must cast over the country, New York, as a Free City, may shed the only light and hope of a future reconstruction of our once blessed Confederacy."

remained a Democrat stronghold. In the presidential elections of 1860 and 1864, Lincoln was heavily defeated in the city. Although it is impossible to isolate any one overriding influence on working class political sympathies, economic self-interest was, again, important. The war effort brought increased economic hardships for already poor communities, due, in part, to rising unemployment.

Drum corps, 8th New York State Militia, Arlington, June, 1861.

New York Enters the War

On April 15, 1861, two days after the surrender of Fort Sumter, President Lincoln issued a proclamation calling for 75,000 militiamen from across the Federal states. As the most populous, New York was issued the largest quota; it was to provide seventeen militia regiments, equivalent to 13,180 men, for the cause. The following day, the New York State Legislature passed an act that approved the enrollment of a further 32,000 volunteers.

Four of the seventeen requested state militia regiments were quickly mustered and dispatched for the defense of Washington, D.C. One of them was the celebrated 7th Regiment of New York Militia – the so-called "Silk Stocking Regiment" – commanded by Colonel Marshall Lefferts. The regiment was given its nickname because many of the men came from New York's elite families – Vanderbilt, Tiffany, Rhinelander, Van Rensselaer, Van Buren, Harriman, Gracie, Fish, and Hamilton.

In the last week of April, under the command of Brigadier General Butler, the 7th Militia played an important role in securing Annapolis Junction, a strategically important railroad connection between the capital and the Northeast.

By the end of the month, New York had sent to Washington another five state militia regiments and also the 11th Volunteer Regiment under Colonel Elmer E. Ellsworth (a personal friend of Lincoln). From that point the threat to Washington appeared to abate and no further New York militia regiments were dispatched. However, on May 3rd, Lincoln issued another appeal for volunteers from New York and by mid-July, the state had mustered thirty-eight volunteer regiments as well as ten regiments of state militia. In fact, eighteen New York volunteer and two militia regiments fought at the First Battle of Bull Run (First Manassas). In this battle, the 101st New York lost a staggering 168, nearly three quarters of its men.

Frederick Douglass.

DEFENDING NEW YORK

Throughout the war, the Union Army garrisoned forts around New York to defend against a possible attack by Confederate troops. The biggest military threat to the city came in late spring of 1863, after Lee's forces invaded the North through the Shenandoah Valley. Union troops, including many volunteers from New York City, marched out to Pennsylvania to defend the Union in the decisive clash at Gettysburg. Had Lee's Confederate Army prevailed at Gettysburg, his next objective would almost certainly have been New York, a few days march away.

Nevertheless, for most of the war, New York remained far behind the front line, its military establishments serving predominantly in a support role. Training for newly-recruited Union troops (many of whom were immigrants recently arrived from Europe) took place at Riker's Island and at Camp Astor. Union troops who were injured or sick were cared for at MacDougall Hospital and De Camp General Hospital. Fort Lafayette and Fort Schuylerm meanwhile were used as prisoner-of-war camps.

FREDERICK DOUGLASS (1818–95)

Frederick Douglass was a former slave who escaped to become a champion of the abolitionist movement, and was one the pre-eminent social reformers of the 19th century.

Born into slavery in Maryland in 1818, Douglass escaped from his plantation master in 1838, and sought refuge in New York, eventually settling in New Bedford, Massachusetts. There, Douglass became active among anti-slavery groups and, discovering his talent for oratory, began to deliver speeches at abolitionist meetings. However, his public appearances also made him a target for pro-slavery groups and he was attacked at public meetings on a number of occasions.

In 1845, Douglass' autobiographical account, *Narrative of the Life of Frederick Douglass, an American Slave* was published, and drew widespread attention. In the following years he traveled to Ireland, then in the grip of the Potato Famine, and also to England, where he met many prominent reformers and gathered support for the abolitionist cause in his homeland.

Returning home, Douglass established a series of pro-abolitionist newspapers and continued to work for the rights of African-Americans. At the outbreak of the war, he appealed through his press for African-Americans to be allowed to fight for the cause that was so strongly identified with their rights. For Douglass, and other abolitionists, the Emancipation Proclamation marked a significant milestone in their political journey, though he felt that it should have extended full suffrage to African-Americans.

Post-war, Douglass had an active political career and continued to speak publicly. This led to him being nominated as vice-presidential candidate by the Equal Rights Party, to contest the 1872 presidential election campaign

During the war, the ranks of both the Union and Confederate Armies were filled predominantly by men who had volunteered for service. However, from 1862, soldiers began to be conscripted, marking the first time that a military draft system had been implemented in the United States. In fact, both sides suffered from manpower shortages and conscription was seen as a means to both maintain numbers and to encourage voluntary enlistments.

The drafts were conducted by lottery. For many ordinary Americans, however, conscription placed excessive authority in the hands of the military and infringed on their citizens rights. Senior soldiers also questioned the value of the conscription system, complaining that it actually discouraged men from volunteering and appeared to be an act of desperation. Furthermore, within the ranks there was considerable hostility towards conscripted men from those who had volunteered.

Because the records of the Confederate Army have been lost, accurate statistics for the number of conscripts it used are difficult to come by. However, it is estimated that conscripts accounted for twenty-five to thirty percent of the Confederate forces east of the Mississippi between April 1864 and early 1865. Of the almost 2.5 million men in the Union Army, we know that only 5.54 percent were drafted: roughly 46,347. It should be noted that about two percent of this total were genuine draftees, and the remainder were paid substitutes. During the war the Union Army called up nearly a quarter of a million men yet only about six percent of them served, the rest paying commutation or hiring a substitute.

The Confederacy, which throughout the war suffered more acute manpower shortages than the Union, passed the first of three conscription acts on April 16, 1862. Under the new law, all healthy white males between the ages of eighteen and thirty-five were liable for a three-year term of service in the Confederate Army. Soldiers that were already under arms had their term of enlistment extended to three years. By the end of the war the age limits for conscription into the Confederate Army had been broadened to cover an age range of between seventeen and fifty.

Less than a year later, on March 3, 1863, President Lincoln signed the Enrollment Act. This required the enrollment of every male citizen between ages twenty and forty-five, including those newly arrived immigrants who were awaiting citizenship applications to be processed.

Continued on page 278.

Secretary of State William Seward and a delegation of diplomats at Trenton Falls, New York. Published in *Harper's Weekly*, September 19, 1863.

New York's Governors

WILLIAM HENRY SEWARD (1801–72)

Seward was a native New Yorker, born in Orange County. He practiced law at Auburn, a profession in which he excelled, and which eventually led him into politics. From January 1839 until January 1843 he served as Governor of New York, and during this tenure was known for his liberal and humanist policy-making. He was also one of the earliest and most active political opponents of slavery. After his term as governor, Seward practiced law again, but returned to politics in 1849 as a Whig senator. From this position he was able to voice his opinions on slave labor. In a speech that was later severely criticized, given at Rochester, New York, in 1858, he stated that there was "an irrepressible conflict between opposing and enduring forces, and it means that the United States must and will, sooner or later, become either entirely a slave-holding nation or entirely a free-labor nation."

After Seward's Whig party had united with the Republicans, he was twice considered as presidential candidate, but failed to receive the nomination. In 1860, Seward's considerable experience and political acumen were, however, acknowledged when Lincoln appointed him secretary of state, a role in which he gave great service to the Union. Perhaps his most important act of diplomacy was to dissuade foreign states from giving official recognition to the Confederacy.

While recuperating from an injury at his home at Washington D.C., an attempt was made on his life by Lewis Powell, an associate of Lincoln assassin John Wilkes Booth. Seward recovered, and became secretary of state for the administration of Andrew Johnson until 1869. During this time he negotiated the purchase of Alaska from Russia. He died at Auburn on the October 10, 1872.

William Henry Seward.

EDWIN D. MORGAN (1811–83)

Edwin D. Morgan arrived in New York City from his birthplace in Massachusetts in 1836 and established himself in commerce. He was a state senator between 1850 and 1853 and, in 1856, was appointed the first chairman of the Republican National Committee, a post he held until 1864, and devoted his efforts to the election of Abraham Lincoln. He was Governor of New York from 1859 to 1862. When the threat of secession loomed, Morgan, like many Republicans, was opposed to the break-up, primarily because of his economic interests. Nevertheless, he played a major role as a recruiter of troops for the Union Army – he raised 223,000 men for the army. For this he was appointed major general of volunteers for the Department of New York between 1861 and 1863.

The Newspaper Men

Henry J. Raymond.

Horace Greeley.

James Gordon Bennett.

HENRY J. RAYMOND OF THE *NEW YORK TIMES*

Henry Jarvis Raymond (1820–69) was a self-made prodigy from Lima, New York. Founder and owner of the *New York Times*, he was called "the godfather of the Republican party" for his role in the party's foundation in 1856. He and Lincoln built a working relationship over the course of the war that was, at times, strained but which ultimately benefited both the Lincoln administration and the Union cause.

As founder of the *New York Times*, Raymond held considerable political power of his own and used it to support Lincoln's bid for the presidency. Nonetheless, after Lincoln's election to office, he rebuked the president on several occasions through his newspaper editorials, notably when he felt that Lincoln was wavering over the abolition issue and, later, for what he saw as a failure to take the war to the enemy. Although the president expressed his aggravation at this treatment, he and Raymond were able to resolve their differences and Raymond and his newspaper ultimately became indispensable to the Union cause. Lincoln later wrote, "The *Times*, I believe, is always true to the Union."

Raymond was elected to the House of Representatives in 1865 and was also one of Lincoln's most important and prolific biographers. He wrote the president's campaign biography as well as a series of books: *The Life of Abraham Lincoln* (1864) *History of the Administration of President Lincoln* (1864) and *The Life, Public Service and State Papers of Abraham Lincoln* (1865).

HORACE GREELEY OF THE *NEW YORK TRIBUNE*

Horace Greeley (1811¬–72) was founder and editor of the *New York Tribune* and an influential Republican politician. His lifelong career as a newspaperman began in his native Vermont, were he worked as a printer's apprentice. After moving to New York City he was engaged as an editor and, in 1841, founded the *New York Tribune*. During the 1850s Greeley's *Tribune* became known for its liberalism and anti-slavery stance. By the end of decade, it could claim the largest circulation of any newspaper in the world.

In the 1860 presidential election, Greeley backed Edward Bates as the Republican candidate and, when Lincoln was elected, expressed serious doubts about the new president's ability to resolve the secession crisis. His own view was that the South should be allowed to secede. However, when war broke out he became a strong supporter of the Union effort – though a frequent critic of the Lincoln administration – and a strong advocate for the Emancipation Declaration. Appalled by the casualties, he backed attempts to negotiate a peace settlement.

THE "MUSTANG" TEAM

The abolitionist Republican presidential ticket and its supporters in the press are the targets of the cartoon, called "the 'mustang' team". Candidate Frémont, wearing an emigrant's smock and carrying a cross (an allusion to his rumored Catholicism), is in the driver's seat of a wagon drawn by the "wooly nag" of abolitionism. On the nag's back sit (left to right) *New York Tribune* editor Horace Greeley, James Gordon Bennett of the *Herald*, and Henry J. Raymond of the *New York Times*. Holding onto the back of the wagon is *Courier & Enquirer* editor James Watson Webb. The wagon also carries Frémont's wife Jessie, who holds a parasol and leans on a sack marked "Bleeding Kansas Fund", a reference to hostilities in Kansas between anti-slavery and pro-slavery advocates. The wagon has reached the "Union Tollgate" (left), which is tended by Brother Jonathan and an unidentified man.

In the summer of 1864, Greeley traveled in person to Niagara Falls to meet Clement C. Clay and Jacob Thompson, who he believed had been authorized to negotiate on behalf of the Confederacy. This turned out to be part of an elaborate plot to discredit Lincoln and Greeley was mauled in the press for his "foolish, if not treasonous, attempt to negotiate with Confederate agents in Canada."

After the war Greeley alienated *Tribune* readers by advocating amnesty for Confederate officials, even paying for a bail bond for Jefferson Davis. As a result subscriptions to the *Tribune* fell by half.

JAMES GORDON'S BENNETT'S *NEW YORK HERALD*

Founder, editor, and publisher of the *New York Herald*, James Gordon Bennett (1795–1872) was at times a supporter of the Lincoln administration and at other moments a scathing critic.

Scottish-born and bred, Bennett came to the United States in 1819. After moving to New York City in 1823, he worked his way up to the position of assistant editor of the *New York Courier and Enquirer* and, in May 1835, founded the *New York Herald*. Over the following two decades, the newspaper – and Bennett's influence – grew exponentially, largely due to his talents as a journalist.

Although he helped shaped public attitudes to the war and its leaders, Bennett was a complex personality for whom nothing was sacred. Through the *Herald* he attacked politicians at will and supported them only when necessary. After Lincoln was nominated, the *Herald* described him as "a vulgar village politician, without any experience worth mentioning in the practical duties of statesmanship." In the crisis before the attack of Fort Sumter the *Herald* was in favor of secession and antagonistic to Lincoln and his administration. After the firing on Fort Sumter, however, Bennett dramatically changed his viewpoint. The *Herald* signaled that it would throw its weight behind the president and Congress in its efforts to bring the war to a speedy conclusion.

Nevertheless, Bennett still vacillated in his support of Lincoln, and was frequently a strong critic. In one stinging editorial he called Lincoln a "joke" and by August 1864, he was looking for ways to have Lincoln ousted. Indeed, the newspaper fell behind George McClellan, the formidable Democrat candidate during the presidential campaign. However, in the last days of the campaign, Bennett once again changed tack, telling his readers that it made little difference for whom they voted. The *Herald* stopped its attacks on the administration and may have thus inadvertently helped Lincoln to victory.

Both Union and Confederate conscription laws contained clauses that exempted certain men from service, due to their occupational, familial, and medical status. Under the Confederate laws, for example, river and railroad workers, civil officials, telegraph operators, miners, pharmacists, and teachers were exempt from the draft on the understanding that they were needed to support the home economy. However, these exemption clauses were open to abuse and were exploited by men shamming illness or disability. While many simply sought to "dodge the draft," there were other ways in which the system of conscription could be exploited for personal gain. Under the Union Enrollment Act, for example, each Northern state was required to fill a set quota, but rather than try to enforce a draft, some chose to offer a payment of between $100 and $500 as an incentive to volunteers. In practice, many men simply took the money and disappeared, only to reappear elsewhere to claim another reward.

However, on both sides, perhaps the most controversial aspect of conscription was the system of commutation. By paying a fee (typically $300) a draftee could commute his service to a hired substitute, usually someone in need of the money, and thus avoid the call-up. This allowed wealthier men to stay out of service and placed the burden for fighting on immigrants and the poorer classes. This circumstance was heavily criticized on both sides, leading one observer to describe the Civil War as a "rich man's war fought by the poor."

THE NEW YORK DRAFT RIOTS

In July 1863, New York City was consumed by five days of rioting, causing widespread loss of life and damage to property. The riots were the most serious civil disturbances of the Civil War, and are seen as "a microcosm of a multiplicity of grievances racking the North during the Civil War.'

Although the riots have been attributed to many causes, they seem to have been triggered by one event. This was the introduction, in March 1863, of a stricter Federal draft law, under which all male citizens between twenty and thirty-five and all unmarried men between thirty-five and forty-five years of age were subject to military duty. The anger that the draft provoked, combined with other simmering tensions and the absence of security personnel in the city, resulted in an incendiary situation.

On Saturday, July 11th, the first draft of 1,200 New Yorkers passed without disturbance. For two days the streets remained relatively quiet. Then, on the morning of July 13th, the first of five days of rioting began when a draft office was attacked. Initially, rioters attacked only military and governmental buildings, and any individual

Called "Enlistment of Sickles' Brigade" this cartoon by Adalbert John Volck satirizes the disreputable class of men allegedly recruited in New York City by Daniel Sickles for the Excelsior Brigade.

MAJOR GENERAL DANIEL E. SICKLES (1819–1914)

Major General Daniel E. Sickles in Washington, D.C.

Probably the most colorful of New York's Civil War commanders, Daniel Edgar Sickles was born in New York City and began his career in the print trade. After graduating from New York University he studied law and was admitted to the bar in 1846. The following year he was elected to the state assembly and later served as a diplomat in London, as a state senator from 1856 to 1857, and, from 1857 to 1861, as Democrat representative to the U.S. Congress. In 1859, already a somewhat notorious figure on the New York political and social scene, Sickles courted further controversy when he was acquitted, on the grounds of temporary insanity, of murdering the man who had cuckolded him. The incident did lasting damage to his political career.

For Sickles, the war offered the chance of a new beginning. He quickly raised four regiments and, in September 1861, was appointed brigadier general of volunteers. He was assigned command of New York's Excelsior Brigade, leading them in the Battle of Seven Pines, during the Seven Days, and was later given command of a division. By December 1862, Sickles had risen to the rank of major general.

As a battlefield commander, he was noted for his bravery, but he was also frequently at odds with his superiors and there are several instances of Sickles making mistakes in the field. During the Chancellorsville campaign, where he led III Corps, his headquarters misinterpreted Stonewall Jackson's movements and ordered movements that left XI Corps completely exposed. Later, at Gettysburg, his men were ordered to cover the Federal left in the vicinity of the Round Tops. In defiance of direct orders, he advanced III Corps into the Peach Orchard, where it was subsequently overrun by General James Longstreet's assault. The corps was virtually destroyed in this action and Sickles was struck by a cannonball during the battle. The ball severely fractured his lower right leg, which had to be amputated just above the knee. Sickles, who might otherwise have faced courts martial, was eventually awarded the Medal of Honor (in 1897) for his services. After his recovery, President Lincoln dispatched him on a fact-finding tour of Union-held Southern territory.

who tried to intervene. But by the afternoon of the first day, personal attacks on African-Americans began to occur, and on their churches, meeting places, shops, and dwellings.

The reasons that the rage of the mob turned so viciously against the African-American population are, again, complex. In part the violence might be attributed to the Emancipation Proclamation, which many New Yorkers believed would result in the rapid influx to the city of freed slaves, increasing competition in an already highly competitive labor market. Another factor might be that African-Americans, who did not have citizenship, were exempt from the draft.

Whatever the cause, throughout the five days of riots, mobs attacked and sometimes killed African-Americans and their white supporters and destroyed their property. One prominent supporter, Abby Hopper Gibbons, saw her home burned to the ground. The mob also attacked white women who were married to black men. However, it was African-Americans themselves who suffered most at the hands of the mob. Near the docks, Irish dockworkers attacked two hundred African-Americans, reflecting workplace tensions that had been brewing between them since the mid-1850s. Elsewhere, an African-American sailor, William Williams, was beaten and stabbed to death while a crowd of men, women, and children looked on. In another brutal episode, coachman Abraham Franklin was dragged through the streets, stoned, and then hanged from a lamppost as a mob cheered. In all, rioters lynched eleven African-American men over the five days of violent protest.

Finally, New York state militia and other troops from the Army of the Potomac were called in to stamp out the unrest. In all, the riots are estimated to have caused between $1.5 and $5 million dollars worth of property damage. The number of people killed is disputed, with some putting the figure as high as 2,000. The riots also had a profound effect on the lives of many African-Americans living in the city. In the aftermath thousands fled the city in fear. By 1865, the black population had plummeted to just under 10,000, its lowest since 1820.

For all the destruction, the riots did nothing to stop the induction of over 150,000 Union troops into the Civil War front-lines.

These scenes from the New York riots show: the ruins of the Provost-Marshal's office; a fight between rioters and military; the charge of the police on the rioters at the *Tribune* office; the sacking of a drug store in Second Avenue; and the hanging of an African-American in Clarkson Street.

Jacob Thompson (1810–85).

THE CONFEDERATE PLOT TO BURN NEW YORK

During the war the Confederate Secret Service made several attempts to strike fear into the Northern population. The failed attack on New York was perhaps the most ambitious.

In the spring of 1864, seeking some way to bring discord to the Union and force it to the negotiating table, Confederate President Jefferson Davis hatched a scheme to terrorize New York through a series of arson attacks. Colonel Jacob Thompson was chosen to execute the plan. During the summer, Thompson infiltrated a group of eight Confederate officers led by Colonel Robert M. Martin into New York City via Toronto, Canada. On the upcoming election day, scheduled for November 8th, they were ordered to carry out diversionary arson attacks while "Copperhead" sympathizers (Northerners who sought an end to the Civil War) seized Federal buildings, municipal offices, and police departments. In unison, operatives in other Northeast cities would engage in similar attacks. However, five days prior to the planned coup Federal intelligence agents received a tip-off from an informer. Union troops were rushed to New York to tighten security, and naval gunboats were sent to protect vital facilities. Against these developments the plan was abandoned, and two of the agents made good their escape.

The six agents that remained now began to plot a new course of action. They resolved to attack several of New York's many hotel buildings, sparking a conflagration that would destroy the entire city. On the evening of November 25th, the day scheduled for the attack, the six conspirators moved to their designated targets around the city. In rooms they had booked, each man built a pile of flammable linen and onto this poured a vial of combustible chemicals (Greek Fire), before fleeing. Fortunately for New York, only half of the planned twenty-four fires were successfully lit, and fire crews successfully extinguished these before they could spread. No lives were lost and there were no serious injuries. Only one Confederate agent was ever apprehended, to be executed four months later.

MAJOR GENERAL JOHN ADAMS DIX (1798–1879)

Born in New Hampshire, Dix entered military service as an ensign with the 14th Infantry in 1813. The following year he was promoted to second lieutenant and transferred to an artillery regiment. After resigning from the service in 1828 as a captain, he was admitted to the bar and established himself in practice at Cooperstown, New York. Subsequently, he became a Democrat politician, served as state adjutant general, state school superintendent, and was a member of the U.S. Senate from 1845 to 1848. During the 1850s he withdrew from politics, while continuing to practice law in New York City.

Shortly before the outbreak of the Civil War, Dix was appointed secretary of the treasury, but resigned the position to return to New York. Appointed by President Lincoln as major general of volunteers, he commanded the Department of Annapolis and the Department of Pennsylvania in 1861, the Middle Department in 1862, the Department of Virginia from 1862 to 1863, and the Department of the East to the end of the war. During this time Dix was responsible for suppressing the New York draft riots. He resigned in 1865, and was appointed minister to France. Dix died on April 21, 1879, in New York City.

New York Regiments

THE "ZOUAVE" REGIMENTS

During the Civil War a large number of units in the Union and Confederate Armies adopted the name and uniform of the "Zouave" Berber riflemen who served in the French Army. Two such units were the 5th New York Volunteer Infantry Regiment, or "Duryée's Zouaves" and the 11th New York Volunteer Infantry Regiment, also known variously as the "New York Fire Zouaves", "Ellsworth's Zouaves", or "First Fire Zouaves".

The 5th New York Volunteer Infantry served in the Army of the Potomac between May 1861 and May 1863. The regiment was raised by Abram Duryée from across New York State but principally Brooklyn. Duryée's Zouaves were particularly noted for their fine drilling, effectiveness in combat, and composure under fire – attributes that won the unit the praise of V Corps commander General George Sykes (1822–80), who said of the regiment, "I doubt whether it had an equal … and certainly no superior among all the regiments of the Army of the Potomac." The regiment took a prominent part in the battle of the Second Bull Run (Second Manassas), where, of 490 members present, it lost 117 killed or mortally wounded, twenty-three percent of those engaged, the greatest loss of life in any infantry regiment in any one battle.

The 11th New York Volunteer Infantry Regiment was raised by Elmer E. Ellsworth, colleague and friend of Lincoln from his time as a lawyer in Illinois, from among the volunteer fire crews of New York City. In one of the first engagements of the war, the unit captured Alexandria, Virginia, though Ellsworth was killed during the action. In July, serving under 2nd Division, Army of Northeastern Virginia, at the First Battle of Bull Run (First Manassas), the regiment suffered severe losses in the fighting at Henry House Hill and during the subsequent retreat. In September 1861, it returned to New York for reorganization before going into camp at Newport News. However,

A soldier in "Ellsworth's Zouaves" regiment.

efforts to reorganize the regiment came to nothing and it was mustered out on June 2, 1862.

THE 121ST INFANTRY REGIMENT

Another common trend was for a regiment to adopt the name of the counties from which it recruited. Following this practice, the 121st Infantry Regiment became the "Otsego And Herkimer Regiment". It was mustered in on August 13, 1862 and attached to VI Corps in McClellan's army, the unit took a limited role in the Battle of Fredericksburg. However, the regiment's first significant action was at Salem Church, in Virginia, where more than half its 453 men were listed as killed, wounded, or missing. These losses were the greatest sustained by any regiment in the battle.

The Otsego And Herkimer Regiment's next major action was the Battle of Rappahannock Station in November, 1863, after which, in the late spring of 1864, the regiment fought in Grant's campaign during the battles of the Wilderness and at Spottsylvania. The regiment was then successively engaged at North Anna, Totopotomy, Cold Harbor, the first assaults on Petersburg, and the Weldon railroad. When General Jubal Early's advance threatened Washington in July, the 121st saw action at Fort Stevens and then in the pursuit of Early through Maryland, into Virginia, and up the Shenandoah Valley, fighting at Charlestown, the Opequan, Fisher's Hill, and Cedar Creek.

At the end of the 1864, the regiment returned to Petersburg and in the following spring took a prominent part in the final assault on the Petersburg fortifications. In the ensuing pursuit of Lee's army, the regiment fought its last battle at Sailor's Creek. It was mustered out on June 25, 1865. The total of 839 killed and wounded was one of the largest sustained by any regiment.

THE 126TH NEW YORK INFANTRY REGIMENT

The 126th New York Infantry Regiment was recruited in the counties of Ontario, Seneca, and Yates and mustered into service for three years on August 22, 1862.

During the siege of Harper's Ferry, the regiment bore the brunt of the Confederate attack and surrendered with the rest of the garrison on September 15th. As was common practice, the men were immediately paroled on the proviso that they took no further role in combat. An exchange deal was completed in December, and the survivors returned to winter camp at Union Mills, Virginia.

In June, 1863, the 126th New York Infantry joined II Corps in the Army of the Potomac and marched to Gettysburg where the regiment redeemed itself through conspicuous gallantry while suffering nearly fifty-eight percent casualties. Much reduced, it went on to fight in the spring campaign of 1864. More losses were sustained during in the battles in the Wilderness and at Spottsylvania. The regiment was subsequently engaged in the Siege of Harpers Ferry, at Gettysburg, North Anna, Totopotomy,

Hon. Horatio Seymour.

Cold Harbor, Petersburg, in the siege of Petersburg, and was also present in the Mine Run Campaign, and, finally, Appomattox. It was mustered out at Washington, D. C. on June 3, 1865. The total of killed and wounded in the regiment was 535.

THE 8TH NEW YORK (HEAVY) ARTILLERY

As well as regiments of infantry, men from New York were also organized as cavalry, artillery, and engineers. The 8th New York (Heavy) Artillery, also known as the "Albany County Regiment" or "Seymour Guard", was recruited in western New York in 1862 as the 129th New York Infantry and later that year converted into a regiment of artillery, the 8th Regiment of Artillery.

The regiment served at Harpers Ferry and several subsequent actions, and also on garrison duties in Virginia. However, its most famous battle was at Cold Harbor in June, 1864, contested between Confederate forces under General Robert E. Lee and Union army of General Ulysses S. Grant. Fighting with fellow New Yorkers as part of the "Corcoran Legion" (4th Brigade under Brigadier General Robert O. Tyler, men from the regiment attacked across open, in places marshy, ground against the well-fortified Confederate lines. The regiment suffered greatly in the storm of musket and cannon fire that poured down on them. Lieutenant Eli Nichols later wrote of the slaughter, "God grant that I may never see [its] like again."

The "Foreign" Regiments

The regimental flag of the Irish Brigade.

THE IRISH BRIGADE

Reflecting ethnic diversity of its inhabitants, New York fielded several "Irish" and "Scottish," and also French, Italian, German, Scandinavian, and Swiss regiments during the course of the war.

Three of the Irish regiments – the 69th, 88th, and 63rd Volunteer Infantry Regiments – and the 2nd Battalion of Light Artillery together formed the "Irish Brigade," which was primarily recruited from among the Irish immigrant communities in New York City, particularly the Lower East Side. It was led by Thomas Francis Meagher (1823–67), an Irish revolutionary who was at that time living in exile in New York City.

The first of the regiments formed was the 69th, which participated in the defense of Washington, D.C. following the First Battle of Bull Run (First Manassas). Meanwhile, the other regiments were assembled and, in early 1862, the fully constituted Irish Brigade joined General McClellan's Peninsula Campaign.

The brigade fought at Yorktown and Fair Oaks, at Seven Pines, and at Antietam (Battle of Sharpsburg), where it achieved lasting glory by mounting a desperate and costly frontal charge against Confederate troops dug in along what became known

as "Bloody Lane". At Fredericksburg, on December 13, 1862, the brigade suffered fully half of its 1,200 men killed or wounded. Nevertheless, the badly mauled brigade found new recruits and was able to field 600 men for the Battle of Gettysburg. Here, again, it saw heavy action, and suffered heavy losses in the area of the battlefield known as The Wheatfield.

By 1864, the Irish Brigade had suffered such losses that the entire brigade had dwindled to the size of a single regiment. Consequently, it was disbanded and the men were allocated to other units.

THE 79TH NEW YORK INFANTRY REGIMENT

The 79th New York Infantry Regiment, also known as "The Highlanders" or "Cameron Highlanders" was raised from among New York's emigrant Scots and Irish communities. In keeping with its Scottish identity, the regimental dress uniform was based on a tartan kilt.

The 79th was originally one of New York's militia regiments and was mustered into Federal service in May of 1861. In early summer, it was stationed in the vicinity of Washington D.C., and participated in the Battle of Bull Run (First Manassas). In this first action, 198 men of the regiment were killed or wounded, including the commander, Colonel James Cameron. The 79th also took part in Sherman's expedition, fighting at Secessionville, and subsequently in engagements near Manassas. The regiment was also active at South Mountain, Antietam, and Fredericksburg. Under Grant, the Highlanders joined in the Siege of Vicksburg, then fought at Blue Springs, at Campbell's Station in Tennessee, and aided in the defense of Knoxville. The regiment fought in the early battles of the Wilderness Campaign and was finally mustered out on May 31, 1864.

ELMIRA PRISON

In May 1864, the U.S. War Department ordered the vacant barracks in Elmira, New York, to be converted for use as a prisoner of war camp. In July, the first 700 Confederate prisoners were transferred from other overcrowded Federal prisons; by the end of August the inmates numbered almost 10,000 men.

Conditions in the camp were poor even by Civil War standards. Only half the internees were housed in the barracks, and others had to make do with tents. Many arrived at camp without clothing and blankets. Sanitation was another problem, compounded by the presence of a large cesspool in the compound and poor drainage. The food ration was barely adequate. Four ounces of light bread and three ounces of salt beef or pork for breakfast; for dinner, the same amount of bread was served with a thin soup.

Under these circumstances, the prisoners' health suffered greatly. By November 1864, it was reported that there had been 775 deaths from sickness, exposure, and associated causes, while over 1,000 per day were on the official sick list. By the end of the war, eight months later, the number of dead had risen to 2,917 (of a total of 12,122 soldiers imprisoned at Elmira). Escapes were rare, but ten men managed to dig a tunnel under the perimeter fence, and on October 7, 1864, crawled through to freedom.

Made by David J. Coffman of the 7th Virginia Calvary while he was a prisoner of war, this map shows Elmira Military Prison in New York. Accompanying records state that Coffman enlisted on April 1, 1862 in Luray, Virginia, was captured May 20, 1864, in Bowling Green, Virginia, and was released June 27, 1865.

New York Union Units Furnished	
Infantry regiments	235
3-month infantry regiments	7
Infantry battalions	1
Sharpshooter units	2
Militia Regiments	7
National Guard regiments	35
Cavalry regiments	33
Misc. Cavalry units	3
Heavy artillery regiments	16
Heavy artillery battalions	5
Light artillery regiments	3
Light artillery battalions	5
Ind. light artillery batteries	42
Engineer regiments	4
Sailors/marine personnel	35,164
Colored troops	4,125

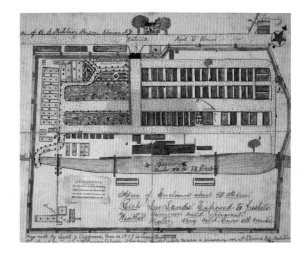

NEW YORK UNION ARMY DEATHS

Troops Furnished	Killed/Mortally Wounded	Died of Disease	Died of Other Causes	Total
409,561	19,085	19,835	7,614	46,534

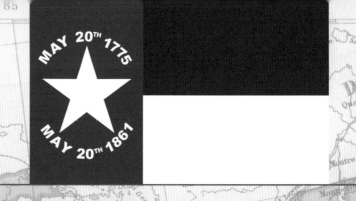

North Carolina

66 I can be no party to this wicked violation of the laws of the country and to this war upon the liberties of a free people. You can get no troops from North Carolina. 99

GOVERNOR JOHN W. ELLIS'S REPLY TO SECRETARY OF WAR
SIMON CAMERON'S REQUEST FOR TROOPS

In the run up to war, as one by one the states declared their allegiances, North Carolina (the "Old North State") proved more hesitant than its southern neighbors in breaking away from the Union. After finally seceding in May 1861, the conflicting loyalties of North Carolinians meant that troops from the state fought for both the Confederacy and the Union.

The majority served with the Confederate Army, however, and by the final surrender the state had provided more troops to the Confederate cause than any other. (North Carolina is also said to have lost more men to the war than any other state.) The strategic significance of the state, and hence the focus of wartime action, lay in her Atlantic ports. Throughout the conflict these were an important conduit for the sea trade with Europe, which supplied the war effort in the South with much-needed arms and equipment.

Like much of the South, in the mid-19th century North Carolina was predominantly an agrarian society, with barely two percent of the 1,000,000 population living in the state's few towns. The largest conurbation, the Atlantic port of Wilmington, was home to only 10,000; in the capital, Raleigh, there were less than half that number. Overall, the vast majority of the citizens made their living cultivating modest plots of land in central region and the mountainous west though, after 1800, a number of plantations had been established for the lucrative cotton trade in the east and on the North Atlantic coast, and a minority class of prosperous and politically influential planters had begun to emerge. The other major population group in North Carolina was the slave workforce, most of whom worked on cotton plantations. In 1860, there were around 330,000 slaves in the state, representing about one third of the total population.

Captain Jesse Sharpe Barnes of F Company, 4th North Carolina Infantry, was killed on May 31, 1862, at Seven Pines, Virginia – one of some 20,000 men of North Carolina who died for the Confederate cause.

The social and economic divisions between the eastern and western parts of the state were reflected in regional political ties. In broad terms, the planter families of the east were Democratic and supported secession, while those in the west tended to favor the Whig Party, and the Union. The rise of the new anti-slavery Republican Party in the late 1850s, and the nomination of Lincoln for the presidency prior to the critical November 1860 election, sharpened the east-west divide. For North Carolina's Democrats Lincoln's nomination was clear evidence of Republican opposition to both slavery and the political influence of the South. Victory for Lincoln, they believed would inevitably compel the state to secede from the Union. Conversely, those North Carolinians who had traditionally supported the Whig Party believed that North Carolina's interests were best served by remaining in the Union, and therefore favored a compromise solution such as advocated by the Constitutional Union Party. Secession, they feared, would lead to a war and all its ruinous consequences.

GOVERNOR JOHN WILLIS ELLIS (1820–61)

When John Willis Ellis took office in 1859, he deplored the notion that secession or civil war was imminent. After Abraham Lincoln became president, Ellis promoted the formation of a confederacy to protect states' rights, slavery, and the South's agricultural interests. At first, Ellis met with resistance. The legislature met in February 1861 and voted down a secession convention. After Lincoln issued a proclamation in April calling for volunteers, Ellis succeeded in forming a convention, and North Carolina seceded on May 20, 1861. Over-working killed Ellis, and he died on July 7th, after consuming all his energy to put the state on a war footing.

THE ELECTION OF 1860 AND THE SECESSION DRAMA

In the November 1860 presidential election, Lincoln's Republican Party was not on the ballot in North Carolina or, indeed, most other Southern states. In the event, John Breckinridge, the Democrat candidate, narrowly defeated John Bell, a former Whig who had helped establish the Constitutional Union Party. Lincoln, however, was able to rally enough support nationwide to carry the election.

On November 20, 1860, two weeks after Lincoln's victory, North Carolina's Democrat governor, John W. Ellis, asked the state legislature to call a public convention to discuss secession. At this point Ellis, and prominent unionists such as *North Carolina Standard* owner William Holden and congressman Zebulon Vance, urged caution. They believed that any decision regarding secession should be based not on fears of what Lincoln might do, but on what the new president actually did. In a state-wide election held in late February, the convention measure was rejected by a slender margin.

The inaugural address that Lincoln delivered on March 4, 1861, contained reassurances for the Southern states that had remained in the Union, and words of appeasement for his supporters in North. For North Carolina's unionists, President Lincoln's address seemed to be a broad endorsement of their cautious approach and, for the meantime, the state remained neutral. However, the attack on Fort Sumter, South Carolina, and Lincoln's subsequent call for volunteers from across the Union to suppress the rebellion, soon forced North Carolina's hand. Few North Carolinians could countenance the idea of taking up arms against fellow Southerners. "You shall get no troops from North Carolina," was Governor Ellis' defiant response to Lincoln's appeal. He then ordered state troops to seize all Federal forts and the Fayetteville arsenal, and indicated in a private telegram to Confederate President Jefferson Davis that the state would support the Confederate government. A secession convention was quickly approved. When the delegates met in Raleigh on May 20, 1861, they voted unanimously to secede from the United States and to join the Confederate States of America.

The following is an extract of the North Carolina Ordinance of Secession, dated May 20, 1861.

"We, the people of the State of North Carolina in convention assembled, do declare and ordain, and it is hereby declared and ordained, That the ordinance adopted by the State of North Carolina in the convention of 1789, whereby the Constitution of the United States was ratified and adopted, and also all acts and parts of acts of the General Assembly ratifying and adopting amendments to the said Constitution, are hereby repealed, rescinded, and abrogated."

The Confederate Department of North Carolina and the Union Department of North Carolina

Both the Confederacy and the Union created an administrative subdivision termed the "Department of North Carolina" to cover the areas of North Carolina occupied by their respective forces. These departments were similar in that each was responsible for the military installations therein and for the field armies in the region, and each was commanded by succession of generals. The Union Department of North Carolina was created on January 7, 1862, under Brigadier General Ambrose E. Burnside and was later reorganized on two occasions. Firstly, on July 15, 1863, the department was merged with the Department of Virginia to become the Department of Virginia and North Carolina. Under this department the Army of North Carolina was formed, commanded by Major General John J. Peck. The Army of the James was also organized from troops from the Department of Virginia and North Carolina and served primarily in Virginia during the Bermuda Hundred Campaign while during the siege of Petersburg it conducted operations against the city of Richmond north of the James River. In January 1865, the department once more became a separate organization, to include Union-occupied areas of North Carolina excluding those occupied by the armies of William T. Sherman. At that time, General John M. Schofield was appointed by Ulysses S. Grant to head the department.

Bethel

One of the earliest actions fought by Confederate North Carolina forces was at Bethel, Virginia, on June 10, 1861. In early June, the 1st Regiment North Carolina Volunteers, under the command of Colonel (later Major General) D. H. Hill, was ordered to move to Yorktown, Virginia, to help defend the Virginia Peninsula. On the morning of June 10th, the regiment marched from its bivouac to meet the advancing Union armies and engaged in the vicinity of Big Bethel Church. After fierce fighting the Union forces were routed. Eighteen Union soldiers died,

General John J. Peck, photographed by Mathew Brady.

for the loss of only one casualty to the regiment – the first North Carolinian to die in battle.

First Battle of Bull Run (First Battle of Manassas)

On July 21, 1861, again on Virginian soil, Confederate North Carolina troops fought in the first major battle of the war, at the Manassas railroad junction outside Washington, D.C. Known variously as the Battle of Bull Run, or First Manassas, three North Carolina Regiments were present: the 11th and the 5th N.C. State Troops with the Army of the Potomac, and the 6th North Carolina with the Army of the Shenandoah. However, only the latter, under the command of Colonel Charles F. Fisher, saw much combat. During the day the tide of battle ebbed back and forth until, finally, late in the afternoon, Union forces began to retreat back toward Washington. Of the 387 Confederate dead, twenty-four were from the 6th North Carolina, including Colonel Fisher.

Burnside's Expedition

In North Carolina itself, Union efforts focused on ways to enforce a sea blockade on the South. At the end of August, Major General Benjamin F. Butler mounted an amphibious assault on the Hatteras Inlet forts, forcing their surrender. The Union War Department now ordered General Ambrose Burnside to mount an expedition to extend Union control over North Carolina's coastal regions. Beginning in September, 1861, Burnside led the North Carolina Expeditionary Corps in a series of attacks against key ports and cities in that locality.

A Kurz & Allison illustration of the attack on Fort Fisher.

The first major success came on February 7, 1862, when a force of 7,500 men led by Burnside landed on Roanoke Island and quickly overcame the Confederate garrison.

A month later, Burnside departed Roanoke Island and, on March 14th, captured the important town of New Bern in Craven County. Subsequently, Union forces used the port town as a base for military operations along the coast and into the interior. From New Bern, Burnside moved against Fort Macon, thirty-five miles to the southeast at Beaufort Inlet in Carteret County. On April 25th, after a month-long siege, the Confederate garrison was forced to surrender.

By the middle of the year, Burnside's expeditionary force had established Federal control over a large swathe of coastal Carolina, including the strategically important Albemarle and Pamlico Sounds. From the security of this position, at end of December, 1862, Union forces under John G. Foster pushed into the state in an attempt to sever the vital Wilmington and Weldon railroad supply line to Virginia. During this "Goldsboro Expedition" Union and Confederate forces clashed at Kinston, White Hall, and at Goldsboro Bridge, which was burned by Foster's troops.

TIDEWATER OPERATIONS

After Burnside's expedition and until the invasion of Sherman and the major actions at Fort Fisher, fighting in North Carolina was largely inconsequential. The most significant action took place the early spring of 1863, when Confederate Lieutenant General James Longstreet, recently appointed commander of the Department of Virginia and North Carolina, launched his Tidewater Operations to try and take the initiative in the theatre. One of Longstreet's major objectives was the Union stronghold of New Bern, and he ordered Major General D.H. Hill, commander of the North Carolina District, to try and recapture the town. After an initial success at Deep Gully on March 13th, Hill marched his 12,000 men against the well-prepared Federal defences at Fort Anderson, but was forced to retire upon the arrival of the Union Navy. During the withdrawal, Hill's army skirmished at Washington, D.C., while Longstreet led a coordinated attack against the town of Suffolk.

THE CAROLINAS CAMPAIGN

In late November 1864, a large Federal army under William T. Sherman marched from Atlanta, Georgia, with the objective of reaching the port of Savannah, to the southeast. Meeting with only sporadic resistance from a much-weakened Confederate army, Savannah fell on December 21st.

In the New Year, Sherman moved north on two lines of advance (XIV and XX Corps under Slocum, and Howard's Army of the Tennessee) through the Carolinas, capturing Columbia, the South Carolina capital, on February 17th, before turning to the northeast and crossing into North Carolina in early March. During the so-called "Carolinas Campaign", the state was spared the destruction that was wrought by Sherman's troops elsewhere.

FORT FISHER AND WILMINGTON

In the meantime, on the southern flank, Schofield moved his Army of the Ohio by sea and rail to attack Wilmington, the most important objective in North Carolina. Union strategists had long known that without the supplies that flowed through this port, the Confederate position would quickly become untenable. However, before any attempt could be made on Wilmington, Schofield first had to secure Fort Fisher, a strongly defended position on the Cape Fear River that protected the Wilmington approaches. It had already been the focus of concerted attacks, beginning with a failed attempt by Butler's Army of the James in December 1864.

In the middle of January, the Fort Fisher Expeditionary Force made a massive, coordinated assault from both land and sea and the fort was finally taken. Schofield then quickly assembled these troops and the XXIII Corps into the Wilmington Expeditionary Force, led this force up the Cape Fear River to capture Wilmington on February 22nd. In doing so, he helped seal the fate of the Confederacy.

One of the English Armstrong guns emplaced in Fort Fisher as photographed by Timothy H. O'Sullivan.

The captured rebel privateer C.S.S. *Florida* and the steamer U.S.S. *Wachusett*.

JOHN NEWLAND MAFFITT OF THE C.S.S. *FLORIDA*

During the war, the Union Navy attempted to force the Confederacy into submission by blockading sea ports on the Atlantic coast and in the Gulf of Mexico. Hence, in addition to providing coastal defense and protection for inland waterways, the main tasks of the Confederate Navy were attempting to break the Union blockade and raiding the Union's own trade fleet. Although several commerce raiders operated under the Confederate flag, two in particular are celebrated. These were the cruisers C.S.S. *Shenandoah*, and C.S.S. *Florida*, commanded, respectively, by James I. Waddell and John N. Maffitt.

In May 1861, Maffitt resigned his U.S. Navy commission and became a first lieutenant in the Confederate States Navy. After serving on Lee's staff as a naval adviser, he ran ships carrying supplies for the Confederacy through the Union blockade. On August 17, 1862, he was given command of the C.S.S. *Florida*, a 700-ton steam-screw cruiser built in England as the *Oreto* and newly commissioned in the Bahamas into the Confederate Navy.

Maffitt joined his ship at Cárdenas, Cuba, and sailed from there to Mobile, Alabama. After running the Union blockade off Mobile Bay under a hail of fire, Maffitt completed the outfitting of the ship and three months later escaped past the blockade again, under cover of a storm. During the next eight months the *Florida* captured twenty-two prizes while operating in the Atlantic and the West Indies, all the time eluding the Federal squadron sent to pursue her. While wintering in Brest, France, Maffit relinquished command of the *Florida* to Charles M. Morris, who took another eleven prizes before October. Anchored a Bahia, Brazil, on October 7, 1864, the Florida was attacked and captured by the U.S.S. *Wachusett*. After the war, Maffitt went to England and worked there as a mariner.

MONROE'S CROSSROADS

From Wilmington, Schofield moved north up the rail lines toward Goldsboro to rendezvous with Sherman while XXIII Corps under Major General

Jacob D. Cox moved west from New Bern. Kinston fell to Cox's forces in mid-March. To the north, Slocum and Howard's first objective after entering North Carolina was the Confederate arsenal at Fayetteville. On March 10th, Slocum's forward cavalry units, under Major General Hugh J. Kilpatrick, were surprised at Monroe's Crossroads by Confederate cavalry. Although this briefly delayed Slocum's progress on the northern flank, with Howard's troops approached largely unhindered on the southern flank, General William J. Hardee ordered the Fayetteville to be evacuated and withdrew to the Smithville Plantation on the Fayetteville-Raleigh Stage Road just south of the town of Averasboro.

AVERASBORO

After entering Fayetteville and destroying the arsenal, Slocum sent Kilpatrick's cavalry forward again. They made contact with Hardee's defensive forces at Smithville on March 15th. By the following morning, four divisions of the XX Corps had arrived to reinforce Kilpatrick's forces and together they assaulted the Confederate lines. Overwhelmed by sheer weight of numbers, the Confederate troops withdrew through successive lines of defences, before rallying for a final stand at Chicora where they had built strong earthworks. Although the Confederate troops withstood numerous Union assaults, they withdrew under the cover of darkness to join the army that General Joseph E. Johnston was gathering at Bentonville for one final Confederate offensive in the Eastern Theater.

BENTONVILLE

At Bentonville, Johnston was able to muster a sizeable force of about 21,000 men, with which he hoped to interfere with Slocum's planned rendezvous at Goldsboro. In the opposing Union camp, Slocum's intelligence staff badly underestimated the strength of this enemy. On March 19th, when Slocum's troops came up against the Confederate troops concentrated at Bentonville, they were caught by surprise. An attack by XIV Corps was quickly

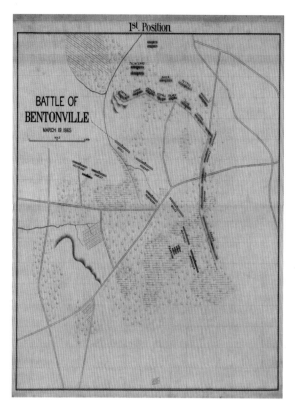

Federal forces encounter Johnston's entrenched army. The Confederate advance pushed Federals and threatened to overwhelm them. Desperate fighting and the arrival of reinforcements saved the day for the Union.

driven back, and the corps overrun in a major counterstrike.

Fighting continued into the next day, when elements of the XX Corps were thrown into the action. Johnston launched several more attacks, which were beaten back, before retreating across the bridge at Bentonville on the night of March 21/22. Union forces took up the pursuit at first light, forcing Johnston to fall back to Raleigh. On April 13th, four days after Lee had surrendered, Raleigh itself fell. Johnston and Sherman began negotiations and finally, on April 26, 1865, Johnston surrendered his army and all of the troops in the Carolinas, Georgia, and Florida at the Bennett Place near Durham. This surrender essentially ended the war in the Eastern Theater.

MAJOR GENERAL ROBERT RANSOM (1828–92)

Robert Ransom, Jr. was a native of Warren County, North Carolina. Like Bragg, he attended West Point and was commissioned into the U.S. Army as second lieutenant in 1850. Assigned to the 1st Dragoons, he was posted to Taos, New Mexico, on the frontier. Promoted to first lieutenant in the newly established 1st U.S. Cavalry, he served later as cavalry instructor at West Point and on the Kansas frontier from 1856.

When North Carolina seceded from the Union in May 1861, Ransom resigned from the U.S. Army and was commissioned captain of cavalry in the Confederate Army, then first colonel of the First North Carolina cavalry (9th Regiment N.C. State Troops). On March 6, 1862, he was promoted brigadier general. During the Antietam Campaign, Ransom commanded a brigade under Longstreet's 1st Corps, in the Army of North Virginia. At the Battle of Fredericksburg in November, 1862, he was division commander under Longstreet's 1st Corps and served with his division in North Carolina until May 1863.

Promoted to major general, Ransom served in Virginia, and was tasked with protecting the important Weldon Railroad. He was successively in eastern Tennessee, and then under Beauregard during the defense of Richmond. In June 1864, he was in command of cavalry during Early's expedition through the Shenandoah Valley against Maryland, Pennsylvania, and Washington, D.C. In August that year, Ransom succumbed to the illness that had plagued him for many years and thereafter served in administrative posts in Kentucky and at Charleston, South Carolina, before surrendering on May 2, 1865.

GENERAL BRAXTON BRAGG (1817–76)

The most celebrated of North Carolina's Civil War military leaders, Bragg was born in Warrenton, North Carolina, and joined the army in 1837. He attended West Point, and served in the 2nd Seminole and Mexican-American wars. Resigning from service in 1856, Bragg became a sugar planter in Louisiana.

On the secession of Louisiana, he was made a brigadier general in the Confederate army and was the first commander of the military forces of Louisiana. In September, he was promoted to major general and given command of the forces in Alabama and West Florida. At the Battle of Shiloh he commanded the right wing of the Army of the Mississippi. Subsequently, he led the Army of the Mississippi (or Tennessee) but after defeat at Stone's River in January, 1863, and Chattanooga in November, 1863, he was relieved of command.

Appointed commander of the Department of North Carolina, he was unable to prevent the fall of Wilmington. In February, 1865, he was with Johnston and surrendered alongside him.

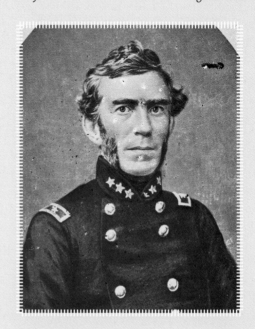

MAJOR GENERAL ROBERT F. HOKE (1837–1912)

The least known but probably the best of North Carolina's Civil War commanders, Robert Hoke fought in nearly every significant battle in the Eastern Theater and is sometimes described as "The North Carolina Lee" as well as "the most distinguished soldier in North Carolina."

Hoke was born in Lincolnton, North Carolina, and graduated from the Kentucky Military Institute in 1854. At the outbreak of the Civil War, he enlisted in the 1st North Carolina Infantry where he received a commission as a second lieutenant. After distinguishing himself at the Battle of Big Bethel, Hoke was promoted to major of the 33rd North Carolina Regiment. He fought through the Peninsula Campaign, the Seven Days, Chancellorsville, Second Bull Run (Second Battle of Manassas), and Antietam (Battle of Sharpsburg).

On January 17, 1863, Hoke was promoted to brigadier general and commanded a brigade at Fredericksburg and at Chancellorsville, where he was severely wounded. He recovered and led a brigade to North Carolina, where he participated in the battles of New Bern and Plymouth. Promoted to major general on April 20, 1864, Hoke led a division at the Battle of Cold Harbor, where his actions played a crucial role in the Confederate victory.

Subsequently Hoke's division participated in the defense of Fort Fisher, the Carolinas Campaign, and finally at the Battle of Bentonville, where he again served with distinction. Hoke finally surrendered to Union forces in April of 1865.

MAJOR GENERAL STEPHEN DODSON "DOD" RAMSEUR (1837–64)

One of the youngest Confederate generals, Ramseur was born in Lincolnton, North Carolina. He fought in the Peninsula Campaign, at Chancellorsville and Gettysburg and died of wounds sustained at the battle of Cedar Creek. Jubal Early's Official Report from Cedar Creek stated that, "Major-General Ramseur fell into the hands of the enemy mortally wounded, and in him not only my command, but the country suffered a heavy loss. He was a most gallant and energetic officer whom no disaster appalled, but his courage and energy seemed to gain new strength in the midst of confusion and disorder. He fell at his post fighting like a lion at bay, and his native State has reason to be proud of his memory."

NORTH CAROLINA TROOPS

North Carolina provided approximately 125,000 men to the Confederate Army during the Civil War: in all, seventy-eight regiments of infantry, plus numerous artillery and cavalry units. Among them were the 26th North Carolina, which lost 714 of its 800 men at Gettysburg – in numbers and percentage the war's greatest losses. On the first day alone this regiment lost 584 dead and wounded; G Company lost all but one man.

In February 1864, twenty-two captured soldiers of the Second Regiment North Carolina Union Volunteers were hanged in Kinston for deserting the Confederate army to join the opposing forces. Others who were captured went to prison, where many of them died. More than 5,000 North Carolina African-Americans joined the Union army during the war.

THE 22ND NORTH CAROLINA REGIMENT

Of the infantry units, the 22nd North Carolina Regiment was one of the longest serving. As part of the Army of Northern Virginia it participated in every notable action in which that army was engaged, with the exception of the First Battle of Bull Run (First Manassas).

The regiment was organized in camp near Raleigh in July, 1861, and until March, 1862, was stationed in support of gun batteries at Evansport, Virginia, which had been erected to block water traffic on the Potomac River to Washington, D.C. In March, 1862, after the Confederate withdrawal from the Potomac to the line of the Rappahannock, the regiment took post at Fredericksburg. Subsequently, it took part in the Williamsburg and Yorktown campaigns, the Battle of Seven Pines, in the Seven Days Battles around Richmond, the battles of Cedar Mountain, Second Manassas (Second Bull Run), Harpers Ferry, Sharpsburg – where it helped repulse of Burnside's attack at the "Stone Bridge" – and Fredericksburg.

The winter of 1862–63 was passed in picket duty on the Rappahannock below Fredericksburg but in May 1863, at Chancellorsville, the 22nd Regiment fought its eighteenth and most costly battle. During Jackson's flank attack on Hooker, the regiment was heavily engaged and suffered very severely. Some 219 men and twenty-six of thirty-three officers were killed or wounded. Nevertheless, the 22nd Regiment went on to fight at Gettysburg, in Trimble's division, supporting Pickett's famous attack on Cemetery Ridge.

In October and November 1863, the regiment fought on the Rapidan River, and at Mine Run in December, after which it went into winter quarters until the spring of 1864. In May of that year, it went into battle at Spottsylvania, then North Anna, at Cold Harbor in early June, and during the summer operated in the vicinity of Petersburg. During the bleak winter of 1864–65, the 22nd North Carolina was in the trenches south of Petersburg, Virginia. At the Wilderness battles of May, 1865, under A. P. Hill's Corps, the regiment was again heavily engaged. As reported in the spring of 1865, the death roll of the regiment amounted to 580.

North Carolina Units Furnished	
Confederate	
Infantry regiments	69
Infantry battalions	4
Cavalry regiments	9
Cavalry battalions	9
Heavy artillery battalions	2
Artillery regiments	4
Light artillery battalions	3
Light artillery batteries	4
Engineer regiments	4
Sharpshooter battalions	1
Sharpshooter independent units	4
Union	
Infantry regiments	2
Mounted infantry regiments	2
Colored regiments	4
Colored heavy artillery	1

The Bennett Place, North Carolina, where General Joseph Johnston surrendered to General Sherman, April 26, 1865.

THE 25TH NORTH CAROLINA REGIMENT

Organized on August 15, 1861, at Camp Patton, Asheville, North Carolina, the men of the 25th Regiment came from counties in the western highlands, including Buncombe, Cherokee, Clay, Haywood, Henderson, Jackson, Macon, and Transylvania. The 25th was alternately stationed in Eastern North Carolina and Virginia, fighting in most of the battles in Virginia and Maryland.

It also served in Carolina coastal defense and fought with Robert E. Lee's Army of Northern Virginia at Antietam (Battle of Sharpsburg), Fredericksburg, Seven Pines, the Crater, and Sailor's Creek. In June 1864, the 25th fought in the trenches of Petersburg, Virginia, and was with the Army of Northern Virginia until the surrender at Appomattox on April 12, 1865. Over the course of the war, as many as a fifth of the unit deserted.

Monument to the 26th North Carolina Infantry at Cemetery Ridge.

NOTH CAROLINA CONFEDERATE ARMY DEATHS

	Killed	Died of Wounds	Died of Disease	Total
Officers	677	330	541	1,548
Enlisted	13,845	4,821	20,016	38,682
Total	14,522	5,151	20,557	40,230

OF 3,156 NORTH CAROLINA TROOPS FIGHTING FOR THE UNION, 360 LOST THEIR LIVES FROM SIMILAR CAUSES

Ohio's flag, adopted in 1902, has a unique shape and an uncomplicated design with a large "O" in the center. The thirteen stars grouped around the "O" represent the thirteen colonies, and the four stars to the right of center bring the count to seventeen, representing Ohio's statehood as the seventeenth state.

Ohio

" The North can make a steam engine, locomotive or railway car; hardly a yard of cloth or a pair of shoes can you make. You are rushing into war with one of the most powerful, ingeniously mechanical and determined people on earth – right at your doors. You are bound to fail. Only in spirit and determination are you prepared for war. In all else you are totally unprepared, with a bad cause to start with. "

WILLIAM T. SHERMAN ON DECEMBER 24, 1860, AFTER HE LEARNED OF SOUTH CAROLINA'S SECESSION

During the American Civil War, the only battle of consequence fought within Ohio's state borders took place at Buffington Island in July 1863. However, in strategic terms, Ohio's geographic location at the heart of the Union, bordering Kentucky and West Virginia, gave it vital importance.

The state's agricultural and industrial output was also essential to the Union effort, and the Ohio River and the extensive railroad network were important arteries for troop and supply movements. Ohio also provided some 310,654 soldiers for the Union Army. More than 260 regiments of men were raised in the state itself, while several more companies of Ohioans served in West Virginia, Kentucky, and Massachusetts regiments. More than 5,000 African-American soldiers also volunteered. Overall, a greater proportion of Ohioans *per capita* served than any other state in the Union.

Despite this, Ohio experienced the same internal political divisions that affected many Northern states. Most Ohioans were opposed to secession and supported the war. In fact, since the time that Ohio was granted statehood, in 1803, slavery had been outlawed in the state constitution and there was considerable sympathy for a nationwide abolition of the practice. Nevertheless, among the population, especially those living along the Ohio River, were many people who had migrated from slaveholding states. Because of a sense of fidelity, or familial ties, these Ohioans felt a greater empathy with the South. Furthermore, prior to the war, particularly in the southern Ohio, trade with the South in agricultural and manufactured products was an important source of income. Many Ohioans, merchants and poor alike, did not want economic links to be jeopardized by war. Opposition to the war was also motivated by hostility to the Union military drafts and another source of contention was the emancipation of slaves, which was advocated by many Northern politicians.

Some Ohioans feared that emancipation would bring a flood of African-Americans economic migrants to the North, including their own state, which would create more competition for jobs.

Ohio, particularly the southern border areas, was also home to a significant "Copperhead" faction. Although, as a group, Copperheads broadly supported the preservation of the Union, they advocated states' rights, vehemently opposed the war, and were one of the most prominent sources of opposition to the Lincoln administration. Ohio congressman Clement L. Vallandigham was the most vocal Copperhead supporters.

The Underground Railway from a painting by Chas. T. Webber.

THE UNDERGROUND RAILROAD

The Underground Railroad was an informal, illegal, network of people, routes and safe houses via which escaped slaves traveled to the North. Between 1810 and 1850, it is estimated that it helped 100,000 slaves to escape.

Its roots can be traced to the end of the 18th century, when the first organized system to assist runaway slaves began to emerge. Operating on the same principles and using the familiar terminology of the railways, it became known as "The Underground Railroad". Safe houses along the escape routes were called "stations" or "depots" and were run by "stationmasters". Financial benefactors were "stockholders", and the "conductor" was responsible for guiding fugitives between waypoints.

For those in held in bondage, the first and often most difficult step toward freedom was to escape the slaveholder. In this act slaves were usually alone and dependent entirely on their own resources. However, sometimes a "conductor" would surreptitiously enter a plantation and aid in guiding the escapee to freedom. Although fugitives would sometimes continue their journey by rail or riverboat, this was both costly and hazardous. Generally, escapees moved on foot, under cover of darkness, transiting between "stations" established at points on the various escape routes that existed. During the day they would rest and eat, and a message would be sent to the next station to alert the "stationmaster" of their imminent arrival.

Financial support, food, lodging, and assistance with resettlement and reemployment was provided both by individual donors and also raised by various philanthropic groups, including so-called "vigilance committees". The latter were organized in many towns and cities in the North, most prominently in New York, Philadelphia, and Boston. However, even after fleeing to the North, escapees were liable to be hunted down by bounty hunters and returned to their "owners".

One of the most notable participants in the Underground Railroad was John Fairfield of Ohio, whose own father had been a slaveholder. The Ohio River, which forms the southern border of Ohio, Indiana, and Illinois, was called the "River Jordan" by slaves who crossed it in their thousands to escape to the North.

CHICKAMAUGA AND CHATTANOOGA

When Major General William S. Rosecrans assumed command of the Army of the Ohio and the Department of the Cumberland in October 1862, the combined force was renamed the Army of the Cumberland. In mid-1863, Rosecrans led his army against Braxton Bragg's Army of the Tennessee in the Tullahoma Campaign in Middle Tennessee and, in the aftermath, Bragg fell back on Chattanooga, an important rail hub and manufacturing center on the Tennessee River. In the meantime, Rosecrans regrouped at Murfreesboro, and began to plan his next move.

In mid-August 1863, he embarked on the Chickamauga Campaign, to wrest Chattanooga from Bragg's forces. Rosecrans split his army into three corps (XXI, XX, and XIV), and sent them southeast from Murfreesboro on separate lines of advance. The army crossed the Tennessee River at points west and southwest of Chattanooga at the end of the August.

On September 8th, with elements of XXI Corps threatening Chattanooga from the north, Bragg withdrew his army south into Georgia. However, with the Army of the Cumberland now dispersed and reliant on tenuous supply lines, Bragg saw a chance to seize the initiative. On the 17th he advanced to engage XXI Corps. Rosecrans' army fell back on to positions near the West Chickamauga Creek and fighting began in earnest on the morning of the 19th, near Jay's Mills. Repeated assaults by Confederate troops pummeled XIV Corps, on the Union left flank, forcing Rosecrans to pull this wing back. The next day, Bragg continued his assault on the left of the Union line. In response, Rosecrans pulled troops out of his right flank to reinforce the left. In late morning, when Confederate forces launched a major assault on the Union right, they encountered a weakened opposition. The right flank of the Union Army collapsed and began retreating northwest toward McFarland's Gap. Fortunately for Rosecrans, the Union left flank under George H. Thomas was able to hold Horseshoe Ridge and Snodgrass Hill and cover the withdrawal. Although the Confederates launched determined assaults on Thomas' embattled lines, they held until Thomas ordered his troops to withdraw under cover of darkness. Although the withdrawal was accomplished in good order, the defeat at Chickamauga was one of the worst maulings the Union Army suffered during the war.

McCLELLAN'S "GRAND SCHEME" – THE PENINSULA CAMPAIGN

In the aftermath of his defeat at the First Battle of Bull Run, McDowell was replaced as commander of the Union Army by Major General George B.

General George B. McClellan with his staff.

McClellan. During his brief tenure as commander, McClellan worked to forge the Army of the Potomac into an effective fighting force. Subsequently, it would become the major Union army in the Eastern Theater.

McClellan was a fastidious planner but vacillated in forming a plan to attack the South. After repeated calls to begin offensive operations, he decided to move against the Confederate capitol of Richmond via the Yorktown Peninsula. The Peninsula Campaign was probably the most ambitious Union operation of the war. McClellan's plan, scheduled to begin in March, 1862, was to outflank Johnston's army in front of Washington (based around Centreville, northern Virginia) by transporting a 100,000-strong army by sea to Urbanna, on the Rappahannock River. Having bypassed Johnston's defenses, McClellan planned to advance towards Richmond.

Before the attack could commence, McClellan's plan was struck by a major blow when Johnston withdrew to south of the Rappahanock River. McClellan had to rethink and chose to land at Fort Monroe on the southeastern tip of the peninsula. The most pressing problem now was the presence of the ironclad C.S.S. *Virginia*, a powerful warship that would become a major threat to Union shipping movements on the James. Nevertheless, working to the revised plan, the huge Union transport fleet sailed from Alexandria on March 17th, bringing 120,000 troops and their equipment to join the men already at Fort Monroe.

The defense of the peninsula was in the hands of Major General John Bankhead Magruder, who had some 70,000 men. As part of his preparations, Magruder built two defensive lines, one anchored on the left on Yorktown and another ten miles back from the first, just in front of Williamsburg.

On April 4th, McClellan began to move up the peninsula and by the next day the Union Army had reached the outskirts of Yorktown. Believing he faced an army at least as strong as his own, McClellan started probing the Confederate defenses on the north bank of the Warwick River and preparing elaborate siege works. By the time these preparations were completed in early May, the Confederates had already withdrawn.

Continuing up the peninsula, McClellan next attacked Fort Magruder and Eltham's Landing (or West Point). By the end of May, the bulk of his army was poised on the eastern outskirts of Richmond. Now, Johnston attacked the Union forces in the vicinity of Seven Pines (or Fair Oaks). Although the battle was inconclusive, it shook McClellan's confidence. He paused to consolidate the Union forces, giving Lee valuable time to bolster Richmond.

The assault on the Confederate capital never came. Instead, in the last week of June, Lee launched a series of savage attacks on the Union forces to the east of Richmond, in what are known as the "Seven Days Battles". McClellan pulled back and returned to Washington, D.C. where he tried to pin his failure on lack of men and support, although he had outnumbered his opponents for the entire campaign.

Important Unionists

Salmon Portland Chase.

Edwin M. Stanton.

SALMON P. CHASE (1808–73)

A lawyer, politician, and leading abolitionist, over the course of his career Chase was a Governor of Ohio and senator for the state as well as secretary of the treasury and, finally, a Supreme Court chief justice.

Born in New Hampshire, after graduating from Dartmouth College in 1826, Chase moved to Washington, D.C., studied law, and was admitted to the bar in 1829. In 1830, he returned to Ohio and practiced law in Cincinnati. There, the deep-held religious and moral convictions that Chase had nurtured as a youth prompted him to join abolitionist and reformist groups. He also used his legal skills to defend escaped slaves.

Although initially a Whig, Chase helped form the anti-slavery Liberty party, and became one of its leaders. He was also a founder of the Free Soil Party and, in early 1849, was elected on a joint Free Soil/Democrat platform to the U. S. Senate. He used this office to protest measures such as the Compromise of 1850 and the Kansas-Nebraska Act.

When the Republican Party began to form in reaction to the Kansas-Nebraska Act, Chase was an early supporter. Elected Governor of Ohio in 1855 and 1857, and a U.S. senator in 1860, he served as secretary of the treasury from 1861 until July 1864 when his radical anti-slavery stance and political ambitions put him at odds with Lincoln. He resigned, but Lincoln appointed him as Supreme Court chief justice. In this role, Chase presided over cases concerning the Civil War and the Reconstruction.

EDWIN M. STANTON (1814–69)

Edwin Stanton was a lawyer, politician, and leading abolitionist, as well as attorney general under the Buchanan administration and secretary of war under Lincoln and Johnson.

Born in Steubenville, Ohio, he graduated from Kenyon College in 1833, studied law, and was admitted to the Ohio bar in 1835. He later practiced law in Pittsburgh and Washington, D.C. While in Ohio, Stanton became involved with a local abolitionist group and, in his professional capacity, represented both the state and the Federal government in legal cases. Two years later, he was part of the team that successfully defended Congressman Daniel Sickles against a murder charge.

In 1860, Stanton gave up his private law practice to become attorney general in the administration of James Buchanan and, in 1862, President Lincoln named him secretary of war. Stanton proved to be strong and effective in the role, instituting practices to rid the War Department of waste and corruption. He was also vigorous in his efforts to rid the government and the army of those who he suspected of harboring sympathies for the South. Although Stanton had ambitions to become Supreme Court chief justice, Lincoln felt that his talents were better employed as secretary of war, and appointed Salmon P. Chase to the post instead.

After rushing to the scene of Lincoln's assassination, Stanton uttered a brief but memorable epitaph to the slain president: "Now he belongs to the ages." He later served in Andrew Johnson's cabinet as secretary of war, but was part of the effort to impeach the new president and remove him from office. Resigning in May 1868, Stanton returned to his private legal practice. That December, his lifelong ambition to sit on the Supreme Court appeared to be fulfilled when President Grant appointed him to the office. He died, however, four days later in Washington, D.C.

William Dennison.

Bust of David Tod inside the National McKinley Birthplace Memorial in Niles, Ohio.

This woodcut from *Harper's Weekly*, December 26, 1863, is based on a photograph of Governor-Elect John Brough.

GOVERNOR WILLIAM DENNISON (1815–82)

Born in Cincinnati, Dennison was a successful railroad promoter and banker. A lifelong Republican, he was strongly opposed to slavery. In 1859, he was elected Governor of Ohio and did a great deal to help recruiting in Ohio. He supported Lincoln's nomination as the Republican candidate for the 1864 presidential election. His reward arrived in September 1864 when he bacame postmaster general. Post-war, he served in the Johnson administration but soon became disillusioned with Johnson and resigned.

GOVERNOR DAVID TOD (1805–68)

Tod was born in Youngstown, Ohio, studied law, and was a member of the Democratic Party. He went into politics in 1838 and became an Ohio state senator, returning to the law on completion of his term. A prominent member of Ohio's Democratic Party, he made two unsuccessful bids to become governor before serving as U.S. minister to Brazil 1847–51.

After Lincoln's election in 1860, Tod joined the Union Party, a newly established party that supported Lincoln's administration and represented the interests of pro-war Democrats and Republicans. The party chose Tod as its gubernatorial candidate in 1861 and he won the election to become the twenty-fifth Governor of Ohio (in office from 1862).

As governor, Tod was required to administer draft measures in the face of strong anti-war sentiment. In the 1863 gubernorial election, the Union Party preferred John Brough as its candidate and Tod's tenure in office ended. In June 1864, he was offered the office of secretary of the treasury. In a poor health, he declined and retired.

GOVERNOR JOHN BROUGH (1811–65)

A newspaper editor and publisher, and twenty-sixth Governor of Ohio, Brough's political affiliation was with the Democrat Party. Like many other "War Democrats", during the war Brough lent his support to the Union Party.

He was born in Marietta, Ohio, and from age twelve, worked for the *Marietta Gazette*. He climbed the ranks of the newspaper business and at age twenty, purchased the *Washington County Republican*, a newspaper with noted Democrat sympathies. Later, he and his brother, Charles Henry Brough, purchased the *Lancaster Eagle*, another traditionally pro-Democrat newspaper. In 1841, the brothers added the *Cincinnati Advertiser* to their assets. While editor of the *Eagle*, Brough became active in politics. He served at the Ohio House of Representatives 1838–39, and was state auditor until 1845.

During the war, Brough joined the Union Party and in the run-up to the 1863 Ohio gubernatorial election stood against the sitting governor, David Tod, as the Union Party candidate. Partly due to his more vocal support of abolition, Brough was chosen to contest the election, subsequently defeating "Copperhead" leader Clement Vallandigham.

Brough strongly supported the Lincoln administration's war efforts, notably in the raising of troops, and backed Lincoln's re-election in 1864. He also worked to improve conditions for Ohio's soldiers. When Salmon P. Chase resigned as secretary of the treasury, Brough was offered the position but declined it to remain as governor. He died in office shortly after the end of the war.

Union Generals

MAJOR GENERAL WILLIAM T. SHERMAN (1820–91)

William Tecumseh Sherman was born in Lancaster, Ohio. In 1836, he entered West Point and, on graduating, was appointed 2nd lieutenant in the 3rd Artillery Regiment. His first field service was in Florida where he gained valuable knowledge of the geography of the Southern states that would prove invaluable during his wartime campaigning.

During the Mexican War (1846–48), Sherman served on the staff of the California military governor and later on the staff of the Commander of the Division of the Pacific. In 1853, he resigned from the army but rejoined as soon as the call for volunteers went out in 1861.

He was appointed colonel of the 13th U.S. Infantry Regiment, then commanded a brigade in McDowell's army. Promoted to brigadier general after First Bull Run, after Shiloh there was a further promotion, to major general. He also formed a bond of friendship with Ulysses S. Grant. In Grant's final Vicksburg Campaign, Sherman commanded the XV corps.

After Grant took command in the west, Sherman succeeded to the command of the Army of the Tennessee. And when Grant became general-in-chief of the Army, Sherman was made commander of the Department of the Mississippi, which included the armies of the Tennessee, the Cumberland, and the Ohio. With these three armies, he invaded Georgia in May 1864, took Atlanta, and then marched to Savannah.

When Grant became president, Sherman became commanding general of the army, a post he held until 1883. He died in 1891.

MAJOR GENERAL GEORGE B. MCCLELLAN (1825–85)

Although McClellan was just thirty-four years old when war broke out, he was already a noted military theorist and logistician. His knowledge of military matters had been nurtured at West Point, then during military service in the Mexican-American War and as an observer in the Crimean War. This experience meant that McClellan was quickly recruited to command Ohio's state militia and, soon after, elevated to command the Department of the Ohio.

In April 1861, soon after Lincoln's call to arms, two Ohio infantry regiments were dispatched to Washington, D.C. On May 3rd, all Federal troops in the states of Ohio, Indiana, and Illinois were combined in the Department of the Ohio, with headquarters in Cincinnati, Ohio. The first commander, Major General McClellan, organized the thousands of volunteers under his command and ordered camps to be built for their training. In early summer, Department of the Ohio troops under McClellan successfully occupied the part of western Virginia which had remained loyal to the Union.

McClellan's early achievements were noted by President Lincoln. Consequently, after the humiliating rout of the Union Army at the First Battle of Bull Run (First Manassas), Lincoln made McClellan the commander the Army of the Potomac. After his departure, the Department of the Ohio was commanded by a succession of generals, dissolved, and then reorganized. Troops from the department were formed into the Army of the Ohio.

GENERAL ULYSSES S. GRANT (1822–85)

A number of Civil War generals hailed from the "Buckeye State" but the most famous was Ulysses S. Grant, who rose to become commander-in-chief of the Union Army and, later, U.S. president.

Hiram Ulysses Grant (later Ulysses Simpson Grant) was born at Point Pleasant, Ohio, on April 27, 1822. In 1839, he enrolled at West Point, after which he joined the 4th Infantry Regiment and served during the Mexican War (1846–48). He resigned his commission in 1854, but offered his services to the Union Army in 1861 and was commissioned as colonel of the 21st Illinois Volunteers. Soon after, he was promoted to the rank of brigadier general and placed in charge of the District of Southeast Missouri. In late September, 1861, Grant moved his troops into Kentucky and established control over the Tennessee and Cumberland rivers – the main waterways into the heartland of the Confederacy. By spring 1862, he had extended Union control over much of western Tennessee. However, in the first week of April, he was beaten at Shiloh by a numerically superior Confederate force. Notwithstanding this loss, Lincoln ordered Grant to prosecute a campaign against Vicksburg. After two failed assaults, Grant laid siege and, on July 4, 1863, the city surrendered. With Vicksburg in Union hands, the western Confederacy was cut off from the eastern and the Union Army had total control of the Mississippi River.

Grant was promoted to the rank of major general and, in October 1863, placed in control of all armies from the Alleghenies to the Mississippi. Although Lincoln had some misgivings about him, in March, 1864, he promoted Grant to lieutenant general and gave him overall command of the Union Army. Although Lincoln appreciated Grant's abilities as a military commander, throughout the war both he and Secretary of War Edwin M. Stanton were frequently at loggerheads with the general over the prosecution of the war.

In the spring of 1864, Grant led the Army of the Potomac across the Rapidan River and entered the Wilderness where, in early May, he met Lee's forces in a series of bloody battles. Grant next

The classic June 1864 image of Lieutenant General Ulysses S. Grant standing by a tree in front of a tent, Cold Harbor, Virginia. The Cold Harbor battle was one of the bloodiest engagements of the Civil War.

moved south to Cold Harbor, which he took at great cost. With his sights set on Richmond, he captured Petersburg, but when Major General Jubal Early moved up the Shenandoah Valley in the summer of 1864, Lincoln demanded that Grant personally take command of the army defending the capital.

On April 4, 1865, the Union Army took control of Richmond after Lee's army and the Confederate government had abandoned it. Five days later, Lee contacted Grant and after agreeing terms on April 9th, surrendered his army at Appomattox Court House. Grant issued a brief statement: "The war is over; the rebels are our countrymen again and the best sign of rejoicing after the victory will be to abstain from all demonstrations in the field."

The last, and perhaps least eminent, of famous Ohioan generals, Irvin McDowell is chiefly remembered for losing the First Battle of Bull Run (First Manassas). McDowell was born in Columbus, Ohio, and, as a young man, studied in France. He graduated from West Point in 1838 and, from 1841, served at the military academy as assistant instructor in tactics. He was appointed adjutant of West Point in 1845. During the Mexican War (1846–48) he was aide-de-camp to General Wood and following that worked in the War Department in Washington, D.C. where he made important contacts with leading Republican Party politicians including Abraham Lincoln and Salmon Chase.

On the outbreak of the Civil War, McDowell was given command of the Union Army south of the Potomac, but in July was heavily defeated by the Confederate Army at Bull Run. Recalled, he was given the task of defending Washington, D.C. In late August, 1862, at the Second Battle of Bull Run (Second Manassas), McDowell commanded III Corps in the Army of North Virginia. Criticized for his performance in the battle, he was relieved on his command. Although he demanded a court of inquiry and was ultimately exonerated, McDowell sat out the next two years of the war. By July, 1864, however, his reputation was rehabilitated and McDowell was given command of the Department of the Pacific. He retired as a major general in 1882 and afterward served as Park Commissioner of San Francisco.

Ohio's Generals as Future Presidents

After the Civil War, the United States was served by a succession of three Ohio-born presidents, all of whom had been Union military commanders. The first of the trio was Ulysses S. Grant, the former commander-in-chief of the Union Army and secretary of war under Johnson. Grant had won many admirers among the voting public for his prosecution of the war and this support helped him to be elected president in 1868, and again in 1872.

Grant's first administration pushed forward Reconstruction in the South, sometimes using the military to enforce unpopular measures. Perhaps his most lasting, but often overlooked, achievement was to secure ratification of the 15th Amendment in 1870. In the words of the Amendment, "The right of citizens of the United States to vote shall not be denied or abridged by the United States or by any state on account of race, color, or previous condition of servitude." This was an early, important, move to secure the freedoms of African-Americans and Native-Americans.

Although widely perceived as a man of scrupulous honesty, Grant was accused of impropriety on more than one occasion. In fact, his presidency was tainted by several prominent scandals, including the Fisk/Gould Scandal that caused panic in the U.S. financial markets. Grant campaigned for re-election in 1872 and, after retiring from the presidency, became a partner in a financial firm that ultimately went bankrupt. He died in 1885, not long after completing his hugely popular memoirs.

In March 1877, Rutherford B. Hayes (1822–93) succeeded Grant to become the 19th President of the United States, holding office from 1877 to 1881. He was born in Ohio and studied at Kenyon College and Harvard Law School. After graduating, he set up as an attorney in Lower Sandusky and

President James A. Garfield.

President Rutherford B. Hayes.

subsequently moved to Cincinnati, where he continued to practice law. Hayes fought in the Civil War, was wounded in action, and rose to the rank of brevet major general. While he was still in the army, Cincinnati Republicans ran him for the House of Representatives. He reluctantly accepted the nomination, believing that as a soldier his place was with his men. Nonetheless, he was elected by a heavy majority and entered Congress in December 1865. Between 1867 and 1876, he served three terms as Governor of Ohio.

In the 1876 presidential election, Hayes stood against Samuel J. Tilden as the Republican Party candidate. The closely fought election had to be decided by an electoral commission. Hayes chose his cabinet on the basis of merit, offending many within his own party because one cabinet member was an ex-Confederate and another a Liberal Republican. In office, he pledged protection of the rights of African-Americans. Hayes had announced in advance that he would serve only one term and after retiring he saw out the rest of his days in Fremont, Ohio.

James A. Garfield (1831–81), president after Hayes, was born in Cuyahoga County, Ohio. He paid his own way through Williams College in Massachusetts and took up a post as a classics professor in what is now Hiram College in Ohio. Garfield was elected to the Ohio Senate in 1859 as a Republican and during the Civil War served the Union Army, rising to the rank of major general of volunteers by 1864. During this time Garfield's

political career was also in ascendance. In 1862, he was elected to Congress and was soon the leading Republican in the House. At the 1880 Republican Convention, Garfield was belatedly chosen as the presidential nominee and in the subsequent election he defeated the Democrat candidate, General Winfield Scott Hancock, by a slender margin of only 10,000 votes. Garfield held office for only a few brief months, however. On July 2nd, 1881, he was shot in a Washington D.C. railroad station. He lay mortally wounded in the White House for weeks, until on September 19th, he died.

President Grant with his family – his wife, Julia, and son, Jesse – at his cottage by the sea.

8th Regiment Ohio Volunteer Infantry
Monument, north side of Bloody Lane,
Antietam National Battlefield.

John Hunt Morgan's Raid
June-July 1863

John Hunt Morgan
June 1, 1825 – September 4, 1864

JOHN HUNT MORGAN'S OHIO RAID, JULY 2-26, 1863

In July 1863, defying strict orders not to cross the Ohio River, Brigadier General John Hunt Morgan led a force of 2,000 cavalrymen from Wheeler's Cavalry Corps on a audacious raid across southern Ohio. Entering the state from Indiana, his force evaded the pursuing Union cavalry for nearly a month as they roved across twenty Ohio counties. Morgan's "Great Raid" penetrated deeper into the North than any other Confederate incursion and, in so doing, his raiders covered over seven hundred miles. On July 26th, after most of his men had been taken prisoner, Morgan himself was finally captured near New Lisbon, Ohio. He escaped from the state penitentiary that November, but was killed the following year in Tennessee. Along with the Battle of Buffington Island, this raid was the only significant military action of the Civil War within Ohio.

OHIO UNION ARMY DEATHS

Troops Furnished	Killed/Mortally Wounded	Died of Disease	Died of Other Causes	Total
309,906	11,588	23,887	0	35,475

Celebrated Ohio Infantry Regiments

49TH REGIMENT

The 49th Ohio was organized in September, 1861, at Tiffin, Ohio, under Colonel William H. Gibson and by the war's end suffered more battle deaths than any other Ohio unit. The men were recruited from several counties, most notably Seneca, and first served in the occupation of Munfordsville during the winter of 1861.

In early spring, 1862, the regiment moved to Nashville and, in April, participated in the Battle of Shiloh. It moved with the Army of the Ohio (Halleck) on Corinth and took part in the siege of that city. After Corinth was evacuated, the 49th Ohio entered Alabama, pursuing Bragg north to Louisville and then went south, reaching Nashville in October. At the end of the year, the regiment distinguished itself in the Battle of Stone's River, where it sustained severe losses.

In September 1863, the regiment was engaged again at the Battle of Chickamauga, and at Missionary Ridge during the Chattanooga Campaign. In May 1864, it embarked on the Atlanta Campaign. Fighting under General Sherman in the 4th Army Corps, Army of the Cumberland, the troops of the 49th Ohio took an active part in the battles of Dalton, Resaca, Dallas, and Pickett's Mill. The regiment then marched north with Thomas's army and fought at Franklin and Nashville.

After Hood's defeat it pursued him across the Tennessee River and, in March, 1865, moved into East Tennessee. The 49th Ohio Infantry Regiment was mustered out November 30, 1865.

8TH VOLUNTEER REGIMENT

Organized on April 29, 1861, at Camp Taylor, Ohio, the 8th Ohio was mustered into service on May 2nd. Its nine companies were chiefly composed of men from the north of the state. The regiment was soon transferred to the (West) Virginia theater of operations, where it participated in the Shenandoah Valley Campaign and, subsequently, in the Maryland Campaign, gaining distinction at the Battle of Antietam (Battle of Sharpsburg). The 8th also participated in the Battle of Fredericksburg and the Chancellorsville Campaign. However, its reputation was made during the Battle of Gettysburg.

On July 2, 1863, the regiment was ordered to take up positions beyond the Emmitsburg Road. It remained in these exposed positions, under constant enemy fire, throughout the 2nd and 3rd July and also during "Pickett's Charge". Reporting on this action, Union Colonel Samuel S. Carroll wrote, "Too much credit cannot be given to both the officers and men of that regiment, as well as their gallant leader, Lieut. Col. Franklin Sawyer, and Captain Kenny, acting major."

Monuments to the 8th Ohio stand at both the Antietam and Gettysburg battlefield sites. According to the monument at Gettysburg, of the 209 men of the 8th Ohio who went into battle that day, eighteen were killed, eighty-three wounded, and one went missing.

Following the Battle of Gettysburg, the 8th was placed on detached duty to New York City to restore order following the Draft Riots. It returned to the Army of the Potomac in September and engaged in a number of small scale actions until spring 1864.

Ohio Union Units Furnished	
Cavalry regiments	13
Cavalry battalions	5
Independent companies	10
Heavy artillery regiments	2
Light artillery batteries	42
Sharpshooter units	10
Infantry regiments	227
Infantry battalions	1
Independent infantry units	5

Oregon

" The news of the attack on Fort Sumter did not reach Oregon until April 29, 1861 – nearly 17 days after the attack – when a steamship from San Francisco delivered the latest headlines from back east. The future General Philip Sheridan, who was at that time commanding Fort Yamhill, Oregon, was ordered to relinquish command of the outpost to a Capt. James J. Archer. Sheridan didn't trust him, writing that Archer "intended to go South" and "I would not turn over the command to him for fear he might commit some rebellious act." Sheridan proved right. Archer resigned his commission to join the Confederate army, and Sheridan was able to turn the fort over to a Union officer. "

FROM *THE COLUMBIAN*

Oregon was peripheral to the main fighting of the Civil War and no military actions of significance were fought between Union and Confederate forces there. At the outbreak of war, statehood had only recently been achieved and Oregon remained largely undeveloped and agrarian.

Oregon's economic contribution was therefore also insignificant. Furthermore, though there was a large influx of migrants to the state during the 1850s, it remained sparsely populated. Only a single regiment of infantry and one of cavalry were raised for the Union Army. Perhaps the most enduring legacy of the Civil War for Oregon is that as many as 30,000 veterans emigrated to the new state after peace arrived.

The first semblance of a state government had been organized in Oregon in 1843, when executive and legislative committees were established. In political terms, Oregon was, like many states, divided over the issue of secession. In the years before the war, when Oregon was a territory seeking statehood, there was much debate over whether it would be a "slave state" or a "free state". Oregonians settled for a compromise solution. In 1857, they voted to make slavery illegal, but also to make it illegal for African-Americans to live in the state. This law was never enforced, but it certainly discouraged settlement by emancipated slaves and African-Americans who had been born free. In August 1857, when delegates met at Salem to draft a constitution for the state, the document they produced contained a clause that banned "negro, Chinaman or mulatto" from voting. This was subsequently approved by the electorate.

Officially, Oregon supported the Union and the war, with Union sympathies being strongest in the northern part of the state. However, there was also considerable secessionist sentiment. In 1860, Oregon U.S. Senator Joseph Lane was the vice-presidential candidate with John C. Breckenridge

JOHN WHITEAKER (1820–1902)

Whiteaker served as the first state Governor of Oregon. Once in office, he concentrated mainly on untangling the huge number of land claims and counter claims on public lands. Although nicknamed "Honest John", this did not deflect his controversial stand on issues of national importance. Whiteaker, a Democrat, held pro-slavery views that conflicted with public abolitionist sentiment. As the nation descended into civil war, Republicans attacked him as a traitor. After serving one term as governor, Whiteaker later became speaker of Oregon's House of Representatives.

U.S. Senator Joseph Lane, the first Governor of Oregon Territory.

Confederate Albert Sidney Johnston refused to aid conspirators in creating a "Pacific Republic" from parts of Oregon and California.

THE DISTRICT OF OREGON DURING THE CIVIL WAR

At the outbreak of war, military affairs in Oregon came under the administration of the Department of the Pacific, which also oversaw California, the Washington Territory, Utah Territory, and the Territory of New Mexico east of the 110th meridian west, (thus including most of modern Arizona and southern Nevada). Regular U.S. troops stationed in the state were withdrawn and sent east. Volunteer cavalry and infantry were recruited in California and sent north to Oregon to keep peace and protect the populace. At that time, the major threat was the escalating conflict between the miners and ranchers and the Paiute, Shoshone, and Bannock tribes in the eastern part of the state. In 1864, this conflict erupted as the Snake War.

THE TWO OREGON UNITS

Oregon raised two units for the Union Army: the 1st Oregon Cavalry and the 1st Oregon Volunteer Infantry Regiment. The former was raised between February and April, 1862, and served until June 1865. In November 1864, 1st Oregon Volunteer Infantry Regiment was organized in response to a national call for volunteers and authorized by the newly elected governor, Addison C. Gibbs.

Each of the eleven companies of the 1st Oregon Volunteer Infantry Regiment was raised from a different region of the state. Training was carried out at Fort Vancouver and the companies were stationed at various posts in the western portion of the state. Detachments of the regiment were at Fort Vancouver, Fort Klamath, Fort Yamhill, Fort Steilacoom, Fort Dalles, Fort Walls, Colville, Fort Hoskins, and Fort Boise (Idaho Territory). The troops patrolled the Oregon Trail and southeastern Oregon but did not experience any major engagements. Instead, they were used to guard travel routes and Indian reservations, as wells as escorting immigrant wagon trains. With the discovery of gold in the Blue Mountains in 1861, the regiment was tasked with protecting the freight trains and miners. Several detachments also accompanied survey parties and built roads in central and southern Oregon.

on the pro-slavery, or "Copperhead", Democratic ticket. In general, support for the Confederacy was concentrated in the counties of southern Oregon, as these were home to immigrants from Southern states who were engaged in mining and farming.

Oregon members of the "Knights of the Golden Circle", a prominent anti-Union group, were reportedly involved in a plot to seize Fort Vancouver, the headquarters of the District of Oregon on the Columbia River. They did not act, however. In another incident, which took place during the Secession Crisis, a group of Southern sympathizers in California made plans to unite with Oregon to form a breakaway "Pacific Republic". Their scheme rested on the cooperation of Colonel Albert Sidney Johnston, commander of the Department of the Pacific. Johnston, however, made it plain that he would not lend his support to the conspiracy and the plan came to nothing.

Fort Vancouver, May 1860. During the war, detachments of the 1st Washington Territory Infantry Volunteers and 1st Oregon Cavalry were stationed here.

Oregon Union Units Furnished	
Infantry regiments	1
Cavalry regiments	1

United States military post, Fort Vancouver, on the Columbia River.

OREGON UNION ARMY DEATHS

Troops Furnished	Killed/Mortally Wounded	Died of Disease	Died of Other Causes	Total
1,810	11	21	13	46

Pennsylvania

❝Now we are engaged in a great Civil War, testing whether that nation, or any nation, so conceived, and so dedicated, can long endure.❞

EXCERPT FROM ABRAHAM LINCOLN'S GETTYSBURG ADDRESS

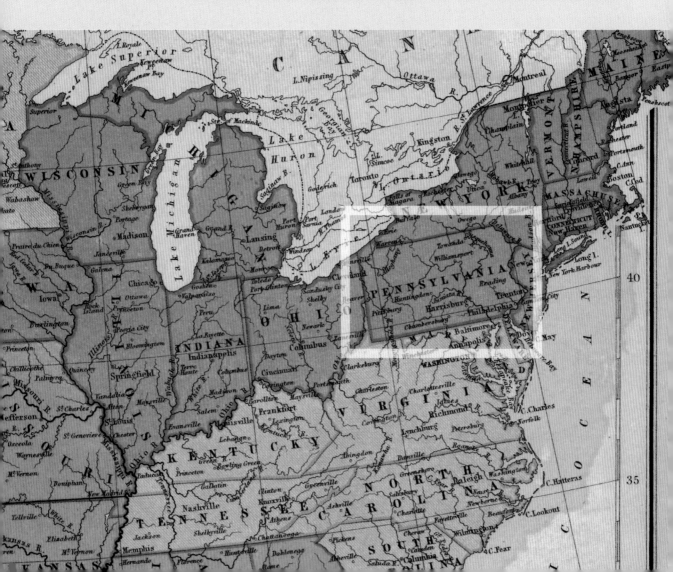

The Commonwealth of Pennsylvania, the second largest state in the Union with a population of 2,900,000, had serious financial problems in 1860 and a budget deficit of $30 million, half the size of the Federal government's.

Its once strong militia had wasted away because of neglect and pacifist influences within the electorate. The state's political landscape had also changed when Andrew Gregg Curtin became governor in October 1860 and Simon Cameron, Pennsylvania's former power broker, began losing his influence in the commonwealth.

Forty-three-year-old Curtin became the first Republican governor, though he ran on the ballot on the People's Party ticket, pledging a policy of "low tariff, free homesteads, and the well-being of the laboring man." Abraham Lincoln had not yet been elected, nor would he be until November, but sounds of secession were already emanating from the South. In his inaugural address, Curtin clearly differentiated himself from Democrats by renouncing the legality of secession. On April 15, 1861, after Lincoln issued a proclamation calling for 75,000 volunteers, Curtin added another $3,000,000 to the commonwealth's budget deficit to pay for organizing and outfitting the state's militia. He personally raised thirteen regiments and on April 18, 1861, established the state training center at Camp Curtin, outside the capital of Harrisburg. Curtin worked relentlessly through the war to bolster the Union Army, and through four years of war raised 270 regiments and enlisted 427,286 Pennsylvanians – including 8,600 African-Americans – roughly fifteen percent of the state's population.

SECRETARY OF WAR SIMON CAMERON (1799–1889)

A master politician, Cameron became powerful by exchanging favors and his contemporaries report that he never forgot a friend or forgave an enemy. In 1860, he displayed his political brilliance by striking a deal with Lincoln without the latter's knowledge. At the time, presidential candidates did not campaign on their own behalf but remained in the background while their campaign managers did the dealing. During the Chicago Republican presidential nominating convention in May 1860, Judge David Davis and Leonard Swett represented Lincoln's interests. Cameron was also on the ballot, along with several others, though he had no chance of winning the nomination because of his tainted reputation. Davis and Swett did not know that Curtin, who despised Cameron, was actually running the Pennsylvania political machine and though Lincoln had ordered his handlers to "make no contracts that will bind me," when Davis and Swett were approached by Cameron's managers they agreed to give the Pennsylvanian a post in Lincoln's cabinet in exchange for the ballots of the state's delegates. Lincoln would not have agreed, but the scheme worked. Lincoln had never met Cameron, knew nothing of the latter's past history of corruption while acting as an Indian claims adjuster in 1833, or his other shady dealings, but felt obliged to offer Cameron one of the lesser cabinet positions, though the wily Pennsylvanian insisted on the treasury department so he could spread patronage among friends. On the eve of his inauguration on March 4, 1861, Lincoln designated Cameron for the war department and regretted doing so within a month. He proved to be utterly incapable of running the post on a war-footing basis and lasted only ten months on the job. Later sent to Russia as minister, Cameron presented his credentials to the Czar, took leave, and returned home to run for the Senate.

GOVERNOR ANDREW GREGG CURTIN (1817–94)

Born in Bellefonte, Pennsylvania, Andrew Curtin gradually wrenched power from Simon Cameron, who had become known as the "Czar of Pennsylvania". The first Republican to be elected governor of the state, Curtin tackled its fiscal problems as well as the horrnedous problems of war. He personally raised regiments, augmenting the 427,000 enlistments recorded during the war. His feud with Cameron, which began in 1950, lasted until the latter's death in 1889. Nevertheless, when Cameron became secretary of war in 1861, Curtin ignored the strained relationship and gave his entire support to the war effort.

GENERAL ROBERT PATTERSON (1792–81)

Patterson had been in the army since the War of 1812, and when Secretary of War Simon Cameron asked Pennsylvania for several three-months militia regiments, Curtin named the seventy-year-old general to command them. Unfortunately, Patterson did not understand the technological improvements made in warfare since the Mexican War, where he had served as a major general. He had a key role to play at 1st Bull Run but failed to engage the enemy in battle. After much criticism, he lost his command six days later and, on July 27, 1861, mustered out.

THE UNION DEPARTMENT OF PENNSYLVANIA

After Lincoln's call for troops, on April 27, 1861, the war department created the Union Department of Pennsylvania, which included the state of Delaware and the western part of Maryland. Sixty-nine-year-old Major General Robert Patterson, a veteran of the War of 1812 and the Mexican War, assumed command of the department from his headquarters in Philadelphia. Patterson moved slowly, badgering Cameron for more men, arms, uniforms, and supplies. By early June his forced consisted of sixteen regiments, and with 13,000 untested men he began advancing toward Harpers Ferry with orders to drive away the Confederates and shore up Union support in western Virginia.

Patterson's militia made slow progress, forded the Potomac River, crossed into Virginia on July 2nd, and immediately clashed with a brigade of General Joseph E. Johnston's Confederates. The sharp one-hour engagement at Falling Waters surprised Patterson, who spent the next two weeks parrying with Confederates without doing much fighting. Ordered by General-in-Chief Winfield Scott to keep Johnston's army engaged in the Shenandoah Valley, Patterson leisurely occupied Harpers Ferry and did nothing. On July 19th, unopposed, Johnston began shifting his forces to reinforce Brigadier General Pierre G.T. Beauregard's army at Manassas Junction. On July 21st, the combined Confederate armies of Beauregard and Johnston defeated a Union Army under the command of Brigadier General Irvin McDowell. McDowell's blueclads ran into a buzz-saw during the afternoon and fled back to Washington. General Scott blamed Patterson for the defeat, relieved him of command, and on August 24th merged the former Department of Pennsylvania into the more expansive Department of the Potomac.

THE CONFEDERATE INVASION OF PENNSYLVANIA: JUNE 1863

On June 3, 1863, one month after the Union defeat at Chancellorsville, advance elements from General Robert E. Lee's reorganized Army of Northern Virginia began edging toward the Shenandoah Valley. Lieutenant General Richard S. Ewell's II Corps crossed through the Blue Ridge Mountains and on June 15th destroyed Major General Robert H. Milroy's Union forces at Winchester, Virginia. Major General Joseph Hooker, commanding the Army of the Potomac, lost contact with Lee's army until around June 25th, when he learned the Confederate force was in Pennsylvania. Ewell continued marching eastward through Pennsylvania, capturing the army post at Carlyle, shelling Harrisburg, and menacing York. Governor Curtin screamed for help from the Federal government and tried to raise another 20,000 volunteers to protect the state.

Lee became concerned on June 28th when he learned the Army of the Potomac, now commanded by Major General George Gordon Meade, had taken a defensive position north of the Potomac near the Maryland border. After Confederates alarmed the entire North by confiscating livestock, food, and clothing and levying tribute on several towns, Lee regrouped his army. Having scattered his forces over

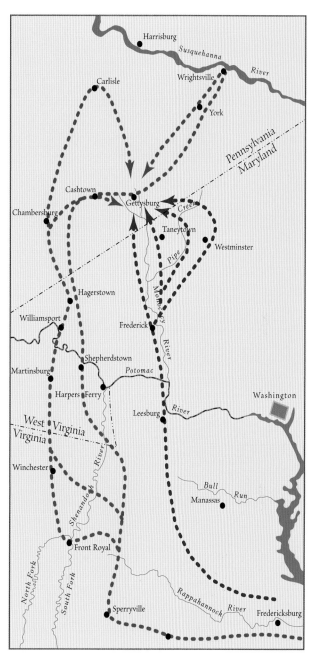

Map showing the routes of the Confederates into Pennsylvania and Gettysburg.

southern Pennsylvania, he ordered them to converge on Hagerstown, Maryland. The fastest route for many led across one of the nine roads passing through Gettysburg. The decisive moment of the Civil War had come.

The Battle of Gettysburg

DAY ONE: JULY 1, 1863

Generals like to choose their fields of battle, but on June 30, 1863, neither Lee nor Meade expected to bring on a major engagement at a Pennsylvania crossroads village called Gettysburg. Because of rumors of a shipment of shoes in Gettysburg, and infantry brigade of barefooted Confederates from Major General Henry Heth's division began marching eastward down the Chambersburg Pike. General Buford spotted Heth's veterans from the cupola of the Lutheran Seminary and dispatched couriers to inform General Reynolds, whose divisions were closest to Gettysburg. Buford dismounted his cavalry, placed his horse artillery near the Chambersburg Pike, and around 8:00 a.m. fired on advancing Confederate skirmishers. Heth's grayclads charged but were several times repulsed. Around 10:30 a.m. General Reynolds arrived with the first elements of the II Corps to relieve Buford and lost his life while directing the placement of reinforcements.

The unplanned battle quickly escalated after Confederate Lieutenant General Ambrose P. Hill ordered William D. Pender's division to join Heth's division in storming the Union line. The Confederates seized embattled McPherson's Ridge and began pushing the Federals back to Seminary Ridge, where the I Corps, now led by Abner Doubleday, regrouped. At noon, Major General Oliver O. Howard came on the field with the Union XI Corps about the same time as Lieutenant General Richard S. Ewell's Confederate II Corps appeared on the roads north of Gettysburg. Ewell charged and Howard's disorganized divisions fled through town about the same time that Hill charged and drove Doubleday's I Corps south of Gettysburg.

The headquarters of General George G. Meade on Cemetery Ridge. Photo by Alexander Gardner, July 1863.

General Winfield Scott Hancock's II Corps, which had reached Cemetery Hill, rallied the fleeing troops and placed them in defensive positions. Lee came on the field, recognized that Cemetery Ridge commanded the field, and ordered Ewell, "if possible," to drive Hancock and Howard off the hill. Ewell hesitated and never attacked. Having won the first day's battle, Lee ordered the Confederates to concentrate on Seminary Ridge, which ran roughly parallel to Cemetery Ridge and a mile to the west. Meade came on the field that night with the rest of the army and with assistance from Hancock placed divisions in defensive positions.

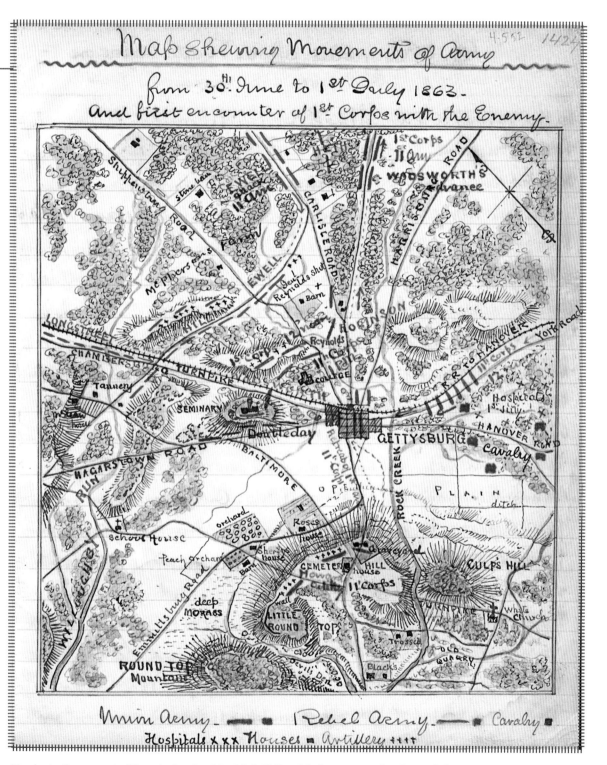

Map showing the movements of the armies from June 30 to July 1, 1863, and the first encounter of 1st Corps with the enemy.

Day Two: July 2, 1863

The Union line on Cemetery Ridge ran north and south and from the air resembled a fishhook. Culp's Hill and Cemetery Hill formed the hook on the right flank, the shank followed the ridge, and the eye on the unoccupied left flank rested on two hills, Little and Big Round Top. Confederates reconnoitered the position in the early morning and found the Federal right flank well defended but the left flank vulnerable. Lee, who could not decide whether to fight or retire, accepted Longstreet's plan to assault the Federal left.

Setting up the assault took time, and the route chosen to avoid Federal observation posts took more time. When Longstreet launched his assault around 4:00 p.m. with Lafayette McLaws' and John B. Hood's divisions, the Confederates ran into Major General Daniel Sickles' III Corps beside the Emmitsburg Road. Sickles had ignored Meade's orders and moved forward to higher ground, inadvertently forming a vulnerable salient that resulted in bloody actions known as the Wheat Field, Peach Orchard, Devil's Den, and Little Round Top. Meade rushed troops to extract Sickles' III Corps from the salient, and a last minute valiant defense saved Little Round Top and prevented Longstreet from breeching the Union left flank. The day ended with a futile Confederate attack on Culp's Hill on the Union right flank, which left both armies bloodied at the end of the day, but with each holding their respective positions.

The defeat of Pickett's Charge shown from the rear of the Union line on Cemetery Ridge, July 3, 1863. A few Confederates penetrated the Union position, only to lose their lives in the effort. Thure de Thulstrup's painting of the charge was published in *Prang's War Pictures*.

Above: Attack on Little Round Top held by the 5th Corps commanded by General Sykes.
Below: The Union lines on the morning of July 3rd during the attack of Johnston's division.

DAY THREE: JULY 3, 1863

As dawn broke on July 3rd, Meade could not decide whether to fight or retire. He held a council of war, during which Hancock urged him to fight. Having unsuccessfully attacked both Union flanks, Lee also decided to fight despite Longstreet's sound objections. He ordered Ewell to assault Culp's Hill to deceive Meade and draw forces while eleven brigades under Longstreet's command assaulted the Union center. Lee believed Union morale had been damaged, so he committed Major General George E. Pickett's fresh division and several other commands to the assault. Ewell's attack on Culp's Hill sputtered

prematurely at noon, one hour before Longstreet's mass bombardment on the Federal center began, thus giving Meade time to make defensive adjustments.

By 3:00 p.m. most of 140 cannon, which had overshot Hancock's position on Cemetery Ridge, were low on ammunition when Pickett's Charge began. After a short lull, 13,000 Confederates broke from concealed positions on Seminary Ridge and advanced across open fields toward a clump of trees on Cemetery Ridge. Union artillery cut great gaps in the Confederate advance, but the enemy closed ranks and crossed the Emmitsburg Road.

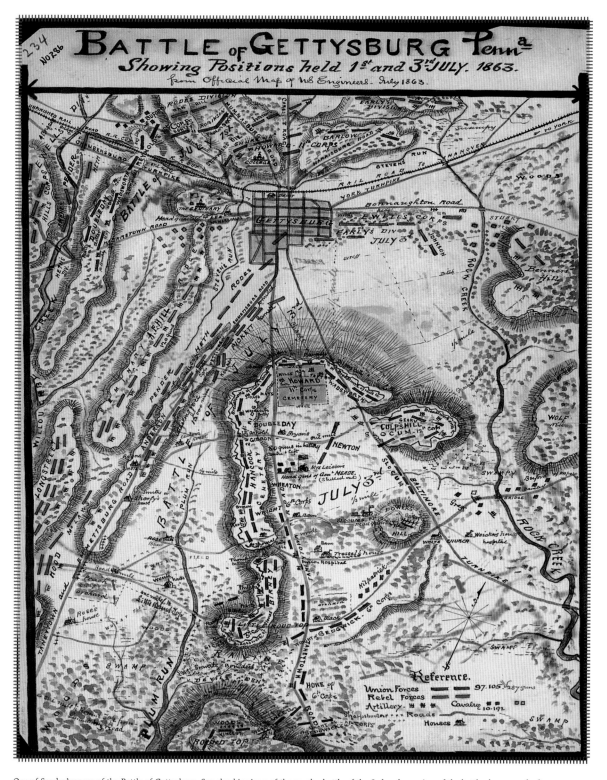

One of Sneden's maps of the Battle of Gettysburg. See also his views of the cavalry battle of the 3rd and overview of the battle shown overleaf.

The grayclads ascended the slope and ran into blazing Federal artillery and rifle fire that cut down hundreds of their trrops in a matter of seconds. A few men reached the clump of trees, only to be killed, wounded, or captured. The survivors streamed back to Seminary Hill. Many of the men never came close enough to fire a shot. Lee understood the defeat, and as the men straggled back into the woods, he met them, and said, "It's all my fault. My fault."

On the fourth day, the two armies stared at each other across the blood-stained fields. That night the Confederate army slipped away and moved toward the Potomac River with the wounded. Weeks passed before Meade followed. Although the Army of the Potomac won the Battle of Gettysburg, the Union lost the opportunity of perhaps ending the war.

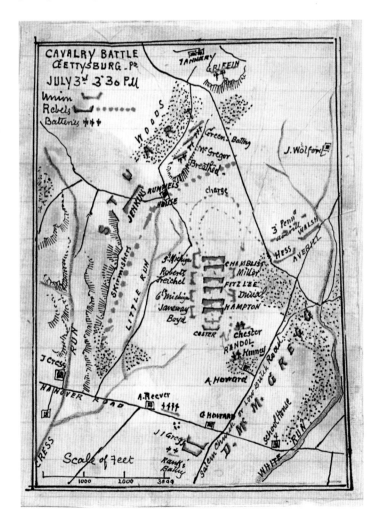

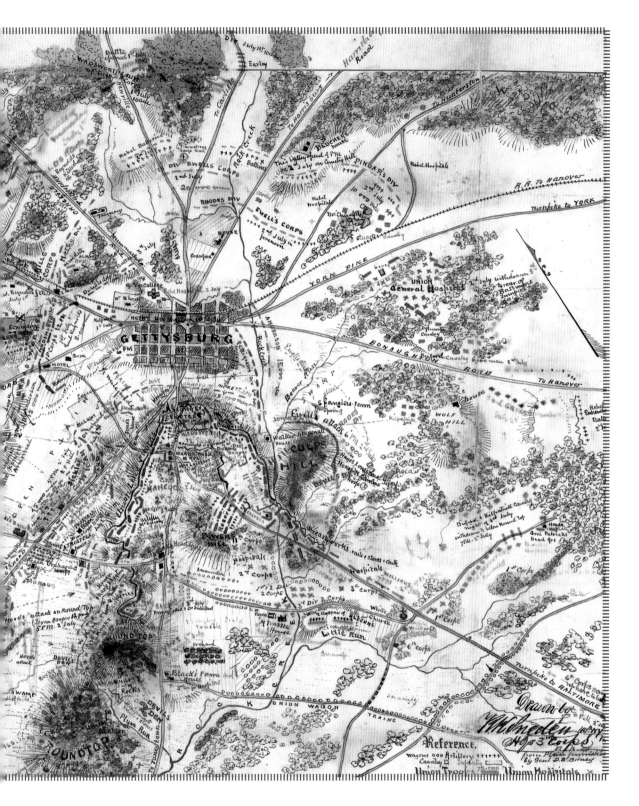

Distinguished Generals at Gettysburg

MAJOR GENERAL JOHN F. REYNOLDS (1820–63)

Born in Lancaster, Pennsylvania, forty-two-year-old John F. Reynolds graduated from the U.S. Military Academy in 1841 and spent the rest of his life in the army. Had Reynolds commanded the Army of the Potomac at the outset of the Civil War, he likely would have chosen an entirely different strategy than his predecessors and there may never have been a Gettysburg. Unlike most West Point men, Reynolds understood offensive tactics while many others, such as Meade and Major General George B. McClellan, preferred fighting defensively.

Reynolds commanded the I Corps in the Army of the Potomac after Lincoln replaced General Hooker with General Meade. On June 30, 1863, as Meade moved slowly toward the Pennsylvania border, Reynolds personally scouted into Gettysburg with Brigadier General John Buford's cavalry and spotted Confederate riders reconnoitering the area. He returned to Meade's headquarters and reported the incident. On the morning of July 1st, he put his divisions on two of the roads leading into Gettysburg shortly after Major General Henry Heth's Confederate brigades began moving toward the town in search of a shipment of shoes. When Major Abner Doubleday arrived with the 1st Division, Reynolds took personal charge of putting regiments in position to check the Confederate advance, thereby providing time for Meade to bring up the army and occupy Cemetery Hill. A stray bullet struck Reynolds in the head and killed him instantly. Reynolds' action at Gettysburg, along with Buford's dismounted cavalry, made Meade's victory at Gettysburg possible. On that day Pennsylvania and the Union lost one of its great generals.

MAJOR GENERAL WINFIELD SCOTT HANCOCK (1824–86)

A Pennsylvanian from a hamlet near Norristown, thirty-nine-year-old Winfield Scott Hancock, named after the venerable and former general-in-chief of the Union Army, graduated from West Point in 1840 and made the army his career. Appointed major general on November 29, 1862, he succeeded to the command of the Army of the Potomac's II Corps.

Hancock played a vital role at Gettysburg on July 1st by selecting the Union position on Cemetery Hill and putting arriving divisions in place in the center of Cemetery Ridge where they could help defend both flanks and the center. The action saved Culp's Hill and possibly the campaign. On July 2, when Lieutenant General James Longstreet attempted to turn the Union left flank in the Wheatfield and the Peach Orchard, Hancock threw in the I Corps. The action saved Daniel Sickles III Corps from being overrun and blocked the Confederate advance on the Round Tops, two previously undefended hills on the far left. On the third day, when Longstreet sent Major General George Pickett's columns in a desperate attempt to break the center of the Union line, Hancock rushed in reinforcements and repelled the assault, thus giving Meade one of the most important victories of the war.

During Pickett's charge, Hancock received a wound from which he never fully recovered when a bullet carried a nail and bits of wood from the pommel of his saddle into his thigh. Nevertheless, he resumed command of the II Corps late that year and distinguished himself and his corps in all the bloody fighting that followed in the Wilderness, Spotsylvania, and Cold Harbor.

Major General John F. Reynolds .

Major General Winfield Scott Hancock.

Major General John Gibbon.

Major General George Gordon Meade.

MAJOR GENERAL JOHN GIBBON (1827–96)

Born in Philadelphia in 1827, John Gibbon grew up in Charlotte, North Carolina, but unlike his three brothers who fought for the South, Gibbon graduated from West Point in 1847 and remained faithful to the North. After serving as McDowell's chief of artillery at First Bull Run, Gibbon became a brigade commander in the Army of the Potomac and led the famous Iron Brigade at Antietam. He commanded the 2nd Division of the I Corps at Fredericksburg, where he suffered a wound. Gibbon recovered in time to lead the 2nd Division of Hancock's II Corps at Gettysburg with conspicuous gallantry until he was again wounded and carried from the field.

After Gibbon recovered, he resumed command of his old division and participated in Grant's 1864 Overland Campaign from the Wilderness to Petersburg. In January 1865, he took command of the XXIV Corps, Army of the James, and was one of Grant's appointed commissioners designated to receive the official surrender of Robert E. Lee's Army of Northern Virginia at Appomattox. Gibbon remained in the army until retiring in 1891, making his home in Baltimore, where he died five years later.

GETTYSBURG CASUALTIES

	Killed	Wounded	Missing	Total
Federal	3,155	14,529	5,365	23,049
Confederate	3,903	18,735	5,425	28,063

MAJOR GENERAL GEORGE GORDON MEADE (1815–72)

Born in Spain of U.S. parents, forty-seven-year-old George Gordon Meade received orders on June 28th from the War Department, expressly issued by President Lincoln, to relieve Major General Joseph Hooker and take command of the Army of the Potomac. Lincoln passed over the more qualified John F. Reynolds because Meade's foreign birth, though he was a Pennsylvanian, disqualified him as a presidential candidate. A West Point man, Meade had served with distinction in the Army of the Potomac, commanded the V Corps, and understood the character and capabilities of the generals under him. Although he demonstrated great skills as a corps commander, he never wanted command of the Army of the Potomac and accepted it only after being ordered to take it. Meade quarreled with his subordinates, who behind his back called him "the old snapping turtle," partly because of his personal appearance and partly because of his acerbic nature. One biographer, Theodore Lyman, also the general's aide, wrote, "I don't know a thin old gentleman with a hooked nose and cold blue eye, who, when he is wrathy, exercises less of Christian charity than my beloved chief."

Despite having only two days to prepare for the Battle of Gettysburg, Meade put his force on Cemetery Hill, running south of Gettysburg, and by doing so occupied the best defensive position in the area. He fought a defensive battle and let Robert E. Lee's Confederates hurl themselves against his infantry and artillery. When Lee gave up the fight, Meade failed to pursue, which annoyed President Lincoln for the rest of the war.

Famous Regiments

THE 6TH PENNSYLVANIA CAVALRY

Known as Rush's Lancers after its commander, Colonel Richard H. Rush, the 6th Pennsylvania was among the first cavalry regiments to volunteer for service. Organized in Philadelphia, the regiment was composed of the city's elite, most of whom were athletes like their West Point commander. The unit entered the war armed with army Colt revolvers and light sabers, but General McClellan, who enjoyed pomp and ceremony more than fighting, suggested the unit adopt five-pound nine-foot-long lances bearing a scarlet swallow-tailed pennant and tipped with an eleven-inch, three-edged blade – an impractical weapon for modern warfare. By June 1863, prior to the Battle of Gettysburg, Rush discarded the lances and replaced them with carbines.

During Lee's movement into Pennsylvania, the 6th Pennsylvania fought Major General James Ewell Brown "Jeb" Stuart's Confederate cavalry on the eastern side of the Blue Ridge Mountains. These clashes kept Stuart from informing Lee of the movements of the Army of the Potomac prior to Gettysburg. Following the battle, Rush's Lancers were one of the few commands in the Army of the Potomac that relentlessly harassed Lee's retreat. The 6th remained in service until the end of the war, first pursuing Lee's army to its ultimate surrender at Appomattox and then riding on into North Carolina to participate in the surrender of General Johnston's Confederates on April 18, 1864.

THE 11TH PENNSYLVANIA RESERVES (40TH PENNSYLVANIA INFANTRY)

Recruited from the western counties of Pennsylvania, the 11th Pennsylvania became one of first thirteen regiments organized, trained, and equipped at state expense by order of Governor Andrew Curtain. On July 26, 1861, the regiment arrived in Washington and became part of General Meade's Pennsylvania

Samuel M. Jackson.

Reserves. In June 1862 the regiment joined General McClellan's Army of the Potomac on the Peninsula and fought in every major campaign from the Seven Days Battles to Gettysburg and Grant's Overland Campaign. Commanded successively by Colonels Thomas G. Gallagher and Samuel M. Jackson, the 11th Pennsylvania had the heaviest losses of any of the thirteen reserve regiments and the eighth highest percentage of killed in action of all Union regiments. Because of irreplaceable losses, the regiment mustered out of service on May 30, 1864.

THE 13TH PENNSYLVANIA RESERVES ("BUCKTAILS")

The Bucktails, known also as the "Kane Rifles", were recruited in April 1861 by Governor Curtin's mandate, and like other reserve units were mobilized and equipped at the expense of the state. Most of the volunteers were called "Lumbermen with a wildcat yell." They were excellent marksmen who brought their own rifles. The earliest recruits wore a bucktail and established a policy that no prospect could join the regiment without first demonstrating his skill with a rifle by bringing with him the tail of a buck. Unlike most volunteer units, the regiment carried long-range Sharps rifles and later adopted seven-shot breech-loading repeating Spencer carbines. After Colonel Thomas L. Kane received promotion to brigade commander, two of his successors were killed, Colonel Hugh W. McNeil at Antietam and Colonel Charles F. Taylor at Little Round Top during the Battle of Gettysburg.

In July 1862 Secretary of War Edwin M. Stanton asked for two more regiments composed of Bucktails, and, by the end of August, the 149th and 150th Pennsylvania mustered in at Harrisburg. Along with the 13th Bucktails, the three regiments participated in all the major campaigns in the East from Chancellorsville to Petersburg. Due to heavy losses the 13th Bucktails mustered out on June 14, 1864; the 149th and 150th in June 1865.

Camp of the 31st Pennsylvania Infantry near Washington, D.C., 1862.

Officers of 50th Regiment Pennsylvania Infantry.

Officers of 3rd Pennsylvania Heavy Artillery at Fort Monroe, Virginia. Soon after the Battle of Antietam, in September 1862, Joseph Roberts, major of the 4th Regular Artillery, received authority from the War Department to recruit a picked battalion of artillery for special service. Recruiting was immediately commenced and the companies were sent to the Fort Monroe where they were drilled by experienced officers in infantry, light, and heavy artillery duty. Early in the spring of 1863, an order was issued from the War Department directing that the two commands of Segebarth and Roberts should be consolidated in one regiment, to be known as the 3rd Pennsylvania Heavy Artillery.

Colonel Strong Vincent.   Colonel Hiram L. Brown.

THE 83RD PENNSYLVANIA

Raised in Erie in the northwestern corner of the state and mustered in on September 8, 1861, the 83rd Pennsylvania joined Major General Fitz John Porter's division on the Virginia Peninsula and during May 1862 engaged in the siege of Yorktown and the Battle of Hanover Court House. The unit became a permanent part of the V Corps and fought in every major battle of the Army of the Potomac from the Peninsular Campaign to the final surrender at Appomattox. After regimental commander Colonel John W. McLane lost his life at Gaines's Mill, Virginia, on June 27, 1862, Colonel Strong Vincent assumed command.

Vincent became a legendary figure at Gettysburg when, on the second day of the battle, elements from Evander McIvor Law's Confederate brigade began storming Little Round Top – the undefended left flank of Meade's position on Cemetery Ridge. The 150-foot-high, steep and rocky hill lay about two miles south of Gettysburg, and most action of the day had taken place around Sickles' salient. Vincent's 3rd Brigade of the 1st Division, V Corps, had been in reserve when, at 5:00 p.m., enemy movement was detected by Major General Gouverneur Warren, who, without waiting for Meade's approval, summoned Vincent. Also without waiting for approval, Vincent rushed the 83rd Pennsylvania and 20th Maine, followed by the 140th New York and 16th Michigan, into position just as Confederates were scaling boulder-strewn Little Round Top. Along with the 20th Maine, the 83rd Pennsylvania bore the

thrust of the Confederate attack. Vincent received a mortal wound repulsing the attack but secured the left flank of the Union line, which otherwise could have been rolled up by Longstreet's divisions and driven off Cemetery Ridge.

During the Civil War, the 83rd Pennsylvania enrolled 2,270 volunteers. Eleven officers and 267 men were killed or died of wounds. Two officers and 150 men died of disease, and another twenty-nine officers and 485 men suffered wounds, bringing total casualties for the regiment to 944. William Fox, who tracked regimental losses during the war, noted that the 83rd's dead "always lay with their faces toward the enemy."

THE 140TH PENNSYLVANIA

Following Governor Curtin's call for twenty-one new regiments, the 140th Pennsylvania mustered into service at Pittsburgh on September 8, 1862 – too late to participate in the Battle of Antietam. The regiment served under forty-three-year-old Richard P. Roberts until July 2, 1863, when the colonel was killed at near Gettysburg's Wheat Field. John Fraser assumed command of the regiment and led it through the next two years as part of General Hancock's II Corps. The regiment lost 360 men in less than three years of service.

THE 145TH PENNSYLVANIA

The 145th Pennsylvania, commanded by Colonel Hiram Brown, was recruited out Erie and arrived at Harpers Ferry on August 13, 1862, without rifles – five days before the Battle of Antietam. The regiment saw no action until the Battle of Fredericksburg on December 13, 1862. Of 505 men who crossed the Rappahannock River at Fredericksburg, 229 were either killed or wounded. Brown suffered a serious wound and turned the command over to Lieutenant Colonel David B. McCreary. At Gettysburg, the regiment took part in the fighting at the Wheat Field and lost eighty-four men out of 200 engaged. Another 172 fell at Spotsylvania. By January 1865, only 156 officers and men out of the original 700 volunteers remained in the ranks.

Lincoln and the Gettysburg Address

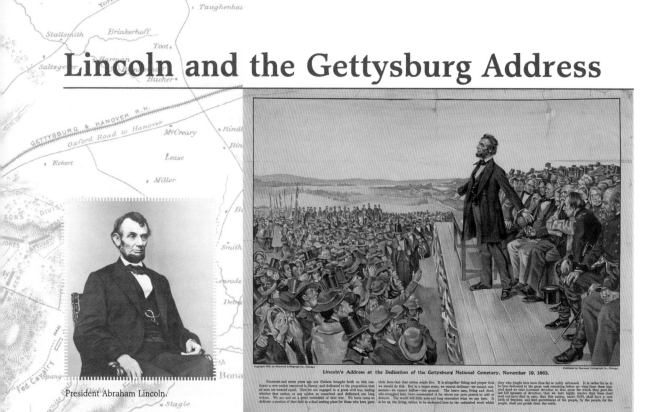

President Abraham Lincoln.

Lincoln's Address at the Dedication of the Gettysburg National Cemetery, November 19, 1863.

THE GETTYSBURG ADDRESS

"Four score and seven years ago our fathers brought forth on this continent a new nation, conceived in liberty, and dedicated to the proposition that all men are created equal. Now we are engaged in a great civil war, testing whether that nation, or any nation, so conceived and so dedicated, can long endure. We are met on a great battle-field of that war. We have come to dedicate a portion of that field, as a final resting place for those who here gave their lives that that nation might live. It is altogether fitting and proper that we should do this. But, in a larger sense, we can not dedicate, we can not consecrate, we can not hallow this ground. The brave men, living and dead, who struggled here, have consecrated it, far above our poor power to add or detract. The world will little note, nor long remember what we say here, but it can never forget what they did here. It is for us the living, rather, to be dedicated here to the unfinished work which they who fought here have thus far so nobly advanced. It is rather for us to be here dedicated to the great task remaining before us – that from these honored dead we take increased devotion to that cause for which they gave the last full measure of devotion – that we here highly resolve that these dead shall not have died in vain – that this nation, under God, shall have a new birth of freedom – and that government of the people, by the people, for the people, shall not perish from the earth."

THE BATTLE OF GETTYSBURG.

The critical moment of the conflict at Gettysburg: 4:00 p.m. on July 3rd.

For several days before delivering the Gettysburg address, Lincoln carried the draft in his hat. According to Ward Hill Lamon, Lincoln's friend and bodyguard, the president prepared several drafts before settling on the final copy. Delivering the speech at the dedication of the Gettysburg Soldiers National Cemetery became another problem when orator Edward Everett, who had been Harvard's president, delivered a two-hour message that exhausted the audience. No one knew quite what to expect when Lincoln took the stand, pulled a sheet of foolscap from his hat, and without looking at the speech, said, "Four score and seven years ago..." By the time the audience finished doing the math, they heard the President say, "... that this nation shall have a new birth of freedom; and that this government of the people, by the people, for the people, shall not perish from the earth." Lincoln then sat down. His address was over. The people were stunned by the brevity, believing it was the preamble to a much longer speech. They never fully heard or comprehended the address until it appeared a day later in the newspapers. Lincoln also believed the address had failed until those who studied the speech came to recognize its greatness. Even Edward Everett, who thought he had won the day, later wrote Lincoln, "I should be glad if I could flatter myself that I came as near to the central idea of the occasion in two hours as you did in two minutes."

The Soldiers National Cemetery at Gettysburg

As wind and rain swept across the Gettysburg battlefield, shallow graves became unearthed and hundreds of decaying bodies lay exposed by the elements. The citizens of Gettysburg conceived the idea of creating a national cemetery and received immediate support from Governor Curtin. Funds provided by the state purchased ground on Cemetery Hill, near the center of the Union line. While architects, masons, and landscapers worked on the cemetery, some of the funds went to Samuel Weaver's laborers, who had the grisly job of disinterring Union and Confederate bodies from field and hospital sites and attempting to identify them before reburial. Many of the Southern dead remained on the field until 1870, when they were transported to cemeteries in the South. The work was not complete by the dedication ceremony on November 19, 1863, but was attended by 10,000 visitors who had come to hear the speeches of Everett, the president, and others.

Entrance to Gettysburg National Cemetery.

Pennsylvania Union Army Deaths

Troops Furnished	Killed/Mortally Wounded	Died of Disease	Died of Other Causes	Total
315,017	15,265	11,782	6,136	33,183

The Soldiers National Monument, sculpted by Randolph Rogers, at the center of Gettysburg National Cemetery.

Once started, work continued on the cemetery. Today it is the Gettysburg National Cemetery, a final resting place for all of America's war veterans. The cemetery is also the site of numerous monuments, including statues of famous Pennsylvanians, like John Reynolds, and Pennsylvania units, like the 83rd Pennsylvania. Also on Hancock Avenue stands the majestic Pennsylvania Memorial, a tribute to all from the commonwealth who fought at Gettysburg.

Pennsylvania Union Units Furnished	
Infantry regiments	217
3-month infantry regiments	25
Sharpshooter units	1
Militia Regiments	81
Reserve regiments	14
Cavalry regiments	25
Cavalry battalions	2
Cavalry militia units	9
Independent cavalry units	8
Provisional cavalry units	3
Misc. Cavalry units	7
Heavy artillery regiments	5
Heavy artillery battalions	1
Independent heavy artillery	6
Light artillery regiments	1
Light artillery battalions	5
Light artillery militia	5
Ind. light artillery batteries	14
Independent Engineer units	1
Sailors/marine personnel	14,307
Colored troops	8,612

Rhode Island

> ❝ Sunday a soldier of Company A died and was buried. Everything went on as if nothing had happened, for death is so common that little sentiment is wasted. It is not like a death at home. ❞

ELISHA HUNT RHODES, 2ND RHODE ISLAND VOLUNTEER INFANTRY

During the Civil War, Rhode Island – like its New England neighbors – remained loyal to the Union. The smallest of the Union states in terms of land area, the "Ocean State" was, nevertheless, prosperous and populous and, as well as providing over 25,000 fighting men, used its considerable industrial capacity to help provision the Union Army.

The state's textile mills supplied troops with uniforms, overcoats, and bedding, while its factories and foundries turned out firearms, cannon, and other vital hardware.

By 1860, the Republican Party was the most influential political force in Rhode Island but its supporters held widely differing views on secession. Many local factory owners ("the lords of the loom") and merchants were engaged in cotton textile manufacturing and had strong economic ties with Southern plantation owners ("the lords of the lash"). Consequently, they sought to avoid war at all costs. At the other end of the social spectrum, Rhode Island had a large Irish immigrant population, which shared the fear of the working classes in other industrial Northern states: that freeing slaves would lead to an increase in competition for jobs. Furthermore, the state's immigrant Irish working class resented the fact that they needed land to vote while blacks were subjected to no such discrimination.

In 1860, the Rhode Island Republican Party nominated the prominent abolitionist Seth Padelford for governor. Consequently, the party split into two factions, one of which remained loyal to the party; the other, made up of pro-Lincoln Republican moderates, formed a "Conservative" alliance with Democrats. They nominated William Sprague, son of one of the "lords of the loom" to contest the Conservative ticket. Sprague won, and was appointed governor.

Although Rhode Island citizens and the new governor were ambivalent about the prospect of war with the South they still felt a strong allegiance to the Union and, after the Confederate attack on Fort Sumter in

Richard Arnold (1828–82) was a Rhode Islander and a brigadier general in the Union Army given the position chief of artillery in the the Department of the Gulf. Isaac P. Rodman was his brother-in-law.

Isaac P. Rodman (1822–62) was a Rhode Island banker who became a brigadier general in the Union Army. He was mortally wounded at the Battle of Antietam.

April 1861, Rhode Island men rallied behind the Federal government. Just three days after President Lincoln issued his call for volunteers, the "Flying Artillery" left Providence for the front. In July, Colonel Ambrose Burnside and Sprague himself led 530 Rhode Island men at First Bull Run (First Manassas).

In Rhode Island itself, a military hospital was established at Melville in Portsmouth while Atlantic House in Newport became the new home of the United States Naval Academy, which had relocated from Annapolis for security reasons. The academy also had training ships and instructional facilities on Goat Island.

Important Unionists of Rhode Island

GOVERNOR WILLIAM SPRAGUE (1830–1915)

The son of a Rhode Island businessman, senator, and governor, Sprague was born in Cranston, Rhode Island, but attended the Irving Institute in Tarrytown, New York, until the age of thirteen, when his father was murdered. He subsequently began to work for the family company, which was engaged in the calico-printing business. Starting at the bottom of the ladder, by the age of twenty-six he was a full partner with his brother and cousin. Under their leadership, A&W Sprague Manufacturing Company became the largest calico printing textile mill in the world. At the same time, like his father before him, Sprague became involved in politics. In 1860, at the age of only twenty-nine, he was elected Governor of Rhode Island. Lincoln liked him, and Governor Sprague was a frequent White House visitor.

In the months preceding the war, Sprague pledged his support to the Union and organized a battery of light artillery that he trained and equipped partly from the family wealth. At the outbreak of the war, his "Flying Artillery" regiment was quickly dispatched to Washington, D.C. Sprague, who had attained the rank of colonel in the Providence Marine Corps of Artillery, appointed himself aide-de-camp to Colonel Ambrose Burnside. At the capital, Governor Sprague's dashing appearance won many admirers, not least Kate Chase, daughter of Salmon P. Chase. John Nicolay, Lincoln's personal secretary was less impressed, remarking the Sprague was "a small man, who bought his place."

Sprague distinguished himself in the First Battle of Bull Run (First Manassas), and returned a hero. From that time he served as a Republican to the United States Senate and in various government positions. He also became embroiled in what became known as Sprague's "Texas Adventure". Supplies of cotton remained vital to his textile empire and, without it, Sprague faced financial ruin. In the fall of 1862, he began to conspire with a Texan named Harris Hoyt, who persuaded him to use his influence on behalf of certain Southern businessmen wanting to bring cotton north. Sprague requested a permit that would allow Hoyt's vessels to pass the naval blockade on Southern ports without inspection. When it was refused, Sprague went ahead with the plans anyway, knowing that he risked death for treason.

The first ship sailed south in December, 1862, carrying arms, ammunition, and other contraband of war to be exchanged with the Confederates for Texas cotton. Initially, the scheme worked well, but when Sprague tried to lobby for official approval his subterfuge was revealed and quickly abandoned. After the war, Sprague made another bid to be elected Governor of Rhode Island, but was unsuccessful and thereafter retired to a farm near Narragansett Pier, Rhode Island. He died in Paris, France, in September 1915.

KATE CHASE SPRAGUE (1840–99)

Katherine (Kate) Chase Sprague was the daughter of politician Salmon P. Chase, and the wife of William Sprague. A noted beauty, she was considered the "social queen" of New York City and, throughout her life, used her connections with the political and social elite to help her father pursue his political ambitions. She was also spoiled, precocious, financially extravagant, and thoroughly disliked by Mary Lincoln, the president's wife. The animosity was mutual.

When Kate married William Sprague, the union was motivated more by political ambition than anything else and by the late 1870s, their lives were a public scandal, culminating in Sprague attacking New York Senator Roscoe Conkling, with whom Kate was romantically involved. The marriage ultimately broke up because of jealousy, infidelity, emotional incompatibility, and bankruptcy.

Governor William Sprague.

Kate Chase Sprague.

Governor Ambrose E. Burnside.

GOVERNOR AMBROSE E. BURNSIDE (1824–81)

Ambrose E. Burnside was one of the most senior Union Army commanders of the Civil War though his battle record is somewhat chequered.

He was born in Indiana and, after schooling, attended the West Point military academy. Prior to the Civil War, he served six years in the regular artillery, during which time he was on garrison duty in Mexico and fought in skirmishes with Apaches in New Mexico Territory. In 1853, Burnside resigned his army commission and moved to Rhode Island to pursue a career in business. His first venture – manufacturing a breech-loading carbine of his own design – was not a success. During this period, however, Burnside also became a major general in the state militia and when war was declared he raised a regiment (the 1st Rhode Island Volunteer Infantry). He was then promoted to lead the 2nd Brigade, 2nd Division, Army of Northeastern Virginia, and fought with this brigade at Bull Run (First Manassas). Four days later he was commissioned a brigadier general and organized an expedition against the North Carolina coast.

By January of 1862, he was commander of the Department of North Carolina and planned the successful Burnside Expedition that led to the capture of Roanoke Island and New Bern. He was twice offered command of the main Union army, firstly following McClellan's failure on the peninsula and again after the Second Bull Run Campaign. He declined the post on both occasions and, instead, was given command of the 1st and 9th corps during the Maryland operations. He fought at the Battle of South Mountain and then at Antietam (Battle of Sharpsburg), at which action his slowness in attacking at the Stone Bridge was criticized.

With McClellan's removal, Burnside was assigned to the command of the army, a position he accepted with reluctance. His tenure as commander of the army was ill-starred. Attacks on Fredericksburg were repulsed and the ill-fated attempt at a winter offensive in January 1863 ("The Mud March") little more than a disaster. Lincoln, who had previously defended Burnside against criticism, was forced to accept his resignation.

With his reputation as a commander badly-damaged, Burnside was assigned to the Western Theater to command the Department of the Ohio. He led the Army of the Ohio during the Knoxville Campaign in the fall of 1863 and, after occupying Knoxville, was besieged there by Confederate General James Longstreet until a column under Sherman came to his relief. Through his prosecution of the Knoxville Campaign, however, Burnside partly rehabilitated his reputation as a commander. Nevertheless, in the fighting in the Wilderness and at Spotsylvania he did not perform well, showing a now-familiar hesitancy to commit his troops. During the Siege of Petersburg he erred once again and was sent on leave from which he was never recalled. After resigning from the service at the end of the war, Burnside became a captain of industry. He was elected Governor of Rhode Island three years running, from 1866 to 1868 and, in 1874, was elected U.S. senator from Rhode Island, in which position he served until his death on September 13, 1881.

Rhode Island Regiments

THE 14TH RHODE ISLAND HEAVY ARTILLERY

Nearly a century before the Civil War, during the American Revolutionary War against the British, African-American troops had fought for the new American nation in the Continental Army. At the start of the Civil War, many African-Americans quickly volunteered to fight in the Union Army. The U.S. War Department, however, refused to use them as combat troops and African-Americans were, instead, given menial jobs as cooks and waiters. Nevertheless, by 1863 the Union Army was experiencing a serious manpower crisis and was forced to revise its recruitment policies, allowing African-American soldiers to fight in the front line. Thereafter, regiments of black troops were raised in several U.S. states. By the end of the conflict, six regiments of U.S. Colored Cavalry, eleven regiments and four companies of U.S. Colored Heavy Artillery, ten batteries of the U.S. Colored Light Artillery, and 100 regiments and sixteen companies of U.S. Colored Infantry had been raised. This represents a total of 179,000 men. Another 19,000 served in the navy.

In July 1863, Rhode Island raised one of the six African-American heavy artillery regiments – the 14th Rhode Island Heavy Artillery though, in fact, the men mustered into the unit hailed not only from Rhode Island, but also Connecticut, New York, and other Northern states. They trained at Dexter Field, Providence, during the summer and fall of 1863 and were assigned to Dutch Island to defend the West Passage in Narragansett Bay, manning eight artillery pieces on the island. In early 1864, they were sent to the coast of Texas and, later in the winter, assimilated into the 11th U.S. Heavy Artillery regiment and posted to the defenses of New Orleans and Baton Rouge. The 14th Rhode Island served bravely and had the highest number of deaths of any black regiment in the Civil War.

THE 2ND RHODE ISLAND VOLUNTEER INFANTRY REGIMENT

On June 6, 1861, Major John Slocum, serving in Colonel Burnside's 1st Rhode Island Detached Militia Infantry Regiment, was recalled to Rhode Island and given orders to form and command the 2nd Rhode Island Volunteer Infantry Regiment. Slocum organized his new troops at Camp Burnside in Providence and, on June 19, 1861, after a brief spell of training, rushed them to Washington, D.C.

Attached to McDowell's Union Army of Northeast Virginia as part of the Rhode Island Brigade, the 2nd fought at the First Battle of Bull Run (First Manassas). Slocum and several of his officers were killed. Although the 2nd fought well, the Confederates routed most of the ill-trained Union army, which retreated back to encampments around Washington, D.C.

The next major actions of consequence came in June, 1862, when the regiment fought in 4th Corps, Army of the Potomac, in the Peninsula Campaign and then, during September, in the Antietam Campaign. In October, 1862, the 2nd was assigned to 6th Corps, Army of the Potomac, and fought with the corps from Fredericksburg to Cold Harbor. After the horrific Battle of Cold Harbor in June 1864, Colonel Elisha Hunt Rhodes assumed command. During the Siege of Petersburg, 6th Corps (under Philip Sheridan) was sent to northern Virginia to stop General Jubal Early from menacing Washington in raids out of the Shenandoah Valley. As part of these operations the 2nd was assigned to defend the capital. It then took part in Sheridan's invasion of the Shenandoah Valley and was garrisoned at Winchester during the battles of Cedar Creek and Fisher's Hill.

Returning to Petersburg in December 1864, the 2nd Rhode Island participated in the subsequent occupation of that city and the battles and pursuit of Lee's Army to Appomattox. After Lee's surrender, the 2nd was deployed in Danville along the Virginia-

Rhode Island Units Furnished	
Infantry regiments	12
Hospital guards	1
Cavalry regiments	3
Misc. cavalry units	1
Heavy artillery regiments	3
Light artillery regiments	1
Other light artillery batteries	1
Sailors/marine personnel	1,878
Colored troops	1,837

William Rogers Taylor (1811–89) was born in Rhode Island. In 1863, he became fleet captain of the South Atlantic Blockading Squadron. During 1864–65 he took part in the operations that led to the capture of Fort Fisher, North Carolina. He died a rear admiral.

North Carolina border until General Joe Johnston's surrender to General Sherman. The 2nd Rhode Island took part in the grand review in Washington, D.C and was mustered out to great celebration in Providence, Rhode Island.

THE 1ST RHODE ISLAND CAVALRY

Organized as the 1st New England Cavalry in the winter of 1861–62 at Pawtucket, the regiment moved to Washington, D.C., in mid-March 1862, and was seconded to Stoneman's Cavalry Command, Army of the Potomac. The first major actions in which it was involved were with Nathaniel Banks' V Corps, Department of the Shenandoah, and then the Army of the Potomac, during Stonewall Jackson's Valley Campaign. In July, 1862, Governor William Sprague appointed French-American colonel Alfred Napoleon Alexander Duffié to command the regiment. Though the 1st Rhode Island's officers initially refused to serve under a foreign-born leader, Duffié soon won them over and reorganized the 1st into a fine fighting unit.

Under him, they fought in Brigadier General George Dashiell Bayard's Cavalry Brigade (McDowell's III Corps), in the Second Bull Run Campaign, and at Cedar Mountain in August. In March the following year, the 1st Rhode Island was at the Battle of Kelly's Ford. It fought with the Army of the Potomac to October 1864, after which it was seconded to the Army of the Shenandoah, until mustered out in August, 1865.

RHODE ISLAND UNION ARMY DEATHS

Troops Furnished	Killed/Mortally Wounded	Died of Disease	Died of Other Causes	Total
19,521	460	648	213	1,321

South Carolina

> " Sir, By authority of Brigadier General Beauregard, commanding the Provisional Forces of the Confederate States, we have the honor to notify you that he will open fire of his batteries on Fort Sumter in one hour from this note. "

LETTER HANDED TO MAJOR ROBERT ANDERSON BY COLONEL JAMES CHESNUT, JR., 3:20 AM, APRIL 11, 1861

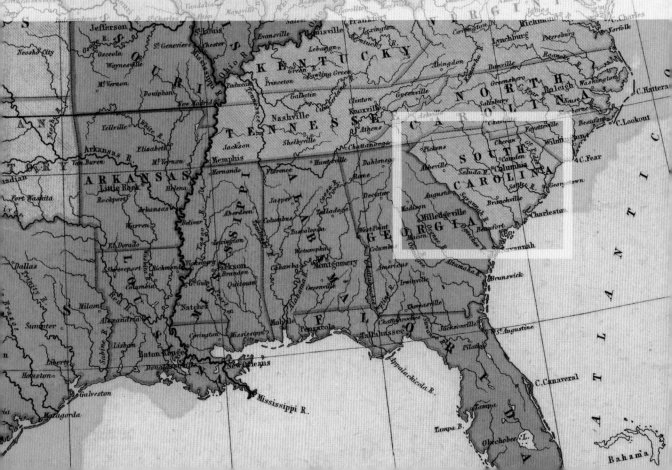

The 1860 U.S. census revealed that the South Carolina's population comprised 291,000 whites and some 412,320 African-Americans, the vast majority of the latter being slaves.

In fact, it is no exaggeration to say that the state's economy would have collapsed without slaves and hardly surprising that South Carolina also had a long history for advocating states' rights and opposition to the abolition of slavery. Many of the state's citizens feared that emancipation would see the destruction of white South Carolina's way of life and culture.

One of the state's leading political lights on the national stage during the first half of the 19th century was John C. Calhoun, a backer of states' rights, especially nullification (the legal theory that a state could invalidate any Federal law that it deemed unconstitutional). Calhoun also believed slavery was a positive good as slave-owners, he argued, had a paternalistic right to rule over "inferior" slaves.

Nevertheless, his voice was, in some respects, moderate compared to others from the state and attitudes in South Carolina began to harden after his death, with extremists becoming ever more vociferous. These advocates of secession were nicknamed "Fire-Eaters" partly due to the increasingly stridency of their oratory, and many had strong connections with the state, including William P. Miles, Louis T. Wigfall, and William L. Yancey. Indeed, the issue brought physical violence to the Senate in Washington, D.C., on May 22, 1856, when South Carolina-born Preston Brooks viciously attacked Senator Charles Sumner, who had recently spoken on slavery and made some derogatory remarks about one of Brooks' relatives.

In fact, South Carolina had passed an ordinance in 1850 that declared it was state's right to secede. A decade later, following Lincoln's election, the firebrands had created an atmosphere in which secession was seen by the majority in the state as the only option. A convention met in Charleston in

GOVERNOR FRANCIS W. PICKENS (1805–69)

Pickens had barely settled into his new job as Governor of South Carolina when delegates at the convention in Charleston signed the ordinance of secession on December 20, 1860. A plantation owner and a member of the state's powerful, well-to-do gentry, he was a staunch advocate of states' rights and believed that they had primacy over any legislation passed by the U.S. Congress. As war became certain and it became inevitable that Fort Sumter would be the tinder box, Pickens ordered state troops to fire on the *Star of the West* as it tried to reach the fort on January 9, 1861. His term of office ended in December 1862 and he returned to his plantation, where he ended the war heavily in debt.

December and voted to secede on December 20, 1860, a decision that put the state at the forefront of the Confederacy.

FORT SUMTER

On December 20, 1860, Union troops occupied Fort Sumter in Charleston Harbor. The following March, Confederate Brigadier General Pierre G.T. Beauregard took command of the forces in Charleston and set about strengthening the forts and shore batteries targeted at Sumter. Powerful guns, most taken from Charleston's Federal arsenal, which had been occupied at the end of 1860, were added to forts Moultrie and Johnson, while new batteries were positioned next to Moultrie and at Cummings Point on Morris Island. Beauregard also drilled 6,000 men and trained many of them to operate the new batteries.

By April, the Union position was untenable. Fort Sumter under Major Robert Anderson was outgunned, outmanned, and short of supplies. The fort was summoned to surrender by Beauregard on April 11, 1861, but Anderson refused. At 3:00 am on the 12th, he suggested his terms, which were quickly rejected by a three-man Southern delegation led by Colonel James Chesnut, Jr., Beauregard's aide-de-camp. The bombardment began at 4:30 am and continued for thirty-four hours until Sumter was in a very sorry state. On the 14th, as it became obvious that further resistance was futile, Anderson surrendered.

REACTION TO LINCOLN'S CALL FOR VOLUNTEERS

At the time Fort Sumter was occupied by Confederate forces on April 14, 1861, just seven states had seceded from the Union. On April 15th, however, Lincoln called for 75,000 volunteers to serve for ninety days to suppress the insurrection. Many wavering governors were appalled, including pro-neutrality Beriah Magoffin, who raged: "Kentucky will furnish no troops for the wicked purpose of subduing her sister Southern states." Other states were even more outraged and four went on to secede – Virginia left the Union on April 17th, Arkansas on May 6th, North Carolina on May 20th, and Tennessee on June 8th. The eleven-state Confederacy was complete (contested Missouri and Kentucky would also be acknowledged as Confederate states by the South).

THE CHARLESTON BLOCKADE AND BLOCKADE-RUNNING

In April 1861, Lincoln proclaimed that Confederate ports would be blockaded by the U.S. Navy and, if possible, occupied by land forces. Over the following years most were closed, but Charleston was one of the last – being occupied in February 1865 – and it therefore became home to many blockade runners. However, the best cargo-carrying boats – those able to sail with heavy, bulky goods like cotton and bring back military supplies – were too slow to evade capture. The best blockade-runners were relatively small and fast, but with limited cargo space. Consequently, they had to make many more trips and thus had more chance of being intercepted. Most were sunk or captured.

The wreck of a blockade-running ship near the shore of Sullivan's Island, South Carolina.

COMMODORE DUNCAN M. INGRAHAM'S NAVY

Along with Wilmington, Charleston was the largest Confederate port to remain open for blockade runners during almost the entire war, thanks in part to a former U.S. Navy captain who had been made commodore of Charleston's naval base in 1861. It was Ingraham (1802–91) who oversaw the creation of new warships, chiefly the ironclad rams *Chicora* and *Palmetto State*, dealt with any Union attacks on the port's defenses, and launched his own attacks on the blockaders menacing Charleston. Due in large part to his skill, the port was never closed by a seaward attack but fell to a landward onslaught in February 1865. At that time, both ironclads were destroyed to prevent their capture.

The blockade of Charleston, 1861.

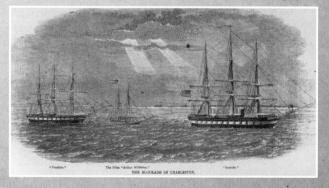

Fort Johnson wth Fort Sumter in the distance. March, 1865.

THE LOSS OF PORT ROYAL SOUND

Union Flag Officer Samuel F. Du Pont was tasked with capturing this coastal inlet in South Carolina in order that it could be used as a naval base from which the Confederacy could be more fully blockaded. His South Atlantic Blockading Squadron duly struck on November 7, 1861. The warships' main targets were Fort Walker on Hilton Head Island to the south of the sound's entrance and Fort Beauregard on Phillip's Island to the north. Walker was put out of action and occupied in the afternoon, while Beauregard was abandoned by its garrison and taken over the next day. Du Pont had gained a major base that would be in Union hands for the rest of the war.

UNION NAVAL ATTACK ON CHARLESTON HARBOR

The U.S. Navy Department ordered Du Pont to capture Charleston Harbor in April 1863 and his force of seven Passaic Class monitors, the broadside ironclad *New Ironsides*, and the experimental monitor *Keokuk* struck on the 7th. However, the warships had hardly made it past the narrow harbor entrance before being caught in cross fire from forts and shore batteries. Some 520 shells struck home in two hours, damaging several of the vessels. In contrast, the warships fired a meager 154 shells. Du Pont, who would resign at his own request in July, ordered a withdrawal. *Keokuk* sank that night and the fleet posted one man killed and twenty-one injured; the defenders had five killed and eight wounded.

SHERMAN'S MARCH THROUGH SOUTH CAROLINA

By December 1864, Major General William T. Sherman's march through Georgia, from Atlanta to Savannah, had been completed and he now turned his attention – and 60,000 troops – against neighboring South Carolina, the cradle of secession. Sherman moved out of Savannah in late January 1865 and advanced on a broad front toward Columbia, the state capital. Weak Confederate resistance was brushed aside and Columbia fell on February 17th, with much of the city soon razed in a controversial fire. Charleston was evacuated the same day and occupied on the 18th. Again, anything of military value was destroyed. Wilmington capitulated on the 22nd and, by the beginning of March, the state was effectively in Union hands.

Three-gun battery on Vanderhorst Wharf, Charleston.

CONFEDERATE DEPARTMENT OF SOUTH CAROLINA

This military department was established in August 1861, but underwent many changes during the war, becoming the Department of South Carolina, Georgia, and East Florida in November, when General Robert E. Lee took charge. He departed in March 1862, replaced by Major General John C. Pemberton. Under Pemberton, it was renamed the Department of South Carolina and Georgia, but in April it was extended back into Florida as the Department of South Carolina, Georgia, and East Florida once more. In September, another change saw Pemberton replaced by General Pierre G.T. Beauregard, who served until October 1864. By October 1863, the department had again been reorganized as the Department of South Carolina, Georgia, and Florida and it was finally reorganized twice in January 1865. Its last commander was Lieutenant General William J. Hardee.

UNION DEPARTMENT OF THE SOUTH

Union operations in South Carolina originally came under the South Carolina Expedition Corps, which was organized during September and October 1861. It was renamed in March 1862, when it became the Department of the South, covering the states of South Carolina, Georgia, and Florida. The Department of Key West was also added on March 15th, but the Department of West Florida was transferred to the Department of the Gulf on August 8th. The department had ten commanders during the war but was dismantled in June 1865.

Generals of South Carolina

LIEUTENANT GENERAL WADE HAMPTON III (1818–1902)

Hampton came from a wealthy plantation-owning family with a strong military background and, at the outbreak of the war, raised and financed a mixed force known as Hampton's Legion. He went on to take part in many of the conflict's major battles as a commander of larger cavalry units and was wounded on five occasions.

LIEUTENANT GENERAL DANIEL H. HILL (1821–89)

Hill served in the U.S. Army until 1849, when he resigned to become a professor of mathematics, but accepted a colonelcy at the outbreak of the Civil War. He was promoted to major general and saw action during the Seven Days Battles and at Fredericksburg in 1862, but his irascible nature saw him clash with Lee, who refused to make him a corps commander. Hill transferred to the Army of Tennessee and was given a corps with the provisional rank of lieutenant general, but again clashed with his superior, this time General Braxton Bragg. When the Army of Tennessee was reorganized, Hill was left without a post and his provisional rank was never confirmed. He spent the rest of the war fighting in minor campaigns and surrendered on April 26, 1865.

LIEUTENANT GENERAL RICHARD H. ANDERSON (1821–79)

A U.S. Army career soldier who had fought in the American-Mexican War Anderson's Southern sympathies saw him begin the Civil War as colonel of a Confederate regiment. During the course of the war, he was destined to see action in most of the Eastern Theater's major battles and campaigns and would go on to command various army corps until virtually the end of the conflict.

Lieutenant General Daniel H. Hill.

Stephen Lee, the youngest Confederate lieutenant general, became commander-in-chief of the United Confederate Veterans. This statue of the general stands at Vicksburg.

LIEUTENANT GENERAL STEPHEN D. LEE (1833–1908)

The Confederacy's youngest lieutenant general when he was promoted to the rank on June 23, 1864, Lee was a West Point cadet and career soldier who resigned from the U.S. Army in 1861. He first saw action in the Eastern Theater, initially in command of artillery and then infantry units. He then transferred to the Western Theater and took charge of the Department of Alabama and East Louisiana in July 1864. He was wounded in late December but returned to service, participating in the Carolinas Campaign before surrendering in April 1865.

THIS MEMORIAL IS DEDICATED
TO THE GALLANT CREW OF THE
CSS HORACE L HUNLEY AND THEIR
COMMANDER 1st LT GEORGE E DIXON
CO A 21st ALA INF CSA WHO
PERISHED DURING THE ATTACK ON
THE USS HOUSATONIC FEB 17 1864

Memorial to the crew of *H.L. Hunley* in Mobile National Cemetery.

C.S.S. HORACE. L. HUNLEY

Although this was not the first Southern submarine, it was the only one to sink a warship. Designed by Horace L. Hunley and built in Mobile, Alabama, the hand-powered forty-foot vessel arrived in Charleston in August 1863. It was not, however, especially seaworthy – it sank on the 19th, killing five of its eight-man crew, and again on October 15th, killing all eight, including Hunley. It was nevertheless raised yet again, and on February 16, 1864, sailed into the harbor under Lieutenant George E. Dixon where it sank the screw sloop U.S.S. *Housatonic* with a spar torpedo – an explosive charge fixed to a bow-mounted wooden spar. Again, *H.L. Hunley* did not make it back to land and its last crew all perished.

Embarkation of exchanged Union prisoners
at Aiken's Landing, February 21, 1865.

View of the Point Battery, Charleston, South Carolina,
showing the gun in the Cheevrs battery.

THE CITADEL MILITARY ACADEMY

This military school can trace its origins back to around to 1822, but the South Carolina state legislature passed a specific act in 1842 to create the South Carolina Military Academy and establish "a public guard of the arsenal at Columbia and of the citadel and magazine in and near Charleston." It was occupied by Union troops when the state seceded though they moved to Fort Sumter on January 9, 1861. Cadets served with artillery units (two were present when the first shells were fired on the fort in April), did guard duties, acted as prisoner escorts, and fought in some battles during the war. The Citadel was reoccupied by Union forces in February 1865 and reopened as an academy later.

A photograph of the Citadel Military Academy in Charleston, with the remains of the concrete wall built in the time of the Revolution in the foreground.

South Carolina Units Furnished	
Infantry regiments	33
Infantry battalions	2
Cavalry regiments	7
Cavalry battalions	1
Heavy Artillery regiments	1
Heavy Artillery batteries	1
Light artillery batteries	28

SOUTH CAROLINA CONFEDERATE ARMY DEATHS

	Killed	Died of Wounds	Died of Disease	Total
Officers	360	257	79	696
Enlisted	8,827	3,478	4,681	16,986
Total	9,187	3,735	4,760	17,682

Tennessee

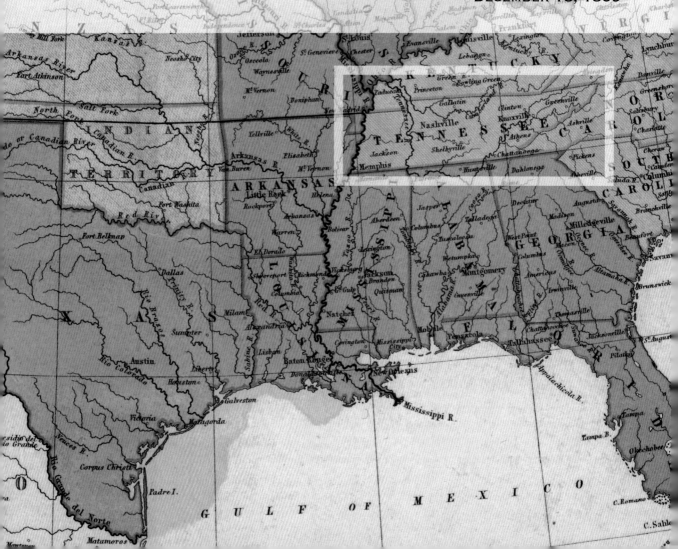

"I voted against him [Lincoln]; I spoke against him; I spent my money to defeat him; but I still love my country."

EXTRACT FROM ANDREW JOHNSON'S ANTI-SECESSION SPEECH TO THE SENATE, DECEMBER 18, 1860

As the crisis between North and South deepened in late 1860 and early 1861, it appeared that the people of Tennessee had little enthusiasm for secession.

In 1860, for example, the state's voters backed Tennessee-born John Bell as their presidential candidate, a member of the recently formed Constitutional Union Party that wished to avoid any disunity over the slavery issue. However, the issue could not be ignored. In January 1861, Governor Isham G. Harris organized a convention and addressed its delegates. He said that the ongoing crisis was the product of "long continued agitation of the slavery question" that had been exacerbated by the "purely sectional" machinations of the Republican Party, and made plain that only the voters of a state could decide whether or not slavery would be permitted within its borders.

On February 9th, there was a state-wide vote on whether or not delegates should be sent to a convention to further discuss the issue of secession. Perhaps surprisingly for a slave-owning state (albeit only twenty-five percent of Tennesseans owned slaves) voters rejected the proposal by a margin of 69,675 to 57,798. More interestingly, if the proposal had been passed, the convention would have been heavily pro-Union as the latter candidates won a total vote of 88,803 while the secessionists polled just 22,749. Yet within a few months the greater part of the political landscape of Tennessee would be wholly transformed.

There were two main catalysts for the turnabout. First, was the attack on Fort Sumter that began on April 12th and ended two days later. Second, was Lincoln's call on the 15th for 75,000 three-month volunteers to suppress the burgeoning insurrection. Harris, who was a staunch believer in the primacy of states' rights, reacted by ordering a mobilization of the state militia, submitting an ordinance of secession to the General Assembly, and establishing contact with the Confederate government. The motion to

A states' rights secessionist and Democrat, Isham G. Harris had retired from politics in 1856, but received the gubernatorial nomination in 1857 and again in 1859. In April 1861, he refused Lincoln's call for troops and urged Tennesseans to pass an ordinance of secession, which on June 8, 1861, they did. By July, he had equipped 100,000 Tennesseans for service with the Confederacy and for defense of the state. Harris did not sit at home during the war. Driven out of Nashville by Union forces, he volunteered as an aide-de-camp and served successively under generals Albert Sidney Johnston, Braxton Bragg, and Joseph E. Johnston in all the major battles fought in Tennessee and Georgia. With a $5,000 dollar reward on his head, he later fled to England but eventually returned to Memphis. During the Reconstruction years, he served three consecutive terms on the U.S. Senate. He died in office on July 8, 1897, in Washington, D.C.

GOVERNOR ISHAM G. HARRIS (1818–97)

Harris was called to the bar in 1841 and his political career began six years later when he was elected to the state's Senate, serving just one term before being elected to the U.S. House of Representatives. He sat in the house for two terms from 1849 until 1853. Harris was the Democrats' candidate for Tennessee governor in 1857 and was re-elected for a further two terms. During his third term, he oversaw the secession of Tennessee from the Union but, when much of the state was overrun in early 1862, Harris's political role diminished and he took the chance to serve as a staff officer.

secede was passed on May 7th. The issue was then put to the public on June 8th. The results showed a marked split. Eastern Tennessee was, as before, largely pro-Union in sentiment, while the west of the state was much more pro-secessionist. The issue was decided by the central region's voters, whose opinions had been utterly transformed between February and June. In the former referendum fifty-one percent had opposed secession, but, in the latter vote, eighty-eight percent favored joining the Confederacy. Tennessee formally left the Union that day.

LINCOLN AND EAST TENNESSEE

Slavery was not widely practiced in mountainous eastern Tennessee and the majority of the local population were opposed to secession. In the July 1861 referendum on the matter, the region voted overwhelmingly to remain in the Union and, when Tennessee did secede, delegates representing twenty-six counties in the east met at Greenville and Knoxville. They petitioned the Confederate state legislature to be allowed to secede from Tennessee. In response, on July 26th, the authorities sent

The capture of Fort Donelson, February 16, 1862.

Felix K. Zollicoffer.

GOVERNOR ANDREW JOHNSON (1808–75)

Johnson served as the seventeenth governor of Tennessee from 1853 until 1857. Thereafter he was a U.S. senator between 1857 and 1862 and the only Southern senator not to resign when the various states of the Confederacy seceded. Johnson was a pro-war Democrat and a firm supporter of Lincoln, and his reward was the military governorship of Tennessee from March 1862 to early 1865. When Lincoln was re-elected, Johnson became his vice-president. He was made president on April 17, 1865, after Lincoln was assassinated.

troops under Brigadier General Felix K. Zollicoffer to prevent such a move.

Lincoln felt a strong moral obligation to his supporters in eastern Tennessee and also saw that its recapture would be an ideal springboard to bring the rest of the state back into the Union. He insisted that it should be freed as soon as possible and, in 1861, an attack was launched from Kentucky. It failed and the region was not freed until much later in the war.

THE CAPTURE OF FORT DONELSON

In February 1862, Brigadier General Ulysses S. Grant launched an offensive against forts Henry and Donelson, on the Tennessee and Cumberland rivers respectively, to break through the first line of the Confederate defenses in northern Tennessee. Henry fell to naval bombardment on the 6th, while Grant moved on Donelson, which was garrisoned by some 15,000 troops under Major General John B. Floyd. An attack by Union gunboats was rebuffed on the 14th, but a Confederate attempt to break out was defeated the next day. Floyd and one of his subordinates, Major General Gideon J. Pillow, escaped by water and another subordinate, Major General Simon B. Buckner, offered armistice terms on the 16th. Grant's reply – "No terms except an unconditional and immediate surrender can be accepted"– brought him to public attention at a time

when the Union needed good news. The capture of the two forts soon bore fruit. Union troops from Major General Don Carlos Buell's Army of the Ohio, which was operating in eastern Tennessee in support of Grant, entered Nashville, the state capital, on the 24th.

The Battle of Shiloh, or Pittsburg Landing.

THE BATTLE OF SHILOH

After the capture of forts Henry and Donelson, and the fall of Nashville, in February 1862, Grant planned to march on Corinth, Mississippi, where Major General Albert S. Johnston was positioned with some 40,000 men. However, Major General Henry W. Halleck, his superior as commander of the Department of the Mississippi, ordered Grant to halt his forces around Savannah in southern Tennessee to await the arrival of the Army of the Ohio under Don Carlos Buell.

This gave Johnston an opportunity to strike first, and a surprise attack was launched on Grant at Shiloh on the Tennessee River on April 6th. The Union line came close to collapse, but, thanks to Grant's efforts, the attack was halted and then driven back. Johnston was killed leading a charge and replaced by General Pierre G.T. Beauregard. Meanwhile, part of Buell's command arrived overnight and was ferried over to the west bank of the Tennessee. Grant counterattacked the following day, forcing Beauregard to order a withdrawal to Corinth after suffering some 10,500 casualties. Grant lost around

13,000 men and there were immediate calls for his dismissal though Lincoln demurred, saying: "I can't spare this man. He fights."

FORREST'S TENNESSEE RAIDS OF 1862

Brigadier General Nathan B. Forrest was sent to Chattanooga to organize a cavalry brigade in June, 1862. The following month, he led his untried troops on a raid into the middle of Tennessee. Departing on July 9th, they made for Murfreesboro, an important Union supply depot on the Nashville & Chattanooga Railroad. The town was garrisoned by some 900 Union troops under Brigadier General Thomas T. Crittenden, who had taken up his post on the 12th. Forrest struck at dawn on the 13th and the surprised new garrison commander surrendered by late afternoon. The raiders destroyed supplies and sections of track but, more importantly, their mission diverted Union troops away from Chattanooga, allowing Confederate forces to be built up there for a major invasion of Kentucky.

The following December, Forrest was ordered into western Tennessee to disrupt the Union lines of communication while Grant was menacing Vicksburg, Mississippi. Again, he demonstrated his brilliance as a raider, striking far and wide. Aside from the materiel damage, his raid forced Grant to delay and revise his plans for Vicksburg.

THE FALL OF NASHVILLE

General Braxton Bragg planned to invade Kentucky in mid-1862 and moved out with the Army of Tennessee from Chattanooga, Georgia, in late July, using the Cumberland Gap to enter Tennessee. His opponent, Major General Don Carlos Buell, commanding the Union's Army of the Ohio (Army of the Cumberland from October), felt his lines of communications with Nashville were threatened and made a headlong retreat all the way to Louisville, effectively surrendering Tennessee and the greater part of Kentucky to Bragg.

In the aftermath, Buell received substantial reinforcements and was told by Washington, D.C. that if he did not counterattack, he would be replaced. He moved in October and soon ran into part of Bragg's army under generals Leonidas Polk and William J. Hardee at Perryville on the 8th. The two generals stood firm all day in the face of attacks by superior forces, yet Bragg decided to withdraw into Kentucky. Buell, however, failed to take advantage of this retreat and was replaced by Major General General William S. Rosecrans on the 23rd. Nashville was re-occupied by Union forces on November 6, 1862.

Army of the Tennessee Memorial, Metairie Cemetery, New Orleans.

THE CONFEDERATE ARMY OF TENNESSEE

The Army of Mississippi was renamed the Army of Tennessee in November, 1862. Its commander, General Braxton Bragg, remained in charge of what was the main Confederate force operating between the Appalachian Mountains in the east and the Mississippi River in the west. Under Bragg the army fought the indecisive Battle of Stones River from late 1862 to early 1863, won the Battle of Chickamauga in September, but was decisively defeated at Chattanooga in November, whereupon Bragg resigned. His replacement was General Joseph E. Johnson, who won a victory at Kennesaw Mountain in June 1864, but was replaced by General John B. Hood the next month. Hood performed badly, abandoning Atlanta in September and losing the battles of Franklin and Nashville in November and December. He resigned in January 1865, and Johnson returned to command the army until its surrender in North Carolina on April 26th.

THE UNION ARMY OF THE TENNESSEE

The title "Army of the Tennessee" was first used in March 1862, when it was under the command of Brigadier General Ulysses S. Grant, who would lead it into action until October 1863. Thereafter, it was led by the equally formidable Major General William T. Sherman until March 1864, when he was replaced by Major General James B. McPherson. McPherson was briefly replaced by Major-General John A. Logan before Major General Oliver O. Howard took charge in late July to May 19, 1865.

Along with the Army of the Potomac, the Army of the Tennessee was the most important of the Union's field armies and fought in all the major campaigns and battles in the Western Theater, ending the war in North Carolina. It was formally disbanded on August 1, 1865.

THE BATTLE OF STONES RIVER

By November 1862, The Union's Army of the Cumberland (formerly Ohio) and the South's Army of Tennessee confronted each other between Nashville and the small town of Murfreesboro on the Stones River. Yet neither of their commanders – Major General Braxton Bragg and Major General William S. Rosecrans respectively – took any offensive action as fall gave way to winter. As time passed, their political masters in Richmond and Washington, D.C. prodded them into action and, finally, at the end of December, both sides attacked at Stones River.

Each general intended to hit his opponent's right flank, but Bragg struck first on the 31st. His troops quickly gained the upper hand, but, thanks to his mishandling of reserves, the advantage was not fully exploited and Rosecrans was able to fashion a second defensive line. Both sides held their ground on January 1, 1863, and Bragg made a final attack on January 2nd, before withdrawing the next day. Both sides had suffered around 12,000 casualties, but Rosecrans still controlled the greater part of Tennessee.

The Battle of Stones River or Murfreesboro. The print shows Union artillery behind infantry lines firing at Confederate troops on the far right.

The Tullahoma and Chickamauga Campaigns

After the Battle of Stones River ended in early January 1863, Major General William S. Rosecrans' Army of the Cumberland remained immobile for some six months while his opponent, General Braxton Bragg with his Army of Tennessee, was based at Tullahoma. Ordered into action or be replaced, Rosecrans moved against Bragg on June 23rd. The Confederates were forced out of Tullahoma and pushed back to Chattanooga by the first week of July, but, now, Rosecrans again delayed and it was not until August 16th that he chased after Bragg.

Supported by Major General Ambrose E. Burnside's Army of the Ohio, which moved toward Knoxville from Lexington, Kentucky, Rosecrans crossed the Tennessee River at Bridgeport, endangering Bragg's communications with Atlanta, Georgia, and forcing him to abandon Chattanooga. Rosecrans then pushed into northwest Georgia, but was unaware that Bragg had received reinforcements: Lieutenant General Longstreet's corps from the Army of Northern Virginia. Bragg struck back along Chickamauga Creek on September 19th, but made only minor gains. Matters changed on the 20th, when Longstreet punched through the Union center. Only the resistance of troops under Major General George H. Thomas prevented disaster and allowed the Army of the Cumberland to fall back on Chattanooga. Bragg followed and besieged the town. Burnside's Army of the Ohio had reached Knoxville, but was stalled by supply problems.

28

THE SIEGE OF KNOXVILLE

As Bragg's Army of Tennessee besieged Chattanooga in late 1863, the general dispatched a force under Longstreet into eastern Tennessee to deal with Major General Ambrose E. Burnside's Army of the Ohio, which was based at Knoxville and was slowly moving to the relief of Chattanooga. The two forces ran into each other outside Knoxville on November 16th at the Battle of Campbell's Station. Burnside subsequently fell back to Knoxville, which he had previously fortified, and Longstreet placed the town under siege.

Confederate forces captured Cherokee Heights on November 23rd, a point just 2,400 yards from Fort Stevens, which Longstreet thought the most vulnerable point in the Union defenses. For some reason, however, he did not bombard the fort from the heights but, instead, launched a surprise dawn assault six days later. The attack was a complete disaster and lasted no more than twenty minutes, during which the Confederates suffering a staggering 813 casualties. The defeat of Bragg at Chattanooga, on November 25th now allowed Grant to send a relief force to Knoxville. Longstreet withdrew on December 4th and the town was relieved on the 6th. It remained in Union hands for the rest of the war.

GRANT AT CHATTANOOGA

After Chickamauga, in September 1863 Rosecrans' Army of the Cumberland was besieged in Chattanooga by General Braxton Bragg's Army of Tennessee, with only a single telegraph line connecting him to the outside world. Within a few weeks both the army and the town's inhabitants were facing starvation. Salvation came in mid-October when Ulysses S. Grant was given command of the whole theater and rushed to Chattanooga. As he traveled to the town he sacked Rosecrans and replaced him with Major General George H. Thomas.

Grant arrived on the 23rd and, four days later, was able to bring part of his command into the town by pontoon. He also opened a supply route, the "Cracker Line", through the Confederate siege lines, which meant that more Union troops and much needed supplies could flow into the town. Grant also ordered Brigadier General William T. Sherman to march from Memphis with his Army of the Tennessee to bolster the forces under his command for a major attack on Confederates holding the commanding Lookout Mountain and Missionary Ridge. The Battle of Chattanooga opened on November 24th. Union troops stormed Lookout Mountain in quick time, though Sherman's attack on the northern end of Missionary Ridge failed. The next day, Grant unleashed his forces against the whole ridge and troops from Thomas's command attacking in the center swept all before them. Bragg retreated, leaving virtually all of Tennessee in Union hands.

This photograph is said to show General Ulysses S. Grant with other Union army officers on Lookout Mountain in Tennessee. Although unconfirmed, the figure on the far left is supposedly Grant.

Thure de Thulstrup's painting of the battle of Chatanooga was published in *Prang's War Pictures*.

BATTLE OF CHATTANOOGA.

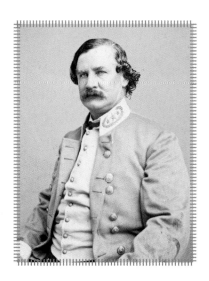

MAJOR GENERAL BENJAMIN F. CHEATHAM (1820–86)

Born in Nashville, Cheatham served in the American-Mexican War and participated in the 1849 California Gold Rush before returning to Tennessee in 1853, becoming a brigadier general in the state militia. He joined the Confederate Army in May, 1861, and saw his first action at Belmont in November. Promoted to major general in March 1862, Cheatham was present at Shiloh in early April, where he was wounded. After returning to service, he fought at Perryville in October and Stones River (December 1862–January 1863). Despite a poor showing at the latter battle, he kept his command and was present at Chickamauga in September. He took over a corps on the 29th and held the right wing on Missionary Ridge at the Battle of Chattanooga.

Cheatham was present throughout the Atlanta Campaign, from May to September 1864, his troops performing well at Kennesaw Mountain in late June, but the general was wounded at Ezra Church on July 28th. While participating in the Franklin-Nashville Campaign in November and December the same year, he mishandled his command at Spring Hill on November 29th, but went on to lead a division in the Carolinas Campaign in the first months of 1865.

LIEUTENANT GENERAL NATHAN B. FORREST (1821–77)

Nathan Forrest was the son of a blacksmith who settled in Tennessee in 1806. He was given little education but, nevertheless, proved a skilled businessman, amassing a large fortune in the pre-war years. When the Civil War broke out, Forrest raised a regiment of cavalry with his own money and served in it as a private. He was promoted to lieutenant colonel by October 1861, and saw his first major action at Fort Donelson in February 1862, where he managed to avoid capture at the surrender.

Further promotions followed – brigadier general in July 1862, major general in December 1863, and lieutenant general in February 1865. After Donelson, he fought at Shiloh, raided Union lines of communications in the west of the state, and guarded the Army of Tennessee's right flank at Chickamauga in September. He was subsequently transferred to Mississippi, but raided Tennessee again in April 1864 – when his troops were involved in the Fort Pillow Massacre – and went on to conduct similar missions in Alabama, Georgia, and Mississippi. He won a notable victory at Brice's Cross Roads, Mississippi, in June, and served in the Franklin-Nashville Campaign in the latter part of the year. Forrest was defeated at Selma, Alabama, in April 1865 and surrendered on May 9th.

MAJOR GENERAL MARK P. LOWREY (1828–85)

After serving in the American-Mexican War, Lowrey trained to be a Southern Baptist preacher. At the outbreak of the Civil War he was a captain in the Mississippi state militia. Soon promoted to colonel of infantry, he commanded a series of regiments in 1862 – at Shiloh in April and at Perryville in October, where he was wounded in the arm. After several weeks recuperating he returned to action, fighting at the Battle of Stones River from December 1862 to January 1863. He was promoted to major general in October, 1863, and went on to serve in the Franklin-Nashville Campaign during November and December 1864. Lowrey had suffered from ill health for some time and resigned in March 1865.

BRIGADIER GENERAL BENJAMIN McCULLOCH (1811–62)

A native of Tennessee who moved to Texas (where he served in the Texas Revolution of 1835–36), McCulloch became a marshal, saw action in the American-Mexican War, and was a member of the state legislature. He received a colonel's commission in the Confederate Army in February 1861, and was given the task of securing the surrender of the main Federal forces in Texas. He was promoted to major general in May and placed in charge of Indian Territory, successfully forging pro-Confederacy alliances with the local Native-American tribes while holding this post. His untrained army was able to win a victory over Union forces at Wilson's Creek, Missouri, in August, but his relationship with a fellow commander, General Sterling Price, was extremely stormy and forced the high command to send Major General Earl van Dorn to keep the peace between them, though to little effect. McCulloch commanded the right wing at the Battle of Pea Ridge (Elkhorn Tavern) in March, 1862, and was killed on the first day.

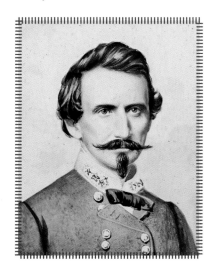

TENNESSEE CONFEDERATE ARMY DEATHS

	Killed	Died of Wounds	Died of Disease	Total
Officers	99	49	72	220
Enlisted	2,016	825	3,353	6,194
Total	2,115	874	3,425	6,414

Clearing Eastern Tennessee

Lieutenant General James Longstreet abandoned his siege of Knoxville on December 4, 1863, and began to move toward Rogersville with the intention of going into winter quarters. He was pursued, if not closely, by Union troops under Major General John G. Parke and the forces clashed in a minor battle at Bean's Station on the 14th, an action that marked the end of the Knoxville Campaign. There were several minor skirmishes thereafter – at Mossy Creek on December 29th and at Dandridge on January 17, 1864, as well as at Fair Garden on January 24th – but the two sides mostly attempted to weather the harsh winter.

Longstreet returned to Virginia in spring, leaving eastern Tennessee free of major Southern forces. Nevertheless, the region suffered a number of Confederate raids in the latter part of the war, chiefly from Virginia. Brigadier General John H. Morgan tried to attack Knoxville in September, 1864, but was killed at Greeneville while trying to avoid capture. Major General John C. Breckinridge followed in November, but, after winning victories at Bull's Gap and Russellville, was halted at Strawberry Fields and fell back to Virginia.

THE FORT PILLOW MASSACRE

The capture of Fort Pillow by Confederate cavalry under Nathan B. Forrest, and the subsequent massacre of the garrison's African-American troops, remains one of the most controversial issues of the war.

The fort, on the Mississippi River about forty miles north of Memphis, had been abandoned by the Confederacy in June, 1862, and was occupied by Union troops and garrisoned with around 600 men – half

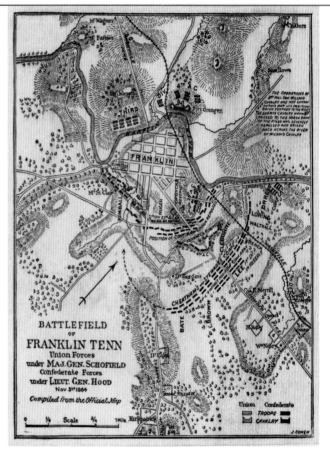

Map of the Battle of Franklin.

African-American and half white – under Major Lionel F. Booth. Forrest arrived at roughly 10:00 am on April 12, 1864, and his sharpshooters soon killed Booth. A note was sent into the fort at around 3.30 pm, demanding surrender within twenty minutes and threatening to take the position by force. Forrest's demand was refused and he subsequently launched a successful assault, taking much of the garrison prisoner.

The massacre began at around 4:00 pm. Confederate losses in the brief fight were fourteen killed and eighty-six wounded, while some 300 of the garrison were killed. About sixty percent of the white garrison were taken prisoner but just twenty percent of the African-Americans survived.

THE BATTLES OF FRANKLIN AND NASHVILLE

Confederate Major General John B. Hood took command of the Army of Tennessee in mid-1864 and crossed the Tennessee River in mid-November. His force struck north rapidly, aiming for Nashville. The state capital was held by the Union Army of the Cumberland under Major-General George H. Thomas, whose command numbered a core of veterans but many more raw recruits.

Needing time to prepare Nashville's defenses, Thomas ordered some 34,000 men under Major General John M. Schofield to Pulaski to delay Hood's advance. Schofield cleverly avoid an attempt to trap him at Columbia on the 26th and 27th, and fought his way out during the night of the 29th to take up defensive positions at Franklin, roughly fifteen

miles to the south of Nashville. Hood's attack the next day suffered appalling casualties. Schofield, as ordered, withdrew to Nashville that night. Undeterred by his losses, the Confederate general continued to push northward, arriving outside the city on December 2nd.

Thomas did not attack immediately, despite his numerical superiority, preferring to complete his preparations. When he finally launched an assault, on December 15th, it smashed Hood's left flank. The battle continued the next day with Thomas menacing Hood's flanks, but the decisive moment came when Schofield's cavalry hit the Confederate left rear. The Army of Tennessee was shattered and never again contested a major battle.

The camp of the Tennessee Colored Battery in Johnsonville.

TENNESSEE UNION ARMY DEATHS

Troops Furnished	Killed/Mortally Wounded	Died of Disease	Died of Other Causes	Total
31,092	744	4,086	1,902	6,777

The 51st Regiment Ohio volunteers on dress parade in Nashville, Tuesday, March 4, 1862.

Union Monument, Knoxville National Cemetery. Completed in 1901, the bronze eagle was shattered by lightning in 1904.

Tennessee Units Furnished	
Confederate	
Infantry regiments	61
Infantry battalions	2
Cavalry regiments	21
Cavalry battalions	11
Heavy artillery regiments	1
Heavy artillery batteries	1
Light artillery batteries	32
Union	
Infantry regiments	9
Mounted infantry regiments	9
Cavalry regiments	16
Cavalry battalion	1
Light artillery battalions	1
Independent mounted scouts	1
National guard	1

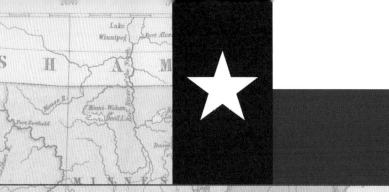

Texas

"The North is determined to preserve the Union. They are not a fiery, impulsive people as you are, for they live in colder climates. But when they begin to move in a given direction, they move with the steady momentum and perseverance of a mighty avalanche."

EXTRACT FROM A PUBLIC SPEECH BY EX-GOVERNOR SAM HOUSTON, GALVESTON, APRIL 19, 1861

The Texas slave population in 1860 stood at 182,566 individuals, roughly thirty percent of its population. Some forty percent of them worked on large plantations while fifty percent toiled on smaller farms. Slaves were, therefore, a key component of the state's economy and Lincoln's election as president in 1860 galvanized the Texas secessionist movement.

Nevertheless, Governor Sam Houston avoided calling a state convention to debate the growing storm until it was clear he had little alternative. It convened in Austin on January 28, 1861. Houston stated that Lincoln's election was "unfortunate" but argued against any "rash action."

The convention agreed to issue an ordinance of secession by an overwhelming majority of 188 votes to eight on February 1st. Those present also released a declaration of causes. These included the Federal authority's inability to prevent attacks

GOVERNOR EDWARD CLARK (1815-80)

At the outbreak of the Civil War, Edward Clark served as Governor Sam Houston's lieutenant. On March 18, 1861, after Houston refused to take an oath of allegiance to the Confederacy, he became governor and suggested raising Indian regiments. Texans decided they wanted someone with a military background to mobilize the state for war and eight months later replaced Clark with Francis Lubbock. Clark soon joined the 14th Texas Infantry as a colonel and later rose to brigadier general. Like many Texans, he fled to Mexico at the end of the Civil War, but later returned home to Marshall, Texas, where he practiced law the remainder of his life.

by Native-Americans and issues relating to the cotton trade, but the document was overwhelmingly dominated by the issue of slavery. The delegates said they were showing "solidarity with sister slave-owning states."

The ordinance was ratified in a popular referendum on the 23rd by 46,129 votes to 14,697. Although a sizeable minority voted against secession, most would go on to tacitly support it. Texas joined the Confederacy on March 2nd, and Houston was replaced as governor by his deputy Edward Clarke on March 18th when he refused to take the new oath of allegiance.

Bob Lemmons was born a slave about 1850, south of San Antonio, Texas. In 1865, he came to Carrizo Springs with his master, John English. After being freed he fell in with Texas rancher Duncan Lemmons and went on to become a cowboy, taking his employer and friend's surname. Photographed in 1936.

Major General David E. Twiggs.

THE SURRENDER OF THE UNION DEPARTMENT OF TEXAS

Major General David E. Twiggs had served the United States loyally since the War of 1812 and, by 1861, commanded all the Federal forces in the Department of Texas. A week after Texas seceded on February 1st, Twiggs met with three Confederate commissioners at San Antonio and agreed to surrender his command without firing a shot. For his actions, he was dismissed from the U.S. Army for his "treachery to the flag of his country." Twiggs briefly served the Confederacy as commander of its Department of Louisiana, but his advanced age forced his retirement in October.

BAYLOR'S "BUFFALO HUNT"

When Texas voted for secession, one of the delegates at the state convention, John R. Baylor, called for 1,000 armed volunteers to go on a "buffalo hunt."

In fact, the volunteers formed the 2nd Regiment of Mounted Rifles. Their objective was opposing any attempts by Federal forces to block secession. The regiment was split in two and moved out to occupy forts abandoned by Union forces. Baylor then pushed into the southern half of New Mexico and, after overcoming the Federal garrison near Mesilla, proclaimed the Confederate Territory of Arizona on August 1st, with himself as governor. He was recalled the next year after seeming to advocate the murder of Native-Americans.

RECAPTURE OF GALVESTON

Galveston, Texas, was taken by Union forces in late 1861, but a year or so later, Major General John B. Magruder, commander of the District of Texas, resolved to recapture the city. He created two cotton-clad warships (wooden steamships lined with cotton bales to protect the vessel from enemy fire), *Bayou City* and *Neptune*, and launched a joint land-sea operation on January 1, 1863. *Neptune* was soon sunk but, despite being out numbered six to one, *Bayou City* captured one Union vessel, while another was destroyed by an explosion. The remainder fled. Four hundred Union troops were captured and around fifty killed while Confederate losses were twenty-six killed and 117 wounded.

SOUTHERN COMMAND CONFUSION AND THE TRANS-MISSISSIPPI

Major-General Earl van Dorn was given command of the Trans-Mississippi (a vast area that included Arkansas, Louisiana, Missouri and Texas, and the Indian Territory) in 1862, largely as a measure designed to stop the feuding between two generals who heartily disliked each other – Major-General Sterling Price and Brigadier General Benjamin McCulloch. Van Dorn successfully unified their two forces into the Army of the West, but was defeated at the Battle of Pea Ridge (Elkhorn Tavern), where McCulloch was killed, in March, and at the Second Battle of Corinth in early October. He was replaced, and Price, who had lost confidence in him, was moved elsewhere.

"Bivouac of Confederate Troops on the Las Moras, Texas, with Stolen U.S. Wagons, Etc.-Sketched by a Member of the Corps." This illustration appeared in *Harper's Weekly* of June 15, 1861, following the surrender of General Twiggs.

Lieutenant General Edward Kirby Smith was made commander of the Trans-Mississippi in March 1863, at a time when the Union was tightening its grip on the river. With the fall of Vicksburg on July 4th, and Port Hudson five days later, Smith was effectively cut off from the rest of the Confederacy. With just 30,000 men spread out of a vast area, he was unable to mount any large-scale attacks but managed to keep personal control of the department until he surrendered on May 26, 1865.

CONFEDERATE DISTRICT OF TEXAS

Command of the District of Texas, later expanded to include New Mexico and Arizona, passed to Major General John B. Magruder in October 1862. He would remain in charge until the war's end, except for a period between August 1864 to March 1865, when he was temporarily replaced by Major General John G. Walker. Both officers faced similar tasks – protecting the district from invasion; keeping the major Gulf ports in Southern hands; managing the cotton trade; raising recruits; and sourcing weapons. Although the district's isolation increased from 1863, when the North took control of the Mississippi, thereby cutting it off from the eastern Confederacy, it remained largely in Southern hands until the final surrender.

Union gunboats on the Sabine River.

UNION COASTAL OPERATIONS IN 1863

France had shown some sympathy for the Confederacy and, in mid-1863, had placed Maximilian on the throne of Mexico. Fearing the ties might grow stronger, the Union sent a combined land and sea force to Texas to prevent the French in Mexico from aiding the Confederacy or, indeed, taking over Texas. The Union actions were also aimed at closing the state's ports, which would curtail the activities of the South's commerce-raiders and blockade-runners.

On September 8th, a force of four gunboats, eighteen troop transports, and 5,000 troops under Major General William B. Franklin launched an attack on Fort Griffin at the mouth of the Sabine River. It was garrisoned by just forty-four men under Lieutenant Richard W. Dowling and protected by six guns. The garrison sank two gunboats and killed, wounded, or captured some 230 Federal men for no recorded loss in a wholly one-sided engagement.

A second Union operation was more successful and saw Brownsville, Corpus Christi, and Fort Esperanza occupied. By 1864, the only major port not in Union hands was Galveston.

Texan Generals

William P. Hardeman.

Jerome B. Robertson.

Lawrence S. Ross.

Louis T. Wigfall.

BRIGADIER GENERAL WILLIAM P. HARDEMAN (1816–98)

Hardeman settled in Texas in 1835 and saw action against Mexico and Native-Americans. He joined the 4th Texas Cavalry Regiment and fought at the Battle of Valverde in early 1862 and went on to lead a brigade during 1864's Red River Campaign. He was subsequently given command of the 4th Texas and promoted to brigadier general in 1865. After the Confederate surrender, he went into exile in Mexico but returned home in 1866.

BRIGADIER GENERAL JEROME B. ROBERTSON (1815–90)

Born in Kentucky, Robertson moved to Texas in 1836. He joined the 5th Texas Infantry Regiment in 1861 and, in mid-1862, was made its colonel. He was promoted to brigadier general the following November and took command of the Texas Brigade. Robertson fought in several major battles, including Gettysburg and Chickamauga in 1863, but lost command of the brigade and took charge of the Texas militia until the war's end.

BRIGADIER GENERAL LAWRENCE S. ROSS (1838–98)

Like many of his peers, Ross's pre-war military experience was in fighting Native-Americans. He joined the Texas Rangers, and led them against the Comanches in the Battle of Pease River in late 1860. At the outbreak of the Civil War, he joined the 6th Texas Cavalry, in 1861, and eventually saw action in 135 battles, including Pea Ridge and Corinth in 1862. He was made brigadier general in early 1864, fought in the Franklin-Nashville Campaign in November and December, but was on leave when the Confederacy surrendered.

BRIGADIER GENERAL LOUIS T. WIGFALL (1816–74)

Wigfall moved to Texas in 1848 and soon became involved in state politics. At the outbreak of war, he became an aide and made a wholly unauthorized approach to the commander of Fort Sumter in April 1861, which secured its surrender on the 14th. Despite his habitual drunkenness, Wigfall was given command of the 1st Texas Infantry Regiment and later, as a brigadier general, of the Texas Brigade, but resigned his commission in 1862 and, thereafter, served in the Confederate Senate.

THE TEXAS BRIGADE

This hard-fighting unit became operational in October 1861, and soon became known as "Hood's Brigade" for its second commander, John B. Hood. Although it primarily contained Texan units, regiments from Arkansas, Georgia, and South Carolina were also part of its establishment at various times. For most of the war, except for a period with the Army of Tennessee, it was part of the Army of Northern Virginia and took part in virtually every one of the major battles in the Eastern theatre with the exception of Chancellorsville in May 1863. Indeed, the Texas Brigade was there at the bitter end and surrendered at Appomattox, Virginia, on April 9, 1865.

THE 8TH TEXAS CAVALRY REGIMENT

This unit was known as "Terry's Texas Rangers" for its founder, Colonel Benjamin F. Terry, who began assembling volunteers in August, 1861. The regiment had one of the most distinguished combat records of any in the war. Terry was killed in the very first battle near Woodsonville, Kentucky, on December 17th, but the rangers went on to participate in many of the war's major battles as well as conducting behind-the-lines raids against Union supply and communication lines. Its last major engagement was at Bentonville, North Carolina, in March 1865. The regiment formally surrendered on April 26th that year.

Samuel Bell Maxey, colonel of the 9th Texas Infantry.

Texas Confederate Units Furnished	
Infantry regiments	22
Infantry battalions	5
Cavalry regiments	28
Cavalry battalions	4
Light artillery batteries	16

TEXAS CONFEDERATE ARMY DEATHS

	Killed	Died of Wounds	Died of Disease	Total
Officers	28	13	10	51
Enlisted	1,320	1,228	1,250	3,798
Total	1,348	1,241	1,260	3,849

OF 1,965 TEXAS TROOPS FIGHTING FOR THE UNION, 141 LOST THEIR LIVES FROM SIMILAR CAUSES.

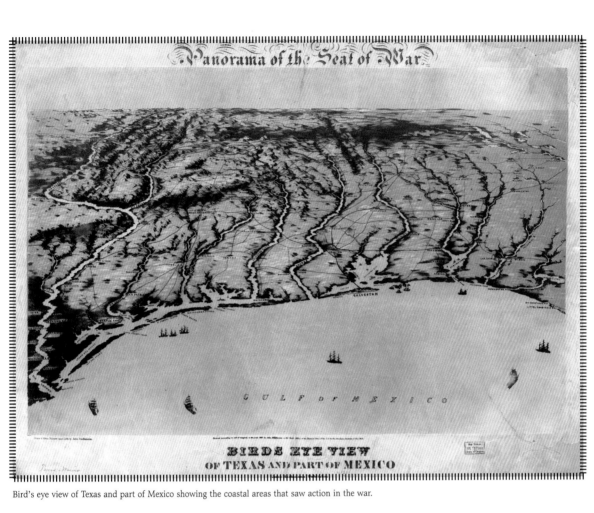

BIRDS EYE VIEW
OF TEXAS AND PART OF MEXICO

Bird's eye view of Texas and part of Mexico showing the coastal areas that saw action in the war.

THE RED RIVER CAMPAIGN

Major General P. Nathaniel Banks and Admiral David D. Porter were ordered to invade Texas by way of the Red River in spring 1864. The admiral put twelve gunboats above the rapids near Alexandria, Louisiana, and made for Shreveport while Banks led 30,000 along the river bank. He was stopped by Major General Richard Taylor at the Battles of Sabine Crossroads on April 8th and fell back on Alexandria. Porter was also forced to turn back in the face of sniping attacks and a falling river. By the time he reached Alexandria, however, the water level was so low his fleet could not float over the rapids. Federal soldiers and sailors built a dam and a flume allowed the vessels to shoot over the rapids. Alexandria was abandoned on May 14th.

THE LAST BATTLE

This engagement occurred after the surrender at Appomattox and took place on the banks of the Rio Grande, about twelve miles east of Brownsville, on May 12-13, 1865. Although there had been an uneasy truce in Texas for a few months, the commander of the Union garrison at Brazos Santiago Island at the mouth of the river, ordered troops to attack Confederate camps at White and Palmito ranches. The assaults were repulsed, with Union troops reporting one dead, nine wounded, and 105 captured; Confederate losses totaled five or six wounded. Texas surrendered on the 26th.

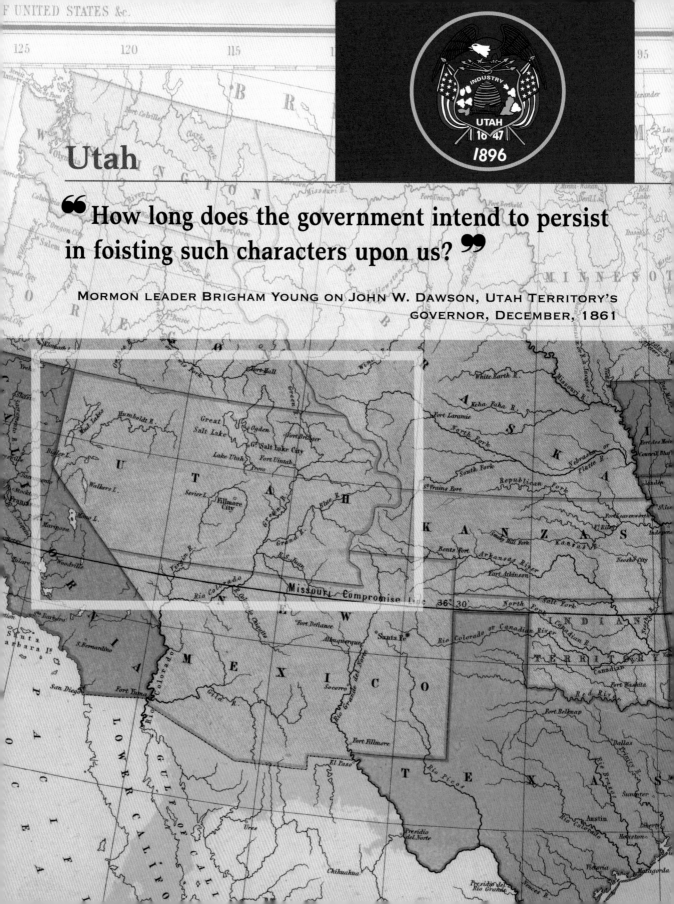

Utah

> ❝ **How long does the government intend to persist in foisting such characters upon us?** ❞

MORMON LEADER BRIGHAM YOUNG ON JOHN W. DAWSON, UTAH TERRITORY'S
GOVERNOR, DECEMBER, 1861

Utah Territory was a vital staging post on the east-west migrant trails linking the western United States with California and, on the outbreak of the Civil War, it became quickly clear that its main inhabitants, the Mormons (followers of the Church of the Latter-day Saints who had been settling in the region since 1847), could not maintain their isolation.

The Federal territory of Utah was formally established in September 1850, and President Millard Fillmore appointed Brigham Young, the church's second leader, as its first governor. Legislation allowing slaves in Utah was passed in 1852, yet the 1860 census records just fifty-nine African-Americans living in the territory, of whom twenty-nine were identified as slaves. If slavery was not an issue, the territory was nevertheless troubled by what could be described as deep mutual suspicion between the Federal government's political, judicial, and military representatives and the Mormon leaders, who had dominated the territory since the late 1840s. From the former's perspective, there were two issues that proved of great concern – the practice of polygamy and the Mormons' seeming lack of commitment to the Union cause as war became ever more certain. As war became a near certainty, the Federal military authorities recreated the Department of the Pacific, in January 1861, and the District of Utah was absorbed into it in early July. Utah was also reorganized during early part of the year and lost some of its vast territory (Colorado Territory was established in late February and Nevada Territory followed a few days later in early March).

However, the U.S. forces stationed in the district were soon withdrawn at the request of Secretary of War Simon Cameron as they were needed elsewhere and their main base at Fort Crittenden

Brigham Young.

UTAH ATTEMPTS TO GAIN STATEHOOD

In 1849, the Mormons attempted to establish a vast state named Deseret. In today's terms, it would cover all of Utah and Nevada, large swathes of Arizona and California, and parts of Colorado, Idaho, New Mexico, and Oregon. Congress rejected the proposal the next year on the grounds it was too big and under-populated. A second attempt came in 1856 but, again, failed, not least because the Mormons had made their acceptance of polygamy public in 1852. Feelings against polygamy grew throughout the decade, with the Republican Party standing on a platform of abolishing the "evils of barbarism, slavery, and polygamy" in 1856. Nevertheless, a third bid was launched in 1862. A third outline state constitution was published on January 20th and was ratified by public vote on March 3rd. A representative traveled to Washington, D.C., but, once again, the proposal was rejected and Congress introduced the Morrill Anti-Bigamy Law on July 8th. Polygamy would continue to be the key issue dogging Utah's bid for statehood and would not be resolved until 1896.

Polygamy was a major issue for Harding and many others who had dealings with the Mormons. These are seven of Brigham Young's wives (he is reputed to have had fifty-four wives and forty-six children) photographed around 1900, some twenty-three years after his death in 1877.

was abandoned. The last departed on August 9th, leaving the Mormons to exert a little more control over their reduced territory for a short time. Nevertheless, as the war intensified the Union Army grew enormously and Cameron's replacement, Edwin M. Stanton decided to reoccupy the territory in 1862. The first troops arrived in July. This move was designed not only to reassert Federal authority over the territory, but to protect mail routes and the recently opened telegraph line that ran through Utah. It also allowed Federal officials to keep an eye on the Mormons for any signs of disloyalty.

THE NAUVOO LEGION

This militia was established in Nauvoo, Illinois, during late 1840 to defend Mormons from attack and, as they moved into Utah during the late 1840s, the legion went with them to protect settlers from Native-American raids. It was officially made the territory's militia in 1852, fought against Native-Americans in the Walker War (1853–54), and opposed an attempt to establish Federal authority in the territory during the Utah War (1857–58). There was, in

Men of the 1st Division of the Nauvoo Legion.

Utah Politics

Alfred Cumming.

John W. Dawson.

President James Buchanan appointed Alfred Cumming (1802–73), a Democrat, as Utah's territorial governor in July 1857. Brigham Young did not approve and ordered all Mormons to evacuate Salt Lake City. Cumming negotiated and successfully eased tensions. He spent the rest of his time as governor curbing Indian raids, building railroads and bridges, and stamping out lawlessness and murder. He disliked the job, however, and left Utah in May 1861.

Abraham Lincoln appointed John W. Dawson (1820–77) territorial governor on December 7, 1861. He resigned three weeks later because of the hostility between himself and the territory's Mormon population.

Lincoln could not find anyone to take the governorship of Utah until July 1862, when Stephen Harding (1808–91) accepted the post. Harding (above) tried to get along with the Mormons, but became critical of the practice of polygamy. The Mormons successfully petitioned for his removal and Harding became another governor to return home in frustration.

John F. Kinney (above) was appointed the chief justice of the Territory of Utah by President James Buchanan and took up his post in June 1860. Kinney and the territory's governor, Steven S. Harding, had a difficult relationship. This was evident when the governor unilaterally pardoned a number of Mormons belonging to a small sect known as Morrisites after some of its members had fired on the local militia in June 1862. Kinney responded by allowing a condemnation of the governor to be put into the public record. Harding, who absolutely opposed polygamy, was not much liked by the Mormons and was removed from his office, in March 1863, at their request to be replaced by James D. Doty, who had been the territory's superintendent of Indian affairs since 1861. The new governor took a more conciliatory line with the Mormons and the relationship improved considerably. Kinney became the territory's Democratic delegate to the 38th Congress in March 1863.

fact, little serious fighting but legion members were implicated in the murder of white settlers passing through Utah, most notably the Mountain Meadow Massacre in September 1857, when around 120 men, women, and older children were killed.

Partly in response to these events, the legion was nominally placed under Federal control in the person of the territorial governor and two of its units were deployed to protect mail routes and telegraph lines during the Civil War. The legion participated in the Black Hawk War (1865–72) but was deactivated in 1870 and formally disbanded as part of the provisions of the 1887 Edmunds-Tucker Act.

UTAH'S NATIVE AMERICANS

The Mormons first settled in Utah's Salt Lake Valley during 1847, in an area that was something of a no-man's land between the local Shoshone and Ute tribes. Relations with the native peoples were fairly amicable at first, but, as more and more Mormons arrived, friction over land rights grew. Matters were aggravated by diseases brought in by the white settlers. Sicknesses often ravaged the locals who had no natural immunity to them. As the Mormon population grew, the increasingly hungry Native-Americans gradually lost their traditional subsistence farming areas and often resorted to small-scale raiding and cattle rustling to secure food. Their raids

were invariably met with force. Federal attempts to establish reservations were not especially successful and tensions simmered throughout the Civil War, though a number of treaties were signed with the Native-Americans.

THE BLACK HAWK WAR

Tensions between Utah's Native-Americans and Mormons broke out into open warfare following an incident at a meeting between the two to broker a negotiated settlement in 1865. The issue was the loss of tribal hunting grounds to domesticated farming but, when one tribal leader at the talks was insulted, chances of peace evaporated. What followed were years of small-scale battles and raids led by Black Hawk, a Ute chief.

The fighting, which was punctuated by atrocities, was at its height during the first two years of the war but incidents continued into 1872. Mormons built forts and raised militia units to defend their farms, while the Native-American raids saw many settlements and farms abandoned and large quantities of livestock run off. The Ute could not sustain the war, however, and many were either killed, settled on reservations, or moved outside Utah. Finally, in 1872, the Federal authorities belatedly agreed to a long-standing Mormon request for the U.S. Army to intervene, effectively ending the war.

Below: Men of the 1st Dicision of the Nauvoo Legion. *Opposite page:* Black Hawk Soldiers.

Above: Fort Douglas. *Below:* Building the Transcontinental Telegraph

Establishing Fort Douglas

In mid-1862, the commander of the Union's Department of the Pacific, Brigadier General George Wright, was ordered to re-establish a Federal military presence in Utah Territory. Accordingly, Colonel Patrick E. Connor led the 3rd Regiment California Volunteer Infantry into the territory during July and headed for the Salt Lake Valley area, where most of the Mormon population was concentrated. His mission was to protect the overland routes that ran through Utah from Native-American attacks and to keep an eye on the Mormons. Much to the chagrin of the locals, he established a base just three miles to the east of Salt Lake City and named it Fort Douglas, after former presidential candidate Stephen A. Douglas. The fort became the headquarters of the District of Utah when it formally opened on October 26th.

First Transcontinental Telegraph

When California was made part of the Union in 1850, it was the first state not to have a mutual border with another Federal state and communications between the West and East coasts was by comparatively slow mail overland route run by the Pony Express or by sea routes. The need to link east and west was a pressing issue and would become even more urgent when the South seceded.

In 1860, the U.S. Post Office was authorized to build a telegraph line and work commenced on July 4, 1861. California's Overland Telegraph Company built the line eastward from Carson City, while the Pacific Telegraph Company worked westward from Omaha, Nebraska. They were to meet up at Salt Lake City. The former company was the first to reach the rendezvous, on October 18, 1861, and the other section of line was completed on the 24th, the day that the first transcontinental telegraph message was sent to Lincoln. The Pony Express business closed two days later.

General Patrick E. Connor, first commander of the 3rd California Regiment.

The 3rd Regiment California Volunteer Infantry

Recruits to this regiment mustered at Stockton and at Benicia Barracks, both in California, between late October and late December 1861. Colonel Patrick E. Connor was its first commander, being appointed on October 31st. The regiment was mostly based at the barracks until June 1862, when elements of it moved through Nevada Territory and established Fort Douglas in the north of Utah, where all of its companies would serve at one stage or another throughout the war. At various times company-sized detachments also served in California, Colorado, Idaho, Nevada, Colorado. The regiment's activities during the Civil War were related to maintaining Federal authority, protecting lines of communication, dealing with threats posed by Native-Americans, and keeping watch on the Mormons. The regiment's biggest battle occurred in January, 1863, when a column from Fort Douglas destroyed a Native-American encampment at Bear River in southeast Washington State. The regiment was reorganized as the 3rd Battalion of Infantry in late October 1863, and was finally mustered out of service in July 1866.

Vermont

66 It is gratifying to realize that each and every call of our country, in her hour of peril, thousands of the young men of our state have willingly and eagerly seized arms and have gone or are going forth to battle for the Union. 99

GOVERNOR FREDERICK HOLBROOK, SECOND INAUGURAL ADDRESS, 1862

Vermont was ceded to Britain by France in 1763 and declared itself an independent republic in 1777. A constitution was unveiled in July of that year and Chapter One, which was subtitled "A Declaration of the Rights of the Inhabitants of the State of Vermont," effectively abolished slavery.

Fourteen years later, in 1791, when Vermont became the fourteenth state of the Union (partly to counterbalance the admittance of slave-owing Kentucky later the same year), the new state's constitution retained the clause.

As the issue of slavery came to dominate U.S. politics over the following decades, Vermont's stance hardened. A Vermont Senate report on the issue in 1854 strongly supported the state's constitution on the matter – so much so that the Georgia General Assembly bizarrely suggested that Vermont should be towed out to sea! And while the country slid toward secession and Civil War, popular feeling moved from supporting the containment of slavery toward its outright abolition in the late 1850s, partly in response to the Whig Party's disarray over the whole issue. At that time, the newly formed Republican Party began to attract support in Vermont and proof that the state had not wavered on the anti-slavery issue came in the 1860 presidential election: president-elect Abraham Lincoln garnered 33,808 votes, while the three other candidates polled a total of 10,732. John C. Breckinridge, the pro-slavery Southern Democrat contender, mustered just 217 votes.

Despite Vermont's stance on slavery, some still sought compromise. State representative Justin S. Morrill proposed an amendment to a pro-Southern proposal in late 1860, seeking "any reasonable, proper, and constitutional remedy to preserve the peace of the country, and the perpetuity of the Union." It was rejected. Vermont also sent five delegates to the Washington Peace Conference,

ERASTUS FAIRBANKS (1792–1864)

Fairbanks became the first of three Vermont governors to serve during the Civil War and set the standard for Vermont's participation in the war.

In mid-April 1861, when Abraham Lincoln issued his first call for volunteers, Fairbanks answered by convening a special session of the legislature to authorize funds for organizing, arming, and equipping the militia. Having personal manufacturing interests, Fairbanks used his industry's credit to subsidize the raising of regiments. He also created state recruiting stations, which drew the thanks of the president and the War Department.

which opened on February 4, 1861. Among them was Lucius E. Crittenden, an ardent abolitionist and official recorder of the meetings. Seven Southern states had already signaled their intention to secede so discussions at the conference largely centered on the eight other slave-owning states, particularly Virginia and Kentucky. A compromise was sought, but satisfied no one, and the Senate rejected the proposals. The House of Representatives did not even vote on the matter. Jefferson Davis was named president of the Confederacy on February 9th and Civil War became inevitable.

VERMONT PREPARES FOR WAR

Like most states on the eve of Civil War, Vermont's own defense overwhelmingly rested with various local militias, which amounted to twenty-two volunteer companies. Many of these men joined the Union Army in 1861 and by the following year just thirteen companies were still available. In response, the state authorities created a new militia – one of able-bodied men aged between eighteen to forty-five – though these units were demobilized on December 2, 1862. Nevertheless, Vermont provided considerable numbers of men for the war effort, in part thanks to the efforts of its state governors. The twenty-sixth governor, Erastus Fairbanks, only served until October 1861 but, when Lincoln made his first call for volunteers in April, his response was "Vermont will do its full duty." Fairbanks convened a special session of the state legislature to procure funds to arm and equip the militia and even used financial credits raised on the back of his family business to furnish units for the regular army. Six regiments of regular infantry and one of cavalry were raised under his governorship.

The next governor, Republican Frederick Holbrook, was equally dedicated to the cause – ten further regiments of infantry, two batteries of light artillery, and three companies of sharpshooters were raised. Three military hospitals were also built in Vermont to aid the wounded and sick. Governor J. Gregory Smith, who held office from 1863 to the war's end, followed a similar path: he was also renowned for his concern for soldiers at the front and raised another infantry regiment, a third light artillery battery, and two companies of cavalry to guard the state's border with Canada.

THE ST. ALBANS RAID

This raid, the most northerly action of the Civil War, was the brainchild of Confederate Lieutenant Bennett H. Young, a Kentuckian who had been taken prisoner in 1863 but managed to escape to Canada. Returning to the South he proposed to lead a raid into Vermont from Canada to seize funds to aid the

war effort and force the Union to station valuable troops along the border. St. Alban's, a small town just twenty-five miles from Canada, was the target.

Bennett returned to Canada, recruited a party of escaped prisoners, and reached St. Albans with two other men on October 10, 1864. More men arrived in twos and threes over the following days until there were twenty-one raiders in all. On the afternoon of the 19th, they robbed three banks of a total of $208,000. A St. Albans citizen was killed and another wounded in the action. Nevertheless, Young's plan to burn the town to the ground was largely unsuccessful.

Leaving only one burning shed behind them, the raiders crossed the border into Canada where they were arrested. A court ruled that they were acting under military orders and, as they were not common criminals, Canada's neutrality prevented them from being extradited to the United States. They were soon freed, though the $88,000 they had with them was returned to St. Albans. Young was expressly excluded from the amnesty proclamation made by President Andrew Johnson in May 1865, and only made his way back to the United States in 1868.

Frederick Holbrook.

Generals from Vermont

Major General William B. Hazen.

Major General Ethan A. Hitchcock.

Brigadier General John W. Phelps.

Brigadier General George J. Stannard.

MAJOR GENERAL WILLIAM B. HAZEN (1830–87)

A West Point graduate who served with the Union Army in the Western Theater, Hazen took part in some of its greatest battles – Shiloh and Perryville in 1862, Stones River in 1862–63, Chickamauga, Chattanooga, Missionary Ridge in 1863, and Resaca, Pickett's Mill, Peachtree Creek, Atlanta, and the March to the Sea in 1864. He was made major general in December 1864 and fought in the Carolinas Campaign the next year.

MAJOR GENERAL ETHAN A. HITCHCOCK (1798–1870)

Hitchcock was a retired soldier who returned to service in 1861 as a major general and held various administrative posts in Washington, D.C. He was a special advisor to the secretary of war, chairman of the War Board, and one of those who found Major General Fitz John Porter guilty of cowardice and disobedience in January 1863, for his actions at the Second Battle of Bull Run (Second Manassas) the previous year. Hitchcock was also the commissioner for prisoner exchange from November 1862 until the war's end.

BRIGADIER GENERAL JOHN W. PHELPS (1813–85)

Phelps was an abolitionist who saw action in Virginia before transferring to the Department of the Gulf. After the capture of New Orleans in May, 1862, he was sent to nearby Camp Parapet where he sought permission to train and arm escaped slaves. His superior, Major General Benjamin Butler, refused and Phelps resigned in August. When the Confederacy's President Jefferson Davis heard of the scheme he declared Phelps an outlaw.

BRIGADIER GENERAL GEORGE J. STANNARD (1820–86)

After commanding a regiment at the First Battle of Bull Run (First Manassas) in 1861, Stannard served in the Peninsula and Maryland campaigns, but was captured at Harpers Ferry and not exchanged until early 1863. Made a brigadier general in March, Stannard led the 2nd Vermont Brigade with distinction at Gettysburg, where he was wounded. When he returned to service, he was present at Cold Harbor, in 1864, and the siege of Petersburg, where he was again wounded. Thereafter, the general undertook light duties in his home state.

Vermont Units

Brigadier General Israel B. "Fighting Dick" Richardson was born in Vermont and mortally wounded at the Battle of Antietam.

THE 54TH MASSACHUSETTS VOLUNTEER INFANTRY REGIMENT

Vermont had a small African-American population at the outbreak of war, with the previous year's census identifying just over 700 living across the state. Records indicate that some 149 of them served in the U.S. Army, and a sizeable number of those men – some sixty-eight in all – elected to join the famous 54th Massachusetts that gained renown for its attempt to storm Fort Wagner in July 1863.

By the war's end, the African-American Vermonters in the 54th had had two men killed in action, both in 1864 – Charles E. Nelson of Bristol in February and Cornelius Price of Underhill in July. Four more recruits had died of disease, twelve were discharged through disability, and just one man deserted. The remaining forty-nine survived.

THE 1ST REGIMENT VERMONT VOLUNTEER INFANTRY

Lincoln called for 75,000 recruits to serve for three months in April 1861. In response, the 1st Regiment mustered at Rutland in May. After being enrolled in the army, the regiment traveled to New York and then sailed for Fortress Monroe, Virginia, on the 13th. Ten days later it made a brief sortie into Confederate-held Virginia, then moved to Newport News on the 26th. Five companies took part in the fighting at Big Bethel in June, the first large skirmish of the war, but were forced back to base. The regiment sailed home in early August and was mustered out on the 15th and 16th. It had suffered six fatalities but only one of those was killed in action.

Vermont Union Units Furnished	
Infantry regiments	18
Sharpshooter units	3
Cavalry regiments	1
Heavy artillery regiments	1
Heavy artillery companies	1
Light artillery batteries	3
Sailors/marine personnel	619
Colored troops	149

VERMONT UNION ARMY DEATHS

Troops Furnished	Killed/Mortally Wounded	Died of Disease	Died of Other Causes	Total
32,549	1,809	1,878	818	5,224

THE 1ST VERMONT BRIGADE

The brigade was organized around five Vermont volunteer infantry regiments in October 1861 and joined the Army of the Potomac in April 1862, becoming part of VI Corps and designated the 2nd Division's 2nd Brigade. It would see intense fighting over the following months: during the Peninsula Campaign, the Seven Days Battles, at Antietam (Battle of Sharpsburg), and at Fredericksburg.

The next year brought little respite: the Vermonters were present at Chancellorsville and Gettysburg. The brigade was again in action in 1864, suffering heavy losses during the Battle of the Wilderness in May. Reinforcements in the shape of the 11th Vermont arrived, however, and the brigade went on to Spotsylvania Court House and Cold Harbor. In under a month its strength had fallen from 2,850 troops to just 1,200.

The Vermonters next participated in the Valley Campaign, winning six Medals of Honor at the Battle of Cedar Creek in October. Six more were won on April 2, 1865, when the brigade helped break through the Petersburg defenses in Virginia. The war effectively ended five days later and the brigade's last act was to take part in the victory parade through Washington, D.C.

Monument to the 1st Vermont Brigade's actions during the Battle of the Wilderness.

THE 5TH REGIMENT VERMONT VOLUNTEERS AND THE SEVEN DAYS BATTLE

During the Seven Days Battles (June 25-July 1, 1862) fought east of Richmond, the 5th Vermont served in Brigadier William T.H. Brooks' 2nd Brigade, part of the Army of the Potomac's 2nd Division. The Confederate attacks during the opening phase of the campaign forced the Army of the Potomac to making a fighting retreat in a southeast direction toward its main base at Harrison's Landing on the north bank of the James River. The regiment's first action came at Garnett's Farm, where there was a sharp skirmish with a division under Major General John B. Magruder on July 27th. Next came the Battle of Savage's Station two days later. As the retreat continued, the regiment was also present during the fighting around White Oak Swamp Bridge on the 30th.

THE 14TH REGIMENT VERMONT VOLUNTEERS AT THE BATTLE OF GETTYSBURG

The 14th Regiment entered service in October 1862, to replace the severe losses recently suffered by the Army of the Potomac. It joined the 2nd Vermont Brigade at the end of October and spent the next several months defending Washington, D.C. The Vermonters became the 3rd Division's 3rd Brigade on June 25, 1863, however, and served as I Corps' rearguard as the Army of the Potomac made its way northward to intercept the Army of Northern Virginia in the Gettysburg Campaign. The regiment reached Gettysburg after dark on the first day, July 1st, and camped near Cemetery Hill. The next day it helped repulse an attack on an artillery battery and, on the 3rd, played a key part in repulsing Pickett's Charge against the center of the Union line on Cemetery Ridge.

The flag of Commonwealth of Virginia
was adopted on January 31, 1861.

Virginia

"Now, therefore, we, the people of Virginia, do declare and ordain, That the ordinance adopted by the people of this State in convention on the twenty-fifth day of June, in the year of our Lord one thousand seven hundred and eighty-eight, whereby the Constitution of the United States of America was ratified, and all acts of the General Assembly of this State ratifying and adopting amendments to said Constitution, are hereby repealed and abrogated; that the union between the State of Virginia and the other States under the Constitution aforesaid is hereby dissolved, and that the State of Virginia is in the full possession and exercise of all the rights of sovereignty which belong and appertain to a free and independent State."

CONVENTION OF VIRGINIA, APRIL 17, 1861

With the establishment of the Jamestown settlement in 1607, Virginia became the site of the first permanent English colony in North America. After initial problems, the settlement began to flourish and the economy of what became the Commonwealth of Virginia was founded on the cultivation of tobacco. Slave labor was considered necessary to harvest this crop, and the Virginia colony grew prosperous by embracing slave ownership.

During the early 19th century industry developed in the state, centred around the new city of Richmond, and railroads linked Virginia to its neighboring states, but these signs of industrial progress were limited – Virginia remained a largely plantation owning and agricultural economy until the outbreak of the Civil War.

As a prominent state in the fledgling United States of America, Virginian politicians were actively involved in the debate over the future course of the country, but they increasingly found themselves at odds with northern politicians, who viewed slavery with distaste. While the tobacco economy declined in the century following independence, Virginia remained firmly in the slave-owning camp. Nevertheless, the number of free blacks in the state increased during this period while settlers also pushed the boundaries of the state further west. Unlike the landowners in the eastern part of the state, these pioneers had no need for slaves and tensions between east and west became pronounced.

JOHN BROWN'S RAID

The abolitionist movement rose to prominence in America during the early 19th century, but most of its supporters advocated a peaceable end to slave-ownership, achieved through political debate. The firebrand abolitionist John Brown advocated a more confrontational approach, arguing that by inciting an armed slave insurrection the whole issue would be brought to a head. On October 16, 1859, Brown and twenty-two supporters raided the Federal Arsenal in Harpers Ferry, Virginia. A detachment of Federal troops commanded by Robert E. Lee cornered the abolitionists and eventually forced them to surrender. John Brown was subsequently tried, convicted, and executed by the Virginia legislature, his death warrant being signed by Governor Wise. While Brown's raid was a failure, it succeeded in polarising American views on slavery, and, therefore, contributed toward the drive to secession and civil war.

Front page of *Frank Leslie's Illustrated Newspaper* of November 19, 1859, with a picture of John Brown captioned "now under sentence of death for treason and murder, at Charlestown, Va."

ROBERT E. LEE'S CRISIS OF CONSCIENCE

Robert E. Lee (1807–70), the general who would become the leading Confederate commander of the Civil War, was born on Stratford Hall Plantation in Northern Virginia. As befitted the son of a hero of the Revolutionary War, he joined the army, and, after graduating from West Point, became a distinguished military engineer, seeing action during the Mexican-American War. Although no supporter of slavery, he crushed the John Brown raid on Harpers Ferry but remained aloof from the political debate over slavery and secession. In March 1861, Lee became a colonel, and the commander of the U.S. Army General Winfield Scott urged him to accept command of the Union Army gathering in Washington, D.C.

The *de facto* secession of Virginia on April 17th placed Lee in a quandary – should he remain a loyal soldier and serve his president and country, or place his allegiance with his native state? It was an agonizing decision but Lee refused the offer of a Union command, and two days later tendered his resignation from the U.S. Army. On April 23rd, Lee was offered command of Virginia's state forces – an offer he reluctantly accepted. The decision to resign his U.S. Army commission had been a painful one, and in the note to General Scott that accompanied his letter of resignation he said; "Save in the defense of my native State, I never desire again to draw my sword." That Virginian sword remained unsheathed through four long and bloody years of conflict.

THE SECESSION DEBATE

In 1860, the Democratic Party split over the slavery issue, and, that June, the Southern Democrats held their own conference in Richmond, Virginia, electing John C. Breckenridge as their presidential candidate. When the presidential election of November 1860 was won by the Republican candidate Abraham Lincoln many Virginians felt themselves torn between the Unionist and Secessionist lobbies, and while Governor Letcher held a peace conference, the Virginia legislature debated the implications of secession.

On February 4, 1861, before the secession debate got properly underway in Virginia, six Southern states seceded from the Union, and formed the breakaway Confederate States of America. Still, Virginian debaters urged a political compromise, and for two months Governor Letcher did what he could to prevent the slide toward military and political confrontation. The hopes for a peaceable solution were dashed following the firing on Fort Sumter in Charleston, South Carolina on April 12th. In Virginia, the secession debate was reconvened and feelings hardened following Lincoln's request for Virginia state troops to help quell the rebellion. On April 17th, a motion to secede was approved by one vote, pending a state-wide referendum.

For many Virginians the argument for secession was clear. The new Republican administration was anti-slavery, yet the right to slave ownership was enshrined in the laws of the Commonwealth of Virginia. Any threat to impose abolition by force or to undermine the legal standing of the state was seen as an attack on the sovereignty of the commonwealth, and, therefore, Virginians felt there was no option but to defend their own sovereign rights.

Governor Letcher mobilized the Virginia militia, not to quell the rebellion but to defend the state's borders against Union aggression. On

May 23rd the referendum was held, and 132,201 Virginians voted for secession, while 37,451 voted to remain in the Union. Consequently, on May 29th the results were announced, and Virginia formally seceded from the United States. The same day it became part of the new Confederate States of America. War was now inevitable.

A TALE OF TWO GOVERNORS

In 1856, Henry A. Wise was elected as the thirty-third Governor of the Commonwealth of Virginia. As a Virginia politician, he had long upheld the right of slave ownership, and as a Democrat he argued for the maintenance of state sovereignty. His greatest challenge as governor came in late 1859, when he ignored political pressure from outside the state and signed the death warrant of the abolitionist John Brown. He was also a leading proponent of secession, and reputedly debated the topic in the Virginia legislature with a cocked pistol in front of him.

In 1860, he was succeeded by former Democratic congressman John Letcher, who began his political career as an abolitionist, but later joined the pro-slavery lobby. Known as "Honest John" in Washington, D.C., Letcher was no supporter of seccession,

and organized political summits in an attempt to avoid conflict, but as a Virginian he also saw it as his duty to implement any decision passed by the Virginia legislature. As a result he supervised the withdrawal of Virginia from the Union, and continued to govern the state on behalf of the Confederate government throughout the Civil War.

Henry A. Wise.

Above: Henry A. Wise (1806–76) served as Virginia's governor from 1856 to 1860. His most remembered act during his administration was overseeing the capture and the hanging of John Brown. His most remembered act *after* leaving office occurred when he stood before the Virginia legislature with a cocked pistol and demanded a vote for secession. Wise became a general during the Civil War with a determination that far surpassed his effectiveness.

Left: A slaveholder and a proslavery spokesman who nevertheless advocated moderation and conciliation, John Letcher (1813–84) replaced fiery secessionist Henry A. Wise as governor in 1860. Letcher tried to dissuade the growing number of secessionists in his state by supporting compromise. When the Deep South began seceding, he helped organize the Washington Peace Conference in an effort to find solutions to the South's perceived injustices. With the firing on Fort Sumter, former Governor Wise addressed the legislature and without Letcher's knowledge secretly sent troops to capture the Harpers Ferry armory and arsenal. Wise's actions eliminated any options Letcher might have had to slow down Virginia's secession. After Virginia passed the ordinance of secession on April 17, 1861, Letcher became governor of the South's most powerful state and cooperated fully with the Confederate government. Financially ruined by the war, at its end Letcher returned to Lexington, Virginia, and resumed the practice of law.

John Letcher.

Ruins of Petersburg and Richmond Railroad bridge, across the James River.

RICHMOND: THE CONFEDERATE CAPITAL

On May 29, 1861, the decision was made to move the new Confederate capital from Montgomery, Alabama, to Richmond, Virginia. Richmond was founded in 1737, and in 1780 became the state capital. By 1861, it had grown into the small city of just under 40,000 people. The new Confederate Congress shared their meeting place with the Virginia Assembly, while a building two blocks away became the home of President Davis, and the "White House of the Confederacy". The population of the city virtually doubled overnight as government departments were established and politicians, civil servants, and military administrators vied for space within the city limits.

Reasons for making Richmond the Confederate capital included its good communication links and its proximity to the leading industrial center in the Confederacy. Once established, it became a major strategic objective for Union commanders, and for four years the state was ravaged by war as the Union army made repeated attempts to advance on the city. Nevertheless, it remained in Confederate hands until April 2, 1865, falling to Union forces only a week before the final surrender of the Confederate Army at Appomattox, Virginia. The war-ravaged city paid a heavy price for Virginia's opposition to the Union. During the final days of the war Richmond was reduced to rubble. Reconstruction was a slow, painstaking process.

An unidentified soldier in Confederate uniform of Company E "Lynchburg Rifles", 11th Virginia Infantry Volunteers holds an 1841 "Mississippi" rifle, Sheffield-type Bowie knife, canteen, box knapsack, blanket roll, and cartridge box.

J.O. Davidson's rendition of the famous battle of Hampton Roads was published in Prang's *War Pictures*.

Virginia's Military Contribution to the Confederacy

At the time of its secession, Virginia maintained a state militia – an organization that had been in existence since the mid-17th century. Before the secession vote, a regiment of ten to twenty companies of Virginia State Rangers had also been raised as a partisan force designed to operate in the western part of the state, where pro-Union feelings were rife. (In addition, from May 1862, a county-based Home Guard was created across the state, to serve as a police force.) On April 27, 1861, the Virginia assembly created the Provisional Army of Virginia, which consisted of nine infantry regiments (one being rifles), a cavalry regiment, and two artillery regiments. These troops were regarded as "militia of the line," but were augmented by numerous additional regiments, classed as "volunteer militia." In practice, there was no real difference between the two groups. In June, 1861, the units – dubbed the Virginia State Line – were transferred to the Confederate army.

In November 1861, the Virginia State Militia was divided into active and reserve classes (also known as First and Second Class militia), but by May 1862 the majority of active militiamen had been drafted into the Virginia State Line regiments seconded to the Confederate Army, and those who remained was reclassified as reserve militia. The reserve class militia – for the most part men over the age of thirty-one – consisted of twenty infantry companies and an artillery company. This force was disbanded in 1864 as the men were called to the colors to replace wartime losses in active units.

The Virginia Navy

On April 27, 1861, the Virginia legislature voted for the creation of the Provisional Navy of Virginia – a grandiose title for an organization that, at the time, possessed no ships. It did, however, form

the basis for a naval force that would be charged with defending the rivers and ports of Virginia. Vessels were soon pressed into service, crewed by former officers and men of the U.S. Navy who had elected to support their home state, and the Virginia Navy was transferred into the Confederate Navy in June 1861.

During the war, the most notable Confederate warship serving in Virginia waters was the C.S.S. *Virginia*, a revolutionary ironclad built from the partially-destroyed hull of the U.S.S. *Merrimac*, a steam-powered warship. *Virginia* is best known for her fight with the Union ironclad U.S.S. *Monitor* during the Battle of Hampton Roads (March 8-9, 1862). She was eventually destroyed by her crew when the Confederates were forced to abandon the naval base of Norfolk, Virginia.

Several other Confederate warships served in Virginia waters, including the steam gunboat C.S.S. *Patrick Henry*, and the ironclads of the James River Squadron, whose task was to defend the capital from naval attack.

Right: Tredegar Iron Works was owned by Joseph Reid Anderson during the war. Today it is houses the Visitor's Center of the Richmond National Battlefield Park.

Below: An example of what was made there – a Brooke rifle defending Dutch Gap Canal. The Brooke rifle was a rifled, muzzle-loading naval defense gun designed by John Mercer Brooke.

Virginia's Industrial Contribution

Virginia was a largely agricultural state, though a handful of regional centers of textile production were producing small quantities of goods before the outbreak of the war. The bulk of Virginia's industry was, however, centred around Richmond. These factories included several woollen mills and wood yards though the most significant factory was the Tredegar Iron Works, sited on the banks of the James River, close to the center of the city. It was the largest iron foundry in the Confederacy, and, throughout the war, provided guns and munitions, locomotives and rolling stock, as well as iron plate for Confederate ironclad warships. The iron works remained in production until Richmond fell to Union forces in April 1865.

Stonewall Jackson Bull Run Aug 17 1861

JACKSON AT MANASSAS

During the battle, Brigadier General Bee tried to rally Confederate troops fleeing past Henry House Hill by exclaiming, "There stands Jackson like a stone wall! Rally behind the Virginians." As a result, Thomas Jackson was given the nickname "Stonewall", and his command – the 2nd, 4th, 5th, 27th, and 33rd Virginia Infantry Regiments – would collectively be known as "The Stonewall Brigade", and considered to be the premier combat brigade in the Confederate Army of Northern Virginia.

OPENING SHOTS

In April, 1861, the U.S. Army retained control of Fort Monroe, located on the tip of the Virginia Peninsula formed by the York and James rivers, providing the Union with a secure base on Virginian soil. On June 10, 1861, a brigade-sized Union force of 2,500 men was repulsed by some 1,200 Confederates near Big Bethel, a hamlet nine miles from the fort. This, the first land battle fought in Virginia was little more than a skirmish, but helped boost Confederate morale.

In western Virginia, a Union force commanded by Major General McClellan drove back a smaller Confederate force in a skirmish at Philippi on June 3rd. This not only made McClellan a Union hero, but it encouraged the pro-Union western Virginians to nullify Virginia's ordnance of secession, and to break away from the state, forming their own political legislature. On June 19th, they declared the foundation of a new state – West Virginia – and this was subsequently ratified by President Lincoln.

A small Union victory at Cheat Mountain (July 11th) led to the withdrawal of Confederate forces from western Virginia, allowing the Union to consolidate its hold over the newly-created breakaway state.

FIRST MANASSAS (FIRST BULL RUN)

Following the bombardment of Fort Sumter, Lincoln called for an army of 75,000 volunteers, willing to serve for ninety days. Lincoln planned to use the gathering Union army to end the war in a single stroke by advancing on the Confederate capital. One decisive battle, he hoped, would win the war.

By July, 1861, Union commander Major General McDowell had 35,000 troops stationed around Washington, D.C. while another 18,000 occupied Harpers Ferry. McDowell was faced by a Confederate army of 22,000 men under Major General Beauregard, while another under 12,000 men under Major General Johnston lay to the west, in the Shenandoah Valley. McDowell advanced on Manassas, hoping to force Beauregard's smaller army back toward Richmond. Instead, the bulk of Johnston's army were sent east by train, which meant that the two opposing armies were roughly of equal size.

The Confederates occupied a position northwest of Manassas behind Bull Run Creek. On July 21st, McDowell attempted to outflank them by crossing the river upstream of the enemy, and then falling on Beauregard's left flank. Meanwhile, pinning attacks along the river held the Confederates in place. The initial attack proved a resounding success, and soon the Confederate left wing was in retreat. A line of

Map of the Shenandoah Valley, from Front Royal and Middletown to Staunton.

sorts was formed on Henry House Hill, but it seemed as if the defenders would break before Johnston's troops could reach the battlefield. Nevertheless, a key position on the hill – occupied by Brigadier Jackson's Virginian brigade – held its ground in the face of the Union attack. When a second attack was launched, for a while the outcome of the battle was in the balance. Then, fresh Confederate troops arrived and slowly the Union army gave ground. By 5:00 pm McDowell's army was in full retreat, and the exhausted Confederates were left in control of the field.

THE VALLEY CAMPAIGN

After its defeat at Manassas, the Union army withdrew to Washington, D.C. and the only significant action in Virginia for the remainder of 1861 was a skirmish at Ball's Bluff (October 21st), on the banks of the Potomac. McDowell was replaced by Major General McClellan, who planned to lead his newly-formed Army of the Potomac in a fresh offensive, again aimed at Richmond. By way of a diversion, the Union force at Harpers Ferry moved to threaten the Shenandoah Valley, which was defended by a heavily-outnumbered Confederate army led by "Stonewall" Jackson.

The Shenandoah was regarded as the "breadbasket of Virginia", and its defense was considered vital. From March to June, Jackson fought what is generally regarded as a brilliant campaign, marching and countermarching his small army to thwart the actions of several larger Union forces. Even his initial defeat at Kernstown (March 23, 1862) proved a strategic victory, as it forced McClellan to denude the Army of the Potomac in order to reinforce the troops facing Jackson. Later Confederate victories – at McDowell (May 8th), Front Royal (May 23rd), Winchester (May 25th), Cross Keys (June 8th) and Port Republic (June 9th) – forced Union troops in the valley to retrench around Harpers Ferry, allowing Jackson to send his army east to reinforce the troops defending Richmond against McClellan.

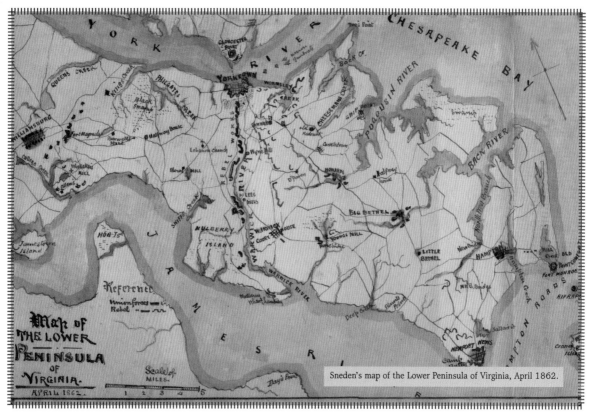

Sneden's map of the Lower Peninsula of Virginia, April 1862.

HAMPTON ROADS

In April 1861, the Confederates captured the Federal naval dockyard at Norfolk, Virginia. The retreating Union garrison left behind the burned-out remains of the steam frigate U.S.S. *Merrimac*, and the fledgling Confederate Navy used the wreck to form the lower hull of a new ironclad warship they dubbed the C.S.S. *Virginia*. Iron plates from the Tredegar Iron Works were used to form her protective armor and, by March 1862, the new ship was ready for action.

During the winter of 1861–62, a Union fleet blockaded Norfolk, and stationed a squadron of steam-powered warships off Hampton Roads, close to the guns of Fort Monroe. On March 8, 1862, Captain Buchanan steered the ungainly *Virginia* into the James River and engaged the Union blockaders. Union shot bounced off her iron hull, and the ironclad was able to wreak havoc on the Union squadron, sinking the U.S.S. *Cumberland* and the U.S.S. *Congress*.

Buchanan hoped to finish off the remaining Union ships the following day, but during the night the blockading squadron was reinforced by the U.S.S. *Monitor*, a small ironclad built in New York and rushed south to face the *Virginia*. While the Confederate ironclad carried her guns inside a large protected casemate, the monitor's two guns were mounted inside a single revolving turret. When battle was resumed the following morning, neither of the two ironclads was able to defeat its opponent. In effect, the two revolutionary warships cancelled each other out.

The *Virginia* was eventually blown up by her own crew on May 9th, when Union troops captured Norfolk. Richmond now had to rely on gun batteries for its defence, but these proved equal to the task when a Union advance up the James River was repulsed at Drewry's Bluff (May 15th).

THE PENINSULA CAMPAIGN

In the spring of 1862, as the Army of the Potomac launched its new drive on Richmond, McClellan moved the bulk of his army by sea to Fort Monroe and began an advance up the Virginia Tidewater Peninsula. He was held up at Yorktown, where Brigadier General Magruder's small Confederate force held the invaders at bay for a month. When Magruder finally withdrew, McClellan gave chase. The two armies clashed indecisively at Williamsburg on May 5th.

The Union advance continued and, by late May, McClellan's army was astride the Chickahominy River, within a few miles of Richmond. General Joseph E. Johnston now launched a counter-attack, falling on an isolated portion of the Union army. In the ensuing Battle of Fair Oaks (May 31st – June 1st) Johnston was wounded, but his surprise attack forced McClellan to go onto the defensive.

The Confederates were reformed into the Army of Northern Virginia, and General Robert E. Lee took command of this force in front of Richmond. He was further reinforced by Jackson's Army of the Valley. In a bloody and fast-moving series of engagements known as the Seven Days Battles, Lee attacked McClellan's larger army and despite bloody reverses at Mechanicsville (June 26th) and Gaines' Mill (June 27th), the Confederates drove the Union forces back toward their supply lines. After further gruelling battles at White Oak Swamp (June 30th) and Malvern Hill (July 1st), McClellan withdrew his demoralized army from the peninsula. Although Lee won the battle, his losses (20,000 men killed and wounded) were, nevertheless, greater than those suffered by his more timid opponents.

SECOND MANASSAS (SECOND BULL RUN)

While the Peninsular Campaign was still underway, Lee sent Jackson's army north to contain a new Union threat, the Army of Virginia, commanded by Major General Pope, which was forming near Manassas. After initial skirmishes at Cedar Mountain on August 9th and Groveton on August 28th, the two armies clashed on the old Bull Run battlefield. In the Second Battle of Manassas (August 29–30, 1862) Pope virtually destroyed his army by launching a

series of uncoordinated attacks against Jackson's line. After Jackson was reinforced by Major General Longstreet, he went over to the attack and drove the remains of Pope's army from the field. The campaign was a strategic triumph for Lee and Jackson, who now held the initiative in Virginia.

Major General Joseph N.E. Johnston (1807–91) was a Virginian who first saw action against the Seminole Indians. When Virginia seceded he was sent to defend the Shenandoah Valley, but his timely intervention at First Manassas (First Bull Run) helped turn the tide of battle. He defended Richmond during the opening battles of the Peninsular Campaign (1862) before being sent to the Western Theater, where his skills as a defensive general were tested to the limit.

STUART'S RIDE

Before Lee launched his offensive outside Richmond during the Peninsula Campaign, he asked his Virginia-born cavalry commander to conduct a reconnaissance of McClellan's army. Jackson excelled himself. On June 12th, he led a force of 1,200 Confederate cavalrymen around the Union Army and over three days harried McClellan's supply lines, destroyed stockpiles of stores, and evaded the troops sent to corner him. On June 15th, he returned to Lee's lines, having ridden his force completely around the Union Army.

JEDEDIAH HOTCHKISS (1828–99)

Hotchkiss is the largely unsung hero of Jackson's Valley Campaign. The Confederate cartographer produced the detailed military maps that Jackson used to outmanoeuver his Union opponents, both in the Shenandoah Valley and during subsequent campaigns in central Virginia. Hotchkiss served under Jackson from 1862, producing maps and directing troop movements (because his mapmaking had made him familiar with the terrain). He served with Jackson at Antietam, Fredericksburg, and Chancellorsville, and after the general's death continued under Ewell and Early, working closely for General Lee. After the surrender Grant paid Hotchkiss for permission to use his maps in his reports.

THE ANTIETAM CAMPAIGN

On September 4, 1862, Lee ordered his Army of Northern Virginia to cross the Potomac and enter Maryland. He was now taking the war to the enemy, to spare the ravaged farmland of Virginia. Moving with uncharacteristic speed, McClellan marched west from Washington, D.C. to confront him.

Lee detached Jackson to recapture Harpers Ferry, which was duly besieged and taken by September 15th. His main army was in western Maryland. McClellan outnumbered him, however, and Lee was forced to fight a defensive battle at South Mountain on September 14th to buy time for Jackson to reinforce him. McClellan's army eventually pushed through the mountains, and, for once, Lee was outmanoeuvred, caught with his army pinned north of the Potomac near Antietam. To survive, his 37,000 men had to stand their ground and fight off a 75,000 strong Union army.

During the ensuing Battle of Antietam (Battle of Sharpsburg) on September 17th, McClellan launched a series of uncoordinated assaults, but Lee's army held its ground. Eventually reinforcements from Jackson's army reached the battlefield, and attacked the Union left flank. The battle was a draw, but an expensive one – the most costly single day of the war, with both sides losing over 12,000 men killed or wounded. Two days later, Lee's army slipped back over the Potomac into Virginia.

FREDERICKSBURG

When McClellan failed to pursue Lee after Antietam, he was replaced by Major General Burnside, who proposed another direct advance on Richmond. In November, while Lee's army was regrouping near Fredericksburg, Burnside advanced south to capture Manassas. He then continued his advance to the Rappahannock River, which Lee turned into a defensive line. Until pontoon bridges could be brought up, Burnside's army was unable to cross the river, which gave the Confederates time to entrench themselves in the heights overlooking Fredericksburg, beyond the southern bank of the river.

On December 11th–12th, Burnside used his long-awaited pontoon bridges to cross the river and occupy Fredericksburg, which was badly damaged by Union shells. Then, on December 13th, he ordered a general assault on the entrenched Confederates. Three uncoordinated assaults were launched, all of which were repulsed with heavy losses. At Marye's Heights, opposite Fredericksburg, repeated attacks were launched against Major General Longstreet's men, who were dug in behind a wall and sunken road. Despite suffering over 10,000 casualties, the Union army never reached the Confederate line. Two days later the humiliated Union Army retreated back across the river.

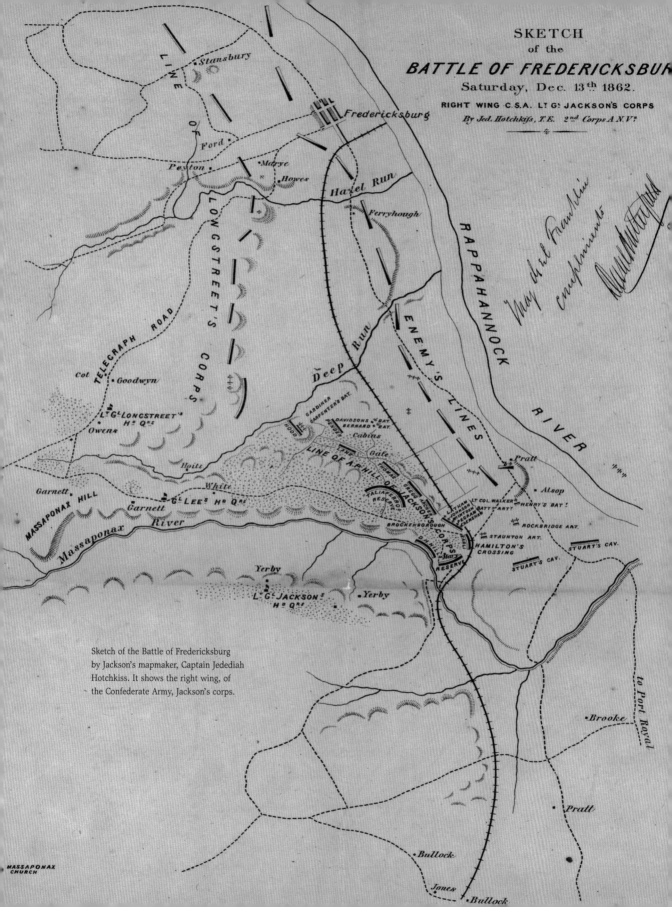

SKETCH
of the
BATTLE OF FREDERICKSBUR

Saturday, Dec. 13th 1862.

RIGHT WING C.S.A. Lt Gl JACKSON'S CORPS

By Jed. Hotchkiss, T.E. 2nd Corps A.N.Vª

Maj Genl Franklin compliments

LINE OF Ford

Stansbury

Fredericksburg

Peyton

Marye

Howes

Hazel Run

Ferryhough

RAPPAHANNOCK RIVER

LONGSTREET'S CORPS

TELEGRAPH ROAD

Col Goodwyn

Lt Gl LONGSTREET'S Ho Qrs

Owens

Hoitt

Deep Run

ENEMY'S LINES

GARDINER CARPENTER'S BAT.
DAVIDSON'S BAT.
BERNARD BAT.
PAYDA

HOOD

Cabins

Gate

LINE OF A.P.HILL'S JACKSON'S CORPS

LANE

THOMAS

GREGG ARCHER

TALIAFERRO RESERVE

Pratt

Alsop

LT COL WALKER

LATHAM JOHNSON McINTOSH PEGRAM CRENSHAW BATT'Y ART'Y

HENRY'S BAT!

ROCKBRIDGE ART.

BROCKENBOROUGH

STAUNTON ART.

DAHL

HAMILTON'S CROSSING

STUART'S CAV.

Garnett

MASSAPONAX HILL

Gl LEE'S Ho Qrs

White

Garnett

Massaponax River

STUART'S CAV.

RESERVE

Star

Yerby

Lt Gl JACKSON'S Ho Qrs

Yerby

to Port Royal

Brooke

Sketch of the Battle of Fredericksburg
by Jackson's mapmaker, Captain Jedediah
Hotchkiss. It shows the right wing, of
the Confederate Army, Jackson's corps.

Pratt

Bullock

Jones

Bullock

MASSAPONAX CHURCH

THE DEATH OF "STONEWALL" JACKSON

On the evening of May 2, 1863, Jackson and a few aides rode forward to probe the Union line near Chancellorsville. As he returned, the group of riders were fired on by men of the 18th North Carolina Regiment. The general was hit by three bullets. The wounds were not seen as life threatening and he was transported to a plantation near Guinea Station, Virginia, where they were examined. It was decided to amputate the general's left arm, but soon afterward "Stonewall" developed pneumonia – possibly the result of spending hours on a stretcher as he was evacuated from the battlefield. He finally died on May 10, 1863. His loss was a grievous blow to the Confederacy, and it may well have contributed to the poor performance of Lee's army at Gettysburg seven weeks later.

CHANCELLORSVILLE

At the start of 1863, the Union Army of the Potomac occupied northern Virginia, while the Confederate Army of Northern Virginia lay behind the Rappahannock River, between the Union Army and Richmond. Additional Confederate forces defended the Shenandoah Valley to the west. In late January, the incompetent Burnside was replaced by a new Union commander: Major General "Fighting Joe" Hooker. The new commander reorganized his shattered army and by the spring he was ready to launch a new offensive.

On April 28th, Hooker crossed the river some twelve miles west of Fredericksburg, driving back the thin screen of Confederates holding the southern bank. His army then advanced into an area of tangled brush and wood known as "the Wilderness", and Hooker established his headquarters four miles

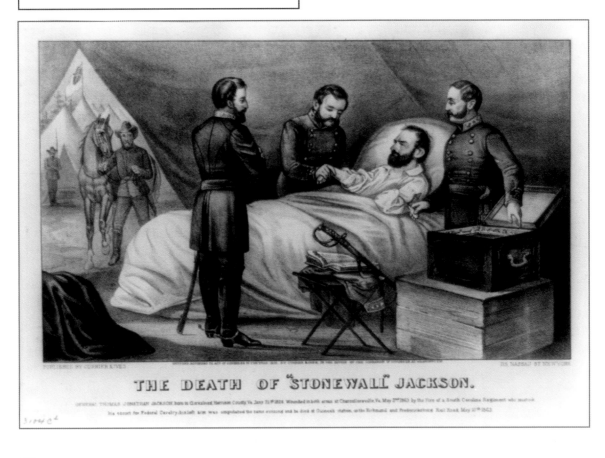

THE DEATH OF "STONEWALL" JACKSON.

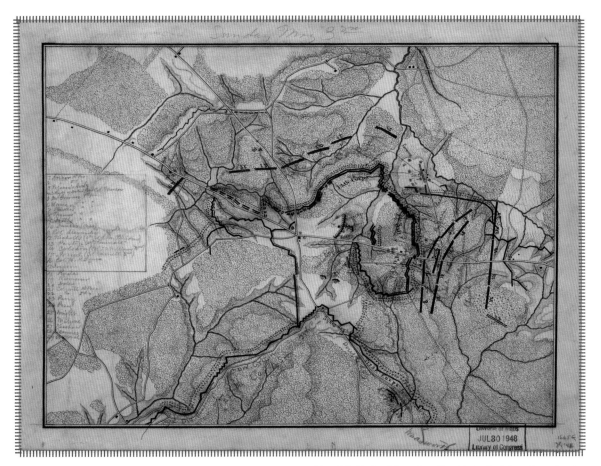

south of the river at the road junction known as Chancellorsville Courthouse. With 104,000 troops he greatly outnumbered Lee's 57,000 men. Instead of advancing, however, Hooker held his ground and waited for fresh supplies.

What followed was probably Lee's greatest victory. Leaving 10,000 men to hold Fredericksburg, he daringly split the rest of his army, sending Jackson's Corps of 28,000 men in an outflanking march around the stationary Union Army, while keeping the rest of his force to the east of Hooker, under his own direct command. At around 5.30 pm Jackson's men fell on the unsuspecting Union right flank, which was deployed to the west of Chancellorsville. The Union commanders on the spot did their best to re-form their line to face the unexpected threat, but, as darkness fell, the Confederates were within sight of Chancellorsville. Confusion reigned supreme and the battle spluttered out after Jackson was severely

Map of the Battle of Chancellorsville with the Confederate forces in red. It shows clearly Jackson's corps to the north and Lee to the east. The Confederate victory was marred by Jackson's death and over 13,000 casualties.

wounded. As "Stonewall" was taken to the rear, Lee advanced his own troops, hemming in Hooker's troops in their salient around Chancellorsville.

The battle resumed the following morning and, after fierce fighting, the Union defenders were pushed back from Chancellorsville toward the river. To take pressure off the army, Hooker had ordered Sedgwick's corps opposite Fredericksburg to assault Marye's Heights, and this time the thinned-out Confederate defences were overrun. Lee detached Major General McLaws to hold Sedgewick at Salem Church, while he continued to put pressure on Hooker's main army. Over the next three days both Hooker's and Sedgwick's forces withdrew back over the river, leaving Lee and his men to savor their spectacular but costly victory.

The Gettysburg Campaign

Despite a spirited, but indecisive, cavalry clash near Brandy Station on June 9, 1863, by June 15th it was clear that the Army of the Potomac was unwilling to renew its offensive. Lieutenant General Ewell's corps defeated a small Union army at Second Winchester on June 14th, which cleared the Shenandoah valley of Union troops and paved the way for a Confederate advance across the Potomac.

On June 15th, Lee launched his second invasion of Maryland, leading his army of Northern Virginia north in what became the opening moves of the Gettysburg Campaign. Hooker had been replaced by Major General Meade, and the two armies finally clashed near the town of Gettysburg, Pennsylvania on July 1st. After an initial day of fighting to the west of the town, Meade occupied the high ground to the south of Gettysburg, forcing Lee to attack him there. On July 2nd, Ewell's Corps to the north and Longstreet's corps to the east launched unsuccessful assaults on the Union position, which was being reinforced as the day wore on. On July 3rd, Lee ordered an all-out attack on the center of the Union line at Cemetery Ridge. The assault – known as Pickett's Charge – was a costly failure, and two days later Lee retreated back to Virginia, after suffering a defeat that turned the tide of the war.

This painting depicts Pickett's Charge, when Confederate forces were repulsed with heavy losses by the Union Army.

PICKETT'S CHARGE: VIRGINIA'S FUTILE MOMENT OF GLORY

On July 3, 1863, Lee ordered a reluctant Longstreet to launch an attack on the Union position on Cemetery Ridge during the Battle of Gettysburg. Although he was only one of three divisional commanders to take part in the assault, the "charge" was named after Major General George Pickett, who commanded three brigades of Virginia troops. A native of Norfolk, Virginia, Pickett fought in Lee's army throughout the battles of the previous year and was known for his courage and colorful appearance. His brigades were shredded by Union fire, suffering more than 505 casualties. One of his Virginian brigade commanders, Brigadier General Lewis A. Armistead, actually reached the Union line, waving his hat on the tip of his sword, but was mortally wounded during the inevitable counter-attack. The spot where the Virginian fell is generally regarded as "the high water mark of the Confederacy." After his shattered troops returned to their starting positions, Pickett reported to his commander, "General Lee – I have no division."

STALEMATE ON THE RAPIDAN

After the Gettysburg defeat, Lee's army returned to Virginia and held the line of the Rapidan River. Meade was content to occupy the area to the north, and, in October, a half-hearted Confederate attempt to outflank the Army of the Potomac was thwarted at Bristoe Station, when A.P. Hill's corps was repulsed by the Union II Corps. Unable to outmaneuver Meade, Lee withdrew back across the Rapidan.

In November, Meade managed to force a crossing of the river, but was halted by Lee's strong defensive positions at Mine Run. Both sides then went into winter quarters.

THE WILDERNESS CAMPAIGN

During the winter of 1863–64, Lieutenant General Ulysses S. Grant assumed command of the Union Army, and established his headquarters with Meade's Army of the Potomac. While Meade theoretically commanded the army, Grant now determined how and when it would fight and in early May, 1864, the Army of the Potomac crossed the Rapidan River to occupy "The Wilderness" near Chancellorsville.

Lee hoped to repeat his success of the previous summer by launching a surprise attack on the Union Army. Instead, during the ensuing Battle of The Wilderness, which was fought from May 5th to the 7th, the two armies fought each other to a standstill.

In previous campaigns, the Union Army had withdrawn to the north to regroup. This time, Grant intended to sidestep Lee's army and march closer to Richmond. Lee was able to divine Grant's intensions, and moved his own army to the east, blocking Grant's advance near Spotsylvania Courthouse. In the battle that followed (May 8th–12th), the Union troops launched repeated attacks against the entrenched Confederate line, but were repulsed with heavy losses. Spotsylvania was a clear defeat for Grant, but, once again, rather than retreating he elected to sidestep Lee by moving his army to the east and south.

Grant now crossed the North Anna River in an attempt to get between Lee and Richmond, but Lee sent Stuart's cavalry to block his path. Stuart was killed during the clash at Yellow Tavern on May 11th, though Lee was able to move his men south to defend the Confederate capital. Further clashes along the North Anna from the 23rd to the 26th May ended in stalemate, so Grant moved sideways again, this time crossing the York River into the Tidewater Peninsula. After several minor clashes, Grant launched another all-out assault on Lee's army at Cold Harbor (May 31st–June 12th), an attack that proved a costly failure, claiming the lives of as many as 5,000 Union soldiers.

The following week Grant moved south again by crossing the James River, thereby threatening Richmond and the nearby city of Petersburg from the south.

EARLY'S CAMPAIGN

In May 1864, Grant ordered Major General Sigel to clear the Confederates from the Shenandoah Valley. Sigel moved to comply but his advance was stopped at New Market on the 15th by an ad-hoc Confederate force that consisted in part of cadets from the Virginia Military Institute. At this point, Sigel was replaced by Major General Hunter, who was defeated in turn at Trevalian Station on June 11th.

The spirited Confederate defence of the Shenandoah was conducted by Major General Jubal Early, whose 14,000-man army then crossed the Potomac to threaten Washington, D.C. Early defeated a Union blocking force at Monocracy on June 9th, but was thwarted by the near-impregnable defences of the Union capital. Six days later, Early withdrew back to Virginia.

Map of Washington, D.C. and northeastern Virginia by the Confederate Engineer Bureau, September 1864.

General Jubal A. Early (1816–94) started the war as a regimental commander (of the 24th Virginia Infantry) before rising to lieutenant general and the command of an infantry corps in the Army of Northern Virginia. He commanded the raid on Washington in 1864 but was relieved of his command by Lee in 1865 after a string of defeats.

THE CADETS OF THE V.M.I.

The Virginia Military Institute in Lexington, Virginia, was founded in 1839, and developed into a military academy of considerable renown. "Stonewall" Jackson taught there before the Civil War and fifteen of its graduates rose to become Confederate generals during the conflict. At the Battle of New Market some 280 teenage students formed a battalion that joined Early's army, and fought alongside the Confederate regulars. Although fifty of them were killed or wounded during the battle, the cadets played their part in ensuring a Confederate victory.

PETERSBURG

From June 1864 until the following spring, the Union campaign bogged down in the mud and trenches in front of Petersburg, Virginia. But before Grant's crossing of the James River in June 1864, General Franklin Butler's Army of the James disembarked at Bermuda Hundred, between Richmond and Petersburg, in an attempt to threaten the Confederate capital. On May 16th, however, the slow-moving Union commander was driven back by a Confederate counter-attack led by General Beauregard and, eventually, Butler's army was withdrawn and used to reinforce the Army of the Potomac.

Grant's drive on Petersburg took Lee by surprise, but the initial Union attempt to capture this key railroad hub was thwarted by the city's brigade-sized garrison. As Lee reinforced the city, both sides dug in for a siege, which dragged on throughout the winter. On June 30, 1864, Union sappers exploded a mine under the Confederate lines, creating an enormous crater. Major General Burnside's corps were ordered to seize the gap blown in the defences, but the assault was mismanaged and some 1,500 of Burnside's men were killed or wounded in what became known as "The Battle of the Crater".

While the siege continued both sides manoeuvred to cut or defend Petersburg's rail links to the southwest and, after a series of clashes, the Union army succeeded in cutting the Weldon Railroad in late August. In these battles, Grant's army took full advantage of its superiority in numbers to isolate Petersburg, and maintain pressure on the city's defences.

By February 1865, the Union Army had been reinforced, and Grant planned to finally destroy Lee's heavily outnumbered force, whose numbers had been dwindling steadily through sickness, desertion, and attrition. However, it was Lee who struck first, launching an attack on the key Union position of Fort Steadman on March 25th. The assault was driven back with heavy losses and Grant responded by attempting to outflank Petersburg to the west,

Richmond after the fall: piles of ammunition in the Arsenal grounds; the Richmond & Petersburg Railroad bridge is at right, a gutted building above.

thereby cutting the last rail link to Richmond and Petersburg. Lee was forced to counter, and the two armies clashed at Five Forks on April 1st. In this last major clash of the war, Pickett's division was destroyed. The following day Union troops broke through the sparsely-held defenses of Petersburg and the city was captured.

THE FALL OF RICHMOND

As Petersburg fell, President Davis ordered the evacuation of Richmond. The Confederate administration was evacuated to the west along the only railroad that remained open and Confederate troops were ordered to destroy the city's remaining stockpiles of arms and ammunition, and to raze the city's industrial centers. The Tredegar Iron Works was spared only because its owner used his workers to defend the site against their own soldiers. As the city emptied, looting was widespread. Panic spread and thousands of residents fled from their homes while fires spread unchecked and large parts of the virtually deserted city were gutted by the flames. On April 3rd, Joseph Mayo, the mayor of Richmond surrendered what remained of his city to the advancing Union Army. The following day, President Lincoln arrived to view the ruins of the Virginian and Confederate capital.

LEE'S SURRENDER

During the two days before Lee surrendered his army, he and Grant exchanged several letters, discussing the need for peace and proposing terms. The final exchange took place during the night of April 8th–9th, and while Grant made clear that he was unable to accept the surrender of the Confederacy, he stated that the surrender of Lee's Army of Northern Virginia would effectively end the bloodshed. As he put it:

"I will state, however, general, that I am equally anxious for peace with yourself, and the whole North entertains the same feeling. The terms upon which peace can be had are well understood. By the South laying down their arms they will hasten that most desirable event, save thousands of human

lives, and hundreds of millions of property not yet destroyed."

Consequently, at 8:00 am, a dignified but downcast Robert E. Lee entered Appomattox Courthouse and was met by his Union nemesis. Terms were agreed, and, finally, at 4:00 pm Lee signed the surrender document. As Lee rode away, Union soldiers began cheering, but Grant ordered them to stop, later explaining: "The Confederates were now our countrymen, and we did not want to exult over their downfall."

Virginia Units Furnished	
Confederate	
Infantry regiments	64
Infantry battalions	19
Cavalry regiments	31
Cavalry battalions	26
(plus 17 smaller independent units)	
Partizan cavalry battalions	13
Virginia State Ranger regiments	1
Artillery regiments	3
Artillery battalions	11
Light artillery batteries	71
(including 5 horse artillery batteries)	
Militia regiments	120
(some of which were only company-sized)	
Union	
Infantry regiments	3
Partizan cavalry battalions	1
Militia regiments (company-sized)	1

Depiction of the capitulation and surrender of Lee and his army at Appomattox, April 9, 1865.

SURRENDER AT APPOMATTOX

Following the loss of Petersburg, the remnants of Lee's army fought a running battle with Union forces as it moved west. After a defeat at Sayler's Creek on April 6th, Lee was cornered near Appomatox Courthouse. There, on April 9, 1865, he surrendered his army to General Grant. After four long, blood-soaked years, the fighting across the ravaged farmland of Virginia had finally come to an end.

VIRGINIA CONFEDERATE ARMY DEATHS

	Killed	Died of Wounds	Died of Disease	Total
Officers	266	200	168	634
Enlisted	5,062	2,319	6,779	14,160
Total	5,328	2,519	6,947	14,794

Washington

Washington's state flag was adopted in 1925.

> **Sir, Unwilling even for a day to hold office under a (so called) 'Republican' president, with my cordial thanks to President Buchanan for the honor of his bestowal, I hereby tender my resignation of the office of Governor of Washington Territory, to take effect from and after the 4th day of March next.**

EXTRACT FROM GOVERNOR RICHARD D. GHOLSON'S RESIGNATION LETTER TO THE
U.S. SECRETARY OF STATE, FEBRUARY 14, 1861

The territory of Washington was created in February 1853 and covered an area the size of New England, though the 1860 census revealed it had a population of just 11,594. It was also isolated, separated from the east by many miles of often difficult terrain. When the Confederates surrendered on April 9, 1865, it took two days for the momentous news to arrive.

Nevertheless, distance did not make Washington's people entirely indifferent to national events, even if their views were less strongly expressed and more moderate than elsewhere.

The territory's local politics before the Civil War was dominated by figures appointed or connected to the Democratic Party. In the 1860 local elections, the voters elected twenty-four Democrats and just nine Republican candidates. However, though local Democrats were mostly against secession, pro-Lincoln sentiments became increasingly evident after his election, not least because political appointees were Republicans. Both sides hoped for compromise not Civil Car.

Slavery was not a major issue within the territory itself, as Washington had been established as free soil. As one pro-Democrat local paper stated, slavery had "long since been settled by latitude and climate." Even so, the general mood in Washington Territory reflected the national sense of unease as war clouds gathered. The pro-Democrat Olympic-based *Pioneer and Democrat* newspaper of March 2, 1860, stated: "It is the firm settled conviction of the public mind that we are approaching, nay, may have reached a crisis in political affairs, compared with which all former ones were as gentle gales to the destroying whirlwind."

Remote, vast, and with a tiny population, Washington territory was never able, in any practical sense, to provide much in the way of support for the Union cause, despite public interest in the conflict. Indeed, in 1861, the locals were more concerned about Native-American raids than fighting on the other side of the continent. The dreadful winter of 1861 and 1862 also became a

Richard D. Gholson, the third Territorial Governor of Washington.

THE "PACIFIC REPUBLIC"

As the national situation deteriorated in early 1861, there were rumors in Washington Territory that an old idea from the 1850s – that of an independent "Pacific Republic" west of the Rocky Mountains – was re-emerging. Newspapers ran stories about unspecified groups of men standing ready to seize political control in the name of the new republic if the Union collapsed – though no such groups ever emerged when the South seceded. Indeed, the local legislature pledged "Washington for the present government."

Grant's Early Duty in Washington Territory

After various postings in the east, Lieutenant Ulysses S. Grant was ordered west in 1852. His first posting was to Fort Vancouver, where he became quartermaster to his old regiment and came into contact with the local Native-Americans, whose plight he viewed sympathetically. Promotion came in 1853, when he was made captain, and he was given command of Company F, which was stationed at Fort Humboldt on the coast of northwest California. However, he abruptly resigned on July 31, 1854, amid rumors that he had been caught drunk on duty and given the option of either facing a court martial or resigning by his commanding officer.

Along with two other officers and some clerks, Grant lived in "Quartermaster's Ranch," while at Fort Vancouver, an imposing, two-storey home with high ceilings and a porch on three sides. In Grant's opinion it was the finest building in the territory. It became the base's social center.

pressing practical problem. Although the legislature did raise some $7,750 for the Union, Washington's contribution in terms of troops was negligible, and it appears that some recruiters were even harassed by local citizens.

WITHDRAWAL OF U.S. ARMY UNITS, 1861

The U.S. Army presence in the whole of the Pacific Northwest was largely based around the 4th Infantry Regiment, which arrived in California during 1853 with a strength of around 900 personnel, including camp followers. The regiment was then split into detachments to garrison existing or new forts and barracks across the Department of the Pacific, which included Washington Territory. When the Civil War broke out, the various detachments were withdrawn from their posts and ordered to make for southern California to stifle any attempted uprising by secessionists. The regiment remained in California until October, when its duties were taken over by local militia units, and then transferred to the east for service with the main Union Army.

MCCLELLAN'S PRE-WAR ENGINEERING WORK IN WASHINGTON TERRITORY

George B. McClellan was ordered to take part in the Pacific Railroad survey in 1853. His task was to identify possible northern routes for the transcontinental railroad from St. Paul, Minnesota, to Puget Sound in Washington Territory. McClellan showed flashes of insubordination in this post, especially toward Washington Territory's governor, Isaac Stevens. Matters came to a head when McClellan suggested Yakima Pass as a suitable route through the Cascade Range without completing a detailed reconnaissance. Stevens demand he check the pass's snow cover in winter and McClellan refused. In fact three other passes, which he had overlooked, were later selected as rail and road routes. McClellan also refused to hand over his log books, most likely because he had been critical of Stevens.

GOVERNOR ISAAC I. STEVENS (1818–62)

Stevens was born in Massachusetts and attended West Point, graduating top of his class in 1839. He joined the Corps of Engineers and saw service during the American-Mexican War. After a series of peacetime appointments, Stevens became active in politics and his support for President Franklin Pierce secured him the governorship of Washington Territory in March 1852. He took up his post in November and, although liked by many, he was unpopular with some for his treatment of the local Native-Americans. He was elected to Congress in 1857 and 1858, but, at the outbreak of war, became colonel of the 79th New York Regiment. Promotions followed and, in 1862, he fought at Secessionville, South Carolina, before moving to Virginia, where he was present at the Second Battle of Bull Run (Second Manassas). He was killed leading his old regiment at Chantilly in September.

THE 1ST REGIMENT, WASHINGTON TERRITORY VOLUNTEER INFANTRY

Also known as the 1st Washington Territory Volunteers, this three-year regiment began enlisting recruits in mid-Oct 1861. The men were not only drawn from Washington Territory but also from California and were mustered at either Alcatraz Island, San Francisco, or at forts Vancouver and Steilacoom in the territory itself. Ten companies had been raised by December 1862, and a regimental headquarters was established at Fort Walla Wall in Washington. The unit was formed into company-sized detachments and served in the territories of Washington, Idaho, and Oregon. Their role was to protect miners, settlers, and emigrant parties, to launch punitive expeditions against various Native-American tribes, and to protect the Nez Perce, a tribe friendly to the United States. The companies were mustered out in 1865.

FORTS IN WASHINGTON TERRITORY

The pre-war forts that dotted Washington Territory were largely constructed at key points to protect white settlers, to help subdue the local Native-American tribes, and to guard various overland trails between the Western and Eastern United States. Thus, these military bases helped extend U.S. Federal authority across the unincorporated northwest of the United States. Some, however, were built in response to particular events. Fort Steilacoom, for example, was founded in 1849 after the murder of Dr. Marcus Whitman and twelve others by the Cayuse, who blamed the white settlers for a smallpox epidemic that left half the tribe dead.

WASHINGTON UNION ARMY DEATHS

Troops Furnished	Killed/Mortally Wounded	Died of Disease	Died of Other Causes	Total
924	0	12	10	22

Council with friendly Nez Percés Indians held by Colonel G. Wright on August 4, 1858, near Fort Wallah Wallah, Washington Territory.

THE BEAR RIVER EXPEDITION

Colonel Patrick E. Connor established Fort Douglas in Utah Territory's Salt Lake Valley in late 1862, largely to protect the growing settler population from attack by Native-Americans. Hostilities between the colonists and the native peoples came to a head when eight miners crossing the Montana Trail were set-upon by the Shoshone. One miner was killed and the rest fled to Connor's fort. He determined to deal with those responsible and, in late January 1863, a 200-strong force of cavalry and infantry stuck out in the depth of winter, marching 140 miles into southeast Washington Territory. The troops attacked the Shoshone on the Bear River on the 29th and what followed was a massacre. Between 200 and 500 men, women, and children were killed, and the body of their leader mutilated. Connor, who had lost twenty-one men killed and forty-two wounded, was made general.

Washington Union Units Furnished	
Infantry regiments	1

BRIGADIER GENERAL BENJAMIN ALVORD (1813–84)

A career soldier who had fought in the American-Mexican War, Alvord subsequently held various peacetime roles before being sent to the West. After a spell building a military road in southern Oregon, he served as the paymaster of the Department of Oregon from 1854 until 1862. That year the head of the Department of the Pacific wanted an experienced regular officer to take charge of the vast, underdeveloped department that, at that time, took in what are now the states of Idaho, Oregon, and Washington. Alvord's chief role was to deal with any friction between settlers and Native-Americans and build forts to establish a stronger U.S. presence in the department, but a lack of local volunteers made his tasks that much harder. He was removed from command in 1865 and resigned his commission.

West Virginia

"We come here to carry out and execute, and it may be, to institute a government for ourselves. We are determined to live under a State government of the United States of America and under the Constitution of the United States. It requires stout hearts to execute this purpose . . ."

ARTHUR BOREMAN, FIRST SESSION OF THE SECOND WHEELING CONVENTION,
JUNE 12, 1861

Virginia seceded from the Union on April 17, 1861, but pro-Union Virginians in the northwest of the country held a series of conventions to discuss breaking away from the state and forming a new one. The decision was agreed in August, and the proposed state called "Kanawha", after a tributary of the Ohio River. One of the delegates attending the first Constitutional Council in December suggested a better name was needed and the delegates voted thirty to fourteen to reject. Several alternative names were put forward, including Allegheny, Augusta, Columbia, New Virginia, West Virginia, and Western Virginia. The issue was put to the vote and thirty delegates selected West Virginia.

On May 23, 1861, a referendum saw over 132,000 Virginian voters back secession from the Union. At the same time a not insignificant minority – some 37,500 voters, most living in the northwest – voted to stay in the Union. The result reflected the split among delegates who had recently attended a convention and issued an ordinance of secession. When they voted, eighty-eight backed the proposal, but fifty-five did not, and, of the forty-seven delegates present from the northwest, thirty opposed secession. In general, although Virginia was a major slave-owning state, the practice was much less common in the poorer northwest.

Those opposed to secession organized conventions in Wheeling from May to August. The Second Convention opened on June 11th. Its delegates swiftly declared that Virginia was still part of the Union; that Virginian officials who had voted for secession had abandoned their posts; and that the

GOVERNOR FRANCIS. H. PIERPOINT (1814–99)

Pierpoint attended the Wheeling Convention that, on September 24-25, 1861, declared Virginia's elected officials had abandoned their posts by seceding, and was elected governor of "Restored Virginia" – the area of the state under Union control. Making Wheeling his capital (until it later moved to Alexandria), he led calls for the creation of a new state in western Virginia. President Lincoln, however, urged Pierpoint to move cautiously as he was concerned over the constitutional position of creating a new state within the borders of an existing one and that new state's stance on the abolition of slavery.

In fact, Congress voted to admit West Virginia in late December 1862, but the president spent a further week or so discussing the matter before signing the bill on the 31st. The issue of slavery was resolved when West Virginians voted overwhelmingly to adopt a process of gradual emancipation on March 23rd. West Virginia joined the Union in June, with Arthur I. Boreman as its first governor. Pierpoint was re-elected as governor of "Restored Virginia" in 1863 and was made the Governor of Virginia when the war ended.

convention would henceforth constitute a legislative body for what was termed the Restored Government of Virginia. Restored Virginia included those parts not in Confederate hands and Francis H. Pierpoint was proclaimed its governor. On August 20th, delegates at the Third Convention decided to put forward a resolution to create a wholly new state.

The pro-Unionists had their cause enhanced that summer, when Major General George B. McClellan overcame the weak local Confederate military presence and support for the decisions made by the conventions was tested on October 24th in a referendum in which 18,408 backed the plan for a new state (just 781 voting against). Restored Virginia would continue as a separate entity until the war's end, but western Virginia had embarked on the long road to full statehood, which was granted in 1863.

McClellan Secures Western Virginia

The Union established the Department of the Ohio in May, 1861, and, by the time Virginia voted to secede on the 23rd, Federal authorities had already issued General Order No. 14, directing the department's commander, Major General George B. McClellan, to save western Virginia for the Union. Various units, mainly Ohio and Indiana regiments, subsequently moved into western Virginia and the Confederates were defeated in a series of battles in June and July. McClellan's stock rose and he was ordered back to Washington, D.C. on July 22nd to receive an even higher command, that of the Department (later Army) of the Potomac.

The Battle of Philippi

Confederate Colonel George A. Porterfield was ordered to take charge of units in northwest Virginia and gather volunteers on May 4, 1861, little knowing that at the end of the month Major General George B. McClellan, head of the Department of the Ohio, would order Union troops under Brigadier General Thomas A. Morris to move into various parts of the same area. Porterfield reached the town of Grafton with 800 volunteers but fell back

Colonel George A. Porterfield.

to Philippi as Morris's troops approached. Morris attacked at dawn on June 3rd and the Confederates broke immediately. The battle was a skirmish, but it had important repercussions: anti-secessionists attending the Wheeler Convention were emboldened to reject Virginia's ordinance of secession.

The Battles of Laurel Hill and Rich Mountain

These two engagements in early July 1861 brought McClellan's campaign to secure western Virginia for the Union to a conclusion. Brigadier General Thomas A. Morris was ordered to move from Philippi to tackle the Confederate troops stationed on Laurel Hill and skirmishing there began on July 7th. McClellan had moved his main force from Clarksburg on June 27th and headed for Lieutenant Colonel John Pegram's force at Rich Mountain. Brigadier General William S. Rosecrans, McClellan's deputy, was ordered to get behind Pegram and the battle was won in two hours on the 11th. The Southern units at Laurel Hill heard of the defeat and retreated.

THE BATTLE OF CHEAT MOUNTAIN

This battle, fought in September 1861, was a small affair but notable in that it marked the somewhat inauspicious Civil War debut of General Robert E. Lee. Lee devised a simultaneous two-pronged attack against Fort Milroy on Cheat Mountain, and against entrenchments held by troops at nearby Elk Water. The attack on the fort was launched on the 12th and was thrown into uncoordinated disarray by a combination of the terrain and weather, as well as the stubborn resistance of the garrison. The Elk Water attack also came to nothing. Lee manoeuvered for advantage the next day, but to no effect. He returned to base on the 17th.

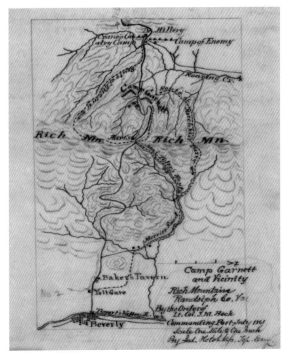

Camp Garnett and vicinity, Rich Mountain.

The burning of the arsenal at Harpers Ferry, April 18, 1861.

Captain Alberts' party attacking the insurgents.

JOHN BROWN'S RAID ON HARPERS FERRY

John Brown was a firebrand abolitionist who was not above using violence to advance his cause. In May, 1856, he and some followers had killed five pro-slavery settlers in Kansas. Three years later he set his sights on the U.S arsenal at Harpers Ferry, Virginia, planning to use the weapons stored there in a slave revolt. Brown and his party stormed the target on the evening of October 16, 1859, but were soon surrounded. The following day the raiders withdrew to an engine house. That afternoon President James Buchanan ordered marines under Brevet Colonel Robert E. Lee to Harpers Ferry. Lee sent an aide, Lieutenant J.E.B Stuart, to request Brown's surrender on the 18th. Stuart was rebuffed and the marines stormed the engine house, capturing survivors. Brown was found guilty of treason and hanged on December 2nd.

Major General Thomas J. Jackson.

Harpers Ferry ruins.

JACKSON'S ROMNEY EXPEDITION

Confederate Major General Thomas J. Jackson took charge of the Valley District of the Department of Virginia in October 1861, and planned an operation to retake western Virginia by launching an attack on Romney. He left Winchester with 9,000 men on a cold January 1, 1862, not knowing that Union troops were simultaneously making for Winchester by way of Romney. Kelley occupied Romney briefly, but, faced with Jackson's advance, retreated on the 10th. Jackson marched into the town on the 14th. Nevertheless, his troops' morale was low due to the weather and, leaving a division behind to garrison the town, he returned to Winchester. His plan to retake western Virginia had failed though he had cleared his district of Union forces.

THE BATTLE OF HARPERS FERRY

In early September 1862, General Robert E. Lee launched an invasion of the North by leading his Army of Northern Virginia northward along the Shenandoah Valley into Maryland. Although he was being shadowed by the larger Army of the Potomac, Lee split his command by sending some 20,000 troops under Major General Thomas J. Jackson to capture Harpers Ferry. The garrison there totaled around 14,000 men, but their commander made the fatal error of not securing the heights dominating the town. Jackson's troops began arriving on the 12th and some fifty cannon were placed on the high ground by the early morning of the 15th. The fierce barrage forced Dixon to surrender quickly.

Dismantling the Baltimore & Ohio Railroad

The Baltimore & Ohio Railroad was one of the Union's greatest strategic assets during the war. It ran from Baltimore to Washington, D.C. and then on to pro-Union West Virginia by way of pro-South Virginia. Thus, the railroad, and its associated telegraph line, were vital in linking the capital with other Northern states, allowing the swift movement of messages, troops, war supplies, and raw materials. When war came in 1861, the railroad's more than 500 miles of track – plus bridges, repair facilities, and tunnels – were plagued Confederate raids that disrupted Union war plans and tied up thousands of Federal troops. Raids by larger bodies of regular Confederate forces and smaller bands of guerrillas or partisan rangers began in the first few months of the war and continued up until the summer of 1864.

Guerrilla Operations in West Virginia

West Virginia was a frequent target of raids by regular Confederate units whose aim was disrupting strategic targets like the Baltimore & Ohio Railroad, destroying industrial sites, and tying up Union forces. Generally, if not always, these operations and the Union's counter-operations adhered to the letter of military law. However, there was a darker side to the Civil War in West Virginia. As the war progressed, bitterly opposed local groups banded together to attack their neighbors. These raids and counter-raids were less about the rights and wrongs of the war and more about local political and economic rivalries. Such conflicts were frequently accompanied by criminality and outright atrocities. Even regular troops sent to deal with the raiders were prone to unlawful acts, as is made obvious in a letter home written by a soldier from Ohio. He wrote: "We do not take prisoners if we can help it."

Railroad construction worker straightening track; pile of twisted rails in background.

The commander of a brigade of cavalry from West Virginia, Brigadier Albert Jenkins was mortally wounded at the Battle of Cloyd's Mountain. He is buried at Spring Hill Cemetery in Huntington, West Virginia.

Union Generals from West Virginia

MAJOR GENERAL GEORGE CROOK (1828–90)

Crook was given command of the Department of West Virginia on July 25, 1864. When he took up his post on August 9th, he renamed the department's main field force the Army of West Virginia. It comprised three divisions and effectively served as a corps within Major General Philip H. Sheridan's Army of the Shenandoah. Sheridan's main goals were dealing with General Jubal A. Early, whose raiders had been striking across West Virginia and Maryland since the beginning of July, and laying waste the productive Shenandoah Valley. The Army of West Virginia fought at the Third Battle of Winchester on September 19th, Fisher's Hill on the 21st and 22nd, and at the decisive Battle of Cedar Creek on October 19th, where Early's force was finally neutralized.

BRIGADIER GENERAL THOMAS M. HARRIS (1817–1906)

Harris was a doctor but shut his practice at the beginning of the war and took command of a Union infantry regiment. Larger commands followed, first a brigade, then a division in campaigns in the Shenandoah Valley. He was present at the Battle of Droop Mountain in November 1863, which effectively ended Confederate resistance in West Virginia, and was made a brigadier general for his actions at the Battle of Cedar Creek in October 1864. He then transferred to the Army of the James, seeing action at the Battle of Fort Gregg at Petersburg on April 2, 1865, and helped trap the Army of Northern Virginia at Appomattox on the 9th.

WEST VIRGINIA UNION ARMY DEATHS

Troops Furnished	Killed/Mortally Wounded	Died of Disease	Died of Other Causes	Total
31,872	1,247	1,878	892	4,017

BRIGADIER GENERAL JOHN McCAUSLAND (1837-1927)

As colonel of the 36th Virginia Infantry Regiment, McCausland (and his unit) managed to avoid capture at Fort Donelson in February 1862. For the reminder of 1862, and into 1863, he fought in the Department of Western Virginia. He was made brigadier general in the various campaigns in the Shenandoah Valley in 1864, controversially razing Chambersburg, Pennsylvania, on July 30th. He then joined the Army of Northern Virginia and fought at the Battle of Five Forks on April 1, 1865. Although he avoided capture at Appomattox on the 9th, he and his command soon surrendered.

MAJOR GENERAL JESSE L. RENO (1823–62)

After serving in administrative posts and on the frontier for several years, Reno was made a brigadier general in late 1861, and went on to fight in the North Carolina expedition from February to July 1862. He opposed Jackson at the Second Battle of Bull Run (Second Manassas) on August 29-30, 1862, and at the Battle of Chantilly on September 1st. Soon after, at the commencement of the Antietam Campaign, he became a corps commander. During a personal reconnaissance at Fox's Gap, during the Battle of South Mountain on September 14th, he was mortally wounded.

West Virginia Union Units Furnished	
Infantry regiments	19
Infantry battalions	1
Independent infantry unit	1
3-month infantry regiment	1
Cavalry regiments	7
Light artillery batteries	8
Sailors/marine personnel	133
Colored troops	196

Wisconsin

❝ **God has preserved me unharmed through another desperate bloody battle. Regiment lost one hundred and sixty men killed and wounded. I ordered a charge and we captured a regiment. Major [John A. Blair] commanding the second Mississippi surrendered his sword and regiment to me . . .** ❞

NOTE FROM LIEUTENANT COLONEL RUFUS R. DAWES, 6TH WISCONSIN, TO MISS MARY GATES, BATTLE OF GETTYSBURG, JULY 2, 1863

Wisconsin became a territory in April, 1835, and by the mid-1840s its population had risen to some 150,000 souls, making it eligible to join the Union.

It voted to move toward statehood in 1846, but the radical document drawn up by delegates assembled to thrash out a state constitution that fall was rejected by the public in 1847. A more moderate document was approved the following year and state statehood was granted on May 29, 1848.

The radicalism of that first constitution suggests that many in Wisconsin had progressive ideals, not least the migrants who had arrived from states in New England as well those from Ireland, Germany, and Scandinavia. Further evidence came in the early 1850s, when Wisconsin became the second state to abolish capital punishment. It was in the same decade that abolitionist groups were established and Wisconsin became a vital part of the Underground Railway that helped slaves gain their freedom. One of the most famous events of this period involved Joshua Glover, a runaway slave from St. Louis, Missouri. He settled in Racine during 1852, but was apprehended by Federal marshals two years later. A fervent abolitionist, Sherman Booth, led a 500-strong crowd to Glover's Milwaukee prison, freed him, and helped him escape to Canada.

The state had either Whig or Democrat governors between 1848 and 1856, but from the latter year until 1866 the post was held by five Republicans. Abraham Lincoln took the state with 56.6 percent of the vote in the 1860 presidential election, while his nearest rival – the moderate Northern Democrat Stephen Douglas – took the greater part of the remainder. The Southern Democrat contender, John C. Breckinridge, garnered a meager 0.6 percent of votes.

Around 90,000 Wisconsin troops served the Union cause, including 272 African-Americans, and they suffered a casualty rate of 13.4 percent. This recruitment total equates to around one in nine of all those eligible and the state was one of few that could always raise new recruits to replace casualties in existing regiments. Wisconsin was also an important source of dairy and brewing products as well as timber for the Union cause.

"OLD ABE" OF THE 8TH WISCONSIN

"Old Abe" was a bald eagle – and the best known regimental mascot of the Civil War – named after the president. The bird was originally trapped in 1861 by a Native-American, Chief Sky, somewhere near the Chippewa River in Wisconsin's Chippewa Country. He was traded with a local farmer, Daniel McCann, for corn and then sold to Company C of the Iron Brigade's 8th Wisconsin Volunteer Infantry Regiment for the sum of $2.50. The soldiers built their new mascot a perch and, thereafter, Old Abe went to war, taking part in several battles. Confederate troops, who nicknamed him the "Yankee Buzzard", made several attempts to capture him but he survived the war with no more than the loss of a few feathers to enemy bullets. He returned home in 1864, and was housed in the state capitol building. Old Abe was asphyxiated by smoke in March 1881, but was preserved and put on display before being wholly consumed by a second fire.

Governors of Wisconsin

Alexander W. Randall.

Lewis P. Harvey.

Edward S. Salomon.

GOVERNOR ALEXANDER W. RANDALL (1819–72)

The state's sixth governor, Randall served from January 1858 to January 1862 and, at the outbreak of the war, made strenuous efforts to raise Federal troops. He exceeded Wisconsin's quota by more than 3,000 men, raising eighteen infantry regiments, ten artillery batteries, and three cavalry units. A training facility, Camp Randall, was named after him.

GOVERNOR LEWIS P. HARVEY (1820–62)

Harvey replaced Randall in January 1862, and, in April, took up the task of gathering together medical supplies to aid troops wounded in the Battle of Shiloh. Harvey traveled with the supplies but met with an accident on the Tennessee River. Stumbling while stepping from a tethered boat onto a moving steamship, he drowned on the 19th.

GOVERNOR EDWARD S. SALOMON (1828–1909)

Salomon took up office after Harvey's death and served until January 4, 1864. He was an ardent supporter of the Union and responded to a call for further recruits that year with alacrity, first asking for volunteers and then setting up a draft. Fourteen extra regiments were raised, but his career was somewhat blighted by draft rioting as he had to call on Federal troops to quell the disturbance. He was succeeded by James Lewis.

Private Horace H. Smith of Company G, 16th Wisconsin Infantry Regiment, in forage cap with bayonet, musket, cartridge box, and musket sling.

Wisconsin Generals

Brigadier General Edward S. Bragg.

Major General Lysander Cutler.

Major General Charles S. Hamilton.

BRIGADIER GENERAL EDWARD S. BRAGG (1827–1912)

Bragg joined the 6th Wisconsin as a captain in July 1861, and had reached the rank of colonel by March 1863. He was wounded at Chancellorsville that year but returned to service and was promoted to brigadier general in June 1864. He commanded the Iron Brigade from the date of his promotion until February 1865, and was mustered out the following October.

MAJOR GENERAL LYSANDER CUTLER (1807–66)

Cutler settled in Wisconsin in 1857 and was made colonel of the 6th Wisconsin in July 1861. Never popular, his troops were glad to see him depart in the summer of 1862. Nevertheless, he was gradually promoted to higher commands throughout the war but was badly wounded at the Battle of Globe Tavern in 1864. He resigned on June 30, 1865.

Wisconsin Union Units Furnished	
Infantry regiments	53
Sharpshooter units	1
Cavalry regiments	4
Heavy artillery regiments	1
Light artillery batteries	13
Colored troops	165

MAJOR GENERAL CHARLES S. HAMILTON (1822–91)

Having served in the American-Mexican War, Hamilton was given command of the 3rd Wisconsin, a regiment that mustered into Federal service in June, 1861. He led the unit until August 10th and was promoted brigadier general, serving in the Peninsula Campaign and at Yorktown. Hamilton then transferred to the Western Theater, seeing action at the battles of Iuka and Corinth in late 1862. Although promoted to major general that October, he resigned in April 1863.

BRIGADIER GENERAL RUFUS KING (1814–76)

King graduated from West Point in the early 1830s, resigned his commission in 1836, and, over the following years, had several non-military jobs. He then moved to Wisconsin Territory and began to dabble in politics. When the Civil War broke out, he was on his way to the Vatican to take up a diplomatic appointment but returned home and was made a brigadier general in April 1861, helping to raise the Iron Brigade. He never led it in battle but was given command of a division in 1862. King's career was blighted by epilepsy and he resigned the following year.

Brigadier General Rufus King.

Howard Cushing.

Alonzo Cushing.

THE CUSHING BROTHERS

These four brothers all had distinguished military careers. Alonzo Hereford Cushing (1841–63) graduated from West Point just as the Civil War began and mostly served in the 4th U.S. Artillery Regiment. He was at the Second Battle of Bull Run (Second Manassas) in 1861 and the Battle of Antietam (Battle of Sharpsburg) in 1862. His battery was positioned on Cemetery Ridge at Gettysburg in 1863 and on the third day of the battle, July 3rd, defended a spot now known as "The Angle", which was the epicenter of Pickett's Charge. Although twice wounded, he continued to operate his battery's two remaining guns until killed by a bullet and was later awarded the Medal of Honor.

William Barker Cushing (1842–72) saw service in the U.S. Navy, and was present at the Battle of Hampton Roads and Fort Fisher. His most renowned exploit was the daring attack on the powerful C.S.S. *Albemarle* that sent the ironclad to the bottom of the Roanoke River on the night of October 27–28, 1864.

William Barker Cushing.

Howard Bass Cushing (1840–71) later became a renowned figure in campaigns against the Native-Americans of Arizona Territory, but was also killed on action service, while the eldest of the brothers, Milton Cushing Jr. (1837–87) served in the navy.

WISCONSIN UNION ARMY DEATHS

Troops Furnished	Killed/Mortally Wounded	Died of Disease	Died of Other Causes	Total
91,029	3,802	7,464	1,935	12,301

BERDAN'S SHARPSHOOTERS

With official support, Colonel Hiram Berdan raised ten companies of marksmen from Michigan, New Hampshire, New York State, Vermont, and Wisconsin between late August 1861 and late March 1862, forming the 1st United States Volunteer Sharpshooter Regiment. Eight more companies were recruited in New Hampshire, Maine, Michigan, Minnesota, Pennsylvania, and Vermont between October and December 1861 to form the 2nd Regiment. The recruits were armed with special rifles and wore a distinctive dark green uniform. They were deployed in small detachments to undertake various tasks that demanded personal initiative, such as skirmishing and sniping. Berdan's regiments fought in most of the major battles in the Eastern Theater from 1862 to 1864, with the 1st recording 153 men killed or mortally wounded in action and 129 deaths through disease. The figures for the second were 188 and 125 respectively. The two regiments were combined in late December 1864, and the new unit broken up in February 1865.

THE IRON BRIGADE

Sometimes known as the "Black Hat Brigade" because of the men's headgear, the Iron Brigade is perhaps the most famous unit to have served in the Army of the Potomac. Unusually, it spent the whole of the Civil War in the Eastern Theater, despite its units being drawn from Midwestern states – three regiments from Wisconsin and one apiece from Indiana and Michigan.

The brigade was activated on October 1, 1861, and its first commander was New Yorker Brigadier General Rufus King. He was, however, promoted before the brigade saw its first action at the Battle of Gainesville in late August, 1862. The brigade fought in some of the bloodiest battles of the conflict and, proportionately, suffered more casualties that any equivalent unit. This was especially true at Gettysburg, where the brigade suffered a sixty-one percent loss rate. The Iron Brigade was disbanded in June 1865.

Hiram Berdan, celebrated commander of sharpshooters.

THE 26TH REGIMENT WISCONSIN VOLUNTEER INFANTRY

This, largely German-speaking, regiment was raised in Milwaukee before entering Federal service in September, 1862. Its first commander was Colonel William H. Jacobs, who resigned his commission in early 1864, while in the latter part of the war it was led by Colonel Frederic C. Winkler – both officers being of German origin.

The 26th Wisconsin served in the Eastern Theater with the Army of the Potomac's XI Corps during 1862 and 1863, being present at Fredericksburg, Chancellorsville, and Gettysburg. It then took part in the Atlanta Campaign, fighting at Wauhatchie, near Lookout Mountain, Resaca, and Kenesaw Mountain between late October 1863 and June 1864. During this period it served in the army's XX Corps. In the latter stages of the war, the 26th participated in the destructive march through the Carolinas, fighting at the Battle of Bentonville, North Carolina, in March 1865. The regiment mustered out on June 17, 1865, having lost 188 officers and men to battle and wounds as well as seventy-seven to disease.

THE 36TH REGIMENT WISCONSIN VOLUNTEER INFANTRY

The 36th Regiment was formed in Madison and taken into Federal service in March 1864, with Colonel Frank A. Haskell at its head. An experienced soldier, he had originally served in the Iron Brigade's 6th Wisconsin before becoming an aide to General John Gibbon and had seen action at both Fredericksburg and Gettysburg.

His new regiment, which was part of the 1st Brigade of the II Corps' 2nd Division, was soon in action during General Ulysses S. Grant's bitterly contested campaign around Richmond in late spring and early summer 1864. It was also present at the battles of Spotsylvania Courthouse, Cold Harbor, and the Jerusalem Plank Road fought in May and June. Haskell was killed by a bullet to the temple at Cold Harbor while leading the 1st Brigade in a charge. The following year the regiment fought at the Battle of Saylor's Creek in April, and was mustered out in July, 1865. It had suffered seven officers and 150 men killed or fatally wounded while three officers and 182 men had died of disease.

Colonel Frank A. Haskell.

INDEX OF STATES